Base

ball
BEFORE WE KNEW IT

A Search for the Roots of the Game

DAVID BLOCK   With a foreword by Tim Wiles

University of Nebraska Press LINCOLN AND LONDON

Library of Congress Cataloging-in-Publication Data
Block, David, 1944–
Baseball before we knew it: a search for the roots of the game
/ David Block; with a foreword by Tim Wiles.
p.   cm.
Includes bibliographical references and index.
ISBN 0-8032-1339-5 (cloth: alk. paper)
1. Baseball—History.   I. Title.
GV862.5.B56 2005
796.357'09034—dc22   2004016099

ISBN-13: 978-0-8032-6255-3 (paper: alk. paper)
ISBN-10: 0-8032-6255-8 (paper: alk. paper)

TO MY LOVING PARENTS

Base-ball

. . . a play all who are, or have been,

schoolboys are well acquainted with.

MARY LEPEL

November 14, 1748, London

CONTENTS

❖

ILLUSTRATIONS

❖

FOREWORD

This whole subject needs elucidation,
and a careful study of the rural sports of the
mother country would undoubtedly
throw much light upon the history
of base ball.

HENRY CHADWICK
"The Ancient History of Baseball,"
The Ballplayers' Chronicle, July 18, 1867

The front page of the Sunday *New York Times* is a forum reserved for the most important news of our nation and culture. So it seems fitting that the edition of July 8, 2001, carried a story on the discovery of evidence showing that young men were playing an organized brand of baseball in Manhattan as early as 1823. This, of course, was twenty-three years before the New York Knickerbockers played the first match under a written set of rules at Hoboken, New Jersey, long considered a watershed moment for the organization of formal baseball teams. It was also sixteen years before the mythic date of 1839, when the game's folklore posits its invention at Cooperstown, New York, by Abner Doubleday. The *Times* reported that New York University librarian George Thompson Jr. had unearthed two newspaper references to baseball games published on April 25, 1823. The alert Thompson, not a scholar of the sport's origins, had noticed the references while pursuing other quarry.

The historiography of baseball's beginnings is dotted with similarly dramatic finds, such as the 1991 discovery of a notice in an 1825 Delhi, New York, newspaper, in which nine men of the town of Hamden sought another group with whom to play "Bass-Ball" for a wager of one dollar per game. And now the latest discovery is David Block's startling revelation of the existence of a German book, published in 1796, that contains seven pages of rules for "das englische Base-ball." These references cast the Knickerbocker Club's accomplishments in a new light, showing that there were organized games and written rules long before 1846. Moreover, the 1796 rules for "English baseball" long predate the earliest print references to that other English pastime, rounders, which calls into question Henry Chadwick's theory that baseball evolved from that game. Yet for all the drama and interest that these new discoveries create, they have seemed ultimately ineffective at changing the popular conceptions of baseball's origins. Though the existing explanations were saddled with problems, no better alternative theory had emerged, at least until now.

The Doubleday Myth, as you will read in these pages, was promulgated by the Spalding Commission in 1908 but shot down immediately and convincingly by the journalist Will Irwin the following year. It was again debunked in 1939 by Robert W. Henderson of the New York Public Library, even as the baseball industry celebrated, with great pomp and circumstance, its "Centennial," the centerpiece of which was the grand opening of the National Baseball Hall of Fame and Museum in Cooperstown. Despite irrefutable evidence to the contrary, the media and the public, encouraged by the flag-waving bluster of the baseball industry, clung to the Doubleday Myth. It seemed they simply preferred the "immaculate conception" of baseball by the war hero Abner Doubleday to the messy evolution that the historical evidence clearly indicated.

Of course, just after 1939 the world plunged into total war, and the sniping in print over baseball's origins stopped dead for several decades. In the suburban peace of the 1950s, it may not have appeared seemly to question the preeminent Doubleday theory. Baseball was experiencing its golden age, and was expanding westward with all the optimism and arrogance that had carried the nation itself along the same transcontinental path a century earlier. This was not a time to challenge consensus. Then again, historians may simply have felt that there was no more debunking to be done: Irwin and Henderson had done a thorough job. The Doubleday Myth, it seemed, would prevail regardless of the evidence.

The myth may also have been buttressed by the pastoral beauty of my home, Cooperstown, New York, and the reverence with which the public and the media have treated the Hall of Fame and Cooperstown since the founding of the shrine. During this same period of "Doubleday consensus," the Hall of Fame, arguably a much less mature institution than it has become, one less concerned with research and education, saw no need to question the Doubleday story. The museum thus tacitly protected the game's creation myth, as Stephen Jay Gould so memorably labeled it.

The publication in 1973 of Harold Peterson's *The Man Who Invented Baseball*, a biography of Alexander Cartwright, was the next milestone in the historiography of baseball's origing. The book had the effect of suggesting that since the Doubleday Myth was untrue, the most logical person to call the "father of baseball" was Cartwright, whom Peterson credited as the prime architect of the Knickerbocker rules. Since Cartwright's club played the first game under written rules at Hoboken's Elysian Fields on June 19, 1846, maybe that was a better place than Elihu Phinney's Cooperstown cow pasture to celebrate as the "birthplace of baseball." Among other effects, this created a good-natured tug-of-war between Hoboken and Cooperstown, between New Jersey and New York, over who had the stronger claim to baseball's beginnings. For whatever reason, Hoboken's valid claim as an important place in baseball's evolution failed to spark the public imagination enough to supplant Cooperstown, and we were ultimately left with a second red herring dragged across the trail of baseball's origins.

Late in the twentieth century came the discovery of the Hamden, New York, reference of 1825, and early in the twenty-first, George Thompson unearthed the Manhattan games of 1823. Even the Hall of Fame, which long clung to the Doubleday Myth, has finally accepted the fact that baseball was not invented in Cooperstown. One of the icons of the Hall's collections, the "Doubleday Baseball," long reputed to be a true relic of that summer day in 1839 when Abner allegedly invented the game, is now displayed as evidence that he did not. The ball is featured in the Hall of Fame's five-year national touring exhibition entitled "Baseball as America"; its exhibit label reads in part: "Doubleday didn't invent baseball, baseball invented Doubleday." Yet despite such blunt clarity, these changes in the historical thinking on baseball's ancestry have been slow to penetrate the public consciousness.

Though no Gallup Poll exists to tell us the public's present opinion of the game's origins, if you ask the average person who invented baseball, you still may get Abner Doubleday as your answer.

Baseball is famously known for the almost religious devotion of its fans, writers, and scholars. Walk into any large bookstore, and you will see many more feet of shelf space for baseball books than for books on other American sports. There are currently more than seven thousand members of the Society for American Baseball Research, or SABR. The game has been studied, analyzed, dissected, poeticized, theorized, and obsessed upon. There is a book that lists the uniform number of every player ever to have worn one. Another book tells what happened on each and every opening day for the New York Yankees. There are books about small-town teams and leagues so obscure that almost no one besides the author recalls them. Compiling a complete bibliography of baseball trivia books would be a daunting task indeed. Don't get me wrong, I love all of these books. But it has often struck me as ironic that so much energy is expended researching and writing about a game whose very origins remain shrouded in mystery, folklore, and misinformation.

Now along comes a book that makes it impossible to ignore the compelling story of baseball's origins any longer. Here is a book that doesn't just push back the darkness by a few years but takes us back centuries, and across the ocean to England and beyond in a fresh attempt to understand the game's beginnings. Here is a book that openly challenges not just the Doubleday Myth but also its most frequent alternatives, the Knickerbocker paternity and the descent from rounders. Here is a book that we have needed since 1867 — in fact, Henry Chadwick himself called for this study, in the quotation that constitutes the epigraph to this foreword. Here also is a book that reveals an intriguing, previously unknown connection between the Doubleday Myth's two towering figures, Abner Doubleday and Albert Spalding.

David Block's prodigious work of scholarship is the most exciting work on the origins of baseball in more than sixty years. What he has to say is of major importance to understanding where baseball came from, and it is truly fascinating. He takes us on a trip far into the English past of games such as tut-ball, stool-ball, cat and dog, munshets, trap-ball, hand-in and hand-out, and even an English game called baseball. Unlike previous historians, he does not rely upon the sketchy memories of old-timers or repeat unproven clichés. Instead he digs deeply into surviving texts and images to reveal the hidden history of games played with a ball, bat, and bases. Learning of these earlier games helps us to understand that, while baseball as we know it is truly American and truly reflective of our national spirit and identity, it was not born in a vacuum. It came from somewhere, and by understanding the voyage of baseball to our shores, and its subsequent development into the fierce sport and big business that it is today, we can appreciate in a new way the universality of a bunch of kids with a ball, bat, and bases, whether they are playing Wiffle ball in Seattle today or tut-ball in England in the seventeenth century.

Block's methodology is a point of interest. A recently retired computer systems analyst, he long pursued his hobby of collecting early baseball books. As his collection grew, he thought it might be a useful service to publish an annotated bibliography of the titles he'd acquired or knew about that referenced baseball and related games. As the bibliography itself reached book length, he realized it needed an introduction to place the books in context.

While looking for material to include in his introduction that could help his readers understand how baseball evolved, Block discovered that little that had been written on the topic was founded on solid historical evidence. His introduction turned into a book as Block realized that the sources pointed to a new and more accurate framework for looking at the early development of the game. He developed this framework over several years of research during which he networked with collectors, scholars, and archivists. He unearthed scores of previously overlooked sources and dusty old volumes containing traces of early baseball and related games. He examined sources not just in early modern English, but also in French, German, and other languages. All the while, I can only imagine that he kept asking himself, "Why hasn't anyone covered this ground before?"

To that question we can add a corollary: What other ground remains to be covered? Block tantalizes us with stories and illustrations of bat-and-ball games of Norse, French, Germanic, and Polish origin. Each of these possible ancestors and possible cousins of baseball bears further scrutiny, though their full analysis falls outside the scope of this work. Perhaps the next step is for baseball researchers to bridge the gap between our research community and the work of European anthropologists and folklorists interested in the games and pastimes of earlier cultures.

David Block and I are firmly convinced that there are further discoveries to be made, and that this book will not be the last word on the origins of baseball. We hope that this book will stimulate much more new thinking and research on the various games that contributed to and became baseball, raising many questions while it answers others. Let the games begin!

Tim Wiles
Director of Research
National Baseball Hall of Fame and Museum

Abner Doubleday invented the game of baseball in 1839 at Cooperstown, New York. This was an unassailable truth of my 1950s
boyhood. It was taught to me by my father. It was inscribed in my
schoolbooks. It was even commemorated by a stamp in my stamp collection. In those days, baseball ruled my world. As its creator, Abner
Doubleday occupied a hallowed spot in my personal hall of heroes.

So when, sometime in the sixties, it finally clicked that old Abner
had nothing to do with the birth of baseball, it was more than a big
letdown. It was a blow that on its own small scale fit right in with the
larger, more somber disillusionments of that decade. Not only was my
country racist and waging a shameful war in Vietnam, it had also lied
to me about baseball's parentage!

Now another thirty odd years have passed, my country has waged
another shameful war, and I find myself writing about the ancestry of
the National Pastime. Perhaps some lingering resentment about the
Cooperstown myth has propelled me in this direction. Maybe I'm annoyed that Abner Doubleday has ascended so effortlessly into the
Folklore Hall of Fame alongside the likes of Paul Bunyan and Rip Van
Winkle. Not that I have anything against Abner personally, but his
myth was not benign. It fooled several generations of Americans
into accepting a deliberate historical falsehood. It also hijacked and
stunted the progress of research into early baseball for many decades.
Historians saw little need to study the origins of the game because the
question appeared to have been resolved. Neither the midcentury re-
alization that the Cooperstown myth was bogus nor the more recent
decision by the Baseball Hall of Fame to cease promoting Doubleday
as the game's inventor seemed to make much of a difference. Researchers continue to skirt the study of baseball's beginnings, perhaps, in part, because the trail has grown so cold.

So here we are in the first years of the new millennium, and the
questions of how, when, and where baseball began remain largely

unanswered. This is an ironic (if not embarrassing) predicament for a sport that has been dissected and studied like none other. And it becomes more and more difficult to remedy with each passing decade. The fossils and relics of baseball's earliest moments were never bountiful, and now such faint traces that may remain are buried beneath three hundred years of historical sediment. In spite of this, new clues about the game's distant beginnings occasionally rise to the surface, the result of painstaking digging by researchers, or simply by fortuitous accident. These findings demonstrate that while the quest for baseball's wellspring may have lay dormant for decades, the prospects endure for its fruitful resumption. My hope is that *Baseball before We Knew It* will renew interest in this unfinished business.

When planning the book I came to realize that the subject of baseball's evolution could not be satisfied by a traditional linear approach. Before I could venture my own investigation and analysis of the historical components that ultimately resulted in our National Pastime, I first had to contend with the considerable body of facts and opinions on the topic that had accumulated over the past 150 years. The challenge was to identify which particles of information within this legacy could be substantiated by historical documentation. The unfortunate reality is that much of what has passed for literal history in the realm of early baseball cannot be corroborated. This applies not only to obvious fairy tales like the Doubleday Myth but also to such widely accepted assumptions as the one that posits baseball's descent from the English game of rounders. Despite their evidentiary shortcomings, these enduring misconceptions of baseball's origins have established deep footholds and are now almost inseparable from the history they purport to explain. Clarifying this muddle became my first order of business, and I devote several chapters to these fallacious theories, shedding new light on their derivations and showing how their respective explanations for the birth of baseball are at variance with known historical evidence.

Separating fact from fancy in the realm of early baseball scholarship was the prerequisite to the second stage of *Baseball before We Knew It*, in which I endeavored to explore the terrain upon which our National Pastime was constructed. Casting as wide a net as possible, and relying almost exclusively on period sources, I sought to identify and analyze every possible early ball game and pastime that might have had a place in baseball's genealogy. I traced most of these games to their roots in the English countryside, but also included some of their continental cousins in the mix. I then focused on the scattered fragmentary clues of baseball's awakening in America during the century preceding 1845. It was only when I brought together the results of my studies from both sides of the Atlantic that I could hazard an educated reconstruction of how the game came to be formed.

My research found me poring through many old volumes of printed works going back hundreds of years. These books covered a hodgepodge of topics, and were united only by their common characteristic of sheltering some hint of early baseball, or one of its relatives. A full itemization of these books, along with detailed commentary on their contents' relevance to baseball history, appears in an annotated bibliography following my final chapter.

In the course of these pages I occasionally point out what I believe to be factual or analytical errors committed by other historians. Among those whom I presume to correct is Robert W. Henderson, who twenty-five years after his death remains the recognized authority in the field of early baseball. In writing history, mistakes are made, even by the great ones like Henderson. Inevitably, despite my best efforts to avoid them, the future will likely reveal that my book too contains factual errors or faulty analyses. History is a collaborative process, and each historian who approaches a topic with a fresh perspective will invariably build upon and correct the findings of those who have gone before.

Through *Baseball before We Knew It* I have tried to expand the universe of knowledge about the beginnings of baseball, while also providing a launch point for further explorations. I hold no illusions that my efforts, combined with those of other present and future historians, will ever connect all the dots of the game's earliest days. Still, my experiences researching this book have convinced me that much more is knowable, and that many more discoveries remain to be made.

ACKNOWLEDGMENTS

❖

In this project I have benefited enormously from the advice and contributions of many individuals. None has contributed more than my brother Philip Block, whose shared interest in the arcane world of early baseball provided a sounding board for me at every step along the way. Aside from his patient counsel and encouragement, Philip's scholarly investigation of the "missing link" between Abner Doubleday and Albert Spalding graces this book with an intriguing new take on a storied old myth.

Another prized contributor to this work is Tim Wiles, whose gracious foreword serves as the perfect keynote to the themes and questions raised within these pages. Tim's thoughtful comments reflect his passion for the history of the game and the insightful perspectives on baseball scholarship gained from his unique vantage point at the National Baseball Hall of Fame. He has also been a generous dispenser of friendship and advice during the course of this project.

I am also extremely grateful for the mentoring of Tom Altherr, whose expertise in the primeval roots of baseball in America is unparalleled. Tom and I became acquainted by telephone and spent long hours discussing minutiae that were fascinating to us but which probably would put most people to sleep. His amazing knowledge and memory, frequent encouragement, and sage counsel were invaluable assets to me and to the book.

This project would never have happened at all if not for Barry Sloate. His article on collectible baseball books, written in 1995, spurred my interest in that area of collecting. In 2001 I called Barry out of the blue, introduced myself, and proposed that we collaborate on an expanded version of his article. He accepted and we started to work. Soon my interest in expanding the effort to a major bibliography and beyond overwhelmed the modest original objective that Barry had signed on for, and we mutually agreed that I would pursue the project solo. Nevertheless, Barry's contributions to the bibliography have been considerable, and I am grateful for his continuing support and friendship.

Thanks are also due to longtime friend Tom Shieber of Cooperstown. Tom has saved me hours of digging by being ever ready to draw upon his lively knowledge of early baseball to answer questions for me. More important, his enthusiastic and contagious embrace of the subject deserves credit for setting me on the course to a similar addiction.

While researching this book I frequently encountered older source material written in languages other than English. SABR member David Ball, whose command of seemingly any language is rivaled only by his generosity and willingness to help, bailed me out by translating numerous passages written in French, German, and Latin. I am indebted to him and his skills as a linguist.

I am also appreciative of the following individuals, whose contributions, large or modest, helped get me to the long-elusive finish line: Gerard Beliveau, Jane Pomeroy, Becky Cape, Walter Handelman, Mary Akitiff, Cory Reisbord, Blanche Zimmerman, Robert Rieder, John Thorn, Mark Rucker, Matt Schoss, Pete Nash, Miryam Ehrlich Williamson, Fred Ivor-Campbell, Peter Morris, Dean Sullivan, Phil Goodstein, Chip Martin, Evelyn Begley, Skip McAfee, Ted Hathaway, Hugh MacDougall, Frank Phelps, Bill Poston, Fred Shapiro, Joe Dittmar, Larry McCray, Robert Strybel, Stas Wnukowski, Barry Popik, Eric Coupal, Daniel Bloyce, John Freyer, Tony Collins, Paul Wendt, Richard Cox, Dave Terry, and the German tourists on the ferry boat to Juneau.

Saving the most emotional for last, I am overawed by the loving support I have received at every step of the way from my family. My brother Mike offered helpful insights after reading my earliest wobbly draft, my brother Joel provided contract advice, and my brother Philip's prodigious contributions I have already acknowledged. I am also deeply grateful for the encouragement and support I have received from Frank, Linda, Karen, Wendy, Camilo, Idania, Laura, Jeremy, Max, Aaron, and Phil.

If riches are measured by the quality of one's children, Bill Gates has nothing on me. My daughter Maggie and her partner Kelly have been steadfast in their advice and encouragement since day one. And Jamie . . . well, if Jamie's energy could ever be harnessed we would solve our dependence on fossil fuels. His unqualified love and enthusiasm have buoyed me through these past few years and have kept me preternaturally young.

Soaring at the head of this wonderful family are my parents, Sam and Frieda Block, whose wisdom has guided me, and whose caring values have been my life-long inspirations. And — credit where credit is due — my mom's foresighted decision not to throw out that shoebox of baseball cards from 1952 triggered my later interest in collecting baseball memorabilia, which ultimately led to this book.

It is also with deep affection that I remember my late mother-in-law, Ruth Duhl, whose love for the joys of language was infectious. She would take heart in knowing that her bequest to me of her treasured full set of the *Oxford English Dictionary* would be applied to such a practical purpose.

To my wife, Barbara, I owe everything. She has been a boundless provider of love, patience, prodding, advice, and every other ingredient needed to propel this first-time author through the scary and challenging ordeal of carrying a book through to completion. While I took an early retirement to write, she continued her dedicated work as a public school teacher despite having to do battle with the colossal frustrations and failings of the system. In every way that counts, she shares full credit for getting me to this point, and for everything this book accomplishes.

BASEBALL
BEFORE WE
KNEW IT

UNCERTAINTY
AS TO THE
PATERNITY

The age-old debate over baseball's ancestry has always been long on bluster and short on facts. Since the earliest days of the game's prominence in America, writers have been eager to expound upon its origins. That they generally had no clue of what they were talking about never seemed to slow them down. As early as 1856 the editors of *Porter's Spirit of the Times*, one of the earliest sporting journals to cover baseball, mused on the game's derivation:

> Notwithstanding the antiquity of Cricket, which was introduced to the U.S. by Englishmen resident among us, we must confess that we feel a degree of old Knickerbockie [*sic*] pride, at the continued prevalence of Base Ball as the National game of the region of the Manhattanese of these diggings. We are not about to write a history of its rise and progress among the early settlers — those sturdy Dutch Burghers, who were in the olden time seen, playing at bowls on the *Bowling Green* — any more than we intend to enlighten the Cricketers on the first match — then we believe termed wickets — which is said by the old chroniclers, to have been invented by the Druids, and was first played at Stonehenge.[1]

The editors' colorful prose appears to imply that the National Game originated with the Dutch founders of New York, rather than the later-arriving English. Continuing the theme, *Porter's* introduced its coverage of baseball's first convention in January 1857 with another burst of enthusiastic verbiage:

Now, for some time past, sensible men have attempted to rouse the attention of "Young New York . . . to the development of their physique;" and yet, beyond the range of the "Cricket Clubs," but little was effected until the past year, when Base Ball started up like the ghost of Hendrik Hudson, who in the veritable history of this village, is represented as having played annually a game of ba'l amid the Kaatskill Mountains. Be that legend, however, fact or fiction, we have to deal with a veritable fact, that a convention of Young New York was held . . . to discuss . . . the best method of encouraging out-door sports, and Base Ball in particular.[2]

But in contrast to the whimsical approach of *Porter's* editors, one of the publication's readers was giving the subject of baseball's beginnings a more literal appraisal. In a letter printed in the October 24, 1857, issue, the correspondent, identified only as "X," wrote: "We find that Cricket was played as early as, and perhaps before the sixteenth century. . . . Base ball cannot date so far back as that; but the game has, no doubt, been played in this country for at least one century." The anonymous writer also stated: "Although I am a resident of the State of New York, I hope I do her no wrong by thinking that the New England States were, and are, the ball grounds of this country," adding: "the boys of the various villages still play by the same rules as their fathers did before them."[3] This measured commentary might have opened the door to an early rational discussion on the origins of baseball in America, but any hope for this was drowned in the tide of bombast that was to follow.[4]

By 1858 other newspapers and magazines joined *Porter's* in offering casual opinions about baseball's heredity. An author writing in the *Atlantic Monthly* that year hailed "our indigenous American game of base-ball."[5] The following year a second writer for the same publication referred to the "Old-Country games of cricket and base-ball."[6] So who was right? Was the National Game a native of American soil or a product of English heritage? In 1859, the year that Charles Darwin published his *Origin of Species*, the game of baseball was spawning its own origins controversy.

While *Porter's* and the *Atlantic* may have been the first to enter the fray, Englishman Henry Chadwick soon turned the issue into his personal fiefdom. Chadwick was a rising sportswriter in New York City who eagerly embraced the young sport which some newspapers were already identifying as the National Pastime. His tireless promotion of the game would soon earn him the sobriquet the "father of baseball." In his introduction to the sport's first annual guide in 1860, Chadwick proclaimed that baseball was of "English origin" and "derived from the game of rounders."[7] With these few simple words, Chadwick set a framework for the debate over baseball's ancestry that still prevails. Over the years the debate has occasionally risen to the forefront of national attention, while at other times, it has completely receded from view. The subject has inflamed passions and patriotism, and along the way engendered its own mythology. Now, more than 140 years since Chadwick raised it, the issue of baseball's provenance remains largely unresolved.

To understand why historians have failed to unlock the mystery of baseball's past, it is useful to study the twists and turns the debate has followed over the years. For a quarter century following Chadwick's anointment of rounders as baseball's predecessor, his theory encountered few challengers, undoubtedly due to the respect he commanded as the game's foremost booster. Most other baseball writers of the era, such as Charles Peverelly, whose 1866 book *American Pastimes* contained the first extensive historical coverage of the game, were content to echo the Chadwick orthodoxy.[8]

One exception to this consensus appeared in the August 26, 1869, issue of *The Nation*. In an article extolling the National Pastime and comparing it to cricket, the author, A. H. Sedgwick, protested the suggestion that baseball was of foreign origin.[9] Instead of challenging Chadwick's rounders theory, however, Sedgwick objected to the notion that baseball derived from cricket. He wrote: "It is a matter of common learning that [baseball] is of no foreign origin, but the lineal descent [sic] of that favorite of boyhood, 'Two-Old-Cat.' . . . He would indeed be an unfaithful chronicler who should attempt to question the hoary antiquity of 'Two-Old-Cat,' or the parental relation in which it stands to base-ball."[10] Although Sedgwick's viewpoint went largely unnoticed at the time, it is of some historical importance in that he was the first observer to suggest that baseball derived from the American "old-cat" games. In the following decades, some of the most prominent proponents of baseball's American birth would eagerly embrace Sedgwick's "old-cat" hypothesis.

In the 1880s the baseball journalist William M. Rankin became the first commentator to confront directly Henry Chadwick's assertion that baseball descended from rounders. In a newspaper article syndicated in 1886, Rankin laid out his argument:

[Baseball's] origin dates back many years, but as to what it sprung from is a matter of conjecture. Some writers advanced the theory that the origin of baseball was in the old game of rounders or town-ball, which was played in many sections of this country before the present game became so popular. As no one disputed this claim it has remained so, or at least it has been accepted by all baseball writers to the present day as a fact not to be disputed. On what basis the claim has been made has never been explained. Unless, however, it is that in each game bases, bats and a ball are required. Thus far and no farther can a comparison be made in the two games.[11]

Rankin then described several ways in which he believed town-ball or rounders differed from baseball: the flat shape of the bat, the square configuration of the bases, the variable number of players involved in the game, and the practice of "plugging" a runner (putting him out by striking him with the ball). "There is nothing in the above description that in any way resembles the national game of baseball," he wrote, "either in its earliest days or in its present form." He went on to mention some basic features of modern baseball, including the diamond-shaped infield, nine men on a side, and three outs per inning. Rankin argued that the rules for the "former games" were "entirely different" from the rules for baseball that had been drafted by the Knickerbocker Base Ball Club in 1845. He concluded:

It can no more be claimed that the game of baseball had its origin in rounders or town-ball than billiards were the issue of pool, or the latter came from bagatelle. It is like Mr. Darwin's theory of the origin of man — it lacks the necessary connecting links to carry out the idea. The game of baseball seems to have sprung up, just as any game has. It has improved each year until it has reached its present state. A claim might just as well be made that rounders had its origin in cricket as that baseball sprung from rounders, and the claim would be just as good in the one case as in the other.[12]

If Rankin held a serious theory for how baseball actually came about, it was obscured by his impassioned efforts to distance the National Pastime from town-ball and rounders. It seems that he was content to assert that baseball simply had "sprung up," for which he offered the faintest of evidence: "It is claimed by several gentlemen, now residing in New York, that they played baseball over fifty years ago. The game at that time had no regular set of rules, but the side getting the first twenty-one aces or runs was declared the victor. There is no doubt whatever but that the game was played in New York over fifty years ago; as it will be seen that the Knickerbockers had no trouble in finding a rival nine so far back as 1846."[13]

In short, it appears that Rankin's theory was that baseball formed spontaneously in early New York sometime before the mid-1830s. His proof was that there were other teams available to compete with the Knickerbockers in the 1840s. His uncompromising opposition to Chadwick's rounders theory apparently precluded even token acknowledgment that baseball could have been influenced by earlier games. In Rankin's defense, however, it is probable that his widely circulated 1886 article represented a distorted version of his actual views. He revealed this in a published letter written more than twenty years afterward: "In the winter of 1885 and 1886 I wrote a brief history of the origin of the game . . . to be syndicated. My version was so much at variance with the then accepted theory that it was 'doctored,' and while it did not say the game had sprung from rounders, it cut out that which I had said. I didn't see the story until after it appeared in print, or it never would have been broadcast over the country."[14]

This alleged censorship could help explain why Rankin's article was so sharply critical of Chadwick's rounders theory, yet never mentioned the legendary baseball writer by name. In fact, if the "doctoring" assertion is true, the motivation of Rankin's editors was very likely their reluctance to print anything negative about Chadwick, who at that time was among the most respected figures in the world of baseball.

Rankin's article was the preliminary skirmish in what was to become a major assault on the rounders theory. The first big gun to join the fray was popular ballplayer and author John Montgomery Ward. Rankin later took credit for Ward's involvement, claiming in a 1905 letter to baseball magnate Albert Spalding: "It was from my article that John M. Ward obtained his ideas about the origin of baseball, and so expressed them in the book he issued in 1888."[15] Whatever the actual catalyst, Ward took up the cause with vehemence. Unlike Rankin, who appeared to be motivated purely by the desire to defend baseball's originality, Ward was driven by extreme jingoism. He was so incensed by Chadwick's notion that baseball was of foreign derivation that in 1888 he devoted the first fifteen pages of his book *Base-ball: How to Become a Player* to "proving" that the sport was, in fact, of American birth. He asserted that those advocating rounders snobbishly believed that "everything good and beautiful in the world had to be of English origin" and that they had come to their conclusion based only upon superficial similarities between the two games. Ward contended that baseball had been played in the United States for at least a century, likely since colonial times, and had, in fact, actually predated the "old" English game of rounders.[16]

After comparing all the features of the two games, Ward, who was also a lawyer, summarized his argument: "In view, then, of these facts, that the points of similarity are not distinctive, and that the points of difference are decidedly so, I can see no reason in analogy to say that one game is descended from the other, no matter which may be shown to be the older."[17]

Having dismissed the rounders theory, Ward now turned to another annoying thorn, the evidence that a game called "base-ball" existed in eighteenth-century England. He maintained that this earlier pastime could not possibly have been an ancestor to American baseball because if it had been, the Anglophiles would have seized on it, not rounders, as the basis for their claim. Moreover, he sneered, this English baseball had been a game for women and girls, and therefore, by definition, could not have been a prelude to the "robust" American sport.[18]

So where did Ward think baseball came from? In answer to this he delivered his famous punch line: "I believe it to be the fruit of the inventive genius of an American boy." He proclaimed baseball to be an American evolution "like our system of government." Ward said old-time players had told him baseball's roots could be traced to the early American game of "cat-ball" — "one-old-cat," "two-old-cat," and so on. While his subsequent descriptions of these games offered scant resemblance to the National Pastime, he nonetheless boldly proclaimed that "from one-old-cat to base-ball is a short step." In summary, Ward laid down the gauntlet: "In the field of out-door sports the American boy is easily capable of devising his own amusements, and until some proof is adduced that base-ball is not his invention I protest against this systematic effort to rob him of his dues."[19]

Later that year, Ward added some fanciful embellishments to his "American boy" theory in an article he wrote for the October 1888 issue of *The Cosmopolitan* magazine:

Exercise Jack must, and this is what he did. Having cut an old rubber shoe into strips he wound these into the form of a small ball. Then he unraveled the leg of an old woolen stocking and wound the yarn around the rubber ball, until the whole was as big around as a good-sized apple. Over this his good mother sewed a petal-shaped leather cover, cut from the soft top of a worn-out boot. And, finally, with the ball thus made, and armed with a broomstick for a bat, he sallied forth ready to take his prescribed medicine upon the village "green."[20]

Because of John Ward's celebrity standing, his dismissal of rounders as baseball's progenitor was accorded considerable coverage in the nation's newspapers. Not surprisingly, it also elicited a spirited response from those who believed the American National Game was of English derivation. Foremost among these, of course, was Henry Chadwick, who wrote the following retort in the *Brooklyn Eagle* of

July 1, 1888: "To say that there is no similarity between [rounders] and our American game of base ball, or to attempt to make the latter a distinctive game of strictly American origin, as Mr. Ward does in his otherwise ably written book on base ball, recently published, is not in accordance with historical facts, to say the least." With more than a modicum of arrogance Chadwick added: "There is no need of presenting any arguments in the case, as the connection between rounders and base ball is too plain to be mistaken."[21]

Chadwick's rebuke of Ward received support from an unexpected quarter, a well-known astronomer named Richard A. Proctor. Like Chadwick, Proctor was an Englishman who had become a naturalized United States citizen; he had gained some renown as the first to publish a complete map of the surface of Mars. Proctor had played rounders in his English boyhood and took umbrage at Ward's excision of the pastime from baseball's historic lineage. He wrote: "Mr. Ward views the evidence as to the antiquity of the game, howsoever called, after what seems to me a strange fashion: but argument on such matters seldom alters opinion, especially when opinion is fanciful to start with." Proctor admitted, "I have not a particle of evidence that the name rounders is as old as, for instance, the settlement of Virginia," but he claimed the game to be at least a hundred years old based upon the recollections of an elderly man he had spoken with decades earlier. He added: "Mr. Ward must not be surprised if, seeing base ball played here in America and finding it to be practically identical with rounders as played in English schools, I regard the two games as one and the same."[22]

The following year, Ward and other professional American ballplayers returned home from the famous six-month Around the World baseball tour organized by former star pitcher, club owner, and sporting goods magnate Albert Spalding.[23] The returning players were honored at a grand banquet held at Delmonico's restaurant in New York, whose attendees included such luminaries as Mark Twain and Teddy Roosevelt. The oft-repeated account of this event places former National League president Abraham Mills at the podium, declaring with nationalist fervor that "patriotism and research alike vindicate the claim that [baseball] is American in its origin."[24] Reputedly the crowd then responded with cries of "No rounders! No rounders!"[25]

Later in 1889 the book *Athletic Sports* appeared, with a focus on baseball and, in particular, Spalding's world tour. The book's first chapter was devoted to baseball's beginnings, with writer W. I. Harris presenting a slightly more balanced approach to the controversy than either Ward or Mills. He wrote: "The origin of baseball is in dispute, and the question will probably never be positively settled. Several writers contend that it came from the old English game of 'rounders,' and there is some evidence to that effect. Others are equally positive that the game is entirely an American product, and the evidence adduced is quite as strong, indeed stronger, that this theory is the correct one." Then Harris put the debate in a context that rang true for many decades, and to some degree still applies today: "To the average devotee of the sport the question does not assume much importance. Only a minority know anything about it, and the vast majority care less. They know they have it, they like it, they wouldn't be without it, and are quite content to believe the game is a home product."[26]

For whatever the reason, 1889 brought a bounty of opinions on baseball's origins. Joining the parade was Professor James Mooney of the Bureau of Ethnology, whose lecture before the Anthropological Society of Washington on December 3 offered what a newspaper described as a "decidedly original" view on the topic. Professor Mooney sided with Rankin and Ward as to the game's domestic roots but reached this conclusion from an entirely different direction:

The modern game of baseball is an American institution, and not, as some might believe, an exotic of foreign growth which has come to us from the older civilizations of Europe and the East. The game from which our present sport is derived had its origin and development among the aborigines of the American continent, who played with bat and ball ages, for aught we know, before the dream of a new world filled the imagination of the Italian adventurer. It is thus American to the core; as distinctively so as the great plains and rivers of the boundless West, or the spirit of freedom and independence which animates us as a people.[27]

Professor Mooney was correct in acknowledging the rich tradition of Native American ball playing but erred in suggesting that any of the truly indigenous Indian games resembled baseball.[28] And despite his stirring paean to America, in which he feted all its glories except Mom and apple pie, it fell to Albert Goodwill Spalding to become the ultimate patriot in the debate over baseball's origins.

Spalding, too, joined the debate in 1889, newly converted to the cause of defending baseball's American patrimony. This represented a big turnaround from his former stance as a booster of Chadwick's rounders theory. The sporting goods giant had made his earlier viewpoint quite evident in a short history of the National Game he had written for the 1878 edition of his annual baseball guide. Taking note of the comparisons to rounders that had followed him and the other American players during the first baseball tour to England in 1874, Spalding stated: "The Englishmen who watched the American Clubs in England, and accused them of playing rounders were not so far out of the way. The game unquestionably thus originated."[29] Now, on the heels of the 1889 world tour, Spalding switched sides. Writing in the October issue of *The Cosmopolitan*, he described his experiences playing in a game of rounders with other Americans when the second tour visited England. He said he was so struck by the differences between that game and baseball that he was now convinced that baseball had to have been of American origin.[30]

In the article Spalding conceded there were differing opinions on the question, and that one unmentioned authority — obviously Chadwick — maintained that baseball "was taken from the old English game of rounders." Then, unexpectedly, he commented that "a French gentleman whom I met in Paris recently insisted that [baseball] was similar to the old French game of *tecque*, introduced into Normandy many years ago."[31] Curiously, three years later, an English sportswriter, Ernest Bell, referring to other Spalding comments on the same French game, came away with the opinion that it was Spalding himself who believed *tecque* to be baseball's ancestor:

Mr. A. G. Spalding, who has devoted much time to an inquiry into the origin of baseball, inclines to the belief that it is descended from the old French game of *tcheque*, which is still played by French schoolboys. According to Mr. Spalding, *tcheque* was imported into America by the French Huguenots, who settled in the Dutch colony of New Amsterdam. It is certainly true that town-ball, the immediate forerunner of baseball, had its largest following in New York city, and that it had been played there for generations before the Dutch and French customs of New Amsterdam had become lost in the modernized New York.[32]

It is hard to know what to make of this passage, since it contradicts Spalding's words of three years earlier, and differs with all of Spalding's subsequent recorded opinions that baseball was of American ancestry. Yet there is no ready explanation for why author Bell would fabricate such an easily disproved story and publish it in an authoritative multivolume work on sports. Bell spelled the name "tcheque," while Spalding had it as "tecque," yet there is no doubt that both were referring to the old Norman ball game identified in nineteenth-century French-Norman dictionaries as "tèque" or "thèque." If in the early 1890s Spalding indeed toyed with the notion that our National Game was influenced by an earlier French pastime, it may indicate only that his views on baseball's origin were at that time still in flux. It also may signal he did not consider an obscure schoolboy's diversion from early New Amsterdam to pose the same affront to American patriotism as English rounders did two centuries later. One final curiosity about Bell's statement is his observation that Spalding "has devoted much time to an inquiry into the origin of baseball." While this was a recognized preoccupation of Spalding, most histories date his great devotion to the subject as arising a full decade later.

Meanwhile, as 1889 drew to a close, Henry Chadwick was undoubtedly growing uncomfortable. The sixty-five-year-old Englishman had reigned as the nation's unquestioned authority on baseball for most of the previous three decades, but suddenly his influence was waning. His long-accepted theory that America's National Pastime had descended from the English game of rounders was under full frontal assault. This could not have pleased the veteran writer whose magnificent knowledge of baseball was matched only by his equally magnificent ego. He sought to counteract the upstart voices claiming baseball was indigenous to America by placing his rounders argument back before the public's view. Chadwick had at his disposal the perfect forum for a rebuttal. As editor of Spalding's widely read annual baseball guide, he had only to insert a reformulated version of the rounders theory into his introduction to the upcoming 1890 issue. Unfortunately, what he offered was so muddled and defensive, and of such questionable accuracy, that he probably did more harm to his cause than good. He wrote:

> As to the origin of base ball, it is virtually quite immaterial whether it sprang from the old English school boy game of Rounders, or not; though the fact that the phase of base ball played by the Olympic Club of Philadelphia as early as 1833 and known as "town-ball," as well as the Massachusetts game of base ball played in the New England States at a far later period, had for their rules a feature of the game of Rounders — viz., the four posts as bases, exclusive of the base where the batsman stood — would go to sustain the claim of its English origin; as also the additional fact that up to the period of the fifties the base ball game in vogue in New York had for one of its rules that of the game of Rounders which put out base runners by hitting them with the thrown ball, there being no base players proper in the game at that time.[33]

Chadwick's defense apparently elicited little notice, and in the months following its publication the fracas surrounding baseball's paternity died down. In the 1890s Chadwick occasionally returned to the rounders topic in local newspaper articles, but he avoided discussing the issue on the pages of the Spalding guide for more than a decade. Then, seemingly out of the blue, the "father of baseball" used his introduction to the 1903 issue of the guide to again lay out his timeworn vision of baseball's ancestry. Perhaps the proud and stubborn writer, now nearly eighty years of age, was personally offended by his friend Spalding's glib and frequent insistence that baseball could not be of English origin. That could explain why he again chose Spalding's baseball guide as the forum for reviving the debate. If Chadwick's intention was to get under Spalding's skin, or to arouse the powerful man's competitive fire over their disagreement, he succeeded to a degree he could never have predicted.

By this time, Chadwick's viewpoint on rounders was more than forty years old, and the times had greatly changed. It was now the dawn of the twentieth century, and newly imperial America was feeling flush with its conquests from the war with Spain. Rampant nationalist fervor invigorated the effort to wrap baseball's origins in patriotic colors, and Albert Spalding was the undisputed champion of the cause. Given his long opposition to his old friend Chadwick's position, he doubtless found it irksome that the latest salvo from the veteran journalist had sprung from the pages of Spalding's own publication.

In 1904 the sporting goods magnate launched a campaign of public speeches and written articles aimed at delegitimizing Chadwick's position for good. On November 17 Spalding delivered a landmark address before a YMCA gathering in Springfield, Massachusetts, in which he laid out an elaborate explanation of baseball's American origins. He later published the text of the speech in a number of newspapers and magazines, including in his own baseball guide for 1905. There he prefaced the speech by ridiculing Chadwick's lack of evidence that baseball was of English descent, stating, "I have been fed on this kind of 'Rounder pap' for upward of forty years, and I refuse to swallow any more of it without some substantial proof sauce with it."[34] In the speech Spalding dusted off a theory he had first tried out in his *Cosmopolitan* article sixteen years earlier. It was modeled on John Ward's speculation that baseball derived from the American colonial era game of "one-old-cat." Spalding contended that one-old-cat had evolved into the companion games of two-, three-, and four-old-cat, the latter featuring a four-base square infield. He theorized that four-old-cat transformed into the game of town-ball, "from which the present game of base ball no doubt had its origin."[35]

There is a touch of irony in Spalding's nomination of town-ball as the immediate evolutionary predecessor of baseball. He needed to provide some kind of intermediary link to justify and explain his awkward hypothesis that baseball had sprung from the remote old-cat games, and the game of town-ball was as well suited for this as any. Yet in making the choice Spalding had to contradict the veteran baseball writer William Rankin, who had inaugurated the campaign against Chadwick's rounders theory twenty years earlier. Rankin had lumped town-ball together with rounders as "former games" that were completely unrelated to baseball.[36]

Spalding sought publicity for his crusade on the pages of newspapers big and small, and the controversy provided lively fodder for the yellow journalists of the day. "Spalding vs. Chadwick" was the focus of column after column, with the debate taking on the aura of a heavyweight championship bout. Journalists took the debate to extremes of fancy. One reported that ball playing originated with the biblical prophet Isaiah.[37] Another wag, not to be outdone, raised the question: "Assuming that baseball originated in America . . . who was the first player? There are good grounds for belief that Adam had no knowledge of the game. Certainly he was unacquainted with 'three old cat.' At the time that Adam swiped the apple there were only two in the garden — Adam and his animated rib. Two cannot play 'three old cat.' There is, however, plenty of evidence that Adam played catch with some of the garden fruit."[38]

Having propelled the issue to the forefront of national interest, Spalding in late 1904 began convening a commission of influential citizens with baseball backgrounds to settle the question of the game's origins "once and for all."[39] He rightly judged that his own prestige as a giant in the field of baseball would endow his handpicked tribunal with all the authority and legitimacy it needed. If any critics questioned the impartiality of a procedure in which one side of the contest selected the judges, their quibbles never made a ripple. Acting with little pretense of objectivity, Spalding's commission solicited testimony from dozens of baseball old-timers, asking them to recall their earliest memories of the game. The following excerpt from a letter Spalding wrote to the Massachusetts baseball pioneer John Lowell typified the tone of his inquiries:

I have become weary of listening to my friend Chadwick's talk about base ball having been handed down from the old English game of "Rounders," and am trying to convince myself and others that the American game of Base Ball is purely of American origin, and I want to get all the facts I can to support that theory. My patriotism naturally makes me desirous of establishing it as of American origin, if possible, and as the same spirit will probably prompt you, I would like your ideas about it.[40]

The responses to Spalding's outreach were varied and contradictory. New Englanders recalled playing the "Massachusetts game," which they usually remembered as "round-ball." Some New Yorkers wrote to the commission describing their memories of playing versions of old-cat. Others reported playing an assortment of other bat and ball games, which bore various names including "base ball," or no name at all. None recalled playing rounders.

Amid all this input, the editors of the *Beacon Journal*, a newspaper in Akron, Ohio, received a letter in April 1905 from an aging mining engineer, a resident of Denver named Abner Graves. He was responding to an article that had appeared in the newspaper under Albert Spalding's byline soliciting information about the origins of baseball. In his letter, a copy of which he forwarded to the commission's secretary, James Sullivan, Graves stated with great conviction that Abner Doubleday had invented the game of baseball sixty-five or so years earlier in Cooperstown, New York. Graves wrote that Doubleday's invention, which featured a four-base infield configuration and two opposing teams of equal size, was a welcome improvement over the cumbersome form of the game of town-ball that he and his friends had been playing.[41]

Seven months later, Graves received a response from Albert Spalding himself. The great man gushed over the contents of Graves's letter and said, "If the statement therein made that the game of Base Ball was invented by Abner Doubleday of Cooperstown, N.Y., can be verified by some supporting facts or evidence, I feel quite certain it will have great weight with the commission in deciding when, and where and how the American national game originated."[42] Spalding also threw in some questions for Graves, including: "Who was Abner Doubleday?" This question was positively strange in that Graves had mentioned in his letter that this was "the same, who as General Doubleday won honor at the Battle of Gettysburg in the 'Civil War.'" Besides, as Philip Block will reveal in Chapter 3, Spalding knew the name Abner Doubleday very well.

Graves responded a week later and provided Spalding with new details about the Cooperstown event. But he admitted, "I am at a loss how to get verification of my statements regarding the invention of base ball" and pointed out that all the other boys who had witnessed Doubleday's presentation were either dead, feeble minded, or aged.[43]

Two years later Spalding's commission submitted its final report. From among the mountain of evidence procured, and notwithstanding the absence of corroborating testimony, the members selected Graves's letters as the centerpiece of their findings. Curiously, certain details from Graves's original comments had undergone transformation. For example, where he had written that Doubleday's version of baseball continued the old-time practice of throwing a runner out by striking him with the ball, the commission announced that Doubleday had replaced this with the innovation that runners be put out at a base. Also, Graves had expressed some uncertainty about the date of the Doubleday event, but the commission placed it firmly in the year 1839.

The report was dated December 31, 1907, but was released to the public on March 20, 1908, packaged within the new edition of the annual Spalding baseball guide.[44] To the surprise of no one except Henry Chadwick, the commission pronounced baseball to be of sound American stock.[45] The Civil War hero Abner Doubleday had invented the game in the year 1839 in the village of Cooperstown. In the commission's view, the great matter was resolved, and a relieved nation could now rejoice in knowing that its beloved National Game was truly homegrown.

The only ripples of opposition to these findings came from two prominent sportswriters. The first was Will Irwin, who in May 1909 wrote a series of articles on baseball history for *Collier's* magazine. He needed but a few short paragraphs to upbraid both sides of the controversy. He proved not only that baseball predated Doubleday but that it predated rounders as well. Irwin wrote: "It was called 'baseball' from the very first, and the name 'baseball' for rounders and its modifications goes back to England." He also stated: "General Doubleday certainly did not invent the name 'baseball,' and in 1839 he was at West Point."[46] The second voice skewering the commission's report was, surprisingly, William M. Rankin, the veteran baseball writer who had been the first to challenge Henry Chadwick's rounders theory a quarter century earlier. Rankin had exchanged letters with Spalding in early 1905, and they had saluted each other as fellow proponents of baseball's American pedigree.[47] Four years later, Rankin still believed the game was American, but he was convinced that its inception dated to the founding of the Knickerbocker Base Ball Club in 1845. In a 1909 letter to Alfred Spink, founder of the *Sporting News*, Rankin said that baseball "owe[d] its origin to [the Knickerbocker pioneer] Alexander J. Cartwright," a viewpoint that was to gain currency later in the twentieth century. Rankin then bluntly expressed his thoughts on the commission's findings:

The latest of all the fakes [among theories of baseball's ancestry] was the one with the Cooperstown flavor in which one Abner Graves of Denver, Colo., declared that the late General Doubleday was "its designer and christener." He said he was a "kidlet" and was on the ground when General Doubleday turned the trick in 1839. What a pity he did not select some other year so that his air bubble could not be pricked so easily. The records of West Point, N.Y., and the War Department at Washington, D.C., were the means of exposing his fake. [Doubleday enrolled in the United States Military Academy in 1838, and military records indicate that he did not take any leaves of absence during 1839 and 1840.][48]

But these critics carried little weight compared to the towering influence of Spalding and his commission, and the American public was quick to welcome Abner Doubleday as the nation's newest icon. The Cooperstown tale rapidly found its way into children's schoolbooks, taking its place alongside other historical anecdotes like Ben Franklin and his kite, and George Washington and the cherry tree. The debate over baseball's origins quietly slid into the shadows. In part this peace was due to the passing of those two old warriors, Chadwick and Spalding, whose personalities and friendly rivalry had so long fueled the controversy.[49] More to the point, in the minds of most observers, there was nothing left to debate.

But in the decades following the commission's report, away from the limelight, a new challenge was stirring. A determined New York librarian, Robert W. Henderson, was quietly pursuing a novel approach to the question of baseball's ancestry: serious historical research. The energetic Henderson had immersed himself in the world of books, simultaneously holding jobs with the New York Public Library and the New York Racquet and Tennis Club. In this latter position, as curator of the club's library, he assembled what may be one of the most important private collections of sporting titles in the world. With great resources at his command, Henderson began researching his favorite subject, the history of ball sports. And as a particular focus, he turned his attention to baseball and the Doubleday story.

Meanwhile, the National Pastime was gearing up for a celebration of its centennial anniversary, which would be highlighted by the dedication of the new Hall of Fame Museum. Naturally, the year chosen was 1939, one hundred years following the presumed invention of the game in Cooperstown. But a few weeks before the big party, Henderson delivered an unwanted birthday present. In an article appearing in the *Bulletin of the New York Public Library*, Henderson proved beyond a reasonable doubt that the Doubleday story was pure fiction. Citing irrefutable bibliographic evidence, he demonstrated that a description of baseball, including a diagram of the diamond-shaped infield, had first appeared in print in the mid-1830s, several years before Doubleday's "invention" of the game in 1839. Furthermore, Henderson showed that these same rules had been published even earlier, in 1828, under the name "rounders."[50]

Once again, the question of baseball's ancestry became a media preoccupation. Henderson had documented his arguments thoroughly, and writer after writer had to acknowledge grudgingly that the librarian was probably correct. Nevertheless, neither the baseball establishment nor even the newspapers were going to allow something so trivial as the truth get in the way of their celebration. With the world on the verge of war, sacred patriotic cows were to be guarded, and Henderson's research was brushed aside. For example, the *New York Times* had this to say on the subject:

> Never mind Europe. Consider what's happening in this country. Baseball officials have been going around making plans for the celebration of the first hundred years of the national pastime. . . . Now Mr. Robert W. Henderson of the New York Public Library staff has dropped a regular bomb on the big baseball program. . . . His researches have led him to the clammy conclusion that baseball was played before 1839, and at other places than Cooperstown. . . . Mr. Henderson has evidence to burn and a lot of baseball officials . . . think that's just what should be done with it. . . . The Cooperstown origin and the date of 1839 have been accepted for centennial celebration by common agreement among peace loving citizens, and disturbance of that peace should be placed in restraint until the big parade at Cooperstown has passed its given point.[51]

Henderson also challenged the propriety of the United States Post Office's issuing a stamp to commemorate the fictitious centennial. In a letter responding to Henderson, an assistant postmaster general acknowledged "the lack of tangible evidence to show that this game originated in 1839." He added, "There is nothing to prove that Abner Doubleday or any other single person is entitled to exclusive credit for the founding of baseball." Nevertheless, he concluded, "the fact remains that 1939 is being universally recognized in sport circles as marking the centennial anniversary of the game. It is on this basis alone that the Department approved the issuance of a commemorative postage stamp."[52]

So baseball celebrated a birthday, the country went to war, and Abner Doubleday remained in the history books. Even today, more than sixty years later, a surprisingly high percentage of Americans still believe that old Abner deserves credit for inventing the National Pastime.

In the years since World War II, historians have been generally reluctant to dip their toes in the waters of early baseball scholarship. The Doubleday story was discredited, but what did that leave? Gradually some researchers began to focus on Alexander Cartwright, a member of the original Knickerbocker club of the 1840s. They credited Cartwright for writing the Knickerbocker rules, which became the basis of the "New York game" that developed into modern baseball.[53] In a 1969 *Sports Illustrated* article, Harold Peterson labeled Cartwright the "Johnny Appleseed" of the sport, based upon his overland journey from New York to California in 1849, during which he supposedly introduced baseball at stops along the way.[54] The author followed up his article with a full book on the subject of Cartwright, *The Man Who Invented Baseball*, in 1973. Peterson, through his detailed research of previously undiscovered sources, clearly demonstrated that, before Cartwright, baseball had been evolving for centuries.[55] He narrowly confined his argument for Cartwright as "inventor" to the Knickerbocker's perceived role of having brought early baseball to a more modern form. In the three decades since Peterson published his book, the case for Cartwright has noticeably diminished. Research into the roles of various members of the Knickerbocker club has suggested that other players may have had as much or more to do with the authorship of the rules than did Cartwright.[56]

Regarding the question of baseball's origins, most recent historians of the game have drifted back to square one, which is Henry Chadwick's original contention that baseball descended from rounders. In fairness, it is not "Father" Chadwick whom most cite as the source for the theory, but Robert W. Henderson, who is credited with providing definitive proof that baseball derived from the earlier English children's game. Because of Henderson's exalted reputation as a researcher and bibliographer, the authors of most popular histories of baseball have repeated his conclusions uncritically. These historians as a group have a well-deserved reputation for careful and accurate research, and it is therefore surprising that none has attempted to corroborate Henderson by conducting a new study on the topic.

At last, in the past few years there has been a small awakening of interest in the search for baseball's roots. The Society for American Baseball Research (SABR) chapter in the United Kingdom has conducted valuable inquiries into the English origins of the game.[57] In the United States, Thomas Altherr, a professor at Metropolitan State College of Denver, undertook a painstaking examination of eighteenth-century documents to trace early footprints of baseball in the colonial era. The new research climate has yielded a number of important revelations. In 2001 the New York librarian George Thompson announced his amazing discovery that young men were playing a form of organized baseball in Manhattan in the year 1823.[58] This predated by more than twenty years the previously known record of such activity. Altherr, in his McFarland/SABR-award-winning paper "A Place Leavel Enough to Play Ball," documented evidence of serious ball playing by Revolutionary War soldiers.[59] My own contribution was uncovering a set of detailed rules for a game called "English base-ball" that was published in a German book in the year 1796. This is the oldest known description of the game, and predates by more than thirty years the earliest known appearance of baseball rules in English.

As these discoveries materialize one by one, they reveal that early baseball history remains a vast unfinished canvas. It is remarkable that so little is understood, and so few studies undertaken, about a topic that would seem to be of interest to so many. Perhaps the next step is to sweep away the remaining myths and misconceptions that still block the way, and finally clear an open field for explorations into the mysteries of baseball's birth.

2

ROUNDERS, SCHMOUNDERS

*Base ball is derived . . . from
the English game of rounders.*
HENRY CHADWICK, 1860

*Baseball . . . is the
descendant . . . directly of the
English game of rounders.*
ROBERT W. HENDERSON, 1939

As it happens, neither Chadwick nor Henderson got it right. I recognize that it might seem presumptuous of me to challenge two of the most revered authorities in the history of baseball. Yet facts don't lie, and every time I take a fresh look at the historical evidence, it always tells the same story: baseball-from-rounders is an impossibility!

It is important to acknowledge, however, that the declarations by Chadwick and Henderson about baseball's paternity carried great weight in the eras when they were written, importance that went well beyond their literal accuracy. Chadwick's comment established a vital beachhead in what was to become a century-long battle to convince the baseball public of the game's European ancestry. Henderson's words were embedded within his historic refutation of the Doubleday Myth. Nevertheless, the merit of these pronouncements regarding baseball's derivation must ultimately be judged upon the weight of supporting evidence, and not solely upon the reputations of the pronouncers.

How did it come to pass that these deans of baseball scholarship anointed rounders as ancestor of the National Pastime? It is time to take a close and careful look at this venerable axiom. What were the circumstances under which Chadwick and Henderson made their respective statements? What was their proof? Why have most modern baseball historians lined up to accept their theory? What can we learn now by taking a fresh look at all the known historical facts?

The "father of baseball," Henry Chadwick, was English born and emigrated to America in 1837, when he was almost thirteen years of age. As a child in England he had played a bat and ball base-running game called rounders. Years later, as an aspiring sportswriter in New York, he was on his way home from covering a cricket match when he witnessed two clubs playing baseball and became immediately enthralled.[1] He soon rose to the forefront of journalists covering the game, and over the next fifty years wrote countless articles, guides, and books promoting the National Pastime.

His assertion that the game derived from rounders first appeared in the 1860 edition of *Beadle's Dime Base-Ball Player*, the initial issue of the first annual baseball guide.[2] Seven years later Chadwick expanded on his position in an article entitled "The Ancient History of Base Ball." Rounders, he wrote, was formed by uniting the old running game of "base" with a ball, and the game took its name "from the fact that the players were obliged to run *round* a sort of circle of bases." Chadwick added: "The game of rounders first began to be played in England in the seventeenth century, and was the favorite ball game in the provinces until it was generally superseded by cricket at the close of the last [eighteenth] century." He then stated his belief that "early emigrants" brought the game to America, where it eventually became known as "base ball."[3] Unfortunately, Chadwick never produced supporting documentation for any of these assertions. In fact, in all the years since, no corroborating evidence for any facet of his rounders yarn has ever surfaced.

Over his lifetime, Chadwick repeated the baseball-from-rounders theory innumerable times. Lacking historical proof, he generally based his case solely upon the apparent similarities between the two games: pitching, batting, fielding, and base running. Because he was introduced to rounders early in his life, before knowing that baseball even existed, he naturally assumed that rounders was the older of the two sports. He then made the logical leap of inferring that baseball descended from the older game.

While it is easy to see how Chadwick came to this conclusion, it is remarkable to realize that the whole idea might never have occurred to him except for the happenstance of his birthplace. Chadwick entered the world on October 5, 1824, in the town of St. Thomas, Exeter, in the county of Devon in western England. In a coincidence reminiscent of a Gilbert and Sullivan plot, the year and location of his birth were uniquely aligned to avail him of the experiences that would lead to his rounders theory. Fate then set in motion the events that eventually led to his famous debate with Albert Spalding over baseball's origins, and ultimately generated the Doubleday Myth.

What did Chadwick's theory have to do with his birth in Devonshire? The answer lies in a remarkable English children's book published in 1828, when Chadwick was four years old. The charming volume, entitled *The Boy's Own Book*, described a wide variety of sports and pastimes and provided helpful instructions for how to play them. The book's section "Games with Balls" included a description of the game of rounders, which bore an uncanny resemblance to baseball, right down to the diamond-shaped infield. Even though Chadwick may never have laid eyes on *The Boy's Own Book*, two factors about the work have a direct bearing on his theory. First, the volume just happens to contain the earliest known historical reference to the game "rounders." Second, the book's description of the pastime begins with the words: "In the west of England this is one of the most favorite sports with bat and ball. In the metropolis, boys play a game very similar to it, called Feeder."[4]

By pure chance, Chadwick's birth occurred in the west of England just four years before the name "rounders" first appeared in print, in the very region of the country where the name had been adopted. Had he been born in London, perhaps the great debate would have been over whether baseball descended from "feeder." Had his birthplace been elsewhere in England, there might have been no debate at all because the game in most locales still bore its original eighteenth-century name — "base-ball." But to young Chadwick it was rounders, and this fact profoundly influenced his opinion on baseball's ancestry and, as a result, thrust him into a controversy that surrounded him for the final quarter century of his life.

It was in Chadwick's waning years that Albert Spalding took steps to erase the rounders theory from the pages of history. Zealously moving to brand baseball as Made in America, Spalding convened his handpicked Special Base Ball Commission to "settle" the question of baseball's paternity. From this sprang the infamous assignment of war hero Abner Doubleday as baseball's inventor. But then Robert Henderson, in "Baseball and Rounders," convincingly repudiated the Doubleday Myth. Henderson, an exalted baseball scholar, produced conclusive proof that baseball derived from rounders. Or did he?

Let's take a closer look at what Henderson actually uncovered, as outlined in his "Summary: How Baseball Developed":

In England, before 1750, a bat-and-ball base-circulating game, known as *base-ball*, was a popular children's pastime. It continued to be played, and called *base-ball*, until well after 1800.

This game was known in America at least as early as 1762, growing in popularity until well after 1800, when it was played, and called base-ball, in many parts of the country.

In England, between 1800 and 1825, similar games were played, and as they developed in different localities, the name *base-ball* changed to *feeder* in some places, and *rounders* in others.

In America between 1800 and 1840 as the primitive baseball developed in different localities, the name *baseball* survived, but forms of the game were also known as *round-ball* and *town-ball*.

In England, in 1829, the first rules of any of these game appeared in print under the name *rounders*, and the game of rounders is played in England to this day.

The rules for rounders were reprinted in America for the first time in 1829. In 1835 identical rules were called *Base, or Goal Ball*, and a revision of these rules in 1839 was called *base ball*.[5]

Based upon these findings, Henderson concluded that "rounders is in direct line . . . as having, by far, the greatest importance in the development of the game. Second only in importance to the game of rounders in the ancestry of baseball was the older game, already known as 'base-ball,' similar to rounders. This game was so familiar to the young men of the 1830s, that when rules began to crystallize in print, the name 'base-ball' was the one chosen for the new game." Or, as more concisely restated in his essay's final sentence: "It seems to be clearly established that the game of baseball as played in America today is the descendant, remotely, of the older English game of 'base-ball,' and directly of the English game of rounders."[6]

Over the years, many historians of the game have embraced this statement of Henderson's as the definitive word on the question of baseball's origins. But despite its renown, there is one small problem with Henderson's conclusion — it doesn't follow logically from his own stated facts. His oft-quoted pronouncement that rounders led "directly" to baseball, and was of greater importance to its development than the older, original game of "base-ball," implies a chronological progression of three distinct games: old base-ball, then rounders, then modern baseball. But his "Summary: How Baseball Developed" clearly demonstrates that modern baseball evolved on a direct line from the earlier base-ball, with the term "rounders" being nothing more than a regional nickname that cropped up in western England at a midpoint in its development.[7] In fact, Henderson offers no evidence in his essay that a game called rounders existed at all before the 1820s. And when, in that decade, a pastime called rounders finally did appear, Henderson says, it was "similar" to the older game of base-ball, and "the name base-ball changed to . . . rounders."[8]

Curiously, Henderson's entire baseball-from-rounders theory teeters on one lone historical circumstance — the appearance of rules for rounders in *The Boy's Own Book* in 1828.[9] No earlier references to rounders in books, letters, journals, or newspapers were cited by Henderson, nor indeed are known to exist. This absence of documentary evidence belies the common perception of rounders' antiquity. Within weeks of the publication of "Baseball and Rounders," this inference caught the attention of the London correspondent of the *Christian Science Monitor*, who wrote: "It is a fair conclusion that Rounders . . . was not played in England before the nineteenth century, for if it had been it would surely have been mentioned by Joseph Strutt when, in 1801, he wrote his elaborate and extremely comprehensive work, *The Sports and Pastimes of the People of England*."[10]

It is noteworthy that among Henderson's several other works discussing baseball's origins, none made a case for the direct lineal role of rounders. In an earlier 1937 article entitled "How Baseball Began," he barely mentioned the word "rounders," and it was nowhere to be found in his summary: "Just as racquets and lawn tennis stem back to the ancient game of tennis, which was played in an oblong court, as badminton is a descendant of the lowly battledore and shuttlecock, so is the great American game of baseball a lineal descendant of the English schoolboy game of the same name."[11]

In his landmark study of ball sports, *Ball, Bat, and Bishop*, published in 1947, Henderson noticeably deemphasized his representation of rounders. Among twenty-nine pages devoted to the development of baseball from infancy through 1840, his comments on rounders focused on the significance of the 1828 rules printed in *The Boy's Own Book* and the subsequent reprinting of those rules as "base, or goal ball" in *The Book of Sports* in 1834. On this he observed: "A comparison of the two books can leave no doubt that here we have the transition of the English game of rounders into the American game of baseball." However, his intention here was almost certainly more semantical than historical. In noting the use of the term "rounders" in the 1828 rules, he wrote: "The fact that the name 'rounders' was selected, instead of the earlier name 'base-ball,' indicates that the former name was in more general use about the year 1829."[12]

Taking everything into account, it seems improbable that Henderson would take much joy in having his lifetime of research reduced to the phrase "baseball descended from rounders." For this simplification to be true, it would have to be demonstrated that rounders was a separate and older game that preceded baseball, and, in turn, gave rise to baseball. As we have seen, the preponderance of Henderson's own findings do not support such a conclusion. Whatever his actual intentions, Henderson's anointment of rounders as baseball's predecessor has become so universally accepted among the baseball historians that virtually no one has chosen to question or confirm his assertion for the past sixty-five years. Nor, for that matter, have scholars challenged the companion notion that rounders is an "old" or "ancient" game, a pervasive belief unsupported by existing historical evidence.

Though arrived at in different centuries, Chadwick and Henderson's misleading appraisals of rounders formed an unwitting alliance to confuse the issue of baseball's ancestry for much of the past 150 years. Curiously, during the same period of time, a similar mix-up was at play in Great Britain. There the confusion over rounders is even more surprising, given that the British nation is normally meticulous about its history. The problem dates to the mid-nineteenth century, when the British public first began taking notice of the gushing noises advertising America's love affair with its new National Pastime. When a team of professional baseball players traveled to England and Wales in the summer of 1874 to show off their fancy new game, Britons were not overly impressed. One letter to the editor of the *Daily News* of London typified the common citizen's reaction: "[Your newspaper's description of baseball] leads me to strongly suspect it is my old friend rounders."[13] True, the game was an old friend, but the letter writer, like most British observers, was apparently unaware that it was baseball, not rounders, which owned a longer history on their island.

The British public's confusion was due to the same memory gap that had misled Chadwick. The term "rounders" had begun replacing the term "base-ball" in England in the 1820s, and by 1874 most Englishmen had forgotten, or had never known, the game's original name. This amnesia was surprisingly abrupt, given that as late as 1840 the authoritative *Encyclopædia of Rural Sports* was observing: "There are few of us of either sex but have engaged in base-ball since our majority."[14] Since it was a matter of pride for Britons to claim patent rights to America's National Pastime, they were more than happy to promote rounders as its venerable and traditional ancestor, and apparently not too fussy about confirming how long rounders had actually been around. This misconception has flourished uninterrupted through the ensuing years of British history and pops its head into surprising corners of popular culture. For example, an English character speaks the following line of dialogue in the classic 1938 Alfred Hitchcock film, *The Lady Vanishes*: "Baseball. You know. We used to call it rounders. Children play it with a rubber ball and stick."

In the United States today, the uncritical acceptance of the rounders theory by baseball historians is largely attributable to their reverence for Robert W. Henderson's scholarship. However, there may also lurk a more subliminal explanation. It is conceivable that some in this country safeguard the theory because, in a certain way, it renews national pride in baseball's American provenance that was formerly stoked by the Doubleday Myth. After all, there's no special glow for Americans if baseball itself was English born and needed only patience to transform gradually into our modern pastime. Instead, if we contemplate an English children's game of a different name, rounders — which alone was nothing remarkable, but then upon arriving on our shores blossomed magically into beauteous baseball — then that is something to crow about.

Whatever the source of its secret power, there can be no doubt of the brainlock that Henderson's theory has engendered. Pick up any baseball history written during the past fifty years and read what it says about the origins of the game. Invariably, if the topic is mentioned at all, the author will echo Henderson. Footprints of original inquiry into baseball's ancestry are nearly nonexistent. Researchers have seemed convinced that there was no need to look further. In the words of the famed authority Harold Seymour: "Baseball stems directly from the English game of rounders. . . . The unquestionable link between baseball and rounders was proved in 1939 by Robert W. Henderson."[15]

Because of the compelling need to stuff everything into the rounders box, some historians have taken an imaginative route to explaining the embarrassing lack of proof that rounders predated baseball. They suggest that it is not really a chicken-or-egg question, but that rounders should simply be understood as a generic name embracing all early forms of baseball played in England, and that these were antecedents to modern baseball.[16] A highly respected authority on early baseball summarized this view as follows: "I see no problem in saying, with Henry Chadwick, that baseball descended from rounders. His point was chiefly that baseball was not a game created out of whole cloth by Americans, but that it descended from an English children's game. Since Alexander Cartwright . . . and many of the other original Knickerbockers were of English descent, there is no reason to suppose they were not strongly influenced by 'rounders,' *whatever the name they knew the game by.*"[17]

Baseball in eighteenth-century England was a simple children's pastime, varying in form from town to town like other folk games of the era. It is topsy-turvy logic to backdate the name "rounders" to embrace all these varieties and then affirm rounders as baseball's progenitor. The extremes of this argument can appear somewhat ludicrous. Consider the following sentence from the generally authoritative *Oxford Companion to Sports and Games*: "The earliest known literary reference to rounders was in 1744 when *A Little Pretty Pocket-Book* included a woodcut of the game and a verse under the name of 'Base-Ball.'"[18] This same phantom reference to rounders has been freely quoted elsewhere, including an appearance on the web site of the English National Association of Rounders.[19] The same Alice-in-Wonderland logic can be found as far back as 1941, when rounders was discussed in a European journal article on the history of "battingball games." The author gave credit to a German author for providing the oldest account of the game in 1796, but then acknowledged that the source "mentions the game as baseball."[20] So the question is: If it looks like baseball, and it is called baseball, what is it? Rounders?

The facts speak for themselves. While the name "rounders" cannot be found anywhere in the historical annals of England or the United States before 1828, the term "base-ball" shows up at least seven times in eighteenth-century writings. The convincing proof that this eighteenth-century base-ball was the predecessor to modern baseball emanates from the first published rules for "English baseball," in 1796. These rules describe a bat-and-ball game in which a pitcher served to a batter, who had three attempts to put the ball in play. Once striking the ball, the base runner ran counterclockwise around the bases with the object of returning home.[21] This familiar pastime, named "base-ball" and resembling baseball, entered the historical record more than thirty years before the first known appearance of rounders.

As for the name "rounders," after taking root in western England in the 1820s as an alternate term for baseball, it then gradually diverged from its parent. While baseball in America was becoming bigger and faster, rounders in England developed its own unique methodology and culture. Today rounders remains an exciting, popular, and highly organized sport in many parts of the United Kingdom, where it is enjoyed by children and adults of both genders.

Meanwhile, in the first years of the new millennium, virtually every baseball history in print, including those by the most respected researchers, continues to carry the same familiar explanation for the origins of baseball: rounders![22] Within the pantheon of baseball mythology, Abner Doubleday may reign supreme. Yet in terms of longevity, durability, and tenacity, the rounders ancestry myth has proven a formidable challenger.

3

ABNER AND ALBERT, THE MISSING LINK

Philip Block

SAINT DOUBLEDAY

The historian Robert W. Henderson may have missed the mark with his designation of rounders as baseball's immediate ancestor, but he was right on target in refuting the Doubleday-Cooperstown story of baseball's origins. In his journal articles of the 1930s, and later in *Ball, Bat, and Bishop*, Henderson unmasked the Spalding commission's failure to provide verifiable proof for its conclusions. He also called attention to the paucity of evidence that General Abner Doubleday ever had anything to do with baseball. Why, then, did the commission (in the words of Henderson) canonize Doubleday as baseball's "Patron Saint"? Henderson charitably pointed out that the commission members, "all men of integrity," were busy men and that they merely read (and did not research) the report submitted by the commission's de facto chairman, former National League president Abraham G. Mills. The decision, according to Henderson, "was a courteous gesture to Spalding, a kind of recognition of his place as a leader in the sporting fraternity."[1]

Nevertheless, the question remains why Spalding and Mills would be so willing to accept Abner Graves's testimony, despite its dubious historical accuracy. With regard to Mills, Henderson pointed out that the Civil War veteran was far from a disinterested party when it came to Abner Doubleday. He noted that following Doubleday's death, Mills had organized the military honor guard that attended the general's body as it lay in state in New York's City Hall on January 30, 1893. In fact, Mills and Doubleday had been members of the same New York post of the Grand Army of the Republic GAR, the Civil War veterans organization.[2]

Yet it was Spalding, not Mills, who initially seized upon Graves's letters, and cited them in his July 28, 1907, report to the commission: "I would call the special attention of the Commission to the letters received from Mr. Abner Graves . . . who claims that the present game of Base Ball was designed and named by Abner Doubleday, of Cooperstown, N.Y., during the Harrison Presidential campaign of 1839."[3] What was Spalding's motivation in backing the Graves story? Up until the time he received a copy of Graves's first letter, Spalding had long advocated an evolutionary development of baseball, which he was convinced was uniquely American. Progressing from one-old-cat to two-old-cat and the other "old-cat" games, through the development of town-ball, Spalding saw the development of the National Game to be one of incremental changes brought to fruition by the efforts of "an ingenious American lad."[4] Spalding even constructed a "Baseball Tree," a schematic showing the progressive development of bat-and-ball games leading up to modern baseball.[5] Following the appearance of the Graves letter, however, Spalding immediately saw merit in ascribing baseball's invention to a single creator, Abner Doubleday.

Certainly, having a Civil War hero as the founder of the National Pastime was a motivating factor, given Spalding's patriotic view of the game.[6] Yet taken alone, this does not convincingly explain why Spalding so readily subordinated his evolutionary theory in favor of the dubious creationist myth put forth by Graves. In truth, a deeper motivation impelled Spalding to enlist the deceased Doubleday to help establish the "American" origin of the great National Game. Newly gathered evidence confirms a curious connection between Abner Doubleday and Albert Spalding, and it is this connection that explains why Spalding was so ready to embrace Abner Graves's apocryphal tale about Doubleday and Cooperstown.

❖

As the great sporting goods magnate looked over the letter in his hands one can only imagine the complex of thoughts and feelings flowing through his mind. For years Albert Goodwill Spalding — ex–baseball player, ex-manager, ex-owner, and for thirty years America's premier sporting goods mogul and expositor of the joys of baseball — had passionately argued that baseball was of American origin. Now, there in his hands, was the evidence. The letter had appeared out of the blue, sent by Abner Graves to the Akron, Ohio, *Beacon Journal*, and then forwarded to Spalding by James E. Sullivan, Spalding's employee and the secretary of Spalding's Special Baseball Commission. Graves's claim that baseball was the invention of the Civil War hero Abner Doubleday could not have found more receptive ears than those of Spalding, and for reasons that until now have been largely hidden from historians of the game.

Despite his later insinuation to the contrary, Spalding was intimately familiar with the name of Abner Doubleday.[7] The New York–born West Pointer was well known in the post–Civil War period for having aimed the first federal guns fired against rebel forces at Fort Sumter, South Carolina, in the engagement that ushered in the Civil War. He also had a major role at Gettysburg, where he took over I Corps upon the death of General John Reynolds on the first day of the great battle. Two days later, troops under Doubleday's command helped repulse Pickett's Charge. General Doubleday himself wrote several books and many articles on his Civil War experiences, especially at Sumter and Gettysburg, and these were in wide circulation in the late nineteenth century.[8]

Yet Spalding's familiarity with Doubleday also sprang from a connection that was literally much closer to home, and much more intriguing. At the time he received Abner Graves's letter, Spalding and his second wife, Elizabeth, had been living for several years in the Point Loma Community, a spiritual enclave in San Diego founded by the Theosophical Society, perhaps the first major organization in America to study and disseminate Eastern esoteric teachings. Established in 1875 in New York by the controversial Madame Helena Petrovna Blavatsky and Henry Steel Olcott, the somewhat secretive organization had been born on the heels of the Spiritualism movement that had spread throughout America and Europe since the late 1840s. The Point Loma Community, or Lomaland, as it was later known, was established in 1897 under the leadership of another controversial Theosophical leader, Katherine Tingley, at whose side Elizabeth Spalding labored as a loyal and trusted associate. Through his wife, A. G. Spalding also became a major supporter of Tingley and the goals of the Theosophical Society, although some have questioned whether he actually was a member of the group.[9] There is no dispute, however, that a few years previous another famous American had been not only a supporter of the Theosophical Society but a prominent member and one of its early officers — none other than General Abner Doubleday.

THE OCCULT ABNER

Following Doubleday's death at the age of seventy-four on January 26, 1893, *Harper's Weekly* ran an obituary, which read in part:

> Since his retirement he has lived quietly at Mendham [New Jersey], writing more or less for the magazines on military subjects and studying the occult sciences. He was one of Madame Blavatsky's first converts, and was a firm believer in the theosophical theories. He was at one time president of the American Theosophical Society, and during all the latter part of his life took the deepest interest in the affairs of the society and the teachings of the leaders. No one could talk with him on this subject without realizing that he was perfectly honest in his faith. Whatever a sceptic might think of the founders of the society, he could not help believing that this old soldier was a genuine Buddhist, and found much consolation in the religion which he had embraced towards the end of his life.[10]

Exactly how and when Doubleday developed his interest in esoteric philosophy has yet to be discovered, but there is circumstantial evidence that this came about early in his life. Doubleday himself described his youth as one in which his chief interests were intellectual: "I was brought up in a book store and early inbibed [sic] a taste for reading. I was fond of poetry and art and much interested in mathematical studies."[11]

As a cadet at West Point, Doubleday was known as "a diligent and thoughtful student, something of a critic, and fond of questions in moral philosophy."[12] Following his graduation, it is known that he subscribed to the Transcendentalist journal *The Dial*, which was concerned with questions of theology and philosophy and included a few translations from ancient Eastern scriptures.[13] As little else is known about Doubleday's early interest in esoteric philosophy, we can only speculate whether Doubleday's reading of *The Dial* indicates that he was already developing curiosity about occult wisdom. Publicly, however, he was single-mindedly devoted to his military career. For the next thirty years Doubleday served almost continuously as an army officer, seeing duty in the farthest corners of the country and beyond, from Maine to across the Rio Grande in Mexico, and from Florida to California. He saw action in the Mexican War, in the Third Seminole War in Florida, and in many of the well-known battles of the Civil War.[14]

Evidence of Doubleday's interest in the occult during his military years is scant. His memoir of his pre–Civil War military service includes a single reference to anything related to spiritual or occult subjects — having an astrologer cast his horoscope for the year 1855, when he was stationed at Old Point Comfort in Virginia.[15] However, during the Civil War Doubleday may have had the opportunity to compare notes with one other famous person whose connection with the occult has been well documented — Mary Todd Lincoln. General Doubleday and his wife, Mary Hewitt Doubleday, met with President and Mrs. Lincoln on numerous occasions during the war.[16] Mrs. Lincoln was attracted to Spiritualism, even to the point that seances were held in the White House following the tragic death of her son Willie in February 1862.[17]

Doubleday's pursuit of esoteric wisdom became a priority for him following his retirement from active service. On December 11, 1873, he left the army, and with his wife made his home (named "Sumter House") in the little Borough of Mendham, New Jersey, thirty-five miles west of Manhattan.[18] Just five months earlier, Doubleday's soon-to-be spiritual teacher, Helena Petrovna Blavatsky, had arrived in New York City. Now in her forties, Madame Blavatsky was already one of the more unusual women of her time. Raised in an aristocratic and wealthy Russian family, Blavatsky was alleged to have demonstrated paranormal powers from an early age. She later traveled widely throughout the world in search of spiritual teachings. She spoke numerous languages and was already recognized as one of the leading teachers in the field of the occult.[19]

Blavatsky's acknowledged purposes in coming to America were to both observe Spiritualist phenomena ("rappings," apparitions, and other spirit manifestations that allegedly had been witnessed in America since the late 1840s) and to provide to the Spiritualists an esoteric understanding of the phenomena they were supposedly witnessing. In 1874 Blavatsky met Henry Steel Olcott, a New York attorney and a former colonel in the Civil War, who had a longtime interest in Spiritualism.[20] Soon thereafter they formed the Theosophical Society, along with another New York attorney, William Quan Judge.[21] Olcott was named the organization's president, while Blavatsky was corresponding secretary, but it was clear that the Russian was the group's spiritual leader.

It was at this early point in the society's history that Abner Doubleday became aware of the existence of Blavatsky and the society's work.[22] After reading her book *Isis Unveiled*, the general was impressed with the "marvelous erudition displayed" by Blavatsky and the "novel explanations given in the work in regard to the psychical and spiritual phenomena." In his words, he "hastened to make her acquaintance."[23] In June 1878 Doubleday officially joined the Theosophical Society and soon became an active member.[24] He attended meetings of the society in New York and met regularly with Blavatsky and Olcott.[25]

The retired Civil War hero must have made a good impression on the society's founders, as he was named president ad-interim of the American society when Blavatsky and Olcott departed to spread the ideas of the society in Asia. On January 17, 1879, Olcott wrote Doubleday, "In making choice of my substitute I cast about for a man of unblemished character, of ripe age, of energy, and moral courage and quick intelligence and found him in you."[26] In his capacity as an officer of the society, General Doubleday kept an official record of correspondence and other documents in several logbooks, now known as the Doubleday Notebooks.[27] These reveal that Doubleday was at the core of the organization's continued work in the United States. Over the course of the next several years Doubleday would be named vice president of the international organization, as well as vice president of the society's newly formed New York branch.[28] However, it appears that in 1884 Doubleday's public activities on behalf of the society began to wane, and the logbooks do not reveal further significant action on his part.

Privately, the erudite general continued his interest in the society as well as his research in the field of the occult, including the translation into English of two French books on magic and the occult.[29] Doubleday remained an active member of the New York branch of the society until the end of his life, constantly writing to the organization and its members.[30] He was ever faithful to his old teacher Madame Blavatsky, even after she came under numerous attacks by her enemies, including charges that she fraudulently produced psychic phenomena and allegations of alcoholism and other "immoral" behavior.[31]

In the late 1880s Doubleday began to suffer from a variety of ailments which seriously curbed his ability to publicly participate in society activities. On January 26, 1893, the old general died from heart failure at Sumter House. Following a funeral service in New Jersey, Doubleday's body was brought to City Hall in New York City to lie in state in the Governor's Room, the same hall where Lincoln and Grant had rested before him. His cortege was accompanied by a military honor guard in part composed of members of Lafayette Post No. 140 of the GAR under the direction of Colonel Abraham G. Mills, commander of the post and a former National League president.[32] Mills, an old friend of Albert Spalding's, was later to play a prominent role as a member of Spalding's Special Baseball Commission. After lying in state in New York, Doubleday's casket was transported to Arlington National Cemetery, where the general was finally buried on January 31, 1893.[33]

In an obituary appearing in the Theosophical Society journal *The Path*, Doubleday was credited with "many strange psychical experiences of his own" in addition to his respected work on behalf of the organization. He was lauded as a "genuine Theosophist" and one who "ever tried to follow out the doctrines he believed in."[34] The mainstream newspapers, however, generally omitted any reference to the general's esoteric interests when describing the funeral services, memorials, and burial. One wonders whether this was due to the efforts of his wife, Mary, who, unlike her husband, was a faithful member of the Episcopal Church, and probably preferred to avoid publicity regarding her husband's occult interests.[35]

THE SPALDING CONNECTION

Unlike General Doubleday, Albert Spalding did not exactly join the Theosophical Society so much as he married into it. In July 1899 Spalding's first wife, Josie (Sarah-Josephine Keith Spalding), suddenly died, and the sporting goods magnate soon took as his second wife Elizabeth Churchill Mayer, a childhood friend from Rockford, Illinois, whose first husband had also died.[36] At the time of the wedding, Elizabeth had been a devoted member of the Theosophical Society for some ten years. The connection to the society through his second wife had a strong influence on how Spalding spent the remainder of his life, and he, in turn, stood in a supportive role, sometimes quite publicly, as an advocate for the Theosophical Society's programs and goals. And it is this connection that later influenced Spalding to anoint Abner Doubleday so readily as the "inventor" of baseball.

Elizabeth Mayer first encountered the Theosophical Society while a music student in London. Around 1890 she joined the London Lodge of the society, which was then under the leadership of Madame Blavatsky, who had relocated to England in 1887 following organizational controversies in British India. According to the society's journal *Theosophical Path*, Elizabeth, as Doubleday before her, was a personal pupil of Mrs. Blavatsky during this early period.[37] At some point after Madame Blavatsky's death on May 8, 1891, Elizabeth Mayer moved back to the United States and became active at the society's headquarters in Manhattan. There she worked with William Quan Judge, who had taken over leadership of a portion of the Theosophical Society in the aftermath of Blavatsky's death.[38] Judge, it should be recalled, was one of the organization's founders and a former colleague of Doubleday's in the society's work in New York.

After Judge's death in 1896, Katherine Tingley ascended to the leadership of the group and Elizabeth soon became one of Mrs. Tingley's closest friends and subordinates. Beginning in the late 1890s Tingley appointed Elizabeth to a variety of important positions, many of which she held for more than two decades. One of Mrs. Mayer's first tasks was as an emissary for Tingley to San Diego, in order to report on the possibilities of acquiring a large property at Point Loma for establishing a Theosophical center of learning.[39] Through the efforts of other society members the ocean-view property was eventually purchased, and on February 23, 1897, the cornerstone for the new community was laid during an elaborate ceremony.[40] Following this, Tingley and Mayer returned to New York to continue the society's work until the facilities at Point Loma could be completed.

It was perhaps during this time in New York that Elizabeth Mayer and Albert Spalding began to talk of marriage, although Albert was still a married man. In his excellent biography Peter Levine reveals that Spalding's intimate relationship with Elizabeth actually began long before Josie died. Based on information received from Spalding's grandniece, Levine has written that Albert and his childhood friend Elizabeth were secret lovers for years, and that their extramarital relationship yielded a son. Prior to Josie's death the son was raised by Spalding's younger sister Mary L. Spalding Brown as one of her own.[41] At the time the boy was known as Spalding Brown. However, on July 5, 1901, one year after the Spalding-Mayer marriage on June 23, 1900, Albert and Elizabeth adopted the boy through a New Jersey proceeding, renaming him Spalding Brown Spalding.[42] At some later point Spalding began to refer to his "adopted" son as "Albert Goodwill Spalding, Jr.," and this is how the boy was known for the rest of his life.[43] After spending his youth at the Theosophical Society's community at Point Loma, Albert Junior moved on to work at the Paris office of his father's sporting goods firm. When World War I broke out, Albert Junior enlisted in the British Army, and he died in combat near Arras, France, on July 1, 1916. Newspaper obituaries indicated that Albert Junior was born in England in 1891.[44] Thus the secret Spalding-Mayer relationship began no later than 1891, and prob-ably earlier.

On June 24, 1900, the *San Diego Union* announced the Spalding-Mayer nuptials as follows: "A marriage, the announcement of which will come as a surprise to the world in general, was that which was consummated yesterday at the home of the bride, Mrs. Elizabeth Churchill Mayer on Point Loma. The groom is Mr. Albert G. Spalding the father of baseball in the great middle-west."[45] Following their hon-eymoon in France (where Spalding led the American contingent at the Paris Olympics), Mr. and Mrs. Spalding returned to California to construct a new family life in the Theosophical community at Point Loma. The family now included Spalding's son by his first marriage, Keith Spalding, and Elizabeth's son from her previous marriage, Dur-and Churchill; newly adopted Albert Junior soon joined them.[46] In Point Loma the Spaldings occupied a luxurious new home, perched within sight of the Pacific. The house was the most prominent resi-dential structure in the community, and was as much a testimony to the family's central position in the Theosophical Society as it was to the great wealth of the sporting goods magnate.

By that time Elizabeth Spalding was established as one of Mrs. Tingley's closest supporters and occupied many positions of im-portance in the organization. Albert was a strong supporter as well, al-though still occupied with his sporting goods empire and continued involvement with baseball. He was one of several wealthy men whose funds kept the society rolling and whose business experience was put to use in managing the swiftly growing enterprise at Point Loma.[47]

Spalding's important status in the organization became quite pub-lic in 1902, when he defended Tingley and Point Loma against nasty allegations from the New York Society for the Prevention of Cruelty to Children (spcc). Following the Spanish American War, Tingley had arranged for a group of Cuban children to be brought to Point Loma for an education. The spcc questioned Tingley's financial responsi-bility as well as her moral suitability for educating children.[48] While the Cuban children were en route to San Diego, the spcc persuaded immigration authorities to detain them at Ellis Island in New York harbor. Albert and Elizabeth Spalding were in New York at the time and quickly leapt into action as high-profile advocates for Tingley and the society. Over the next five weeks, Albert Spalding appeared before a succession of tribunals to defend the integrity of the Point Loma community. His intervention proved to be the decisive factor, and F. P. Sargent, commissioner general of U.S. Immigration, ordered the release of the children after conducting his own special inquiry.[49]

Albert Spalding's high profile role in the Cuban children affair demonstrated his commitment to the Theosophists and their experiment at Point Loma. It also suggested that Spalding had more than just a passing familiarity with the group during the ten years or more of his affair with Elizabeth that preceded their marriage. Indeed, the lengthy relationship (extramarital and marital) between Albert and Elizabeth Spalding before 1905 provides a telling backdrop to the later selection of Theosophist Abner Doubleday as baseball's creator. The Spalding-Mayer relationship was consummated at the time Elizabeth was still a pupil of Madame Blavatsky's, and it is hard to imagine that Albert Spalding would not have been aware of his lover's discipleship under such a well-known and controversial figure. It is also clear that even at this early period Elizabeth was probably aware of the role that Abner Doubleday had played in the prior history of the organization. When Elizabeth joined the society, Doubleday was still alive, and a member of the New York branch, although his illness had already limited his activities in the group. After her move from London to New York, Elizabeth became an active member of the society, working under the direction of William Quan Judge, Doubleday's former colleague. Presumably Elizabeth was also a reader of the society's organ, *The Path* (published by Judge), which carried a prominent obituary for Doubleday in 1893. While the Spaldings' likely familiarity with the name Abner Doubleday may not have seemed of consequence at the time, it proved important a decade later, when one Abner Graves stepped into the picture.

SMOKING GUN?

Let us now review the sequence of events that followed the arrival of Abner Graves's first letter, in which the old mining engineer claimed that Doubleday had invented baseball at Cooperstown. On April 3, 1905, Graves wrote to the Akron, Ohio, *Beacon Journal*, responding to Albert Spalding's appeal for information on the origin of baseball.[50] On the same day Graves posted a copy of his letter to the secretary of the Spalding baseball commission, James Sullivan. Sullivan immediately wrote back to Graves at his Denver office address, confirming receipt of the letter, thanking him, and telling Graves that his information would be transferred to the Special Baseball Commission "at the proper time."[51]

It has yet to be determined exactly when and how Sullivan sent Graves's April letter to Albert Spalding in Point Loma. Evidence of its transmission is borne out, however, by the appearance of a newspaper article four months later, on August 13. The *New Century Path*, a Theosophical Society weekly published at the Point Loma community, contained a story entitled "Major-General Abner Doubleday." The article ran alongside a photo of the deceased general and began with the words, "Every member of the Universal Brotherhood and Theosophical Society knows of and honors the memory of Major-General Abner Doubleday." It went on to reproduce the Doubleday obituary from the March 1893 issue of *The Path*. But it also added: "It is of interest to note the fact that it is to this stanch Theosophist, well-known army officer and author, that the national game of Base Ball owes not only its *name*, but also in large degree its development from a simpler sport; or, indeed, according to some writers, its *very invention*."[52]

And on whom did the unsigned article rely for this claim? None other than "Mr. Abner Graves, a mining Engineer of Denver, Colorado." The story goes on to quote several sentences from Graves's letter as it appeared in the *Beacon Journal* (without referring to the newspaper by name), beginning with those famous words, "The American game of 'Base Ball' was invented by Abner Doubleday of Cooperstown, New York, either the spring prior, or following the 'Log Cabin & Hard Cider' campaign of General Harrison for President." Yet the article did not stop there. It went on to recognize one other member of the society whose impact on baseball was indisputable: "It is also of interest to note that another well-known member of the Universal Brotherhood and Theosophical Society, Mr. A. G. Spalding, of Point

Loma, California, is universally known as the patron of the development of Base Ball and athletic sports generally; and it is certainly due to Mr. Spalding that so large a proportion of our American youth have a love for the health-giving and manly games."[53]

The significance of the *New Century Path* article cannot be overstated. Published more than two years before the Special Baseball Commission made its official proclamation, it demonstrates how the Theosophical Society provided the link that led Spalding to crown Doubleday as baseball's inventor. The article was published at the society's general offices at the Point Loma colony, within walking distance of the Spaldings' home, at a time when the family was in residence. The material in the article about Graves's identification of Doubleday as baseball's inventor was not public knowledge at the time (except, perhaps, two thousand miles away in Akron) and most certainly arrived in Point Loma via a communication from Sullivan to Spalding. The circumstances surrounding the article's publication strongly suggest that Spalding was fully involved with it, and may have even written it himself. It is also noteworthy that the *New Century Path* story explicitly draws a connection between Doubleday and Spalding, proudly describing them as well-known members of the Theosophical Society who both had made major contributions to the development and growth of baseball.[54]

Records of Spalding's Special Baseball Commission suggest that publication of the *New Century Path* article marked the moment that Spalding began to adopt Graves's baseball creation story as his own. On August 13, 1905, the day the Doubleday article appeared in the Theosophist newspaper, Spalding sent two letters from Point Loma in which he expressed great interest in the Doubleday-Cooperstown theory. The first, addressed to James Sullivan in New York, included some correspondence on the "Base Ball-Rounders theory" and then went on to add, "That Doubleday Cooperstown tip is worthy of careful investigation and corroboration. Enclose find article about Doubleday."[55] The article he enclosed was undoubtedly the just-published *New Century Path* biographical piece on Doubleday.

The second letter of that day was sent to Albert Pratt, an old baseballer who previously had written Spalding about early baseball in

Ticonderoga, New York. Spalding wrote Pratt, "The enclosed may interest you. Note what Abner Graves says of Genl. Doubleday of Cooperstown, N.Y. From this it would seem that Doubleday was the real father of 'Base Ball' and Cooperstown N.Y. its birth-place. Can you corroborate or throw any light or evidence on the Doubleday Cooperstown history? From this it would seem that Doubleday gave base ball its name."[56] As with his letter to Sullivan, the item Spalding enclosed in the Pratt letter was almost certainly the Point Loma article, fresh off the presses.

The evidence of the *New Century Path* story, together with his written communications of August 13, 1905, leave no doubt that Spalding was fully aware of Doubleday's relationship to the Theosophical Society. Yet despite his own involvement with the society — rather, probably because of it — the sporting goods magnate never publicly divulged the organizational ties he shared with the man he was anointing as baseball's inventor. On July 28, 1907, Spalding addressed a lengthy letter to the Special Baseball Commission carefully repudiating the "rounders theory" and giving his endorsement to Abner Graves's Cooperstown creation story. "I am very strongly inclined to the belief that Cooperstown, N.Y., is the birthplace of the present American game of Base Ball, and that Major General Abner Doubleday was the originator of the game," wrote Spalding.[57] This letter, sent from the Spalding residence at the Theosophical Society's colony at Point Loma, needless to say made no reference to the mutual connection of Doubleday and Spalding to the society. In contrast, Abraham Mills's letter to the Special Baseball Commission readily acknowledged Mills's former relationship to the Civil War general through the GAR.[58]

Had Spalding been as candid as Mills, the Doubleday baseball creation story might never have gotten off the ground. It is doubtful whether the other commission members would so readily have rubber-stamped Spalding's recommendation had they been aware of his personal motives for promoting the late general. But even if they had, it is a good bet the press and public would have greeted the Doubleday tale with skepticism when confronted with Spalding's glaring conflict of interest. For the great sporting goods mogul, the Cooperstown creation story would have spun rapidly from a source of pride to a source of embarrassment.

Years later, perhaps we should marvel at Spalding's chutzpah in championing Doubleday as baseball's inventor, all the while refraining from disclosing the Theosophical connection. To the old ballplayer, the Graves story was a convenient means to the end of "proving" the American roots of his beloved game. And if it also elevated to baseball sainthood an esteemed former member of his wife's spiritual organization, well, that was all right too. That the Cooperstown myth would keep several generations of Americans in the dark as to the true origins of their National Game was hardly a concern of its most famous promoter.

PLAYING BALL AT CAMP DOUBLEDAY

An engraving depicting Camp Doubleday shows two members of the Seventy-sixth Regiment of New York State Volunteers playing a baseball-like game (see detail next page).

Abner Doubleday? Bats and balls? Could it be? Fantasies aside, the visual evidence of soldiers playing a game resembling baseball at a Civil War military post named in honor of its commander, General Abner Doubleday, falls well short of reopening the question of whether he invented the pastime. Nonetheless, the placement of two young men armed with bat and ball in the center of this engraving underscores just how commonplace that sort of play was during the War between the States.

The illustration comes from an 1867 book chronicling the exploits of one of the military units that served under the command of General Abner Doubleday during a series of major battles in the war.[1] The

1. A. P. Smith, *History of the Seventy-sixth Regiment of New York State Volunteers* (Cortland NY: Truair, Smith and Miles, 1867).

Seventy-sixth Regiment of New York State Volunteers played a key role in these battles, and their respect for their commander was of such magnitude that they changed the name of their encampment from Fort Massachusetts to Camp Doubleday. In the engraving, two men in the midst of the parade ground are shown to be playing an unusual game. Using baseball bats, they appear to be hitting a ball back and forth in a manner similar to tennis. None of the other soldiers in the scene are involved in the game, which would tend to rule out the well-known two-batter informal "scrub" game known as two-old-cat.

In all likelihood, the two men were engaged in an obscure pastime called drive ball. As described in *The Boy's Book of Sports*, published in 1835, the game consisted of two players facing each other with bats, who took turns striking a ball back and forth. Each player hit the ball from the spot where he retrieved it, with the objective being to advance ground on the opponent.[2] This could be done by preventing a batted ball from getting too far behind you, or, when it was your turn, by driving the ball as far as possible beyond the other player. According to *The Boy's Book of Sports*, "the space of ground passed over will readily show who is the victor."

Searching for a genuine association between Abner Doubleday and baseball is akin to combing through Beatles lyrics for clues that Paul McCartney is dead — you know there is nothing to it, but it offers amusing entertainment nonetheless. The historians Tom Heitz and John Thorn unearthed one bit of historical minutia that might be adjudged a Doubleday-baseball connection, a report that in 1871 he included baseball equipment among a list of requested supplies for the

2. *The Boy's Book of Sports* (New Haven: S. Babcock, 1835), 12.

"colored regiment" under his command at Fort McKavett in Texas.[3] Other than this thin example, careful scrutiny of Doubleday's life has not yielded even the most tenuous tie to the game he was reputed to have invented. So it may well be that the picture of "drive ball" being played at the encampment named after him is as close as we ever shall get.

3. Thomas R. Heitz and John Thorn, "Early Bat and Ball Games," SABR UK, Web site for Society for American Baseball Research (UK Chapter), http://www.sabruk.org/history/bat.html.

4

WAS
ABNER
GRAVES TELLING
THE TRUTH?

Even after the passage of one hundred years, the Abner Graves story about Abner Doubleday still resonates with weirdness. Graves's recollections of his Cooperstown childhood appeared lucid and precise in his letters to the Spalding commission in 1905, yet they became the foundation of the National Pastime's most memorable hoax.[1] His testimony about Doubleday, abetted by the Spalding commission's endorsement, sent baseball history coursing on a wild goose chase from which it did not recover until late in the twentieth century. While historians eventually discredited the Doubleday story by demonstrating that the Civil War hero never had anything to do with baseball, the mysterious behavior of Graves himself has proven more difficult to decipher. What could possibly have motivated the Denver businessman to fabricate a yarn that would fall apart under minimal scrutiny? Is it possible that, despite his misidentification of Doubleday as baseball's inventor, Graves was actually telling what he believed to be the truth? Or, given the bizarre and tragic events that consumed the final years of his life, was Graves's baseball story an early portent of impending insanity?

Graves's road to notoriety began when the seventy-one-year-old Denver resident made a business trip to Akron, Ohio, in the spring of 1905. On the morning of April 3, while reading in his room at the Thuma Hotel, he spied an article in the local newspaper, the *Beacon Journal*. The story was entitled "The Origin of the Game of Base Ball" and carried the byline of the famous sporting goods magnate Albert G. Spalding. In the article, Spalding summarized the ongoing controversy between Henry Chadwick, who theorized that baseball had evolved from the English game of rounders, and others, including Spalding himself, who believed the game had originated in America. Spalding announced the formation of a special commission to settle the question of baseball's ancestry "for all time." He requested "that everyone interested in this subject transmit as soon as possible to Mr. Sullivan [secretary of the commission, James Sullivan] any proof, data or information he may possess or can secure bearing on this matter."[2]

Graves responded immediately. Placing a sheet of paper in his type-writer, he pecked out a letter to the editor of the *Beacon Journal*, with a second copy to Sullivan, offering "data on the subject" of Spalding's article.[3] Here he wrote his immortal words: "The American game of 'Base Ball' was invented by Abner Doubleday of Cooperstown, New York." Graves laid out the now famous story of how Doubleday, then a student at Cooperstown, but "the same, who as General Doubleday won honor at the Battle of Gettysburg," transformed and modernized the old game of town-ball·and renamed it baseball. In his letter, Graves never actually stated that he had witnessed the "invention" firsthand. In fact, the only indication he gave of his own concurrent presence in Cooperstown was a brief comment that he could recollect some of the best players in town and the locations where they played. It is understandable that the old-timer's memories of that long-ago event might have been fuzzy, as he was only six or seven years old when it had occurred.

The editor of the *Beacon Journal* knew a good story when he saw one and published Graves's letter the next day atop the sports page under the headline: "Abner Doubleday Invented Base Ball."[4] Apparently the Ohio paper lacked national influence in those days, or suffered from limited distribution, for there is little evidence that its big scoop traveled anywhere outside the Akron city limits. Most of the baseball public would not learn about Graves's amazing testimony until March 20, 1908, nearly three years after the *Beacon Journal* story, when the Spalding commission finally released its findings.

Meanwhile, on November 17, 1905, in response to a communication from Spalding, Graves wrote a second letter to the commission in which he provided additional information about the Doubleday invention. This time, he placed himself in the middle of the plot, describing how he and a group of friends in Cooperstown were playing marbles when Doubleday approached them and explained the new game of baseball by diagramming it in the dirt with a piece of stick.[5] Graves's inclusion of new details in his story may have only been an innocent effort to round it out, but it signaled a curious impulse to embellish his original tale with each retelling.

By the time of his entry into the debate over baseball's origins, Graves had already lived a long, adventure-filled life. At age fourteen he had departed Cooperstown for the California gold fields, and then spent much of the next fifty years pursuing a variety of occupations and business schemes. He had farmed in Iowa and prospected in Colorado, and by the time he took up permanent residence in Denver in 1894, he apparently had attained modest success as a mine owner and real estate investor. According to the historian Phil Goodstein, Graves was twice hospitalized in asylums during his years in Iowa, which suggests that the demons that plagued his final days were already at work long before he wrote the Doubleday letters.[6]

Whatever his mental state, Graves basked in the attention that came his way when Denver discovered his role in unveiling Abner Doubleday as baseball's inventor. Local journalists flocked to interview him and found him to be a colorful and quotable subject who was not shy about regaling them with stories of Cooperstown, or any of his other past adventures. The newshounds readily accepted whatever Graves told them at face value, reporting even those tales that were of dubious accuracy. For example, the elderly businessman was quoted as saying that, following his travels to California as a forty-niner, he became a rider for the Pony Express in 1852. This was just the kind of Old West yarn that appealed to readers, and the fact that the Pony Express did not actually start up until 1860 was not the kind of detail that anyone would bother checking.[7]

One noted interview with Graves appeared in the *Denver Post* on May 9, 1912. He again recounted his story about the invention of baseball, but the tale had matured in the seven years since he first related it in 1905. No longer was Graves a mere bystander to the event, but as the headline to the interview exclaimed, "Denver Man Played

First Baseball Game in History of Sport." Whereas in his earlier accounts Graves had been a little boy at the time of Doubleday's invention, now he had grown to be a college student. "I was a student at Green College in Cooperstown, New York, at that time," he expounded. "Abner Doubleday, the man who invented the game, if you call it an invention, came to our school and interested us boys in his idea. We went out on the college campus and Doubleday drew out his diagram of his game in the sand." Graves went on to provide a flood of new details that were missing from his earlier accounts, then concluded: "Yes sir, I played in the first baseball game ever played in the United States. I am proud of it."[8]

Clearly Graves was getting so caught up in his baseball fable that he couldn't resist upgrading himself from bit player to leading man. He had come a long way from the marginalization he had expressed seven years earlier in his second letter to the commission. There he had complained that Doubleday's new game placed him at a disadvantage because it restricted the number of players on each side. He had written: "We smaller boys didn't like it because it shut us out from playing, while town-ball let in everyone who could run and catch flies."[9] By 1912 he had forgotten that inequity, allowing him to crow: "You know, they don't play ball like they used to. Why, I played in the very first game of ball that was ever played. And that game — well, it was some baseball, young man."[10]

The 1912 article included a photograph of Graves looking as cocksure as he sounded. The bearded old-timer was shown with a jaunty homburg on his head, a smirky grin on his face, and a half-smoked cigar sticking out the corner of his mouth. Above his head he waved a chamber of commerce pennant promoting the state of Colorado. In his interview, Graves made a point of saying that, even at his advanced age, he was still playing baseball, boasting, "I expect, Saturday, to play in the game between the chamber of commerce and the real estate exchange. I guess I'll be shortstop or something like that." The *Post* interviewer soaked it all up, hailing Graves as "one of the most enthusiastic followers of a baseball game in the country. There are mighty few of them that he misses in Denver, and he is usually seen in the front row of the grandstand, yelling with all of his might for the Grizzlies."[11]

*Abner Graves seemed very pleased with the celebrity
he gained from his contribution to the Doubleday story.*
Denver Post.

As a sidenote, the author of the 1912 article commented that during the interview Graves was clutching a copy of the newly published
book *The American National Game*. It is reasonable to speculate that
the volume had been given to Graves by its author, Albert Spalding.
Certainly Spalding must have felt deep gratitude toward Graves,

whose Doubleday story had provided Spalding an attractive figurehead for his crusade to prove baseball's American genesis.

Four years later, when Graves was well into his eighties, he was still proclaiming his fitness as a ballplayer. This came in a letter he wrote to the *Freeman's Journal* of Cooperstown on December 18, 1916. He was responding to an article that appeared in that newspaper a week earlier, proposing that a commemoration of Doubleday's one hundredth birthday be held in 1919. Graves reminded the newspaper's readership that he was one of the "boys that Doubleday showed his completed diagrams and plans of the new game and whom he instructed as helpers to play the first game and test out his plan, and I helped in those games as one of the players." He added: "I think that by all means the suggested celebration be held at the place where the game was first played, and if so held, a game should be played just like those original games were, and if such is done I wish now to enter my name as one of the players." As to his advancing years, Graves acknowledged: "Of course, at that time I will have passed more than a fifth of a lifetime beyond the old time allotment of 'three score years and ten' as a man's life limit, but I expect to be able to run and dodge the balls the opposing players throw at me sufficiently well so as to make a 'home run' under those old rules of the game."[12]

As an octogenarian, Graves clearly relished playing the role of colorful eccentric, but as the years wore on he grew increasingly irascible and irrational. In 1924 he became embroiled in a bitter quarrel with his second wife, Minnie, who at forty-eight was barely half his age. They were arguing about whether to sell their home, and Graves, who was becoming increasingly paranoid, apparently convinced himself that Minnie was trying to poison him. Suddenly, in the midst of their argument, he pulled a gun and shot her four times. Still in a fury when arresting officers arrived on the scene, Graves slapped one of them before being restrained. When a prosecutor asked him why he shot his wife, he replied, "You never mind sir. It's no business of yours. I only protected myself." When the same prosecutor accused him of murder, Graves flew into a rage and tried to attack him, shouting, "I'll get you!" For her part, as she lay on her deathbed, Minnie's final words were "Tell Abner I forgive him."[13]

Graves's mental condition continued to deteriorate while he was in custody. At his trial he emphatically denied that Minnie was dead. The jury found him mentally unbalanced and not responsible for the murder, and the judge committed him to the state asylum for the insane.[14] Graves quickly slipped out of the public's view, and his death in the asylum two years later at the age of ninety-two went unreported in the newspapers until several months had passed. Graves's obituaries echoed the familiar canards about his background that reporters saw no more need to confirm than they had when he was alive. For example, the editors of the *Denver Post* wrote: "He became a pony express rider in 1852, and for years was one of that daring crew that fought hostile Indians in pushing Uncle Sam's mail thru to the Pacific Coast."[15]

The obituary also stated that "Graves played on the first baseball team ever to exhibit in this country. He was one of a team organized at Green College, Cooperstown, N.Y., in 1840." Ironically, the editors made no mention of Abner Doubleday's role in the story. What a shame Abner Graves wasn't alive to see his twenty-year campaign finally come to fruition! Thanks to the *Denver Post*, he finally managed to supplant his namesake Abner as the story's hero. Another curious aspect to the obituary was that, just two paragraphs before mentioning that Graves played college baseball in 1840, the newspaper reported his birth date as February 27, 1834. Evidently, the *Post's* editors assumed their readership was so conditioned to outlandish stories involving Graves that none would blink at the implication he had advanced to college as a six-year-old.

The entire Graves affair remains something of an enigma. We may never know what motivated him to sit down in that Akron hotel room and describe Abner Doubleday's invention of baseball. One possibility is that the whole thing was a practical joke, and when everybody fell for it he just rode along on its tail for the remainder of his life. It is even possible that at some point, given his mental vulnerabilities, he started believing the story himself. A more cynical analysis is that the Doubleday yarn was a deliberate deception by Graves. Knowing that the Spalding commission was seeking to prove baseball to be of American origin, the opportunist Denver businessman may have seized the chance to promote himself as an important witness to history. He may have crafted the fable knowing full well that General Doubleday was long departed and therefore unable to set the record straight.

A more plausible scenario is that Graves was not trying to mislead anybody in his 1905 letters. Those recollections of the events in Cooperstown were written when he was seventy-one years of age, describing scenes he had witnessed when he was as young as five. The accuracy of details remembered across so many decades must be considered tenuous at the least. Factoring in the effects of time, his letters to the commission could have been exactly what they appeared to be in 1905, genuine good-faith attempts to recall an actual long-ago incident. Graves may well have retained a warm boyhood impression of a youth showing up and presenting him and his playmates an improved version of ball play, called "base ball." To young Abner Graves and elder Abner Graves alike, lacking any information to the contrary, this occurrence could certainly have resonated as an original invention.

With the passage of nearly one hundred years since he told his tale, the only way to test Graves's veracity is to compare the factual details of his story to what we now know about the history of early baseball in the days of his youth. Of course, his identification of Doubleday was off the mark, but what about other specifics he described, such as the features and rules of the baseball game he perceived being invented? Evaluating his accuracy on these points may illuminate the question of his general truthfulness. It seems improbable that Graves, on the spur of the moment, would have been able to fabricate a whopper of a story about Abner Doubleday and then have the presence of mind to surround it with obscure but accurate historical detail.

Itemized below are the "facts" of baseball's invention according to Abner Graves. Listed first are the Spalding commission conclusions that were based upon Graves's testimony. Following these are other specific points that Graves revealed in his 1905 letters.[16]

COMMISSION CONCLUSIONS

1. Baseball was of American origin: Graves didn't actually say this, but it is implicit in his letters. It is well documented

elsewhere in this book that baseball originated in Europe. Graves, however, could not have been expected to know this.

2. The inventor was Abner Doubleday: This is the hardest fact to explain. There is some genealogical evidence that a second Abner Doubleday, a cousin of the famous general, lived in Cooperstown at the time in question. The namesake, Abner Demas Doubleday, was born in Otsego County on March 9, 1829, and lived in the Cooperstown area until moving to Kalamazoo, Michigan, following the Civil War.[17] Additionally, according to Graves's own words in his second letter to the commission, a second Doubleday cousin, John, also lived in Cooperstown and was a ballplayer. Perhaps it was one of these alternate Doubledays who diagrammed a new game that day in Cooperstown, and over time Graves confused him with his better-known cousin.

3. The new game was called "base ball": Use of the name "base-ball" in England dates as far back as 1744, when it appeared in the classic children's book *A Little Pretty Pocket-Book*.[18] In America the term appeared no later than 1762, when the first pirated edition of the same work was issued in New York; the name may have arrived even earlier in the company of English immigrants. A reference to "base ball" appeared in the town records of Pittsfield, Massachusetts, in 1791, and as we have seen, young men in Manhattan were playing an organized game of that name in 1823.[19] Publishers in New England produced at least three books in the mid-1830s describing the game and calling it "base ball."[20] Whomever Graves perceived introducing the game could have obtained the name by reading about it, encountering it somewhere outside of Cooperstown, or learning of it from someone who had traveled to New York City.

4. The year was 1839: Actually, in his first letter Graves recalled the date being in "the spring prior, or following the 'Log Cabin & Hard Cider' campaign of General Harrison for President." This would place it in 1840 or 1841. In Graves's second letter he acknowledged that the year could have been

either "1839, 1840 or 1841." Clearly it was the commission that decreed the date to be 1839, for reasons that remain a mystery. In any case, the exact year of this event is irrelevant because it has nothing to do with baseball's invention. Graves's uncertainty about the year supports his overall credibility: if he were making up the Doubleday story, why would he be so positive about some details and waver about others?

5. The location was Cooperstown: It is a lovely town, and the only quarrel anyone has with it is the claim that it was baseball's birthplace.

6. The "Doubleday" infield was diamond-shaped: Graves described it as a square with bases at each corner. A diamond-shaped base layout appeared in print in America as early as 1829, in the first Boston edition of *The Boy's Own Book*, and then reappeared in at least three other books during the 1830s. It is plausible that the mysterious "Doubleday" could have seen one of these books, or learned about the feature in his travels.

7. In the "Doubleday" game, base runners could be retired by being struck with a thrown ball: Graves's exact words were, "Anyone getting the ball was entitled to throw it at a runner and put him out if [the fielder] could hit him." This, in fact, was a long-standing feature of early baseball and its predecessors that dated back centuries.[21] Commission member Abraham Mills, in a letter accompanying the final report, erroneously credited "Doubleday" with the innovation of "substituting the existing method of putting out the base runner for the old one of 'plugging' him with the ball."[22] In fact, the revolutionary innovation of tagging or forcing runners at a base was introduced by the Knickerbocker Base Ball Club in 1845.[23]

8. Before the "Doubleday" event, the boys were playing "town-ball": There is no reason to doubt this, since "town-ball" was one of the common names for early baseball in America. Interestingly, the version described by Graves was particularly

primitive, played without dividing players into teams even when a large number of boys were present. Players arrayed in the field would converge on any batted ball, and the lucky one who caught it was rewarded with a turn at bat. The flat-faced bat and high-lob style of pitching he described were also forms that were fairly old-fashioned for 1840.[24]

9. "Doubleday" invented the concept of "sides" with eleven players on each: In 1840 or thereabouts, the practice of having two teams was a familiar feature of the game in many places in America, and it dated back for centuries in Europe. It is surprising this was unknown to Graves, but perhaps considering his young age and the relative isolation of Cooperstown, he was simply unaware of what went on elsewhere. The concept of a fixed number of players was a relatively modern concept for the time, although it is likely that some of the more organized baseball / town-ball / round-ball matches held in Philadelphia, New York, or Boston during those days had guidelines for team sizes. The specific number of players on each team that Graves attributed to "Doubleday," eleven, may have been borrowed from cricket.

10. "Doubleday" introduced three strikes and out: As Graves wrote, "Great furore and fun marked opening of the game on account of the then unprecedented thing of 'first man up, three strikes and out.'" Regardless of who introduced this game to Graves and his friends, the three-strikes concept was hardly new, dating back to at least the end of the eighteenth century in England, and perhaps much earlier.

SO WHAT'S THE VERDICT?

Was Abner Graves being truthful with the commission? In my opinion, the only evidence to the contrary (other than his misidentification of Doubleday) lies in a snippet of opinion with which he concluded his second letter. He wrote: "Just in my present mood I would rather have Uncle Sam declare war on England and clean her up rather than have one of her citizens beat us out of Base Ball." Wow! Here was an unabashedly jingoistic slam directed against Henry Chadwick, which revealed Graves's partiality toward proving baseball to be America's own. But was this his motive for cooking up a tall tale, or just an impetus for conveying his honest recollections to the commission?

Aside from this outburst, the evidence of Graves's letters supports his veracity. While he was mistaken about the identity of the "inventor" who presented the new game to him and his friends in Cooperstown, in virtually every other respect his reminiscences have the ring of truth. All the elements of the game of "base ball" that he perceived to be newly minted, including the name, had already existed before that moment. While the Spalding commission took Graves's testimony and made it the centerpiece of an historic revelation, the actuality of what happened in Cooperstown may have been less grandiose.

Here's one possible scenario: An older student, possibly Abner Demas Doubleday, the general's cousin, had traveled outside Cooperstown, or perhaps he simply had conversed with someone who had returned from a trip downstate. One way or another he acquired knowledge about a new variety of ball called "base ball." He was bursting to share the details of the game with the boys of Cooperstown, since it was an obvious upgrade from the dowdy form of town-ball they had been playing. Young Abner Graves, with neither experience nor perspective to know any better, perceived the older student as having invented the new game.

True, this is only shameless speculation, but I may as well stick by it until some archeologist digs up a long-buried security camera from a nearby minimart that recorded the entire event.

WHERE DO THEY FIND THESE GUYS?

Consider the following:

In the late nineteenth and early twentieth centuries, two older gentlemen submitted letters to newspapers purporting to describe historic baseball scenes they had witnessed as children many decades earlier.

One sent his letter forty-eight years after the experience, the other
  sixty-six years after.
One of the events had taken place in 1838, the other in 1839.
The two long-ago baseball memories emanated from small towns
  in the eastern part of the continent, but both individuals were
  residents of Denver at the time they sent their letters.
Their descriptions provided great detail about the rules of the
  games they had witnessed, including the equipment, the
  venues, the names of many players, and even diagrams of
  the playing fields.
Both of them must have possessed extraordinary powers of recall,
  for each was at most seven years old when the incident he
  wrote about occurred.
Both had acquired modest fortunes at the time of their letters,
  but by their deaths had frittered them away.
Both were suspected of committing sensational murders which
  scandalized their communities, though neither was convicted
  for the crime.

By now you will have identified one of these uncanny recollectors
as the notorious Abner Graves. One would think his tour de force of
summoning up the Doubleday story could not be rivaled, but not only
did someone do just that, but he did it nearly twenty years earlier. This
accomplishment was the work of Dr. Adam Ford, who in 1886, while
a resident of Denver, submitted an amazing letter to *Sporting Life*
newspaper. In it he recounted a baseball game he had observed in
the small town of Beachville, Ontario, forty-eight years earlier, in
June 1838.[25]

Ford's recollective powers may have been even more prodigious
than those of Graves because his reminiscence was laden with far
greater intricacy of detail. He described the rules and order of the
long-ago game, the manufacture of the equipment used, and the precise dimensions of the playing field. He also furnished a diagram of
the infield configuration and supplied the names of fourteen of the
participants. Like Graves, his startling act of memory centered upon

an event that transpired when he was very young, in Ford's case when he was barely seven years of age!

In the United States, Abner Graves's fable about Abner Doubleday was accepted as literal history for many decades. The deception led to the establishment of the National Baseball Hall of Fame and Museum at Cooperstown, and the issuance of a U.S. Postal Service stamp in 1939 to commemorate the centennial anniversary of the famous deed. A parallel process transpired in Canada. Based upon Ford's testimony, it became axiomatic that the first baseball game played in that country, perhaps the first baseball game played anywhere, was the one he described at Beachville in 1838. Today the Canadian Baseball Hall of Fame has taken up residence in the nearby community of St. Mary's, Ontario, where Ford resided after returning from college. In 1988 a Canadian stamp was issued to commemorate 150 years of baseball in that country.

The absence of corroborating evidence ultimately doomed Abner Graves's Cooperstown tale to disrepute. In Canada it has been a different story. Ford's recollections remain unchallenged, despite the fact that no other proof has come forward to confirm that the 1838 game ever occurred. Which is not to say that Ford's letter has escaped scrutiny. In 1988 two Canadian sports historians, Nancy Bouchier and Robert Barney, conducted a study of the details contained in Ford's letter and reported their findings in an article in the *Journal of Sports History*. They concluded that the doctor's account of the Beachville game was credible, based upon an analysis of the extensive nonbaseball supporting information Ford had provided.[26] They determined that the doctor correctly identified the date of the contest as a local holiday, and that the individuals he identified as players and observers genuinely resided in the vicinity of the game. Because of this, they concluded there was no reason to doubt his veracity, and, by extension, presumed him to have faithfully recounted the details of the game.

This seems like an inordinate leap. It assumes that because a portion of Ford's testimony was verifiable, his entire story must be taken as truth. Ford grew up in Beachville, and would certainly have been familiar with the names of his neighbors as well as other details about the small community. If he had wanted to fabricate a tale about early baseball, he could have easily drawn upon his hometown knowledge to provide a believable backdrop. As for the particulars he provided about the 1838 game, these could have been the product of an inventive mind utilizing information about the early days of baseball readily available when he wrote his letter in 1886. Above all, the legacy of the Doubleday fiasco should caution sports historians to remain skeptical when considering any early baseball reminiscence that is not corroborated by firm evidence. It should not be forgotten that Abner Graves provided accurate details about individuals and venues in Cooperstown and yet was totally off base in his claim about Abner Doubleday.

A more judicious handling of the Beachville game appears in William Humber's excellent history of baseball in Canada, *Diamonds of the North*, published in 1995. Humber gives respectful consideration to Ford's reminiscence, hailing it as "the most famous account of an early baseball type game in Canada." But although he devotes several pages to describing the reputed 1838 contest and evaluating its place in the history of the era, he also acknowledges that Ford's account of the game was "almost too good to be true." In Humber's view, "the greatest veracity" of Ford's recollection lay "in the boundaries of its detail — the time, the general format and the players." The author regards Ford's explanation of the rules "more questionable," however, and describes the doctor's precise description of the distances between bases as "somewhat preposterous."[27]

While there is no conclusive evidence that the Beachville game actually transpired, there is also no contravening proof that Ford made the whole thing up. Ultimately, it is a matter of whether one trusts his story, which goes to the question of his character. It is interesting that Bouchier and Barney, who embraced Ford's tale at its face value, also revealed seamy details about the doctor's life that raise serious doubts about his rectitude. They referred to Ford's "careless use of alcohol," which led to other troubles, the worst being the discovery of a dead man in his office. This turned out to be an officer in the local temperance association who had spent the night drinking with Ford. Following a closed-door inquest, the doctor escaped murder charges, but the resulting scandal forced him to leave Ontario and take up residence in Colorado. The Canadian researchers also mentioned that Ford's last years were "wrought with drug and alcohol dependence."[28] It was in the midst of this period of his life that the doctor wrote his letter describing the 1838 game in Beachville. While some may choose to believe him, I find it less than credible that a person with serious substance problems could recall in great detail an elaborate event that had occurred forty-eight years earlier when he was only seven years of age.

Of course, there are other possible explanations, such as that Ford had some remembrance of observing a baseball game when he was a child, then availed himself of knowledge acquired later in life to embellish the long-ago memory. Whatever the true story, the authorities of Canadian baseball have inexplicably chosen to commit themselves to the same type of dubious fable about a "first" game that the collapse of the Doubleday story should have warned them against. National pride has always been a powerful motivator, and perhaps the allure of preempting their American neighbor as the earliest country to host a baseball contest has blinded some Canadians to the precarious value of Ford's narrative. While we can hope that the tale of baseball at Beachville in 1838 stands on firmer ground than the North Woods legend of Paul Bunyan and Babe his blue ox, in the end it may be that both are equally apocryphal.

And what about the intriguing circumstance that Dr. Ford and Abner Graves were concurrent Denver residents for several years immediately before and after the turn of the twentieth century? SABR member Chip Martin finds this somewhat suspicious, given the similarity of their stories. In an article entitled "The Adam Ford–Abner Graves Connection in Their Stories on the Origins of Baseball," Martin quotes another SABR member, Jay Sanford, as saying: "It is safe to say that they traveled in the same circles in the Denver business community and quite possibly in Denver social circles as well." Martin goes on to write: "It is quite reasonable to assume Ford and Graves knew each other, shared an interest in sport and drink, and were no doubt fond of swapping stories from their youth." He speculates that Graves, having heard Ford's "yakking" about the Beachville game so often, was inspired to come up with his own tale when he learned that the Spalding commission was soliciting testimony.[29]

While the circumstantial possibilities are tempting, there is no hard evidence that Graves and Ford were acquaintances, much less drinking buddies. If Chip Martin's suspicions are correct, they would certainly suggest that Graves's story about Abner Doubleday was premeditated, and not a spontaneous response to the commission as has heretofore been supposed. Still, until and unless someone can actually prove that the two men with the mighty memories crossed paths, the notion that one's story gave rise to the other's must remain a delicious "what if?"

In 1796, the same year that George Washington delivered his farewell address, a young educator in Germany was making history of another type. In the tiny hamlet of Schnepfenthal in the duchy of Gotha, Johann Christoph Friedrich Gutsmuths published a remarkable book that was the first of its kind in any language, a comprehensive guide to all the popular games and sports of the day. One of the games Gutsmuths wrote about probably did not garner much attention at the time, but two hundred years later it seems of towering importance. There, beginning on page 78, were seven pages of German text unveiling the earliest known rules for a game called baseball! It should not come as a surprise that this 1796 version of baseball was decidedly primitive compared with our modern National Pastime. Yet even at that stage the game was recognizable, and, thanks to Gutsmuths's detailed account, we have a vivid and long-lost record of baseball at an early evolutionary moment.

J. C. F. Gutsmuths was a visionary in the embryonic field of physical education. His book harboring the baseball rules bore an impressive title: *Spiele zur Uebung und Erholung des Körpers und Geistes für die Jugend, ihre Erzieher und alle Freunde Unschuldiger Jugendfreuden* — Games for the exercise and recreation of body and spirit for the youth and his educator and all friends of innocent joys of youth. Gutsmuths called the game *Ball mit Freystäten (oder das englische Base-ball)*, which literally translates to "ball with free station, or English base-ball."[1] Many of the details revealed in his account have undergone considerable change over the past two hundred years. For example, the bat was only two feet long and had a four-inch flat face at the hitting end, the number of bases varied with the number of players, and the batting team was entitled to only one out before the side was retired. Home base was an area rather than a specific spot, and apparently all players from the hitting team gathered there, not just the individual who was batting. Yet despite these disparities, at its core *das englische Base-ball* is strikingly familiar. A pitcher served to a batter, who had three attempts to put the ball in play. After hitting the ball, the batter ran counterclockwise from base to base as far as he could safely go without being put out. His objective was to complete a circuit of the bases and return to home. Outs were recorded by catching the ball on the fly, touching or striking the runner with the ball, or throwing to a base.

What foresightful urge could have motivated Gutsmuths to write about baseball? Certainly in his wildest dreams he could never have predicted the auspiciousness of his act. Being an expert in the field of exercise and recreation, however, he may very well have glimpsed in the incipient game a special quality worthy of promotion. Otherwise, his inclusion of baseball in 1796 makes little sense. His book was directed at parents and educators in Germany, and there is little evidence that baseball was played anywhere in continental Europe during that era. Even in eighteenth-century England, where the game originated, nary an author had as yet undertaken to describe it in print. Gutsmuths's appreciation for baseball is suggested by his comparison of its merits to those of a related pastime, *das deutsche Ballspiel* (the German ball game). The latter game, which also involved use of a bat and ball, as well as base running, had achieved considerable popularity in late-eighteenth-century Germany. Gutsmuths wrote that English base-ball "is smaller in scale and requires less strength in hitting, running, etc. At the same time, it demands an equal amount, if not more, attentiveness."[2] He added, "The German ball game will never be able to fully repress English base-ball, as pleasant as ours may be." Gutsmuths's prophecy about baseball's resilience has been fulfilled, while the German ball game, pleasant or not, has since faded into extinction.

It may be hard to appreciate today just how innovative Gutsmuths's work *Spiele zur Uebung und Erholung* was within the context of his times. Nowadays, in any large bookstore, we can find shelves of titles pertaining to sports and games, but in 1796 the topic was truly revolutionary. Publishers of that era released occasional volumes devoted to such gentlemanly pursuits as hunting and fishing, or to such indoor pastimes as card games and chess. But that was about all. Books were expensive commodities in eighteenth-century Europe, and publishers apparently regarded children's games and ball sports as far too trivial for commercial consideration. Moreover, the still potent influence of conservative Protestantism cast a disapproving pall over efforts to promote frivolous play.

Gutsmuths looked beyond those barriers. Devoted to educating his students in both mind and body, he embraced the radical notion that sports and exercise were essential complements of classroom learning. In attempting to implement his curriculum, however, he encountered an obstacle. No materials were available for instructing youth in how to play the popular games and sports of the day. It was to fill this vacuum that he wrote and published *Spiele zur Uebung und Erholung* in 1796.

To say the least, I was astounded when I came across the book and its unheralded baseball content.[3] While not totally unknown, Gutsmuths's work has largely escaped the notice of American and English sports historians. This in itself is perplexing. Not only was his collection of pastimes apparently the first of its kind, but its detailed instructions for playing the various games were not to be rivaled by any book in any language for another fifty years. By contrast, Joseph Strutt's well-known folio work *The Sports and Pastimes of the People of England*, published in 1801, is a scholarly history of sport intended for an adult audience. Although impressive in size and content, it suffers from stuffiness and lacks the practicality of the Gutsmuths book in providing explicit guidance for how to play the games. Mention should also be made of William Clarke's *The Boy's Own Book*, published in 1828, which, though designed as a guide for children, did not compare to Gutsmuths's work in depth of detail.

Spiele zur Uebung und Erholung consists of nearly five hundred pages packed with every imaginable children's game and activity, more than one hundred in all. These range from hopscotch to bowling, kite flying to charades, and include fifteen different games of ball.

It is the book's time capsule of baseball, however, that reverberates most eloquently through the intervening years. More than any other early text yet discovered, the description of *das englische Base-ball* opens a small window into the game's "dark ages," the century-long span that followed baseball's inception in the early 1700s. Previous research has yielded few clues about the game's maturation during those years, especially about the manner in which it was played. The Gutsmuths rules not only add precious detail to this landscape but also inject new fuel into the debate over the game's origins. The recognizable features of *das englische Base-ball* lend compelling circumstantial support to the contention that eighteenth-century English base-ball was the immediate predecessor of nineteenth-century American baseball. The 1796 rules also help controvert the popular notion that baseball derived from the English game of rounders.

Gutsmuths's rudimentary brand of baseball was positively diminutive when compared to our modern pastime. The pitcher positioned himself only five or six steps from the batter and lobbed the ball in a gentle arc. On the base paths, runners had to navigate a distance of only ten to fifteen paces to travel from one station to the next. In other respects, however, the characteristics of the 1796 game were not dissimilar from those of other early forms of baseball, including the storied practice of placing out a runner by "soaking" him with a thrown ball while he was between bases. Moreover, Gutsmuths describes a second method of retiring base runners that was perhaps a little more sophisticated than normally found in early baseball. This was called "burning," and came into play when a fielder observed that an opposing runner had overrun or neglected to touch a base. The fielder could then place the runner out by obtaining the ball and throwing it at the base, while at the same time calling out the word "burned!"[4] This innovation of directing the ball to the base, rather than at the runner, was an early prelude to the modern baseball method of forcing or tagging a runner at a base, a practice that was not to be introduced for another fifty years.

In fact, base running, with all its myriad possibilities, seems to have been the feature of English base-ball that Gutsmuths found most intriguing, and he cites the following example to illustrate its complexity (keep in mind that the number of bases in *das englische Base-ball* often exceeded four):

> When several hitters have already hit and run, then several bases are occupied. Let us assume that this is the case with bases three and four. Thus it sometimes happens that when a new hit occurs, the person on three runs further, whereas the person on four stands still (either due to inattentiveness or because the serving team is too near to him with the ball) the result of which is that two people are standing on base four. This once again calls for the order of the game: there can only be one person at one base at any time. If, in this case, the person at base four does not quickly run to base five, or if the recently arrived runner does not return to base three, then the best positioned member of the serving team in possession of the ball can run toward them and either touch one of the individuals or burn one of them in the manner described above, in which case the at-bat is lost.[5]

The embarrassing predicament of two runners finding themselves on the same base (due to inattentiveness!) is certainly not unknown today. But Gutsmuths goes on to present another colorful scenario that did not survive the test of time. He describes a rule in English base-ball whereby the batting team could retain its at-bat even after making out. All they had to do was run onto the field, grab the ball, and then either tag or throw the ball at a straggling member of the fielding team before he was able to get off the playing field. In response, the defenders then had the opportunity to return the favor to the batting team before they made it back to the home plate area, and so on. Gutsmuths clearly enjoyed this feature of early baseball. He wrote: "In this way a fun, short-lived fight ensues, and the team that wins at the end is the one that has the last throw. This is the reason why, when one catches the ball, one must throw it backwards, and why when one burns or touches a runner for an out, the ball must be thrown such that no one from the opposing team can grab it and thus throw it again."[6] This "retaliation rule" was not unique to *das englische Base-ball* but was, in fact, a recurring feature among several of baseball's early European relatives, including the French pastime *la balle empoisonée*, or "poisoned ball."[7] Over time the colorful practice faded quietly into oblivion, quite possibly, baseball's critics might argue, to the detriment of our modern game.

Gutsmuths knew that baseball was completely alien to his German audience, so he wrote: "In the description of this game I can be brief, for it is mostly equivalent to the German ball game. Thus I am aiming my description at those players who already understand the German game."[8] Understanding baseball's cousin *das deutsche Ballspiel* took some doing, however, and Gutsmuths devoted twenty-one pages to the task. In its own right, the long-vanished German game holds considerable importance to baseball history in that it descended from an earlier northern European family of bat-and-ball games called "longball," which constitutes an influential branch in the lineage of our National Pastime.

Gutsmuths's description of *das deutsche Ballspiel* reveals that the game had many points of similarity with baseball. Two opposing teams took turns at batting and fielding, and the basic ingredients of pitching, hitting, and catching the ball were all to be found. One noticeable difference was that only two bases were used, a home plate and a "resting" base. Furthermore, the act of base running was governed by different rules and required different strategies than in baseball. For example, if one or more players from the batting team were retired, they could still have an opportunity to run the bases. This happened if a subsequent batter in their lineup hit safely, in which case the previously retired batters simply followed on the heels of their successful team member to the resting base. Because of this feature, any number of players could occupy the resting base at any given moment. The batting order in this game was not static as in baseball but was reordered frequently during the course of an at-bat. This was to take advantage of a rule that enabled the batter who came to the plate after all other team members had made out to have a final opportunity to drive home all remaining base runners. Teams would try to maneuver their best player into this slot. This "cleanup hitter" would then get three tries to strike the ball and fulfill his task (other batters had only one chance to hit the ball).[9] However, a team's opportunity to manipulate its lineup to get the best hitter up at the right moment was further complicated by another rule. This directed that base runners who successfully navigated the bases had to take their next turn at bat in the order that they had returned to the home base area. So teams not only had to juggle the sequence of batters waiting their turns but also had to try to control the order in which they crossed the plate.

The methods of retiring base runners in the German ball game were generally identical to those practiced in early baseball, such as catching a ball on the fly or striking a runner with the ball between bases. Gutsmuths also describes a number of minor rules that could result in a player's being put out. In fact, the author's elaborate presentation of detail about *das deutsche Ballspiel* strongly suggests that it was a fairly complex activity, perhaps best suited for older children or young adults. This, in turn, raises a question about whether Gutsmuths was also in possession of many more details about English base-ball than he elected to divulge in the book. How else to interpret his comment that, in comparison with the German game, baseball "is much more bound by numerous small rules"?[10]

Gutsmuths devoted a separate short chapter in *Spiele zur Uebung und Erholung* to promoting his ideas for an improved hybrid game that would "unite both forms." He said it would be based upon the superior rules of English base-ball but would adapt the longer, stronger bat of the German ball game so that the ball could be hit with greater power. He also recommended, in addition to a home base, a fixed layout of four bases arranged in a square pattern. (In fact, his proposal is similar to later configurations of early baseball in the United States, such as those of New England round-ball and Philadelphia town-ball.) Gutsmuths believed that these improvements would make the game more appealing to German players.

Other than their surprising appearance in a German-language book from a small town in central Germany, there is nothing historically incongruous about discovering baseball rules dating from the late eighteenth century. By then the game had become a popular children's pastime in England and was finding a home in America as well. While no other written rules from the 1700s are known to have survived, such codes, written or not, must certainly have abounded. On ball fields of that era, as in any era, the probable first order of business for any two groups of youths squaring off for a contest was to agree on a set of parameters to govern their play. Because few specifics are known about eighteenth-century baseball on either side of the Atlantic, we can only speculate to what degree these rules remained consistent from game to game. A logical guess is that ballplayers in communities where baseball had become a favored pastime would be more likely to develop established forms and traditions for playing the game, while, in other locales, impromptu rule making may have been the norm.

Even allowing for some local standardization, the inherent informality and boundless variety of baseball during this stage of its evolution would have presented difficulties to any editor seeking to capture the game's rules for publication, not that many would have been inclined to do so. Eighteenth-century society generally dismissed children's folk games as frivolous distractions, and baseball, as a new kid on the block, was likely to get as little attention from publishers as any. One delightful exception to this was the landmark juvenile classic *A Little Pretty Pocket-Book*, first released in 1744. This little book contains the earliest known reference to the word "base-ball," and also endeavored a brief description of the game:

The ball once struck off,
Away flies the boy
To the next destined post,
And then home with joy.[11]

These lines can hardly be described as rules, but they do offer the first simple attempt to document the order of play. Almost exactly one hundred years later, in 1845, members of the Knickerbocker Base Ball Club of New York codified what have been characterized as the first "official" rules of baseball. Obviously, a great deal of history transpired in the intervening century between *A Little Pretty Pocket-Book* and the Knickerbockers, and the evolution of rules was part of this. Previous studies charting the progression of baseball's rules have neglected this formative period, particularly the fifty-year stretch before 1845 when authors, beginning with Gutsmuths, began to chronicle the game. Overlooking these earlier contributions has unwittingly fostered the impression that the Knickerbockers created their famous rules out of thin air.

Baseball evolved from a matrix of early English folk games, and it follows that baseball's rules were borrowed and shaped from those same traditional pastimes. The process involved unknowable numbers of children and youths experimenting in fields and churchyards and village greens over a period of centuries, with the resulting wisdom passing unobtrusively from one generation to the next. As far as is known, Gutsmuths in 1796 was the first writer to transfer this cumulated folk knowledge to the printed page, and over the next fifty years several other children's authors made modest attempts to do the same. These subsequent endeavors did not approach the German author's work in richness of detail but were important historical contributions nonetheless. Including Gutsmuths's inaugural effort, attempts to describe various forms of baseball-like games are known to have appeared in at least eight books published before 1845. (The full text of each of these descriptions appears in appendix 7.)

Given that the earliest of these accounts was published in German, can it come as a surprise that the second was written in French? This was a description of the game *la balle empoisonée* — poisoned ball — in the children's book *Les Jeux des jeunes garçons*. The earliest known edition of this title dates from about 1815. Strictly speaking, poisoned ball should not be equated with baseball because the game did not employ a bat. Instead, the hitter at home plate relied upon his bare hand to strike the ball. In all other respects, however, the composition of the French pastime was remarkably baseball-like, including its four-base, diamond-shaped infield.

It was not until 1828 that an English-language account of a sport resembling baseball first appeared. This was the well-documented description of the game rounders that made its debut in the second London edition of *The Boy's Own Book*, a guidebook of sports and pastimes that achieved considerable popularity in both England and the United States. Despite being labeled "rounders," with the alternate name of "feeder," the game depicted was unmistakably baseball. Featuring a diagram of a diamond-shaped infield, the concise, paragraph-long explanation of rounders became the basis for all subsequent descriptions of baseball published in the United States during the 1830s. The first of these imitators was *The Book of Sports*, written by the Boston author Robin Carver and issued in 1834. Carver reprinted the rounders text from *The Boy's Own Book* virtually intact but renamed the game "'base,' or 'goal ball.'" The following year, a Providence, Rhode Island, children's publisher, William Daniels, copied Carver's "base, or goal ball" word for word in a chapbook entitled *The Boy's and Girl's Book of Sports*. In the same year the New Haven publisher Sidney Babcock took the project one step further. Using the same rounders text as his starting point, he updated the description of the game to reflect current practices, such as fixing the base-running direction as counterclockwise. He also named it definitively as "base ball."

Perhaps the most unusual of all the early representations of baseball made its appearance in 1837. It surfaced in the fictional work *Female Robinson Crusoe*, which professed to be the narrative of a young woman, Lucy Ford, who had lost her way in the American wilderness. In the story, a companion of Lucy's named Tommy also gets lost and finds himself captured by Indians. When later reunited with Lucy, Tommy reports witnessing his captors practicing a sport played with bat and ball. He describes the game in considerable detail, and there is no mistaking its uncanny resemblance to baseball. The anonymous author of *Female Robinson Crusoe* clearly had some familiarity with the pastime, and he apparently was trying to connect it to the ball-playing adeptness of North American Indians that was already widely celebrated in the United States by the 1830s. As we have seen, however, none of the many ball games practiced by the indigenous peoples of this continent actually resembled baseball. While the suggestion of native roots for the game in *Female Robinson Crusoe* may have been fanciful, the author's portrayal stands as the earliest detailed description of a baseball-like activity wholly original to America.

The three remaining examples of baseball-like games published before 1845 were English pastimes recounted in English books. Although the delineated activities resembled baseball, they also presaged the growing differentiation of the English branch of the pastime from its American counterpart. The first of these was an account of the game "squares" found in the pages of the *Youth's Encyclopædia of Health* in 1838. This was a simple presentation of bare-boned early baseball, not very different from the game first outlined in *The Boy's Own Book* in 1828 and restated in several American books in the 1830s. The lone idiosyncrasy of this entry lay in its name, "squares," which as an alternate label for baseball or rounders, cannot be found elsewhere in the historical record.

The Every Boy's Book of 1841 contains the final two pre-Knickerbocker descriptions of games resembling baseball. The author treats the pastimes "rounders" and "feeder" as two separate activities, not, as William Clarke had in *The Boy's Own Book* thirteen years earlier, two names for the same game. Indeed, the two were now played differently, with feeder having become a simplified version of rounders — a scrub game, as such informal pursuits were called — characterized by having only one player, the feeder, positioned in the field at any given moment. The representation of rounders in this book is of particular interest because the game was shown to have begun its divergence from American baseball. Notably, the number of bases had expanded to five, and the concept of hitting for a "rounder," a feature unknown in baseball, made its published debut.

The foregoing collection of published descriptions, though small, constitutes the most reliable existing body of knowledge about the development of baseball's characteristics before 1845. Taken separately, however, each account should be considered no more than a fleeting snapshot of the variant of baseball that the author happened to witness, if indeed his portrayal was based upon firsthand observation. Given that uniform standards for playing baseball were nonexistent during those early years, the tiny pool of descriptive examples that have survived may be compared to nine snowflakes plucked from a blizzard, perhaps representative of the whole, but hardly comprehensive.

The authors of these sketches of early baseball reflected the game's many faces in the mix of names they attached to it. Whether they chose "rounders" or "base-ball" or something else depended upon the year and place of publication. A majority of the accounts were published in Europe, a ratio concordant with the game's English up-bringing. Although it can be argued that the development of baseball as a sport in the United States had grown largely independent of European influence by the 1820s or 1830s, the same cannot be said of its representation in print. With one lone exception — the fictional Indian game depicted in *Female Robinson Crusoe*— the descriptions appearing in American books during those years obtained from material first published in England.

It should also be noted that, regardless of their country of publication, these early descriptions were directed almost exclusively at juvenile audiences. Although young men in the United States had already begun experimenting with the game, baseball in the early nineteenth century was still widely regarded as a diversion for children. It took several more decades before writers and editors began to contemplate the profitability of publishing baseball rules for adults.

In their various descriptions of the early game, Gutsmuths and his mostly anonymous cohorts provided random glimpses of a work in progress. At first a casual and many-faceted pastime, baseball was gravitating toward fewer and more clearly defined forms. Ultimately, one resulting prototype of this process found its way to the ball fields of Manhattan in the early 1840s. There, groups of young tradesmen and professionals, including those who were soon to make up the Knickerbocker Base Ball Club, mixed in their own field-tested modifications.

Suddenly, the informality that had governed baseball for many decades was about to give way to a new era of structure and standardization. The Knickerbocker Club adopted a formal constitution and by-laws in 1845 that were based upon those of men's social clubs of the era. When other baseball clubs began to form in the New York City area in the early 1850s, they chose the Knickerbocker structure as their model. In 1857 representatives of seventeen clubs met in Manhattan in the sport's first convention and agreed upon a uniform code of rules. Enthusiasm for their approach to the game spread rapidly to cities in upstate New York, to nearby Philadelphia, and up into New England. Following the Civil War, organized baseball based upon the New York model surged into every corner of the nation.

Thankfully, this phenomenon did not suppress the creative energies that had given birth to the game and shaped its spirit. While parents and older siblings filled the ranks of organized baseball teams in towns and schools and factories, youthful players continued to find ingenious new ways to adapt the game to their immediate playground conditions. By no small measure it has been the discovery and enjoyment of boundless varieties of scrub baseball by each new generation of American children that has helped bond them to our National Pastime, and in this way preserve the game for generations to follow.

6

HOW
SLICK
WERE THE
KNICKS?

❖

In September 1845 the newly chartered Knickerbocker Base Ball Club of New York agreed upon a set of twenty rules to guide its play. Historians ever since have hailed that moment as the birth of modern baseball. In the 1850s, the Knickerbockers and other newly formed New York clubs began to tinker with these original rules, ushering in an era of almost constant reevaluation and adjustment that continued for the remainder of the century. This process ultimately resulted in the rules that, a few tweaks aside, still guide the sport today.

For more than 150 years following its founding in 1845, the Knickerbocker club had borne the designation of "first organized baseball team." Then an important discovery announced in 2001 revealed that other organized teams existed in New York City at least as early as 1823.[1] Notwithstanding this, the Knickerbockers are still generally credited with devising the first baseball rules codified and accepted for organized competition. But what about the oft-repeated tag that these rules "lie at the heart of modern baseball?"[2] Certainly the Knickerbockers played an important historical role, but do their rules truly merit their reputation for originality and longevity?

In order to evaluate the proper place in history of the Knickerbocker rules, it may be helpful to take a fresh look at them, their relationship to preexisting features of baseball, and their life span in the official rule book. This review will be confined to the fourteen rules that governed play on the field, bypassing the six (rules 1, 2, 3, 5, 6, and 7) that addressed equipment descriptions or off-field issues.

Rule 4: The bases shall be from "home" to second base, forty-two paces; from first to third base, forty-two paces, equidistant.

Many respected historians have credited the Knickerbockers with introducing the diamond-shaped infield and ninety-foot base paths.[3] In fact, neither of these claims is well-founded. The four-base square or diamond configuration was almost certainly a known commodity to the young Knickerbockers, having already appeared in at least four descriptions of early baseball-related games published in America before 1845.[4]

Regarding the base paths, there is no direct evidence that the Knickerbockers intended their cross-diamond measurement of 42 paces to specify a baseline of 90 feet. Since the days of the Roman Empire, the length of a pace had been commonly defined as 2.5 feet. By this measure, the Knickerbocker distance across the infield was 105 feet, which equates to about 75 feet between bases. Some historians have disputed this point, maintaining that a healthy young athlete's stride in 1845 would have been closer to 3 feet than 2.5, which would equate to a home to second measure of 126 feet, and a home to first distance of about 90 feet.[5] This argument appears to assume that "pace" in 1845 was a variable unit of measure that was dependent upon the length of a person's foot, yet it also suggests that for the Knickerbockers the term had a functional value of about three feet. This interpretation runs counter to the definitions of "pace" found in most dictionaries of the era. For example, Noah Webster's dictionary of 1828 defines the term as: "(1) A step. (2) The space between the two feet in walking, estimated at two feet and a half."[6] Given that the Knickerbockers chose to designate a precise number of paces (42), not a round number like 40 or 45, it seems unlikely they intended their infield measurements to be variably dependent upon the stride length of the person stepping off the distances. Nor does it make sense for them to have bypassed the common unit of measure "yard" and chosen "pace" if their actual intention was to denote a length of three feet, rather than 2.5.

The Knickerbockers' 42 paces (or 75-foot base paths) was a logical increment in the gradual expansion of base-to-base dimensions that began in the eighteenth century, when the first published baseball rules stipulated a distance of 10 to 15 paces (25 to 38 feet).[7] By the 1820s and 1830s, the separation between bases had extended to 36 to 60 feet.[8] Then came the Knickerbockers in 1845, and while theirs remained the official measurement for the ensuing decade, it is likely that some ball clubs, including their own, experimented with alternate distances during that interval. On December 6, 1856, the rules of the Putnam Base Ball Club were printed in *Porter's Spirit of the Times*, and these reiterated the Knickerbocker measurement of 42 paces across the infield. However, the diagram printed in conjunction with the rules identified the distance as "42 paces or yards," thus signaling that a change was in the works. Less than two months later, the first formal "Base Ball Convention" meeting in New York officially declared the dimension between bases to be 90 feet, the familiar distance that remains in effect today.

❖

Rule 8: The game to consist of twenty-one counts, or aces; but at the conclusion an equal number of hands must be played.

Obviously, this method of deciding a game's outcome did not endure. This rule, like the one preceding it, was replaced at the 1857 baseball convention. At that time it was initially proposed that victory be awarded to the team with the higher score after seven innings. Fortunately in the end, for those of us who enjoy the pleasures of three- to four-hour ballgames, the convention opted for the familiar nine innings.

It is interesting to note that the Knickerbockers did not define what was meant by a "count" or "ace." Perhaps by that time the terms were so commonplace that no explanation was necessary. It remains a mystery, though, why the club did not choose the word "run" to identify a score in rule 8, even though that term appeared on their preprinted score sheets in 1845. "Run," like several other baseball terms, had been borrowed from cricket.

Curiously, in the various descriptions of early baseball and kindred pastimes that preceded the Knickerbocker rules, scant attention was paid to the method of scoring. One exception was the historian Joseph Strutt's account of a multibase version of "tip-cat" which noted that a base runner could "claim a score towards their game every time they quit one hole and run to another."[9]

❖

Rule 9: The ball must be pitched, not thrown, for the bat.

By "pitched," the Knickerbockers meant that the ball needed to be tossed underhand, as in horseshoes. This method of serving the ball, of course, did not endure in baseball, although it has survived to the present in nearly all forms of softball. In 1845 the Knickerbockers codified it as a feature of New York baseball, distinguishing their game from New England round-ball, which allowed overhand "pitching." This soon emerged as one of the key differences in the competition between the two forms of baseball. An advocate of round-ball, by then known as the Massachusetts or New England game, touted the overhand method in an 1856 newspaper article:

> The ball was thrown, not pitched or tossed, as a gentleman who has seen "Base" played in New York tells me it is; it was thrown, and with vigor, too, that made it whistle through the air, and stop with a solid smack in the catcher's hands, which he directly held in front of his face. I have frequently heard the catcher tell the thrower, and have made the same request myself when catching, to throw as swift as he wished, and aim for my face. One of these swiftly-delivered balls, when stopped by a skillful batsman, is sure to give the outmost scout employment, and the striker to go his rounds in safety, and score one tally as he reaches home.[10]

Within a few years after these words were written, the Massachusetts game disappeared, and the New York version of baseball became preeminent. With their manner of serving the ball to a batter, however, the New Englanders eventually scored a posthumous victory.

Underhand tossing remained the official method of pitching in baseball until 1883, when sidearm throwing was admitted; the following year, the game finally embraced the overhand delivery.

While the Knickerbockers codified the underhand style in 1845, they certainly did not originate it. That method of serving the ball was evident in all known descriptions of early baseball before 1845. The only variable was in the distance separating the pitcher from the batter. In 1796 this separation measured only twelve to fifteen feet, and over the next fifty years it gradually lengthened.[11] The Knickerbockers' rules of 1845 make no mention of how far from the home base they expected the pitcher to stand. In 1854, however, when members of the Eagle Ball Club of New York issued revised by-laws and rules that were similar in most respects to those of the Knickerbockers, they stipulated the pitching distance to be not less than fifteen paces, or approximately thirty-seven and a half feet.[12]

❖

Rule 10: A ball knocked out of the field, or outside the range of the first and third base, is foul.

The inclusion of foul lines differentiated the Knickerbocker game from the many other varieties of baseball played in 1845. The normal practice then was to consider a ball in play regardless of the direction it was hit. Although it was innovative to baseball, the concept of foul territory was not in itself an original idea. The game of trap-ball, which played a role in baseball's evolution, had introduced foul lines many decades earlier. Strutt provides a clear description of this feature: "It is usual in the present modification of the game, to place two boundaries at a given distance from the trap, between which it is necessary for the ball to pass when it is struck by the batsman, for if it falls withoutside of either, he gives up his bat and is out."[13]

The practice of a batter being ruled out for hitting the ball foul reappears in the first description of rounders published in 1828, although this proviso was limited to a ball hit directly behind home plate.[14] Six years later, when the rounders rules were reprinted under the title "base or goal ball," the foul-out feature had disappeared.[15]

Possibly it was the act of reducing the penalty from an out to a strike that made the foul ball concept successful when applied to baseball in 1845. (Rule 10 does not actually specify that a foul ball is counted as a strike, but the wording of rule 18 affirms that the Knickerbockers intended it so.) Nevertheless, it was a radical concept and initially did not spread beyond the New York area. Practitioners of other forms of baseball, such as town-ball, round-ball and rounders, not only were defining tipped balls as being in play but were honing the skills to play them. In rules for rounders published in *The Every Boy's Book* in 1841, the catcher's role was described as playing missed balls and "tips." In case of the latter, the catcher was to retrieve the ball and attempt to strike the runner before he reached first base.[16]

This same general idea was inherent in Massachusetts round-ball, whose boosters prided themselves on practicing a more challenging game than the one in New York. They maintained that the action was more exciting when a struck ball could take off in any direction, and considered the art of tipping a ball over the catcher's head to be one of a batsman's greatest skills.[17] Whatever merit this claim may have had, it was lost with the demise of the Massachusetts game, clearing the way for the Knickerbockers' foul-strike concept to take hold as a core feature of modern baseball.

❖

Rule 11: Three balls being struck at and missed and the last one caught, is a hand-out; if not caught is considered fair, and the striker bound to run.

Long before the advent of the Knickerbocker Base Ball Club, three-strikes-and-yer-out was an indelible feature of the game. In fact, the rule may actually derive from some of baseball's earliest ancestors. The folklorist Alice Gomme has described a variation in the medieval English game of "kit-cat," in which "a certain number of misses (not striking the Cat) may be agreed on to be equivalent to a put out."[18] Similarly, in reference to an "ancient" Irish version of "cat," she comments: "The hitter is out if he fails three times to hit the cat." The same general proviso existed in other bat-and-ball pastimes, such as one variety of trap-ball in which "if (the batter) makes more than two unsuccessful efforts at striking the ball, or touches the tongue more than twice without being able to hit the ball, he is out."[19]

J. C. F. Gutsmuths, the author of the 1796 rules for *das englische Base-ball*, specified that "the batter has three attempts to hit the ball while at the home plate."[20] In this rendition of the game, a batter was obliged to run if he swung and missed at strike three. Since there was no catcher, the batter had a sporting chance of reaching first base before the pitcher or another fielder was able to retrieve the ball and strike him with it. In the half century preceding the Knickerbocker rules of 1845, every published description of early baseball embraced some variant of the three-strike rule as a fundamental tenet of play.[21]

❖

Rule 12: If a ball be struck, or tipped, and caught, either flying or on the first bound, it is a hand out.

The rule that a batter is out on a caught fly ball is, perhaps, the oldest in the game. It characterized all of baseball's principal ancestors, including stool-ball, trap-ball, and most varieties of cat. As further evidence of its antiquity, the act of catching a batted ball was pictured in several medieval illustrations depicting bat-and-ball play.

Unlike the familiar fly out, however, the bound rule is seldom found in the history of bat-and-ball games. Usually thought of as a Knickerbocker innovation, the rule may actually have been a legacy of earlier pastimes. A glimpse of it appeared in the poem "Stool Ball, or the Easter Diversion," published in 1733, in which the task of the fielders was described:

To seize the ball before it grounds,
Or take it when it first rebounds.[22]

Other than this lone eighteenth-century reference, however, no known evidence of the bound rule exists prior to the Knickerbockers' adoption of it 1845. But a description of the game rounders published in London in 1856 suggests that the rule might have had other unseen roots. The 1856 description states that a batter could be retired "if [the ball] is caught before it falls to the ground, or after a single hop or rebound."[23] Since the bound rule had not appeared in any of the earlier known descriptions of rounders, its sudden arrival in 1850s England might have been somebody's inspired idea to copy what the Knickerbockers were experimenting with in America. A more likely explanation is that the old stool-ball rule was simply one of many interchangeable features of children's bat-and-ball games that had been practiced on English playgrounds for decades, and then briefly, in the 1850s, someone made an effort to establish its use in rounders. For naught, apparently; twenty years later, when the newly formed English rounders associations began codifying standardized rules, the bound-out rule was nowhere in evidence.

As for American baseball, by the late 1850s the bound rule had became a source of controversy. The Knickerbocker club, having determined that the practice negatively affected the game, in 1857 began seeking its elimination. A majority of the other clubs continued to favor the rule, and it wasn't until 1865 that it was finally done away with. Before that date, however, many games were played under the "fly rule" when both clubs consented to its application.

❖

Rule 13: A player running the bases shall be out, if the ball is in the hands of an adversary on the base, or the runner is touched with it before he makes his base; it being understood, however, that in no instance is a ball to be thrown at him.

Without a doubt, this rule is the Knickerbockers' single greatest contribution to the game of baseball. The elimination of the practice of soaking or plugging — striking a runner with a thrown ball — was a critical step in sculpting the balance and grace of the modern game. It was sparklingly original, given that a central feature of every previous description of baseball and related games mandated throwing the ball at base runners to put them out. The Knickerbocker practice of putting runners out at a base, or tagging them between bases, has remained a fixture of baseball from 1845 until the present day.

It should be noted that the Massachusetts game of round-ball, played widely in New England, continued to embrace the practice of soaking base runners throughout the 1850s. It is not unreasonable to conclude that the failure of New Englanders to embrace the Knicker-bockers' greatest innovation doomed the Massachusetts game to obsolescence.

❖

Rule 14: A player running who shall prevent an adversary from catching or getting the ball before making his base, is a hand out.

It is possible the Knickerbockers were first to introduce this prohibition against interference, as it cannot be found among any of the earlier descriptions of baseball or rounders. It is more likely, however, that the rule was practiced earlier but that chroniclers simply didn't consider it important enough to include in their brief overviews of the games. This supposition is based upon a general picture of early baseball that can be drawn from the handful of surviving descriptions. Most commonly, in those days, the game was an activity for children or teenagers and was played with a soft ball on a field considerably smaller than in modern baseball. There is no indication from any source that it was a rough-and-tumble sport. Given this, it seems unlikely that the practice of disrupting or preventing a fielder from catching a ball would have been tolerated as fair play.

❖

Rule 15: Three hands out, all out.

In the accounts of early baseball, there were several different methods for determining the termination of a team's at-bat. The "three out, all out" rule adopted by the Knickerbocker club was a break from the most common of these. In effect, it was a compromise between the two most prevalent systems at use before the 1840s, which can be summarized as follows:

> One out, all out: Only a single out had to be recorded before a team lost its at-bat. The earliest recorded forms of baseball

employed this method. It appears in the rules for *das englische Base-ball* published in 1796 and in the description of *la balle empoisonée* that appeared about 1815.[24] In those days it was relatively difficult for the fielding team to put out an opponent. With the exception of fly outs, base runners had to be struck with the ball between bases, a more challenging feat than forcing or tagging them at a base. Also, these early versions of baseball featured the archaic retaliation rule. This provided a means for the batting team, after making an out, to retain its at-bat. To accomplish this, one of its members had to retrieve the ball and successfully use it to strike one of the players on the fielding team before he succeeded in exiting the field. In this way, an at-bat could be extended well beyond a single out.[25]

All out, all out: All members of the batting team had to make out before the at-bat was ended. This method first surfaced in the rules for rounders published in *The Boy's Own Book* in 1828, and was repeated in all descriptions of baseball and related games that appeared in the 1830s.[26] It was probably borrowed from cricket where entire games consisted of one or two interminably long innings that continued until every player on both sides was retired. It is probably no coincidence that the "all out, all out" method made its baseball debut just when the retaliation rule was disappearing; undoubtedly it gave a very different look to the game than the previous practice. Going through the batting order, once a player was put out, he was finished for the inning. However, those who reached base earned the right to bat again when their turn came up, and this continued until every member of the team had been retired. In some cases the entire game would consist of each team batting only once, with the side scoring the most runs declared the winner.

Three out, all out struck a harmonious balance between these two very different approaches. As to the rule's origins, the only hint that it predated the Knickerbocker era stems from the description of an obscure form of the game "kit-cat" that included the following directive: "If there be only six players, it may be previously agreed that three put outs shall end the innings."[27]

Aside from this, even assuming the emergence of the three-out, all-out rule coincided with the formation of the Knickerbocker club, it is far from certain that the team deserves credit for its invention. The doubt arises from evidence that other New York teams were applying the rule in games played in New York City in October 1845, only a few weeks after the publication of the Knickerbocker rules.[28] It is possible that members of the Knickerbocker club, who participated in these contests, introduced three out, all out to the other players on the spot. But it is more likely that the practice had already come into general usage among the city's baseball fraternity during the early 1840s, and that the Knickerbockers simply formalized it in their rule book.

William Cauldwell, who as a reporter for the *New York Mercury* initiated the first regular baseball coverage in 1853, offers further support for this notion. In a letter of reminiscence written later in his life, Cauldwell recalled playing baseball in New York City when he was "knee high to a mosquito," at a time "when 14th St. was considered out of town." The game he remembered was called simply "three out all out."[29] Ultimately, whatever the pedigree of the practice, it is to the credit of the Knickerbockers that they recognized the efficiency of three outs per side per inning, and their codifying of the rule fixed it as a fundamental and enduring feature of the game.

❖

Rule 16: Players must take their strike in regular turn.

This is an obvious and intuitive rule that flows from the order of the game. Without it, teams could simply have their best players bat over and over. It is no surprise that most descriptions of early baseball preceding the Knickerbockers mention that members of the batting team take their places "in turn."

A slight variation of this rule was established in all-out, all-out baseball, in which every member of the batting team had to make out before the side was retired. In this version, players batted in a certain order, but once through the lineup only those individuals who had reached base safely were able to bat again, in which case "they play at the ball in rotation, until they all get out."[30]

Clearly, this Knickerbocker rule is still in effect today, but it can hardly be deemed an innovation.

❖

Rule 17: All disputes and differences relative to the game, to be decided by the Umpire, from which there is no appeal.

How comforting to know that the visage of the stern-faced umpire walking away from the arguing ballplayer dates to the earliest moments of organized baseball! More surprising is the fact that this rule predates the Knickerbocker club. Article VI, section 3 of the *Constitution of the Olympic Ball Club of Philadelphia*, published in 1838, describes the following as one of the duties of the team recorder: "He shall be the umpire between the captains on Club days, in the event of a disputed point of the game, and from his decision there shall be no appeal, except to the Club, at its next stated meeting."[31]

Baseball borrowed the concept of umpires from the game of cricket, which had become an established pastime in the Philadelphia and New York areas by the 1830s.

❖

Rule 18: No ace or base can be made on a foul strike.

The Knickerbockers' innovation of the foul strike concept has already been discussed under Rule 10 above. Their prohibition against advancing a base on a foul was an amplification of the earlier rule and has no precedent among any of the earlier descriptions of baseball and related games.

❖

Rule 19: A runner cannot be put out in making one base, when a balk is made on the pitcher.

This is another rule that apparently originated with the Knickerbocker club, as there is no known mention of it in any earlier accounts of baseball. Then again, it could have existed earlier but not been considered important enough to record. Given how many changes have affected the pitching and base-running components of baseball since 1845, it is somewhat surprising that the balk rule has survived virtually unscathed.

❖

Rule 20: But one base allowed when a ball bounds out of the field when struck.

This is another relatively inconsequential rule that the Knickerbockers saw fit to record. "Out of the field" probably meant beyond either fair or foul territory, where the ball could no longer be played because of some obstruction or hazard. Perhaps a fair ball entering into one of these off-limits areas was treated somewhat akin to the modern ground-rule double. Whatever its true significance (or insignificance), the rule appears to be original to the Knickerbockers.

❖

This review brings one striking peculiarity about the Knickerbocker rules to the fore: the list is not complete. There are fundamental aspects of the 1845 game that the authors chose not to address. For example, they made no mention of the number of players on a team, or of the arrangement of defenders on the field. They said nothing about positioning of the batter or pitcher, or which direction a base runner was to run (whether first base was to the left or right of home plate). They failed to explain how a score was tallied; only that it was called a "count or ace." Despite these glaring omissions, the Knickerbockers addressed such minor rules as balks and base-runner interference. What was going on? Tom Shieber of the Baseball Hall of Fame has offered the opinion that these rules were never intended to be a complete code but simply designed to clarify those aspects of baseball that were not standardized in 1845. He further suggests that the rules were presented with the presumption that players of the era were familiar with the basic tenets of the game.[32] Tom may well be correct, or perhaps there is some other as yet undiscovered explanation. Whatever the answer, it is apparent that, even in their own time, the original Knickerbocker rules did not present a full blueprint of the game.

In summary, it is evident that some of the claims glorifying the Knickerbockers' place in history have been exaggerated. The famous list of rules they created in 1845 contains an interesting contrast of restatements and innovations, bull's-eyes and duds. Were these rules an important contribution to the progress of baseball? Undoubtedly. Did they signify the birth of our modern game and constitute its lasting foundation? Not quite.

7

IN THE
BEGINNING

The roots of baseball were planted the moment the first cave kid hit a stone with his club. Since then, the game's progression has been a little more difficult to figure out. Supermarket tabloids and serious scholars alike have placed the pastime in Egypt at the time of the Pharaohs.[1] The Greeks, the Chinese, and the Vikings have all been reputed to play, and representatives of many other cultures have stepped forward in recent decades to claim a share of baseball's provenance.

In a broad sense, many of these suitors may have a case. The elements of baseball — throwing, batting, fielding and running bases — are so natural and intuitive that the youth of many lands have been combining them into games for countless generations. Nobody has done more than the author Harold Peterson to tickle our imaginations with the far-flung possibilities of this experimentation. In his unique 1973 book *The Man Who Invented Baseball*, Peterson leaps from century to century and continent to continent with a dazzling panoply of intriguing games that he contends were part of baseball's genetic pool. He cites a game called *svinka* from Poland, one known as *titschkerl* played in Austria, *turca* from Italy, and a pastime called *pulat* that hails all the way from India.[2] The great frustration in trying to delve further into these and other discoveries of the late Mr. Peterson is that he neglected to document his source material for most of them. Despite this shortcoming, and allowing that his analytical leaps tying some of these early games to baseball may have been overly fanciful, Peterson nonetheless is among the few American historians to have recognized that the roots of our National Pastime meandered across many cultural and historical boundaries.

Peterson was the heir of several earlier attempts by scholars to probe the historical origins of games played with bat and ball. Most of these studies were conducted in Europe within a decade-long span beginning in the late 1930s, a body of work that has gone largely unnoticed by American baseball historians. The improbable catalyst for these efforts was the astounding discovery made by an Italian researcher working in an isolated region of North Africa in 1937. Professor Corrado Gini, a prominent demographics specialist, was conducting a field study among Berber tribesmen living in a remote village in Libya, which was then an Italian colony.[3] He was investigating the origin of a mysterious trait for blond hair among the villagers when one day he observed a group of them playing a ball game that to him appeared remarkably similar to American baseball. The Berbers called the game *ta kurt om el mahag*, which literally translates to "the ball of the pilgrim's mother." While the name might not ring a bell, the game itself was a familiar mix of batting, fielding and base running. It used only two bases, home and a resting base, and the pitcher stood just a few feet from the batter and served the ball in a gentle arc. After putting the ball in play, batters were retired in the manner typical of most early baseball-like pastimes, by having their struck ball caught on the fly, or by being hit by a thrown ball while running between bases. The Libyan game even featured the colorful retaliation rule, where members of the batting team, after making out, could retain their at-bat if one of them was able to seize the ball and use it to strike any of the opposing defenders before they vacated the field.

Gini carefully documented his discovery, a process which, according to his records, included taking film footage of the game.[4] He then tackled the vexing question of how a remote settlement of Berber tribesmen came to be practicing a sporting activity that was unknown in any other region of North Africa. He ultimately concluded that the game's arrival in the village almost certainly coincided with the introduction of the genetic strain that had been the primary focus of his study. Gini presented his results in 1938 to an anthropological conference in Copenhagen and subsequently published them in American and Italian journals. His conclusion caused quite a stir. He determined that the game, *om el mahag*, was a cultural legacy of blond

Europeans who visited the region during the Stone Age, thousands of years before Christ!

Gini acknowledged that his startling deduction was partly the result of having eliminated all other possible explanations for how *om el mahag* found its way to the isolated village. He believed the game's remote location and obvious great age excluded any likelihood that it was a recent implant and therefore could not have derived from the same English roots as baseball. (For the same reasons, Gini ruled out the improbable counterhypothesis that baseball descended from the North African pastime.) The Italian scholar also dismissed the possibility that the two games, *om el mahag* and baseball, were of independent origin, saying that this "was difficult to accept in view of the marked and detailed similarities between the two complex games." This left him with only one other feasible supposition: that the two games derived from a common ancient source. He tested this premise by examining two possible scenarios. In one, he hypothesized that the long-ago ancestor of the two games at one time had spread over a wide area of Europe and North Africa but had eventually disappeared in all but a few scattered locations, including England and the tiny Berber community in Libya. His second model, which he implied was the far more likely of the two, held that the ancestor game had never expanded beyond a relatively small area of Europe, and then migrated directly to the Berber community "in a form more or less resembling the present game." Implicit in this alternative was that the game at some point also made its way from its original home area to the British Isles, and from there eventually to America. Gini added: "To accept this hypothesis, we should have to admit (and this is not difficult) that the game dates back to much earlier times than is generally supposed."[5]

In supporting his extraordinary claim of *om el mahag's* antiquity, Gini cited various evidentiary clues from the language and rituals of the Berber tribesmen. But the heart of his argument rested upon the circumstance that the single isolated grouping of people known to play the game was also the only community to display the blond-hair trait. He maintained that his findings were supported by other scholars' studies of ancient records of the Libyan population that demonstrated that the light-skinned migrants who imported the blond hair to the remote region had arrived "up to some thousands of years before our era."[6]

A Danish historian named Per Maigaard was seated in the audience when Gini presented his paper on *om el mahag* at the 1938 conference in Copenhagen. At the time, Maigaard was hard at work on his own research project, delving into the history of European sports played with bats and balls. He was amazed to learn about Gini's discovery, although he quickly recognized that the Italian scholar's knowledge of ball games fell well short of his expertise in the field of demographics. In December 1941, amid the darkest days of World War II, Maigaard published the results of his studies in an article entitled "A History of Battingball Games."[7] Notwithstanding the breadth of his topic, the Danish scholar devoted a select portion of his article to *om el mahag* and to his reflections on Gini's theories about the game. Maigaard's composition, written in somewhat labored English, made its appearance in the journal *Genus*. Since this just happened to be the official publication of Gini's population organization in Rome, it is obvious that the two scholars had maintained contact with each other following the Copenhagen conference. Unlike his Italian counterpart, Maigaard was well versed in the history and classification of ball sports, and he attempted in his article to set straight some of Gini's misleading suppositions regarding *om el mahag*. Foremost among these was the Italian's description of the Berber game as "an elementary baseball."[8] Maigaard instead categorized it as a variant of the ancient European game of longball, a game he afforded patriarchal stature in the evolution of bat-and-ball sports.

In organizing his history, the Danish researcher divided bat-and-ball sports into three broad classifications. He wrote: "*Longball, rounders* and *cricket* are the most complicated games of ball ever seen. They evidently make one common group, typologic and also genetic. The similarities are too many to justify the belief in an independent origin for any of them."[9] Maigaard placed baseball in the rounders category, which, along with cricket, he considered of relatively modern derivation — that is, within the past five hundred years. Longball, by comparison, he deemed to be far older, and he identified numerous regional variations of the game that he claimed had been played for centuries across a broad swath of northern Europe. He even provided a detailed diagram of each longball variety, showing the respective playing fields, the positions of competitors, and the shapes of the bats.

Maigaard's article included a composite instruction for practicing the sport of longball, which virtually mirrored Gini's observations of how the Berbers played *om el mahag*. It also matched the basic elements of Gutsmuths's eighteenth-century guidelines for playing the German pastime *das deutsche Ballspiel*. Maigaard theorized that longball was thousands of years old and credited members of the "blond North-European Race" as its most likely inventors. More precisely, he judged Sweden or his own country of Denmark to have been the game's birthplace. He obviously felt self-conscious about this claim, because he followed it with a disclaimer: "In view of the general inclination of authors who have written about these games to attribute their origin to their own country, I am not very glad to draw this conclusion."[10]

Maigaard held that longball was the common ancestor of all bat-and-ball sports. He believed that the "newer" games of rounders, baseball, and cricket had come to be formed on Europe's western edge through a confluence of longball and various Celtic games, among which he included stool-ball and varieties of the game cat. His endeavor to classify these sports and provide a structured prehistory to baseball and cricket was a rare and noble effort. The fact that his work was published in Europe during World War II may account for its continued obscurity among contemporary sports historians. Maigaard's historical analysis of the little-known game of longball, if accurate, fills a measurable gap in the family tree of ball sports. On the other hand, his failure to provide documentation for most of his findings leaves us without the ability to corroborate them. Even the existence of the term "longball" lacks substantiation.

Maigaard also leaves us uncertain of the extent to which he accepted Gini's claim that the game *om el mahag* was brought to North Africa thousands of years before the common era. Attributing an approximate date to that event is important for estimating the window of time when sophisticated bat-and-ball games first emerged or, at least, for dating the class of games that Maigaard describes as long-ball. Referring to "battingball games," the Danish scholar admits: "Hitherto I have supposed them not to be more than some 1500 years old." He appears to agree with Gini in commenting, "They may be of a rather ancient date," and then, "Professor Gini is right. It is not probable that om el mahag is a recent importation." But then Maigaard goes on to make an elaborate case for the game's likely migration to Libya from Germany in the company of Vandal tribesmen in the fifth century, thousands of years later than Gini's estimate. Although he qualifies his remarks by saying that "the Berber-Longball game came to Africa with the Vandals *at the latest*," it is evident that he is distancing himself from Gini's argument.[11]

Gini quickly picked up on this disagreement-couched-as-an-agreement and prepared a response to the Danish historian, which he included in an article he wrote to appear alongside Maigaard's in the December 1941 issue of *Genus*. Gini dismissed the Vandal theory by asserting that the European tribe's occupation of Berber territory was brief and superficial.[12] He argued that if the Vandals had been responsible for importing the game in the fifth century, they also would have left behind other residues of their culture, especially in less remote locations. He further contended that om el mahag was originally associated with ancient spring rain rituals of the Berbers, which he claimed was confirmed by the Greek historian Herodotus in the fifth century BC. While Maigaard's knowledge of games may have been superior to that of Gini, the Italian was clearly an expert in matters of demographics and cultural history. Because of this, there is every reason to place credence in Gini's claims of great antiquity for baseball's obscure African cousin.

A third European researcher, Erwin Mehl of Germany, expanded upon the work of Gini and Maigaard in a 1948 article entitled "Baseball in the Stone Age."[13] Mehl focused on the long and rich history of bat-and-ball games played on the European continent, drawing upon a number of earlier studies by German historians of the nineteenth and twentieth centuries. He examined and evaluated the features of a wide range of early Indo-European games stretching from Lapland to India but seemed predisposed to a conclusion that Germanic and

Slavic ball games were the most important influences on the development of what was ultimately to become baseball.

Despite the author's home-team favoritism, "Baseball in the Stone Age" was highly informative and offered some rare and fascinating examples of early bat-and-ball games. The jewel among these was an unnamed but curiously familiar pastime that Mehl found described in a German book from the year 1610. The author of that work was an Austrian doctor named Hippolytus Guarinoni, who stated that he had played the sport with students in the city of Prague. His account of the game appeared within a ponderous 1,300-page treatise advising people how to live healthy and pious lives.[14] What follows is an English translation of Guarinoni's description:

The third ball game, which I have seen only in Bohemia but never in Italy. The ball is of the same size as the ball in the preceding game (the size of a quince) and is hard and made of leather. Two sides divide up in the field here and there, in all directions, in the middle, to the side, and to the back, at a distance of seventy, eighty, and a hundred paces, and wait for the ball coming in the air, that they may catch it. The second side hits it to them with a club four feet long. The club is round, and the handle is thinner and the end is thicker, so that the ball is struck with greater force and driven to a distance. In batting, there are two [players] — one who throws the ball to the batter in such a way that it strikes the bat, and the batter, who, if he hits it right, drives it high and far. If it is caught in the air by the opponents, then the batting side must leave off batting and go to catching. Such a game is not one of the most violent exercises, because it requires no particular skill, variety of motion, or bending of the body except usually running. It is good for tender youth, which never has enough of running back and forth without one giving another a friendly push or tripping him unexpectedly while running, so that whoever believes himself to be sure of foot finds himself lying on the ground. Such a game was very popular in Prague, and we often played it. The cleverest players were the Poles and Silesians, so I believe that it may have come from there.[15]

It is unusual to find such a detailed explanation of any game from the early seventeenth century, even rarer for the pastime to be one with familial ties to baseball. It is a mild disappointment that the author did not furnish us with sufficient clues to know whether the Prague game incorporated base running. He may have been indirectly suggesting this by his comment that the game "usually" included running, and that this was "good for tender youth." It is worth mentioning that two Hungarian authors, who refer to Guarinoni's description in a 1985 book entitled *Fun and Games in Old Europe*, paraphrase him as stating that the batter, after hitting the ball, "attempted to make the circuit of the bases without being hit by the ball."[16] Unfortunately, no evidence of this is found in Mehl's excerpt.

What may be the most remarkable aspect about the game described by Guarinoni was its proximity in time to a second recorded instance of early-seventeenth-century bat-and-ball play involving expatriate Poles and Silesians. This second example appeared in a most unexpected location: colonial Jamestown, Virginia. It is a little-known fact that the early English colonists at Jamestown imported a small group of Polish workers to the settlement to assist with such specialty tasks as glassmaking and the production of pitch and tar. The Poles, who sought to balance their hard work with well-deserved recreation, brought with them a popular Silesian folk game called *palant* or *pilka palantowa*, meaning "bat ball." We know this from the journal kept by one of the Polish settlers, Zbigniew Stefanski of Wroclaw, who published his Jamestown experiences as a memoir in 1625. The Polish-American researcher Arthur Waldo discovered the memoir and reprinted parts of it in his 1977 work *The True Heroes of Jamestown*. Of particular interest is a Stefanski entry from the year 1609: "Soon after the new year, I, Sadowski, Mata, Mientus, Stoika, and Zrenica initiated a ball game played with a bat. . . . Most often we played this game on Sundays. We rolled rags to make the balls. . . . Our game even attracted the savages who sat around the field, delighted with this Polish sport."[17]

So should true credit for introducing baseball to America go to those early players from the Silesian fields? Possibly, although it is fair to say that even if this game was an ancestor of baseball, it did not successfully plant a toehold in America in 1609. The Polish workers at Jamestown returned to Europe in 1610, fed up with the terrible conditions in the colony and their disrespectful treatment at the hands of their English employers. More time passed before other English migrants to the New World imported forms of bat-and-ball games with which they were more familiar. As for the game of *palant*, it is still occasionally played today in Poland and is among the few survivors of the family of northern European games labeled by Maigaard as longball.

Meanwhile, in "Baseball in the Stone Age," Erwin Mehl enthusiastically echoed Maigaard's view that baseball had been spawned in Northern Europe, although he would not have been too keen on ascribing importance to the Polish game *palant*, nor any other game born outside of Germany. In his article, Mehl exhibited an undue fixation on his own country's role, tracing his case for the Germanic origins of baseball back to the ancient Berber game discovered by Gini. Perhaps feeling a need to reclaim vestiges of national pride after his country's defeat in World War II, Mehl missed no opportunity to promote Germany's contributions to ball sport history and maintained that this influence had spread in all directions. Starting to the north, he asserted that the language and culture of Scandinavian ball games were actually Germanic in origin, to which he added: "A striking counterpart to these northern radiations of Germanic ball games is seen in the south. After the Germanic migrations all the Western Romance languages borrowed the word for ball from the Germanic languages with which they were in contact, although the Latin *pila* was available and the people played ball games. Obviously, the Germanic ball games made so great an impression in both the north and the south that the terminology as well as the games were borrowed."[18]

In introducing the ball game that Guarinoni witnessed in Prague, Mehl felt compelled to establish the doctor's Germanic credentials: "Notwithstanding his Italian name, which is of Germanic, probably Lombard, origin and is akin to the German *Werner* (protector of the army) in its older form *warinhari*, Guarinoni spoke and felt like a German."[19] Mehl's conspicuous nationalism raises inevitable doubts about his objectivity as a scholar.

It is no great surprise that Mehl took considerable pride in J. C. F. Gutsmuths's epic anthology of sports and games, the 1796 *Spiele zur Uebung und Erholung*. But while paying brief notice to Gutsmuths's coverage of "the older English form of baseball," Mehl's fondest words were bestowed upon his fellow German's twenty-one-page description of *das deutsche Ballspiel*. Mehl observed that calling it "the *German ball game* . . . indicates its wide distribution in Germany," and he echoed Gutsmuths's words that the game "preeminently deserves an exact description." While it is true that the German game warrants recognition both as a relative to baseball and in its own right, it doesn't merit the lofty significance that Mehl attached to it. Still, his lament for the game's twentieth-century demise was undoubtedly heartfelt ("It is nevertheless beyond doubt that the oldest form of batting games is dying out among the Germans"), as was the sincerity of his epitaph ("The contrast between its fate and the success of its highly esteemed cousins, cricket and baseball, gives one food for thought").[20]

It is worth repeating that Mehl, as well as Maigaard, made mention of Gutsmuths's historic description of English base-ball. It also "gives one food for thought" that this information has been almost completely absent from the writings of baseball historians in all the years since Mehl's article. The unfortunate truth is that American researchers during the past half century have made only minimal effort to document baseball's early history and for the most part have not been inclined to go looking to European sources for clues. I have little doubt that the pioneering American baseball historian Robert W. Henderson would have been an exception to this tendency, but he conducted his research from the late 1930s to the mid-1940s, before "Baseball in the Stone Age" was published. Because Maigaard's article and one of Gini's went to press in Europe during World War II, it is doubtful whether Henderson would have had the opportunity to read them.

Although Henderson's explorations into the roots of baseball were taking place in the same decade as the studies of the three Europeans, a literal and figurative ocean separated them. And whereas modern baseball historians have long overlooked the writings of Gini,

Maigaard, and Mehl, their American counterpart's work has been placed upon a pedestal. As we have seen, Henderson's conclusions about the origins of baseball have been so universally accepted within the scholarly community that for decades no one conducted independent research to verify his findings. Henderson's pivotal work *Ball, Bat, and Bishop*, published in 1947, showcased the results of his long investigation into the history of bat-and-ball sports. Reexamining his sources and arguments after the passage of a half century may reveal an occasional error, yet there is no doubt that Henderson's study still deserves recognition as the single most authoritative work on the subject.

The combined efforts of Henderson, Gini, Maigaard, and Mehl in the 1930s and 1940s unveiled the sweeping evolutionary tableau of games played with bat and ball. Enhanced by Harold Peterson's revelations of baseball-like games descending from many cultures, these studies support a hypothesis that baseball did not spring from a single linear evolutionary path but is the ultimate product of a common cultural memory extending back thousands of years. This helps explain why the solution to baseball's origins has been so elusive. It also helps decipher the paradox of why any number of bat-and-ball games from so many countries appear to be part of baseball's ancestry, and yet only scant circumstantial evidence exists to show how the American game directly descended from any single one.

Irrespective of this ancient and global pedigree, there is little doubt that baseball's implantation and nourishment in colonial America was almost exclusively the immediate product of English cultural influence. In the following chapters I will explore a spectrum of early English bat-and-ball games that preceded baseball, evaluating which among them most directly contributed to the development of our National Pastime.

8

STOOLS, CLUBS, STOBS, AND JUGS

CLUB-BALL

Historians and anthropologists take particular satisfaction in identifying the oldest or earliest example of whatever phenomenon or subject they happen to be studying. It is no surprise, therefore, that this same fascination holds true for researchers of bat-and-ball games. The pioneering English sports chronicler Joseph Strutt appeared to have fulfilled this requirement for baseball scholars in the pages of his 1801 masterwork *Sports and Pastimes of the People of England.* Strutt described and documented an ancient game called "club-ball," which he identified as the oldest ancestor of cricket, and, by extension, the granddaddy of all other related games played with bat and ball.[1] In recent decades, authors of baseball histories have often cited Strutt's patriarchal nominee in their capsulated treatments of the game's origins. Yet, circling back to take a closer look, it now appears that old Joseph Strutt may have taken some serious liberties with his scholarship. It turns out that his heralded game of club-ball, like so much of the lore pertaining to baseball's ancestry, may be more fanciful than factual.

Writing in 1801, all Strutt could offer in describing club-ball was that it was distinguished from "goff" by its use of a straight bat rather than a curved one. For evidence of the game he quoted a fourteenth-century proclamation from the reign of Edward III that required county sheriffs to prohibit the playing of various games on the Sabbath, including *"pilam manualem, pedinam, et bacculoreum, et ad cambucam."*[2] Strutt translated this medieval Latin to read "playing at hand-ball, foot-ball, club-ball and cambucam [golf]." His identification of "club-ball" as a distinct game, however, was overly imaginative. The words *pilam bacculoreum* translate simply as "ball play with a stick or staff" and most likely alluded to a variety of early bat-and-ball games, not any one in particular.

Strutt's bestowal of forefather status upon the otherwise unknown game of club-ball may have been a self-serving attempt to explain the origins of cricket and other bat-and-ball games for which he had no alternate theory. Although Strutt is generally held in high regard as a scholar, his sleight of hand in this matter did not go unnoticed by other sports historians of his era. One of them, William Maxwell, argued that cricket was far older than Strutt acknowledged and that "the game of club-ball appears to be none other than the present, well-known bat-and-ball."[3]

In his 1801 book Strutt also furnished what he described as visual evidence of club-ball: two illustrations of ball games that he had copied by hand from medieval manuscripts. One depicted a player getting ready to fungo a ball — toss it in the air and hit it as it falls — to a waiting fielder. The second was more baseball-like, portraying a woman seemingly pitching a ball to a male batter. As a proof for Strutt's club-ball theory, however, this second image had an inherent disadvantage — it was nto English in origin. Strutt copied it from an illuminated French manuscript of the period, which casts serious doubt on whether it could really have illustrated the game banned by Edward III.

To further confuse the issue, Robert W. Henderson in *Ball, Bat, and Bishop* displayed the original French image along with a second similar illustration of a bat-and-ball game taken from the same manuscript.[4] Both images at first glance appear to show a woman pitching to a male batter, with a cluster of fielders waiting with arms outstretched. Henderson called one of the games "stool-ball" and the other *la soule*. The original French manuscript dating from the year 1344 is housed in the Bodleian Library at Oxford. The library describes Henderson's *la soule* image as "monk holding a bat, and nun holding a ball; watched by two monks and two nuns with hands raised." Henderson's stool-ball image, however, which also happens to be the one

Image from fourteenth-century French manuscript "The Romance of Alexander." Henderson described the game as la soule. MS. Bodl. 264, fol. 44r (detail), by permission of the Bodleian Library.

copied by Strutt and called club-ball, the library describes as "woman holding wide-mouthed jug; youth brandishing a club. . . . A group of children look toward the centre."[5] A jug?

I obtained digital copies of both images from the Bodleian Library. An examination of the one that was Strutt's club-ball and Henderson's stool-ball confirms the library's description. The illustration has absolutely nothing to do with ball playing! The woman's hands are plainly holding a jug, and there is no way Strutt could have missed it. It is bizarre to think that he would have been so driven to establish club-ball as an ancient game that he would fabricate evidence to prove it, but no other explanation presents itself. Strutt's trickery has been taken as truth for much of the past two hundred years, with Henderson being only one of many to repeat it as fact. As early as 1891 the English author P. H. Ditchfield, in his book *Old English Sports*, provided an elaborate description of the 1344 Bodleian image of "club-ball."[6] Obviously, he had never actually seen the manuscript first-hand, and was simply basing his commentary upon Strutt's earlier interpretation.

Curiously, the second image from the 1344 manuscript, the one ignored by Strutt and called *la soule* by Henderson, appears to be a genuine baseball-cricket predecessor. It is puzzling that Henderson iden-

A second image from the fourteenth-century manuscript "The Romance of Alexander." Henderson identified the game shown as "stoolball," but it is evident the woman is holding a jug. MS. Bodl. 264, fol. 22r (detail), by permission of the Bodleian Library.

tified it as *la soule*. According to his own description, *la soule* was played by driving the ball along the ground with the foot, the hand, or a stick, while the Bodleian illustration clearly shows a ball being pitched and a bat being held upright.

Returning to Strutt's club-ball, except for his questionable extraction of the term from the fourteenth-century Latin proclamation, there is absolutely no evidence that a particular game of that name ever existed. Yet notwithstanding this mirage, clues found within the writings and records of medieval England confirm that the common folk of that era were already mixing balls and bats into their repertoire of recreational alternatives. One early and unusual reference was noted in the records of the Hustengs Court at Oxford for March 17, 1292:

> Henry le Soper and Rose his wife make complaint of Godfrey Faber and John Faber, that when the said Henry and Rose were in their shop for the purposes of selling their goods, viz., girdles, gloves, silk, and other mercery, on Wednesday, the feast of St. Gregory, after dinner, in All Saints' parish, there came

Strutt used the second "Romance of Alexander" image pictured as the model for his hand-drawn illustration of "club ball,"; in his version the woman appears to hold a ball in her hand.

Godfrey and John playing in the street with a club and great ball, and with the club and ball they knocked into the mud the goods of Henry and Rose that were in their shop, and trod upon them; and not content therewith they took the said Henry and smote him and beat him and evil entreated him, and Rose likewise they beat and evil entreated, and threw her on the ground, to the damage of Henry and Rose to the value of twenty shillings.[7]

After all this beating and evil entreating it is easier to understand why Edward III issued his edict banning games with balls. One must assume that this sort of hooliganism represented exceptional behavior, or bat-and-ball pastimes might never have survived the Middle Ages. Illuminated manuscripts of the era depict additional examples of these games; in addition to the Bodleian Library's ball-playing monk and nun, an illustration from a work in the British Library pictures two players with clubs in hand, one getting ready to fungo a ball.[8] Unfortunately, we have no specific information about how these games were played or what they were called. Perhaps Strutt's fictitious term "club-ball" could be put to good use, recoined as a generic catchall for those anonymous games of bat and ball played in England during the medieval era.

HAND-IN AND HAND-OUT

The earliest indication of this pastime comes from another edict banning the practice of various games. King Edward IV complained in the year 1477 that his subjects were losing the necessary military skills needed to defend the kingdom. Instead of practicing archery and swordplay they were diverting themselves with all sorts of frivolous pastimes. The king outlawed the "old" games of "Dice, Coits, and Tennis," as well as some "new imagined games called Closh, Kailes, Half Bowl, Hand-in and Hand-out, and Queckboard."[9] Or as written in the original Norman French that was still the official language of the English court: "*novelx ymaginez Jeuex appelez Cloishe Kaylez half kewle Hondyn & Hondoute & Quekeborde.*" Hand-in and hand-out is briefly defined in the Oxford English Dictionary as the "name of a game with a ball in the fifteenth century."[10] A further description is provided by Joseph Baldassarre in his article "Baseball's Ancestry": "Two holes are cut in the ground at opposing positions and the dog (batsman) tries to keep the cat (ball hurled by bowler) out of the hole."[11] If this portrayal is accurate, it identifies hand-in and hand-out as being nearly the same as the ancient game of "cat and dog," which, as we shall see, was a likely forerunner of the American scrub game of two-old-cat.

The name "hand-in and hand-out" may have been the source of the terms "in party" and "out party," which distinguished the batting team from the fielding team in cricket, and then later in baseball. Another baseball term, "hand out," may also have derived from this ancient game. (A "hand out," later shortened simply to "out," was a statistical category that appeared in baseball's earliest known box scores in October 1845.[12] The same term also appeared in several of the Knickerbocker Base Ball Club's rules, again denoting an "out" or "putout.")[13]

STOOL-BALL

The game of stool-ball dates at least as far back as the Middle Ages and is known to have taken multiple forms that varied by location and time. The folklorist Alice Gomme suggested that its ancestral name was "bittle-battle," with the "bittle" being the bat used to defend the stool.[14] The *Oxford English Dictionary*, however, lists no entry for this construction and, in fact, cites no usage of the word "bittle" in any context. (Henderson cites an unnamed author as having claimed that bittle-battle was mentioned in the Domesday Book in the year 1086.)[15]

Stool-ball was played widely in the British Isles and was a diversion for both sexes. References to the game appear in many English books over hundreds of years, dating back at least to 1450.[16] Until the eighteenth century, authors mentioning the game tended to dwell on its role in the cultural order rather than as a sport. Henderson theorizes that stool-ball originated as a Christian adaptation of pagan ball play that was part of spring fertility rites.[17] As evidence he demonstrates that virtually all early references to the game portray it as an Easter-time pastime practiced in churchyards, but infused with strong suggestions of courtship and sex.

Literature of the seventeenth and eighteenth centuries bears out this theory. Shakespeare employed the phrase "playing stool-ball" as a euphemism for sexual behavior.[18] George Chapman, in his English translation of Homer, suggested that the lovely Nausicae used her powerful stool-ball stroke to splash the ball in the water, thereby causing her companions to shriek, and rousing the nearby sleeping Ulysses, whom she was intended to seduce.[19] Generally, writers celebrated the game as a joyful and sometimes bawdy spring pastime in which the victors were rewarded with pungent tansy cakes, kisses, and, on occasion, sexual pleasures.

Samuel Johnson's *Dictionary* in 1755 defined stool-ball as "a play where balls are driven from stool to stool," which suggests that at least two stools were involved.[20] An illustration of the game appearing in the slightly earlier *A Little Pretty Pocket-Book* depicts three male players and one stool.[21] One player is pitching underhand to a batless batter standing next to the stool, while a third player waits in the field. A piece of verse beneath the image reads:

The *Ball* once struck with Art and Care,
And drove impetuous through the Air
Swift round his Course the *Gamester* flies,
Or his *Stool's* taken by Surprize.

The poem implies that multiple stools or bases must have been involved, or else what course would the gamester be flying around? The stool being taken by surprise suggests that if a fielder returned the ball to the home stool before the runner, the latter was retired.

Strutt described two versions of stool-ball.[22] The first method consisted simply of a single stool with one player positioned next to it, while a second player standing "at a distance" tossed a ball with the intention of striking the stool. It was the object of the first player to prevent this by beating it away with her hand. Points were scored every time the batter struck the ball. If the ball was missed, the players exchanged places and then the former tosser was entitled to bat and score points.

Strutt's second method employed multiple stools spaced around a circle. A player was situated at each stool and a tosser was involved as before, but in a slightly expanded role. The tosser pitched the ball to a stool, where a defending player attempted to smack it by hand. If the ball was struck, the batter and all the other stool tenders circled around the stools (bases) while the tosser ran to retrieve the ball. Once having the ball in hand, the tosser tried to throw it and hit one of the runners between stools. If successful, the tosser earned the right to guard a stool, and the runner who had been struck became the next tosser.

Strutt was the recognized late-eighteenth- and early-nineteenth-century English authority on games and sports, and his representation of stool-ball as a game played without a bat has long been assumed to be accurate. However, this and other long-held suppositions about the game are challenged by a remarkable poem that appeared in an English magazine sixty-eight years before the publication of Strutt's work in 1801. The poem, entitled "Stool-Ball, or the Easter Diversion," captures vivid details of one contest from the early eighteenth century, including:

The earliest confirmed evidence of a stool-ball player actually using a bat.

New particulars about the method of play. In the poem, the batters are young women divided into two teams. Each member of the "in" team remains at bat until she is retired. This happens if any of her batted balls is caught on the fly or on a bound by one of the defenders. Additionally, a batter is out if a fielder retrieves any ball in play and, in the process of throwing it back in, manages to strike the stool. The poem does not reveal whether the ball is served to the batter by a pitcher or self-served, fungo style. In the field, the first line of defenders comprises other young women, who attempt to catch fly balls in their aprons. The row of outfielders behind them is made up of young men, whose stronger arms, according to the author, are more suited for making the long, accurate throws needed to strike the stool. The version of stool-ball described in the poem apparently did not include base running.

A wonderful poetic description of the game's setting, including the playing field and the cheering assembled audience.

Attention to such details as the design of the stool and the coin toss to decide who bats first.

A dramatic narration of the contest itself, the building tension and the climactic role of individual players, somewhat anticipatory of "Casey at the Bat."

A paean to the benefits of good clean fun, fresh air, and exercise,

which the author contrasts to the "crim'nal" behavior of those
who would stay up all night gambling.

An enticing clue in the search for baseball's birthplace.

STOOL-BALL, OR THE EASTER DIVERSION

When now the time of penance past,
The self-denying days of fast,
Nature with vigour blooms a-new,
And shews a more enlivening view.
Cold wintry seasons far retir'd,
And all with vernal warmth inspir'd,
The beauteous maids, and willing swains
In scenes of frolick croud the plains;
And to the spring their honours pay,
In rites of customary play.

Then Swanzey, in thine each fair street
Parties of sport and pleasure meet.
The beaux and belles of first degree
Possess the place of dignity;
And in the market's guarded square
Whirl the swift ball thro' liquid air.
The tribe of an inferior test
The second privilege arrest;
They chuse that open area most,
Where stand the stocks and pillory post;
Where justice shows a worn-out face,
And sinners seldom meet disgrace:
While servile bands, of mean renown,
Enjoy the out-parts of the town.

Yet sometimes here confusion reigns,
And chance each station ascertains.
Describe, my muse, the annual play
In which they waste the festal day.

Soon as the sun from noon-day's height
To western regions bends his flight,
A throng of spreading hoops is seen,
Assembled round the sportive scene;
Obsequious youths their pleasure wait,
Each proud to chuse a lovely mate.
At upper-end is fix'd the stool,
In fam'd heroick games, the goal;
Not sacred tripod, as of old,
But quadruped of modern mold.
Hence is the missive engine born,
And hither speeds its swift return.
Two gen'ral parts the match divide,
Proportion just on either side.
Who have the fortune to begin,
Obtain a lucky chance to win;
Which the decisive shilling shows
By cross or pile to these or those.

Now let the fair in just array
Perform the functions of the play!
See at the goal Pulcheria stand,
And grasp the board with snowy hand!
She drives the ball with artful force,
Guiding thro' hostile ranks its course.
Subtly it creeps along the ground,
Or flies aloft with whizzing sound.
Then see the milk-white aprons rise,
And turn their beauties to the skies,
(Some in native cambrick plain,
Some wrought in flow'rs of various stain)
In round capacious figure bent,
And stretching to a wide extent,
To seize the ball before it grounds,
Or take it when it first rebounds.
The youths their stations have a-far,

Enjoin'd to guard the distant rear,
With nimbler limb, and manly strength,
To strike the mark from utmost length,
To watch the ball that farthest speeds,
And tow'rs above the ladies heads.

While it eludes the thrower's aim,
Pulcheria carries on the game,
In triumph o'er the envious foe,
Still numb'ring each auspicious blow;
Till, erring in some fatal way,
The ball becomes a legal prey.
Yet if a cause of doubt appear,
Shrill clamours rend the trembling air;
Each female tongue in self-defence
Exerts its tuneful eloquence;
The men in well-bred silence wait,
And leave the ladies to debate.
Then should her rival's right be shown,
Pulcheria lays her weapon down.
Again the adverse bands retreat,
A second heroine to defeat,
Who join'd in the confed'rate cause,
Pursues the game with loud applause.
If haply fortune join the foe,
And give her but a single blow,
Chagrin'd she quits th' unlucky post,
And mourns her toil and glory lost.

Then starts a more successful fair,
The vast dishonour to repair;
While still a lovely tribe remain,
The growing conquest to maintain.
Their tender breasts for triumph burn,
And each impatient waits her turn.

The ladies gallant labours done,
We finish what they well begun.

Nor does it small ambition raise,
To hear the shining circle praise.
Women, if void of martial fire,
The noblest heats of soul inspire;
And greater vict'ries ne'er were earn'd,
Than where a Helen was concern'd.

The tidings of the final blow
Give shame and terror to the foe.
Their hearts in trembling measure beat,
Repining at their near defeat.
In the last efforts of despair,
They watch the ball with stricter care.
The ball securely glides along,
Nor falls expos'd amid the throng.
Loud triumphs from the goal proclaim
The prosp'rous issue of the game;
While those without reluctant yield
The honours of the sportful field:
Yet urg'd by rage, and fond desire,
A second proof of skill require.
Small remnant of the victor-crew,
Now left the combat to renew,
Yet custom justifies the claim.
Commences then another game.
Where the same feats of valour shown
Both sides with equal vict'ry crown.
Then the blest joys of female smiles
Conclude the well-rewarded toils.

Ye blooming nymphs of Cambrian race,
Distinguish'd by each softer grace,
Protect the muses grateful theme,
Nor blush to own the rural game.
Where does the shame or crime appear
Of harmless romping once a year?
No rule of virtue it offends;

And health on exercise attends.
Such motion brings delightful rest,
Nor kindles passions in your breast;
Quickens the fluids in their pace,
And spoils no charm of woman's face;
While open day-light, and fresh air
Chase gloomy vapours from the fair.
More crim'nal they, not more polite,
Who shake the guilty box all night;
Their fortune, fame, and peace expose,
And stake their all on casual throws.[23]

The venue for this colorful contest is identified in the poem as "Swanzey"— the Welsh seaport of Swansea.[24] The town sits directly across the Bristol Channel from the English county of Devonshire, the corner of England where the name "rounders" as a pseudonym for baseball first came into local usage in the early nineteenth century. Because use of a bat was not an evident feature of English baseball in its earliest manifestations, it is possible that bat usage in the nearby Swansea version of stool-ball became familiar in Devonshire and influenced the more advanced form of baseball that evolved there. (An earlier hint that Wales may have been one pole of baseball's fertile crescent is suggested in the writings of John Taylor, "the water poet," who on a journey to that part of Britain in 1652 observed people playing "the lawful and laudable games of trap, cat, stool-ball, racket, &c., on Sunday."[25] It is intriguing for so many of baseball's antecedents to be identified together in one locale.)

A likely legacy of this hotbed of stool-ball is the remarkable game of Welsh baseball. In the early twentieth century, organized teams playing a form of baseball reminiscent of nineteenth-century Massachusetts round-ball took root in Wales and parts of western England. For several decades this game enjoyed great popularity, and given its proximity in form and geography to earlier English variants of baseball, it is almost certainly a modern reemergence of those older pastimes.

After many hundreds of years of preeminence as a traditional folk game, in the late nineteenth century stool-ball finally ascended to the ranks of organized sport, complete with town associations and published rules. Use of a bat was now formally codified. Stools were replaced with "targets": round pieces of wood about a foot wide that were attached to posts in the ground.[26]

No other single game contributed more to baseball's early formation than stool-ball. The game was a popular fixture on the English scene for centuries, and in its multiple base version featured a familiar combination of ball play and circular base running. Players needed to advance to the next stool without being struck by the ball and put out. Add to this the skills of fielding, throwing, and, in some varieties, striking the ball with a bat, and stool-ball had most of the elements of baseball-in-waiting. A further linkage was that, in its infancy, the game of baseball in England was known to be a shared activity for girls and boys, which may have directly carried over from the earlier stool-ball, in which interaction of the sexes was commonplace.

STOBBALL AND STOW-BALL

To say there is no common assessment of the games of stobball and stow-ball would be an understatement. Despite a number of literary references to one or both of these dating back nearly five hundred years, neither historians nor etymologists can agree on what the games were or how they were played. It is not even certain whether they were two names for the same game or two completely unrelated pastimes.

Here's what the various authorities have had to offer. *The English Dialect Dictionary*, released in six volumes between 1898 and 1905, equates stobball with the game of stool-ball. Alice Gomme agreed, stating in her *Traditional Games of England, Scotland, and Ireland* that the earliest references to stool-ball were from the sixteenth century, and that the game then was called stobball. Taking an opposite tack, the *Oxford English Dictionary* maintains that "the corruption of stool-ball into stoball [and] stobball seems hardly probable," and deems stobball to be an old form of stow-ball, an entirely separate game. The OED's only citation offering even a vague description of stow-ball, however, is a phrase plucked from the works of the historian Joseph Strutt:

"A pastime called stow-ball is frequently mentioned by the writers of the sixteenth and seventeenth centuries, which, I presume, was a species of goff; at least it appears to have been played with the same kind of ball."[27]

So is stobball stool-ball or stow-ball or both? And where does golf fit in? Perhaps a look at some of the historical clues will help unscramble this conundrum. A good place to start is the tantalizing reference to stobball found in John Aubrey's *Natural History of Wiltshire*, completed in 1685:

> They smite a ball stuffed very hard with quills and covered with soale leather, with a staffe, commonly made of withy, about three and a halfe feet long. Colerne Down is the place so famous and so frequented for stobball playing. The turfe is very fine and the rock (freestone) is within an inch and a halfe of the surface which gives the ball so quick a rebound. A stobball ball is of about four inches diameter and as hard as a stone.[28]

The author's emphasis on the quality of the playing surface might be more applicable to golf than stool-ball, but the same cannot be said of that four-inch-thick "stobball ball." Furthermore, Aubrey's description of the stobball staff makes no mention of a curved head, as we would expect on a golf club. On the other hand, if stobball was a variant of stool-ball, then the presence of a straight bat, or any bat at all, would be of some historical significance. Another author, Edward Chamberlayne, implied a distinction between "goffe" and "stow-ball" when delineating a list of popular recreations in the 1669 edition of his work *The Present State of England*.[29]

The location of stobball play is also noteworthy. Aubrey wrote that the game was popular in "North Wilts, North Gloucestershire, and a little part of Somerset near Bath."[30] These venues, like Swansea and Devonshire, are located near Bristol Channel in the southwest corner of Great Britain. An earlier reference to the same game in the same region of the country can be found in John Smyth's *Berkeley Manuscripts*, in which he tells of the Earl of Leicester coming down to Wotton in 1573 with a large number of attendants and "thence . . . to Wotten Hill where hee played a match at Stoball." Elsewhere in the same work Smyth named additional neighboring locales, taking pains to point out that the pastime was not solely the province of nobility:

The large and levell playnes of Slimbridge warth and others in the vale of this hundred: And the downes or hilly playnes of Stintescombe, Westridge, Tickruydinge, and others in the hilly or Cotteswold part, doe witnes the inbred delight, that both gentry, yeomanry, rascality, boyes and children, doe take in a game called Stoball, The play whereat each child of 12.yeares old, can (I suppose) aswell describe, as my selfe: And not a sonne of mine, but at 7. was furnished with his double stoball staves, and a gamster therafter.[31]

The fact that hilly "playnes" were deemed appropriate for this sport seems to suggest a closer relationship to golf than to a base running game, as does the necessity for players to possess double staves. On the other hand, Smyth's portrayal of stobball as a suitable activity for fairly young children does not mesh with golf's status in its early history as an adult pastime.

A strong argument for relating both stow-ball and stobball to stool-ball comes from David Terry, an English sports researcher who has studied the early history of cricket. Terry writes that "stow" and "stob" were both "dialect names for a stump, being the lower part of a tree or its remaining stump."[32] The OED and other dictionaries affirm his definitions. A stump would have been a plausible alternative to a stool as a home base, and that explanation, if true, would distance the games of stobball and stow-ball from any affinity to golf. Terry hypothesizes that a stump might have been the original cricket wicket but acknowledges that evidence illuminating these early games is quite thin.

Perhaps the earliest surviving reference to stobball is found in the rolls of the court baron of the Royal Manor of Kirklington for the year 1525 under the heading "trespass." As translated from the original archaic French-tinged Latin, the document reads: "Item, that Peter Franklin put twenty-four cattle in the Stoballfield contrary to the order of this court previously enacted."[33] So whatever the true nature of the game, this entry confirms that, at least in this one locale, the mysterious game of stobball enjoyed the rare and lofty stature of having legal protection for its playing field.

PRISONER'S BASE, OR THE GAME OF BASE

The game of prisoner's base, also sometimes known simply as "base" or as "bars," is quite old, with references going back to at least the fourteenth century, when another one of those annoying edicts of Edward III banned its play on the grounds of Parliament.[34] It is not a ball game but rather a simple chase exercise, which Strutt described as follows:

> The performance of this pastime requires two parties of equal number, each of them having a base or home, as it is usually called, to themselves, at a distance of about twenty or thirty yards. The players then on either side taking hold of hands, extend themselves in length, and opposite to each other, as far as they conveniently can, always remembering that one of them must touch the base; when any one of them quits the hand of his fellow and runs into the field, which is called giving the chase, he is immediately followed by one of his opponents; he again is followed by a second from the former side, and he by a second opponent; and so on alternately, until as many are out as choose to run, every one pursuing the man he first followed, and no other; and if he overtake him near enough to touch him, his party claims one toward their game, and both return home. They then run forth again and again in like manner, until the number is completed that decides the victory; this number is optional, and I am told rarely exceeds twenty.[35]

As a children's recreation, prisoner's base enjoyed considerable popularity and is described in many of the early books on games and amusements. Strutt wrote that it also was held in high repute by adult men in several English counties and recalled witnessing a contest played in 1770 between two teams of a dozen players each.[36]

Despite the similarity in names, it is improbable that prisoner's base had any influence on baseball's evolution. Historians, however, have occasionally confused the two games. References to "a game of base," or "playing at base" in early texts have sometimes been assumed to be evidence of baseball, without the presence of corroborating indicators. Some writers have gone so far as to promote prisoner's base as a distant antecedent of baseball. No less a figure than Henry Chadwick elected this easy course in lieu of a serious inquiry into the origins of the National Pastime. In a newspaper column devoted to baseball's ancestry, Chadwick portrayed prisoner's base as requiring competitors to run from one base to another, a claim for which there is no supporting evidence.[37] He compounded his error by asserting that prisoner's base changed into the game of rounders when someone thought of "uniting with it the game of ball," a leap that likely existed only in Mr. Chadwick's fertile imagination.

9

TRAPS
AND
CATS

❖

TRAP-BALL, OR TRAP, BAT, AND BALL

Largely unknown today, the age-old game of trap-ball, also called trap, bat, and ball, enjoyed wide popularity over a period of many centuries. References to its play hark back to the 1400s and possibly earlier. As late as the nineteenth century it was still a common recreation throughout Great Britain, but in recent years it has survived in the backyards of but a few scattered pubs.

Trap-ball play is fairly simple. A ball is placed on the ground in a "trap," which is a device for elevating the ball into the air. After activating the trap, the batter swings at the served ball and drives it as far as possible. From that point the game can be pursued in one of several ways. Strutt described one variety in which the striker, employing a flat-faced bat, gained one point for each successful hit. The batter's turn ended if any of three events occurred: (1) he hit the ball out of bounds, (2) the ball was caught on the fly, or (3) a fielder retrieved the ball and when throwing it back either hit the trap or succeeded in getting the ball to rest within a bat's length of it.[1]

A second method of play is the Essex variety, which Strutt also described. In this version a round bat very similar to a modern baseball bat was used. Batters using this instrument, in Strutt's words, "frequently drive [the ball] to an astonishing distance."[2] The scoring method was something like *The Price is Right* in reverse. After hitting the ball, the batter called out any number he chose. Then when the fielder returned the ball, the players measured how many bat lengths from the trap the ball had come to rest. If it exceeded the number the batter called out, he won that many points. If it was less than his number, he received no points and lost his at-bat. A third variant, reported in some children's books of the nineteenth century, simply tested which player could hit the ball the farthest.

The design of traps changed over the course of centuries. An early example consisted of an eight- to twelve-inch stick or bone, with one end flattened and fashioned like a shallow spoon. This served as a lever when positioned to protrude from a short trench in the ground. It could also be propped like a seesaw on a piece of wood or stone, or attached in the V of a wooden cradle atop a short elevated platform. The batter placed a ball in the spoon portion, then struck the opposite end of the lever with the bat, propelling the ball into the air. In the eighteenth century, a mechanized trap was devised that looked something like a shoe. Typically it utilized a simple lever device, but sometimes it housed a spring catapult that was activated by a trigger.

Trap-ball bats, also called trapsticks, were of differing sizes and shapes. Strutt illustrated one, purportedly from the fourteenth century, that looked like a Ping-Pong paddle. Most references in literature from the sixteenth century through the eighteenth suggest that trapsticks then were typically thin and round. In the late eighteenth century, the growing popularity of cricket influenced a gradual shift to flat-faced bats, except, as previously noted, in Essex. By the mid-nineteenth century, trap bats, as illustrated in children's books, appear to have reverted to Ping-Pong-paddle size.

Trap-ball's longevity and enduring popularity in England undoubtedly contributed to baseball's development. Certainly, the concept of boundaries marking foul territory was an important innovation. While trap-ball did not include a base-running component, the game's required skills of batting and fielding transferred readily to baseball. In fact, since there is some evidence that baseball did not incorporate use of a bat in its earliest days, it is quite possible that the game of trap-ball influenced that all-important enhancement.

While trap-ball was a pervasive pastime in England, it never attained significant popularity in the United States.[3] Varieties of the game old-cat surpassed it as a form of scrub. As we shall see, however, a circumstantial case can be drawn that the old-cat games themselves resulted in part from trap-ball's influence on another old English game, tip-cat.

NORTHERN SPELL

Sports historians occasionally identify the English game of northern spell as one of baseball's ancestors. The term "northern spell" itself has a curious history, in that it is a modernized spelling of a composite of earlier names pertaining to an ancient pastime that, as it turns out, was not a separate game at all. Leading nineteenth-century authorities on games agreed that northern spell required a trap, a bat, and a ball, and that the object was to hit the ball as far as possible once it had been served by the trap.[4] The winner was the batter who hit the ball the farthest. Clearly, this was nothing but good old trap-ball in its simplest form. Why it was called northern spell and other names is probably more a function of history and location than a reflection of any material difference in the games themselves.

Before it gained the common designation "northern spell" in the nineteenth century, the pastime had worn almost as many labels as there were counties in Britain. According to Alice Gomme, these included *nur and spel; nor and spell; knurr and spel; knur, spell, and kibble; spell and ore; buckstick, spell, and ore; spell and nurr; spell and knor; dab and stick; kibel and nerspel; trippet and koit;* and so on.[5] The nur (knurr, nor, and the like) was a small wooden ball; the spell (spel) was the trap; and the bat was variously called a kibble, tribbet-stick, or buckstick. These terms are derived from old Norse or Danish words that arrived in Britain in the twelfth or thirteenth century and were preserved in rural areas. While the term "trap-ball" applied to the game played in population centers, the various forms of northern spell were rustic equivalents played in more isolated parts of the country. Besides the simpler rules, the only significant difference between northern spell and trap-ball was the ball itself, with northern spell generally using one carved of wood, while trap-ball used one with a core of wool or feathers covered in leather.

Tip-cat and numerous other varieties of the game of cat were staples on the English scene beginning in the Middle Ages and were probably of Celtic origin. Although typically no ball was involved, these games' collective influence on baseball's origins may be of greater significance than generally recognized.

Tip-cat employed two basic pieces of equipment, a bat and a "cat." The cat was normally a piece of wood four to eight inches long. This could be a simple straight stick or a sculpted shape that was two to three inches thick in the center and tapered to a point at the ends.

Strutt described two principal methods of playing the game.[6] In the first, a straight piece of stick was placed on the ground near the batter's feet and laid over another small piece of wood, creating the same type of seesaw as in trap-ball. The tapered cat could also be used, as it did not require any supporting fulcrum. The batter struck one end of the cat with the bat, sending it spinning up into the air. He then hit the airborne object as far as possible, again similar to trap-ball. His object, at the minimum, was to drive the cat outside a large ring that had been marked on the ground surrounding the batter's station. If he failed to accomplish this, he was out, and another batter took his place. If he succeeded he called out a number to be scored toward his game. Then a measurement was taken of how many bat lengths from the starting spot the cat actually had landed. If the number measured was less than the number the batter had called out, he was out; otherwise he counted his called number toward his score and continued to bat. This is similar in some respects to the method of scoring used in the Essex variety of trap-ball.

Strutt described the second method of tip-cat as follows:

Make four, six, or eight holes in the ground in a circular direction and as nearly as possible at equal distances from each other, and at every hole is placed a player with his bludgeon: one of the opposite party who stand in the field, tosses the cat to the batsman who is nearest him, and every time the cat is struck the players are obliged to change their situations, and run once from one hole to another in succession; if the cat be driven to any great distance they continue to run in the same order, and claim a score towards their game every time they quit one hole and run to another; but if the cat be stopped by their opponents and thrown across between any two of the holes before the player who has quitted one of them can reach the other, he is out.[7]

This form of tip-cat combined the elements of pitching and base running, as well as the concept of retrieving a batted object and throwing it to retire runners. It couldn't have been easy to throw the cat with accuracy, which probably explains why fielders had only to toss it between two bases in order to retire any runners in the vicinity. The positioning of batters at every base was a feature common to many English forms of cat and resonates when compared with the following description by Albert Spalding of the "old colonial" American game of four-old-cat:

> Four old cat was played by eight or more boys, with grounds laid out in shape of a square. Four old cat required four throwers, alternating as catchers, and four batsmen, the ball being passed from one corner to the next around the square field. Individual scores or tallies were credited to the batsman making the hit and running from one corner to the next. Some ingenious American lad naturally suggested that one thrower be placed in the center of the square, which brought nine players into the game, and which also made it possible to change the game into teams or sides, one side fielding and the other side batting. This for many years was known as the old game of town-ball, from which the present game of baseball no doubt had its origin, and not from the English picnic game of rounders, which is first cousin to that other juvenile pastime of drop the handkerchief.[8]

Four-old-cat stationed four batsmen at four bases, and scores were tallied each time a runner reached the next base. Both of these features are identical to the four-hole version of tip-cat. Spalding credited an "ingenious American lad" with the bright idea of a single thrower, which, he claimed, introduced the possibility of two sides. Yet Strutt's description of four-hole tip-cat may have suggested exactly the same thing in the phrase "one of the opposite party who stand in the field, tosses the cat to the batsman who is nearest him."[9]

It would be too much of a coincidence to presume that these two games evolved independent of each other. A far more likely scenario is that English immigrants to the American colonies in the eighteenth century imported varieties of the game cat. Perhaps it was Spalding's ingenious American lad who substituted a ball for the wooden cat, but more likely this idea was also of European derivation. Several eighteenth-century varieties of cat using a ball instead of a stick are described by the baseball historian Harold Peterson, although he neglects to identify his sources.[10]

A confirmed example of the term "cat" equating to a ball appears in an 1846 English work entitled *Every Boy's Book of Games, Sports, and Diversions*. The anonymous author of this book described a game nearly identical to Strutt's multiple-hole version of tip-cat, but with two embellishments. While mainly using the term "cat" to describe the object being struck, the author also stated that "a smooth round stick is preferred by many boys to a bat for striking the *ball*."[11] Second, although normally runners could be put out by throwing between bases, as was the case in tip-cat, the author added that sometimes players changed the rule so that fielders had to actually strike the base runners with the ball. Most surprising of all was the name of this game: rounders! Here we have, in one unusual package, a game bridging Spalding's four-old-cat and English tip-cat, and bearing the unexpected name of "rounders." This, of course, is magnificent irony, given that rounders was precisely the name of the English game that Spalding scornfully belittled while upholding the "American" old-cat games as baseball's true ancestors.

To be certain, the version of rounders mentioned here is something of an anomaly, differing considerably from most descriptions of the game bearing that name. But this example underscores the complex evolutionary underpinnings of all these pastimes and demonstrates that, like baseball, the American old-cat games are almost certainly of European origin.

Though tip-cat was probably the best known of the English family of cat games, its many cousins also dotted the landscape. These included cat i' the hole, cudgel, lobber, scute, and catchers.[12] Cat and dog was among the oldest in the family and resembled the American game two-old-cat, with two bases, two batters, and one pitcher. (Cat and dog was also mentioned in a nineteenth-century cricket history as being the progenitor of the double wicket.)[13] The game was described as an "ancient sport" in the 1808 edition of Jamieson's *Etymological Dictionary of the Scottish Language*:

> Three play at this game, who are provided with clubs. They cut out two holes, each about a foot in diameter and seven inches in depth, with a distance between them of about twenty-six feet. One stands at each hole with a club, called a *dog*, and a piece of wood about four inches long and one inch in diameter, called a *cat*, is thrown from the one hole towards the other, by a third person. The object is, to prevent the *cat* from getting into the hole. Every time that it enters the hole, he who has the club at that hole, loses the club, and he who threw the *cat* gets possession both of the club and the hole, while the former possessor is obliged to take charge of the *cat*.[14]

Yet another variety was called kit-cat. This was probably a forerunner of the American game three-old-cat, featuring a triangular base layout and three batsmen. Even one-old-cat appears to have had an English antecedent, a game called munshets, which was described in a nineteenth-century Yorkshire glossary as follows:

> It is played by two boys in the following manner: One of the boys remains "at home" and the other goes out to a prescribed distance. The boy who remains "at home" makes a small hole in the ground, and holds in his hand a stick about three feet long to strike with. The boy who is out at field throws a stick in the direction of this hole, at which the other strikes. If he hits it he has to run to a prescribed mark and back to the hole without being caught or touched with the smaller stick by his playfellow. If he is caught he is "out" and has to go to field. And if the boy at

field can throw his stick so near to the hole as to be within the length or measure of that stick, the boy at home has to go out to field. A number of boys often play together; for any even number can play.[15]

Undoubtedly, there was great variation in how the assorted medley of cat games were practiced from locale to locale across the English landscape, with the numbers of players, the distances between bases, and virtually every other factor subject to myriad improvisation. The lengths of the bats ranged from two-foot versions intended for one-handed use to heavier three-foot-long cudgels that required two hands. The wooden cats were typically about three to five inches in length and in most of these pastimes were pitched underhand to the batter. The exception, as we have seen, was the game of tip-cat, in which the cat had to be slightly longer to enable the batter to tip it up in the air.

Overall, it is quite obvious that the family of English cat games were early contributors to baseball's evolutionary enrichment. Despite being simple children's diversions, they collectively employed the familiar elements of batting, pitching, base running, and fielding. These skills transferred readily to games played with balls, whose spherical shapes proved to be easier to throw, catch, and hit than the wooden cats.

ONE-, TWO-, THREE-, AND FOUR-OLD-CAT

The legendary American old-cat games were direct descendants of the English cat games. While prevailing wisdom dates the American games to the colonial era, there is no actual evidence to show whether this is fact or fable. In fact, almost all of what is known about the early history of the old-cat games comes from later nostalgic recollections, rather than from primary accounts. The informal scrub status of these pastimes may explain their scarcity in the printed record, but it seems curious that they are also absent from diaries and letters before the 1850s. Although reference to the game "cats" is found in North America as early as the late eighteenth century, mention of the more explicit term "old-cat" does not appear until 1837, when a published children's story briefly alludes to boys playing "one-old-cat."[16] Despite the lack of contemporaneous evidence, however, there are ample indications that the games enjoyed widespread popularity during the early decades of the nineteenth century. These come from the abundant reminiscences of old-time ballplayers, recorded many years afterward, of having played versions of old-cat during that era.

Because of the lack of primary documentation, the true history and evolution of old-cat in America remain somewhat obscure. Albert Spalding labeled one-old-cat an "old colonial game," and John Ward referred to "cat ball" as "the original American ball game," adding "the time when it was not played here is beyond the memory of living man."[17] However, it is beyond the realm of plausibility to imagine, as these gentlemen implied, that the old-cat games sprouted spontaneously on American soil, and just coincidentally resembled in name and method the cat games of Europe, which had prospered for the previous six centuries.

In 1905 Spalding published brief descriptions of how he believed the old-cat games were played.[18] Even that undertaking was unusual because, despite the frequent allusions to the games by authors and old-timers of the late nineteenth and early twentieth centuries, few bothered to offer any illuminating details. In fact, the earliest known description of how to play any of the old-cats was so brief that you wonder whether the scribe had been challenged to write it in as few words as possible. In *Atlantic Monthly* in October 1866 he wrote that one-old-cat was "played as a trio, boy A throws the ball at boy B, standing opposite, whose duty is to smite, while boy C, behind B, catches B out in case of a miss."[19]

Baseball historians have sometimes suggested that the word "cat" in one-old-cat is a shortened form of the word "catapult," and that the game was originally called "one hole catapult."[20] This premise totters on shaky footing. It rests upon the assumption that one-old-cat derived from the games trap-ball and tip-cat, in which a ball or cat was popped into the air by a lever inserted into a "hole" in the ground that acted like a catapult. While this might be a tidy and satisfying explanation, it does not appear to be supported by historical evidence. I have not found a single reference in the nearly seven hundred–year history of cat games that points to "catapult" being the original name. The *Oxford English Dictionary* traces the root of "cat," the game, to the same ancient Anglo-Saxon root as "cat," the animal.[21] In virtually all varieties of the game, the word "cat" is associated with the short object hit by the bat, and not the propulsion mechanism.[22] In fact, in most versions of cat, the object being hit by the striker is served by a person, not by any type of a device. Finally, it seems unlikely that one of the oldest members of the cat family, the game "cat and dog," would have paired the names of two animals to describe the game if the "cat" really stood for "catapult."

The playing of old-cat games in early America was a parallel occurrence to the play of baseball itself. As with most varieties of scrub, these games were simple, entertaining activities in their own right, but they also allowed youth to practice the baseball skills of batting, fielding, and base running. There is no evidence that "old-cat" either preceded baseball in America or materially influenced its evolution.

One final note on cat. In a recent conversation with my father, who turned ninety-four in 2004, he described a game he played as a youth on the streets of New York City. He recalled that he and his friends would cut off a short length of a broom handle and lay it on the ground on top of another stick or a rock. Then, using the remainder of the broom handle as a bat, they would tip the short stick up in the air and swing and hit it as far as they could. While this almost exactly describes one form of English tip-cat, my father's name for the game was "one-old-cat"!

10

IT'S
STARTING
TO LOOK
FAMILIAR

ROUNDERS

In chapter 2 I demonstrated how the game of rounders could not have been baseball's progenitor. Briefly stated, I found that the earliest known historical reference to the English pastime did not appear until 1828, and despite oft-repeated pronouncements that rounders is an "old" or "ancient" sport, there is no documented evidence that the name came into usage any earlier than the beginning of the nineteenth century.

Initially, the term "rounders" was a regional pseudonym for English base-ball, a fact borne out by the features of the game described in *The Boy's Own Book* in 1828.[1] There the pastime was unmistakably baseball-like, with a four-base diamond-shaped infield and a recognizable method of play. As new versions of rounders began to appear in English books in the 1840s and later, however, their similarities to baseball diminished. The game took on a fifth base, which was positioned sometimes as part of a disjointed square layout similar to the variety of early baseball played in the New England states, sometimes as part of a pentagon configuration. The bat grew shorter in length and evolved into a one-handed implement. By the early 1870s, when the first tour of American professional baseball players visited England, rounders and baseball had diverged into two separate sports.

While rounders may be only a footnote to baseball's evolution, the game itself stands on its own considerable merits and has been enjoyed by generations of adults and children in the United Kingdom.

To this day it remains a popular organized activity in many parts of that nation.

TUT-BALL

Perhaps instead of rounders, historians would have been closer to the mark nominating tut-ball for the role of baseball's predecessor. Tut-ball? Although its name is unfamiliar to even the most ardent students of baseball, this forgotten English folk game may have played an integral role in the evolution of our National Pastime.

The *Oxford English Dictionary* defines "tut" thus: "Each of a number of objects set up as 'bases' in rounders or similar games; also, a kind of stool-ball in which the player at each base must move to the next base each time the ball is struck; also called tut-ball; also the game of rounders."[2] With their usual thoroughness, the editors of the OED have literally and figuratively covered all the bases, identifying tut-ball as both stool-ball and rounders. The dictionary's most valuable revelation about tut-ball, however, lies in the list of literary references that follow the game's definition. Here the OED's editors demonstrate that the name "tut-ball" is nearly as ancient as stool-ball; they provide examples of its usage dating back to the early sixteenth century. By contrast, the dictionary offers no such early evidence for the name "rounders," which did not find its way into print until three hundred years later.

The earliest reference to tut-ball comes from the records of the Priory of Hexham, in northern England, where the pastime was among several looked upon with considerable disfavor. In an entry for the year 1519, a scribe wrote (as translated from the Latin): "Dishonorable games are played within the cemetery, that is, hand and foot ball games, such as tuts and handball and Pennyston. Let them stop games of this sort, under penalty of excommunication."[3]

Although headstones no doubt made for terrific bases, the penalty appears to have been a little steep for the crime. The severity of the warning suggests that the transgressing players may have been adults, for it is difficult to believe that the church, even in those days, would excommunicate children simply for playing ball in the cemetery.

Tut, or tut-ball, makes a second sixteenth-century appearance in the poem "Fruites of Warre," written in 1572:

Yet, have I shot at maister Bellums butte,
And throwen his ball although I toucht no tutte:
I have precase as deepely dealt the dole,
As he that hit the marke and get the gole.[4]

Can you tell from this snippet of Renaissance verse that the word "tut" has the exact same meaning as the word "base"? Even if that isn't evident, nineteenth-century dictionaries consistently defined "tut" as a small chunk of brick or sod used for a base. Consensus on how the game was actually played, however, was not so forthcoming. As with other folk games, tut-ball's features undoubtedly varied from location to location. The editors of the OED were not the only scholars of their time who could not settle on whether the game more closely resembled stool-ball or rounders. The collective problem facing dia-lectologists and folklorists attempting to describe tut-ball in the late nineteenth century was that by then the game was nearly extinct. As a result, they had to depend upon older sources that were not neces-sarily reliable. For example, the authoritative *English Dialect Dictio-nary* cited quotations about tut-ball that had appeared in two different folk glossaries from the county of Yorkshire.[5] One of these, an 1888 work from Sheffield, described a version of the game as it was sup-posedly played at a girls' school fifty years earlier:

The players stood together in their "den," behind a line marked on the ground, all except one, who was "out," and who stood at a distance and threw the ball to them. One of the players in the den then hit back the ball with the palm of the hand, and im-mediately ran to one of three brick-bats, called "tuts." . . . The player who was "out" tried to catch the ball and to hit the runner with it while passing from one "tut" to another. If she succeeded in doing so she took her place in the den and the other went "out" in her stead. This game is very nearly identical with rounders.[6]

It is noteworthy that the author made the comparison to rounders despite the clear absence of a bat. (It would have been more accurate to point out the similarities between this version of tut-ball and another English game described later in this chapter — an early-eighteenth-century children's pastime known as base-ball.)

The second Yorkshire reference, written in 1877, stated that tut-ball was "now only played by boys, but half a century ago by adults on Ash Wednesday, believing that unless they did so they would fall sick in harvest time. This is a very ancient game and was elsewhere called stool-ball."[7] At the least, tut-ball appears to have been a simple hit-the-ball, catch-the-ball, run-the-bases type of game. But what about use of a bat? The 1888 description cited above clearly states that a batter's bare hand was used to strike the ball. However, a secondary definition of "tut" from the *English Dialect Dictionary* indicates that in the county of Cornwall the word served as a verb meaning "to bat at cricket."[8] This appears to be consistent with a terse definition of tut-ball offered by James Orchard Halliwell-Phillipps, who in his authoritative *Dictionary of Archaic and Provincial Words* simply called the game "a sort of stobball."[9] Stobball, you will recall, was played with a bat or club and was perhaps a variant of stool-ball. The evidence is thin, but it is possible that bat usage in tut-ball varied by location or was employed only by older and more skillful players.

One additional reference illuminating tut-ball's history is found in a Devonshire manuscript from the year 1777. This described "tut" as "a sort of stool ball much practised about the Easter holidays, particularly at Exeter."[10] Not only does this corroborate the game's evolution from stool-ball, but it also places tut-ball in a most suggestive location. The town of Exeter in the western English county of Devonshire was the birthplace of Henry Chadwick, the "father of baseball." We have seen that Chadwick's recollection of playing rounders there as a child in the 1830s precipitated the debate with Albert Spalding over baseball's origins. Now we learn that this town had been identified fifty years earlier as the epicenter of tut-ball, a game virtually identical to what was later called rounders.

The evidence regarding tut-ball is intriguing but highly circumstantial. As early as 1519 the name "tut" was associated with ball games, and the OED alone cites four examples before 1800. This closely parallels the richly documented career of stool-ball and lends support to the notion that tut-ball was a spin-off of the better-known game. Another link is that both games apparently could be played with or without a bat (although the only actual account of tut-ball players hitting the ball by hand was recorded in 1888, by which time the game was nearly extinct.) On the other hand, an obvious and important distinction between stool-ball and tut-ball was that one used stools and the other used tuts. The change from one to the other was probably the impromptu solution of some sixteenth-century ballplayers who found themselves without sufficient stools to complete an infield. That long-ago modification may well have signified the dawn of the modern base.

It would be an inordinate leap to assign tut-ball the role of baseball's evolutionary predecessor based solely upon the foregoing evidence. Yet, other than stool-ball, there is a notable lack of alternate candidates. At the least, the curious history and baseball-like features of tut-ball place it within the front rank of pastimes meriting further study.

FEEDER AND SQUARES

The brief explanations of the pastimes feeder and squares that appeared in English children's books of the early to mid-nineteenth century constitute virtually all that we know about the two games. An 1838 book, *The Youth's Encyclopædia*, describes the game of squares as having features roughly identical to those of rounders and baseball from that era.[11] No other evidence of squares is known to exist. Feeder appeared ten years earlier, in *The Boy's Own Book*, the same 1828 work in which rounders made its debut. The author identified "feeder" as being an alternate name for rounders, the one in use in the London metropolitan area.[12] In 1841 the game feeder reappeared in *The Every*

Boy's Book, where it was given its own separate listing.[13] The pastime was portrayed as a simpler version of rounders, with the entire defensive team consisting of one player, the feeder, who not only had to pitch but also had to field the ball wherever it was hit. The feeder had to stay on the field until he retired a batter, either by catching a fly ball or plugging a base runner between bases. Once that happened, he joined the batting party, and the player who had been put out became the new feeder. Without additional information it is hard to know how to categorize this simplified pastime. It could have been no more than a scrub version of rounders, which at that time was entering a period of rapid development and differentiation from baseball. In many respects, however, this 1841 description of feeder harks back to earlier, more primitive forms of ball play, and is actually more reminiscent of pastimes children played during the eighteenth century, such as tut-ball and varieties of cat.

ENGLISH BASE-BALL

There are at least five surviving examples of the word "base-ball" having been used to describe an English pastime in the eighteenth century. Was that game a direct forerunner of American baseball, or is the use of the same word simply coincidental? The answer may lie in an examination of clues from each example.

The first known historical use of the word "base-ball" was in the classic English children's book *A Little Pretty Pocket-Book* in 1744. This work, as mentioned earlier, includes a small woodcut entitled "Base-Ball," which depicts three well-dressed young men arrayed on a field with three bases marked by posts. One player is preparing to pitch a ball, while a waiting striker, with no bat in his hands, stands ready to hit the ball with the flat of his palm. A short verse beneath the illustration reads:

The ball once struck off,
Away flies the boy
To the next destined post,
And then home with joy.[14]

A Little Pretty Pocket-Book reveals that baseball in its day was a multiple-base activity in which the objective was to strike the ball, run around the bases, and return to home. The similarity to our modern game is extraordinary considering that the book is more than 250 years old. The major disparate element, of course, is the absence of a bat. The fact that baseball was selected for inclusion in *A Little Pretty Pocket-Book* suggests that it was already a familiar pastime by the year 1744.

The second known reference to baseball in the eighteenth century was in a letter written on November 14, 1748, by a close acquaintance of the British royal family. The author Mary Lepel, known by her title Lady Hervey, was describing the activities of the family of the Prince of Wales. She wrote: "In the winter, in a large room, they divert themselves at base-ball, a play all who are, or have been, schoolboys are well acquainted with. The ladies, as well as gentlemen, join in this amusement."[15] This passage confirms the point that baseball was an already familiar activity in the mid-1740s in England. Lady Hervey did not offer any new insights into the features of the game, although the fact that family members were playing indoors suggests a smaller scale than is customarily associated with baseball. Perhaps indoor play was made feasible because batters of the era used their hands, rather than bats, to strike the ball. Then again, "a large room" for these particular citizens could have been a ballroom of grand dimensions. Although Lady Hervey described baseball as a "schoolboy" activity, her characterization of the participants as "ladies" and "gentlemen" suggests that older children or adults may have been engaged in its play.

Following Lady Hervey, it was nearly fifty years until the next known surviving reference to English base-ball. This was preserved in J. C. F. Gutsmuths's 1796 German book *Spiele zur Uebung und Erholung*. As elaborated in Chapter 5, the German author's specification of rules for *das englische Base-ball* was a blend of familiar features — such as pitching, batting, and base running — with antiquated characteristics that have long been forgotten. Nevertheless, Gutsmuths's representation of early baseball endures as the most detailed insight into the game before the Knickerbocker rules of 1845.

The fourth known example of baseball from eighteenth-century

England appeared in the manuscript of Jane Austen's first novel, *Northanger Abbey*. Although the book was not published until 1818, Austen wrote it between 1798 and 1799. The book contains the following sentence: "It was not very wonderful that Catherine . . . should prefer cricket, base ball, riding on horseback, and running about the country at the age of fourteen, to books."[16] While this selection reveals little about the nature of the game, it does confirm Lady Hervey's information that females in England were, on occasion, practitioners. One final eighteenth-century English application of the term "base-ball" is found in the little-known historical novel, *Battleridge*, published in 1799. Near the opening of the book, a character named Sir Ralph Vesey laments: "No more cricket, no more base-ball, they are sending me to Geneva."[17] As with the Austen example, this reference provides no insight on the composition of English base-ball, 1790s style. It does suggest, however, that the game by then had enlisted some adult adherents.

In 1888 the renowned ballplayer John Montgomery Ward, in his book *Base-ball: How to Become a Player*, devoted nearly a full chapter to denouncing the idea that our National Pastime was not indigenous to America. In the course of his argument he commented: "It is now intimated that base-ball itself, the same game and under the same name, is of English origin." He proceeded to quote from Lady Hervey's letter as well as the passage from Jane Austen, and then, employing shamelessly tortured logic, attempted to belittle the implications. First, he said that the word "base" stemmed from the game prisoner's base, and that any other activity using bases and a ball would naturally be called base-ball. Next, commenting on the participation of girls, he stated: "Base-ball in its mildest form is essentially a robust game, and it would require an elastic imagination to conceive of little girls possessed of physical powers such as its play demands."[18] Finally, he asked rhetorically, if American baseball was derived from English base-ball, why were proponents of the game's English origins instead pointing to rounders as its predecessor?

It is a shame that Ward was so obviously predisposed to a conclusion that American baseball and English base-ball were unrelated, because he showed unusual resourcefulness as a researcher. He may, in fact, have been the first American baseball historian to report upon the Hervey and Austen references.[19] He also unearthed a rare description of early baseball in an obscure children's book that, ironically, served to undermine the very argument he was trying to make. The book was *Jolly Games for Happy Homes*, published in 1875 and featuring the charming subtitle: "to amuse our girls and boys; the dear little babies and the grown-up ladies."[20] Contained under the heading "base-ball" was the following passage:

> The one who is "out" throws the ball, which the one who is in receives "in" her hand as if it were a bat, bats it away and starts for the first base, or station. The garden or field has previously been divided into bases or stations, duly marked at convenient distances.
>
> The business of the followers of the leader who is "out" is to act as scouts, to catch up the ball thrown — after which they can all start if they like — and hit the runner with it as she passes from base to base. If she is so hit she is "out," and must remain dormant till there is a change in the ministry of the game. Her business is to make good her passage from base to base without being hit, and for this purpose to keep an eye on the enemy and the flying ball. If she is hit on reaching or whilst stationary at a base, it counts for nothing. Each member of a party runs in turn. When all members of a party are out, the game recommences, passing into the hands of the other party, and so on.[21]

This description is noteworthy for several reasons. It depicts an extremely early and primitive form of baseball that was long out of vogue by the book's publishing date of 1875. The absence of a bat, and the identification of the players as female, both strongly suggest that this was the variety of baseball alluded to in the eighteenth century by Lady Hervey and Jane Austen. Strangely, Ward came to a very different conclusion. While recognizing that this "base-ball . . . is very similar in essence to our game," he blithely presented it as unrelated to the eighteenth-century girl's baseball he had derided only two paragraphs earlier. Instead, he made the unconvincing assertion that the simplified pastime described in *Jolly Games for Happy Homes* was not old at all, but "is doubtless a modern English conception of our National Game."[22] In fact, Ward's unheralded discovery proves just the opposite. The game was called "base-ball," it was played without a bat, it was played by girls, and, as he himself observed, it resembled the modern American game. The innocent "jolly game" that found its way into print in 1875 was essentially a time capsule of how baseball was played when *A Little Pretty Pocket-Book* first mentioned it in 1744.

Notwithstanding Ward's protestations, the family resemblance of English base-ball and American baseball is self-evident. The characteristics introduced in *A Little Pretty Pocket-Book*, and elaborated by the Gutsmuths work, have attained full maturity in our modern game. No other pastime more directly contributed to the development of American baseball than its diminutive eighteenth-century English namesake.

CRICKET

When the subject of baseball's origin comes up in casual conversation, it is not unusual for someone to suggest the game of cricket as a likely ancestor. A veneer of logic attends this viewpoint, for the two sports exhibit certain similarities and share a common English heritage. Moreover, the fact that baseball inherited such basic terms as "runs," "outs," "umpires," and "innings" from cricket also bolsters the premise of a lineal relationship. This circumstantial connection is so enticing that even the occasional baseball historian will uphold cricket as a viable progenitor of our National Game.[23]

Peeling back the layers of history does indeed reveal a familial link between the two pastimes, but certainly not on the order of parent-child. Perhaps calling them distant cousins would be a more appropriate analogy. Cricket is the older of the two, with evidence of its play dating to the sixteenth century, or possibly earlier. As with baseball, the early history of cricket remains veiled and elusive, with little unanimity among historians on when and how the game derived. A recent study by the English researcher David Terry, however, has begun to untangle part of the mystery. Writing in *The Sports Historian*, the journal of the British Society on Sports History, Terry acknowledges that cricket in its most primitive forms bore similarities to other early folk pastimes, such as stool-ball, hand-in and hand-out, cat and dog, and stobball. But then, drawing on various references, he observes that the emergence of cricket at particular sites in sixteenth- and seventeenth-century England was not a random phenomenon, but followed a pattern that correlated with the geographical locations where immigrants from the country of Flanders established settlements during the same era.[24]

The Flemings arrived over a period of several centuries, crossing the English Channel to avoid religious persecution at home. They were mostly involved in the wool trade, and their settlements followed established trade routes in southeast England. It was there, primarily in the counties of Kent, Surrey, and Sussex, that cricket became established in the seventeenth century. Terry finds no evidence that cricket had been played originally in Flanders, but he hypothesizes that the Flemings combined elements of a hockey-type game they had played at home with the rustic ball games they encountered in their adopted society. He also cites a theory advanced by a European language expert named Heiner Gillmeister that the word "cricket" was a shortened form of the name the Flemings called their hockey game: *"met de krik ketsen."*[25]

We know that baseball traces its roots back to many of the same folk games that gave rise to cricket. Nevertheless, no evidence exists to show that cricket contributed in any direct way to baseball's evolvement. In fact, most signs suggest that that such a role was highly improbable. The two games appear to have been separated geographically, with baseball's emergence having centered in the western parts of England while cricket hailed from the southeast. Their intrinsic characteristics also varied. For example, the use of a bat, from the first, was a defining feature of cricket, whereas that was not the case with the earliest forms of baseball. This suggests that baseball's immediate antecedents were pastimes such as stool ball, in which a player's bare hand sufficed to strike the ball. Also, from its beginnings baseball's action centered upon a player running around a circuit of bases. This is an attribute that differs markedly from the up-and-back running between wickets practiced in cricket. Had children of the late seventeenth or early eighteenth centuries been seeking to emulate cricket by creating a smaller, simplified version, it seems unlikely they would choose to alter such an easily imitated feature.

That said, baseball and cricket possess a significant historical association, but one that is cultural rather than derivative. By the second half of the eighteenth century, both had became popular recreations in England, albeit among different segments of the population. Both migrated to America with English settlers and gained footholds in their new surroundings. While baseball at first remained primarily a children's game, cricket was played predominantly by adults, as had been the case in England. By the 1840s organized competitions among cricket clubs had spread up and down the eastern seaboard of the United States, with particular concentration in the New York and Philadelphia regions. When, in that same decade, adult baseball players began to organize formal clubs of their own, they freely borrowed terminology from cricket, a game with which many of them were familiar. Until the onset of the Civil War, the number of organized clubs practicing the upstart sport of baseball lagged behind the number playing cricket, but that changed immediately after the conflict, when baseball exploded in popularity. Cricket did not disappear in America at that juncture but retained a loyal and active following, especially in the Philadelphia area, where it is still practiced today.

WICKET

During the late eighteenth and early nineteenth centuries, when a few adult Americans were beginning to take notice of baseball as an enjoyable diversion, another upstart ball sport was also gaining some adherents. This was the game of wicket or wicket ball, a pastime that is virtually unknown today but which, at the time, had an avid following in some local areas, particularly in the state of Connecticut. Because so little has been written about wicket, mention of it invariably effects puzzlement. The most common assumption is that "wicket" is simply another name for cricket. Occasionally, because of its New England history, some speculate that wicket was related to round ball, the variation of baseball practiced in that region.

In fact, wicket was a game unto itself, although more closely related to cricket than to baseball. In a way, it was cricket democratized. When that old English game arrived in America in the company of eighteenth-century colonists, it tended to retain the formal qualities it possessed in the mother country. Cricket clubs formed in metropolitan areas like New York and Philadelphia, and the sport assumed a regimented character. This type of formality was unsuited to the down-home culture of smaller communities and rural areas, and wicket sprang up as a uniquely American adaptation of the English sport. It differed from cricket in a number of ways, most notably in that the wickets were wider and much lower to the ground, and the ball was literally bowled on the ground, not pitched through the air.[26] Perhaps the biggest difference was that, unlike the eleven-man teams found in cricket, wicket employed thirty players on a side. In some places this enabled virtually the entire community to take part.

Even at the height of wicket's popularity in the early to mid-nineteenth century, newspapers tended to ignore the game while affording coverage to its more famous cousin. The game's proponents bristled at this lack of respect and recognition, and in 1857 two of them voiced their dissatisfaction in letters sent to the editor of *Porter's Spirit of the Times*. The first came from a Troy, New York, wicket player who complained on February 7 of the publication's lack of response to questions about wicket he had submitted in an earlier letter: "I infer that you either did not receive the letter, or you thought that the 'Troy Wicket Club' was a 'myth.'" The second correspondent, from New York City, wrote: "I would like to see the old game of WICKET (not cricket), played. It is a *manly* game, and requires the bowler to be equal to playing a good game of ten pins."[27]

There are parallels in the respective roles played by wicket and early baseball in the first half of the nineteenth century. Although the games were not closely related, both had populist appeal and served as counterpoints to cricket. Both satisfied a yearning within local communities for a competitive team pastime that was relatively easy to organize, and could be enjoyed by players with differing levels of ability. When wicket all but vanished at the end of the 1850s, it may have been the result of some inherent shortcoming, such as the difficulty in forming thirty-player teams. A more likely explanation, however, is that the game's demise was an inevitable consequence of baseball's explosion in popularity at that very moment of history.

However else others may attribute the origins of baseball, the French own a singular viewpoint on the subject. At least that is the impression conveyed by various dictionaries and sporting encyclopedias published in France during the past century, which aver, matter-of-factly, that baseball was an outgrowth of an old Norman game called *thèque*.[28] As we have seen, this claim was first raised as far back as 1889, when Albert Spalding reported learning about *thèque*'s similarity to baseball from "a gentleman I met in Paris."[29] Could there be any substance to the outlandish French allegation? It stands directly counter to the broadly held assumption that baseball was chiefly of English derivation. Yet to discard the *thèque* theory we would have to prove it wrong, and therein lies the challenge. The history and genealogy of *thèque*, as extracted from the limited available references, are so fragmented and contradictory that they frustrate any solid findings one way or the other.

Published descriptions of *thèque*, mostly from within the past century, depict a game that broadly resembled rudimentary forms of baseball from an earlier time period. One noticeable difference is that, in the French game, the pitcher was actually a member of the batting team. The following representative account appeared in an 1899 issue of *Le Soleil*, a French-language daily newspaper from Quebec City:

> "Grande thèque" and baseball are two different games that have their own rules. "Grande thèque" is played with two teams with a maximum of ten players each. It is played on a field of 300 to 400 square meters. Instead of the baseball diamond, the "grande thèque" ground has a pentagon shape. On every angle they put a wooden base or sand bag to mark the five bases. The pitcher and batter are from the same team. The pitcher will throw nicely so the batter will be able to hit the ball. Generally,

the game is played in two innings of forty points. Like "bat and ball," to call someone "out" you have to hit him with the ball between two bases.[30]

Aspects of this description, such as the pentagon infield and the practice of throwing the ball at base runners, are indicative of what you might expect to find in any account of English rounders from the same time period. Given these similarities, there is a temptation to assume that the Norman game was adapted directly from its English counterpart, or at least strongly influenced by it, and thus of relatively recent vintage. Yet this premise is deflated by indications that a ball game called *thèque* was played in France as early as the fifteenth century. One such clue appeared in a French letter written in the year 1447 and cited in a seventeenth-century Latin dictionary. The author of the letter stated: "The supplicant was playing with Pierre le Sort at 'Jeu de tecon,' otherwise called ball." A second letter, written eight years later and quoted in the same dictionary, contained a similar observation: "These companions were encouraging one another to play a game called 'touquon.' . . . Gaillart . . . held in his hand a small wooden mallet with which he would strike the ball."[31]

Obviously, these snippets revealed little about the nature of the game, and, unfortunately, the search for useful references to *thèque* from the ensuing four centuries has proven equally unproductive. During that long span of years, the pastime was occasionally mentioned in French literature as a children's ball game, but without further elucidation. Finally, in 1856, a description of the game appeared in a juvenile work entitled *Jeux des adolescents*. The book's author labeled the pastime *la balle au bâton*, or stick-ball, but it was almost certainly *thèque* by another name. The play of the game was fairly simple, in contrast to the version of *thèque* described forty-three years later in the Quebec newspaper. Instead of two opposing teams, each player fended for himself. Once batting, a participant could remain part of the home party until he was put out. At that point he joined other players in the field, and his former spot in the batting lineup was taken over by the fielder who had gotten him out. No pitchers were involved, with each batter serving the ball to himself fungo style. The identifi-

Illuminated miniature from Cantigas de Santa Maria, a thirteenth-century Spanish manuscript of medieval songs produced under the sponsorship of Alfonso X. The pitcher's proximity to the batter in this image suggests the artist may have been depicting the ancient European game of longball. Artistic license may explain the simultaneous gathering of the other players to catch a pop-up.

Illuminated miniature from The Ghistelles Calendar, Flanders, ca. 1301, W.851 ff. 5–8, The Walters Art Museum, Baltimore. Great arm extension! You can kiss that one good-bye.

Image from the fourteenth-century manuscript Decretals of Gregory IX, *written in Italy and illuminated in England. Royal 10 E IV Folio 94v, by permission of the British Library. This fungo-like activity seems to anticipate the obscure nineteenth-century game drive-ball portrayed in the Camp Doubleday engraving in the sidebar following chapter 3.*

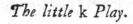

The little k *Play.*

BASE-BALL.

THE *Ball* once ftruck off,
 Away flies the *Boy*
To the next deftin'd Poft,
And then Home with Joy.

MORAL.

Thus *Britons* for Lucre
 Fly over the Main;
But, with Pleafure tranfported,
Return back again.

TRAP-

A Little Pretty Pocket-Book, *11th ed., 1763, courtesy Lilly Library, Indiana University, Bloomington. This book, first published in 1744, contains the first known appearance of the word "base-ball" in print.*

3. Ball mit Freystäten.
(oder das englische Base - ball.)

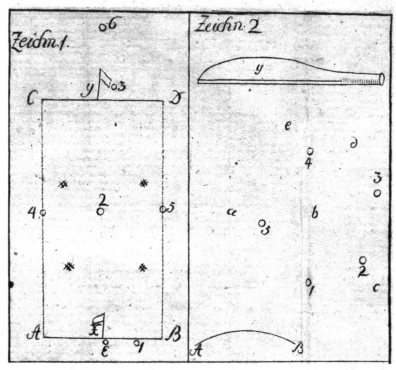

Diagrams illustrating the games das deutsche Ballspiel *(the German ball game)* on the left, and *"ball with free station,"* or das englische Base-ball *(English base-ball)*, on the right, taken from the book Spiele zur Uebung und Erholung, 1796. In the English base-ball diagram, the uppercase letters A and B mark the home plate area, the numbers 1–5 indicate the bases, and the lowercase letters a through e show the positioning of the defensive players. In the German ball game, the two flags indicate the batting base and running base, respectively. The four double crosses signify the author's suggested base layout for a hybrid English-German ball game.

Illustration of "trap-ball" from Youthful Sports, *1804.*

Trap Ball.

The Book of Games, *1805.*

In Remarks on Children's Play, *1811, this game was identified as "trap-ball," but it more closely resembles baseball.*

Illustration for the month of April in the children's almanac Taschenbuch für das Jahr 1815 der Liebe und Freundschaft, *1815.*

PLAYING BALL

With bat and ball some boys we find,
'T' amuse themselves are much inclin'd.

Engraving by the pioneer woodcut artist Alexander Anderson. Children's Amusements, *1820, courtesy American Antiquarian Society.*

The Boy and the Looking-Glass.

Good Examples for Boys, *1823. Yes, disaster looms, but rest assured that the boy will learn an important moral lesson.*

The Young Florist, *1833. No references to baseball are found in the text, which is true to the title.*

This scene of boys playing baseball on the Boston Common appeared first in The Book of Sports, *1834, and in several books afterward.*

This engraving by Alexander Anderson first appeared in Mary's Book of
Sports, *1832, and subsequently made its way into numerous other chapbooks.
This impression was taken from* Sports of Youth, *1835.*

The Book of Seasons, A Gift for the Young. Autumn, *1840.*
Note the short bat and the one-handed batting style.

The boys play with balls.
John has a bat in his hand.
I can hit the ball.

Reading lesson from McGuffey's Newly Revised Eclectic First Reader, *1844.*
The text also seems to encourage positive thinking for batters.

"Boys Playing Bat and Ball," from Sanders's The School Reader, First Book, *1853.*
The primer includes a full-page lesson describing the game.

THE THROWER.   THE STRIKER.

THE CATCHER.   BASE TENDER.

The first and, perhaps, only contemporaneous illustrations of adults suited up to play the Massachusetts variety of baseball. The Base Ball Player's Pocket Companion, *1859.*

cation of the game is established by the author's comment that "the stick is of moderate length and fairly thick, and is called *tèque* in Normandy, the principal place where this game is played."[32] While this equates *la balle au bâton* with *thèque*, it also raises the question whether the term *thèque* identified the ball, as indicated by earlier references, or the bat, as in this one.

In fact, the etymology of the word *thèque* is about as mixed up as it can be. The two very old references to the ball game cited in the seventeenth-century Latin dictionary were linked to the Latin word *tudatus*, which is a derivative of the word *tundo*, meaning "to pound."[33] In an 1849 French-Norman dialect dictionary, however, the word *tèque* was defined as "a children's ball game, stemming from the English word *take*."[34] And, compounding the confusion, two twentieth-century French dictionaries stated that the name of the game *thèque* derived from the ancient Scandinavian word *tekja*. One of these references said *tekja* meant *butin* — in English, "booty" — whereas the other equated *tekja* to *lutin*, which means "elf" or "goblin."[35]

The identity quandary doesn't stop there. A new element of misdirection was introduced by the author of a comprehensive 1909 French guidebook on sporting activities called *Le Livre des sports athletiques et des jeux de plein air*. The book included a three-page description of *thèque*, but the author called it *la balle au camp (ou grande thèque)*. The phrase *la balle au camp* was hardly unfamiliar to the French public, as it was the common label for a ball game described in children's books during the nineteenth century. In those cases, however, it was synonymous with the name *la balle empoisonée*, or "poisoned ball," a separate baseball-like activity, which, unlike *thèque*, did not use a bat. The word *camp* in *la balle au camp* has customarily been translated as "field" (as in "field-ball"), but examination of the original texts suggests that defining the term as "home base" would be more accurate. If applied generically, this might explain why both *thèque* and *la balle empoisonée* would share the same pseudonym — *la balle au camp*, or "base ball." Regardless, this casual naming convention complicates the identification of these games.

In introducing *le grande thèque* in 1909, the author of *Le Livre des sports athletiques* stated: "This is an old French game that was still being played in Normandy and Beauce about fifty years ago. Then, fallen out of use in France, it passed to England where it is played a great deal. We were wrong to let it pass away. The English, on the other hand, have perfected it."[36] It is hard to know what to make of this lament over the loss of *thèque* to England. Clearly, the author was implying that English rounders and base-ball originally derived from France, but if a Channel crossing in that direction had occurred at all, it obviously had to have taken place many decades, if not centuries, earlier than he suggested.

So given all this, what the heck was *thèque*? It would be an awfully big coincidence for its considerable resemblance to English base-ball and rounders not to be the result of some historical migration across the Channel. But precisely when that occurred, or in which direction, cannot be divined from the available evidence. So apparently the field is clear for the French to go on claiming parental rights over America's National Game. In the absence of any new evidence to the contrary, who can prove them wrong?

❖

Like *thèque*, the roots of *la balle empoisonée* (poisoned ball) are uncertain. When books about children's activities first began appearing in France in the first decades of the nineteenth century, *la balle empoisonée* was invariably one of the pastimes included. Because nothing earlier is known about the game, and because of its marked resemblance to base-ball, there is a natural tendency to assume it was an offshoot of its English relative. Yet there is no actual evidence that this was the case.

Rules for *la balle* first appeared in the book *Les Jeux des jeunes garçons*, published about 1815.[37] The game's features were similar in some respects to the version of rounders described fifteen years later in *The Boy's Own Book* by William Clarke, including the revolutionary diamond-shaped, four-base infield.[38] A player could be retired if his struck ball was caught on the fly, or if, as a base runner, he allowed himself to be struck by the "poisoned" ball.

In his book *Ball, Bat, and Bishop*, Robert W. Henderson expressed the opinion that the rules for *la balle* from *Les Jeux des jeunes garçons* were the earliest ever published for a bat and ball base running game.[39] While there is no denying the rules' historic importance, Henderson apparently erred when stating that a bat was utilized in the game. The French text is somewhat ambiguous on the point, saying only that the player at home "repels" the ball — Henderson translated the word as "strikes".[40] A color illustration of the game that appeared in some editions of *Les Jeux des jeunes garçons*, however, clearly shows a striker using his open palm to hit the ball, and reveals no evidence of a bat. Since Henderson reprinted this image in *Ball, Bat, and Bishop*, it is inexplicable why he classified *la balle empoisonée* as a bat-and-ball game. Subsequent illustrations of the game printed in later books, such as the one in *Jeux des adolescents* from 1856, confirm the absence of a bat.

If, in fact, *la balle empoisonée* migrated to France from England, the missing bat might help date its window of travel. As mentioned in the section on English base-ball above, when the game in eighteenth-century England was still a new and primitive children's pastime, the use of a bat was optional. If the game crossed the Channel in those years, it could explain why hitting the ball with the open palm was the only major feature distinguishing *la balle* from other forms of early baseball. This, however, is speculation, and like almost everything else about baseball's French cousins, the history of *la balle empoisonée* remains an enigma. The game continued to appear in French books until the mid-nineteenth century, and, as is the case with *thèque*, is still played in residual forms today. Neither of these variations, however, ever stirred passions among the French citizenry that in any way resembled America's torrid love affair with baseball.

11

BASEBALL
BEFORE WE
KNEW IT

It seems difficult to believe, but in the entire history of baseball only one previous researcher has conducted a comprehensive scientific inquiry into the origins of the game. This distinction belongs to Robert W. Henderson and his landmark 1947 study of ball sports, *Ball, Bat, and Bishop*.[1] Henderson infused his chapters entitled "Baseball: Infancy" and "Baseball: Adolescence" with such vivid historical and bibliographic detail that to this day they constitute the starting point for any discussion of the game's beginnings. In the decades since the publication of *Ball, Bat, and Bishop*, advancing technology has revolutionized historical research. Tools such as online library catalogues, email, digitized books and newspapers, and microfilm readers have enabled scholars to explore resources with a span and tempo unimaginable in Henderson's day, which makes his accomplishments all the more remarkable.

Writing now with the advantages of the past fifty-plus years, and upon the solid foundation laid by Henderson, I offer my own interpretation of baseball's birth and childhood. Ideally, what follows would be a step-by-step literal history of the game's earliest days. Unfortunately, the fragmentary surviving evidence from that era does not support such an undertaking. Instead, I'll attempt the next best alternative, a plausible reconstruction of baseball's odyssey based upon existing historical clues. In this regard, I have chosen to be somewhat selective. My model is based almost exclusively upon documented evidence that I have been able to verify with my own eyes. Furthermore, I rely primarily on source material that was written in the applicable historical periods, and place less confidence in the recollections of

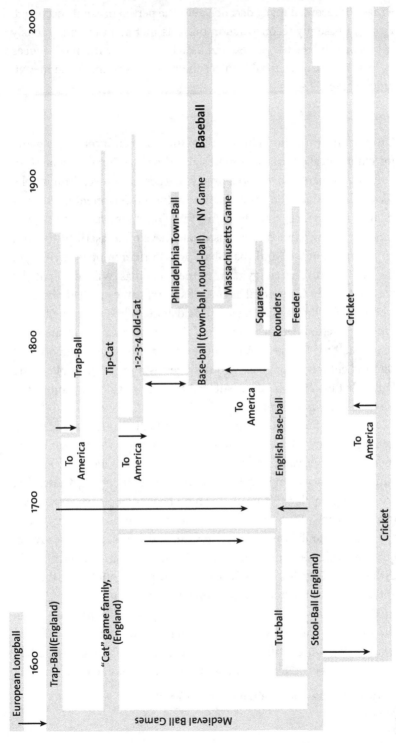

Theoretical Flowchart of Baseball's Evolution.

witnesses recorded many decades after the pertinent events occurred. Finally, I base my reconstruction on facts that point unambiguously to baseball and related games, and tend to discount written references to "base" or "playing at ball" unless their contexts confirm that they allude to baseball.

❖

Once upon a time, in the first half of the eighteenth century, a game for children called base-ball materialized on the English scene. Pinpointing the game's debut to a precise decade has proven impossible. We can hardly fault the writers of the era for not documenting the momentous milestone, since to them it no doubt bore as much significance as a new game of tag. Historians have often ascribed the first known usage of the word "base-ball" to a Puritan minister writing in the year 1700. The clergyman, named Thomas Wilson, reputedly mentioned it in his journal as one of several games he had observed when visiting the English town of Maidstone. While many books and articles in recent decades have cited this pioneering use of the word "base-ball," the Reverend Wilson is undeserving of the attention. The claim is entirely erroneous, and it serves as a prime example of the fables that too often have substituted for history when the subject of baseball's origin is discussed.[2]

In fact, the first documented references to the name "base-ball" did not appear until the 1740s, and their content suggests the pastime by then was well beyond its infancy. The most direct basis for this assumption comes from Lady Hervey, who told us in her 1748 letter that "base-ball [is] a play all who are, or have been, schoolboys are well acquainted with."[3] With no reason to doubt her words, it follows that if "all" current and former schoolboys of the 1740s were already acquainted with the game, it must have originated at an indeterminately earlier time. Exactly how early we can only guess, but late in the seventeenth century is not an unreasonable possibility.

This toddler called base-ball, like many juvenile pastimes, was shaped by the children who played it. In its simplest form, as inferred from period sources, the game consisted of one player serving a ball to a waiting second player, who was situated at a home goal. The second player attempted to strike the ball and, if successful, proceeded to run as far as possible around a circuit of bases. Additional players either fielded the ball or took turns as strikers, or both. Outs were tallied if balls were caught on the fly, or if fielders were able to catch runners off base and strike them with the ball.

Base-ball's youthful founders were most likely attempting to imitate features of other games they witnessed in the English countryside, activities that were the domains of older youth or adults. Undoubtedly the pastime most mimicked was stool-ball, which in its varied forms had crisscrossed the English landscape for centuries. Children observing the frolicking pleasures of the multiple-base version of stool-ball may have been inspired to adapt its features to their own capabilities and scale. Dimensions were reduced, and in place of stools the children used simple sticks or markers for bases. Running the base paths was limited to the striker and his successors, replacing the permanent bases-loaded arrangement of stool-ball. And the act of throwing a ball at a runner to get him out replaced the more difficult task of having to hit the home base (or stool) with the thrown ball.

This explanation, of course, is purely conjectural. No known eyewitness accounts of base-ball's genesis have survived the centuries. Nevertheless, logic suggests that something similar to this scenario must have happened, because when baseball appeared it bore many of the features of stool-ball. One possible variation is that the game of tut-ball played an intervening role. Tut-ball, we recall, was also a likely spin-off of stool-ball, and its antiquity almost rivals that of its parent pastime. Surviving evidence about tut-ball, though limited, indicates that the game's features were nearly identical to those of early baseball, and dictionaries of the nineteenth century confirm that the words "tut" and "base" had precisely the same meanings. All of this suggest a hypothesis that tut-ball was a fledgling version of base-ball which had separated from stool-ball as early as the sixteenth century. The appearance of base-ball 150 to 200 years later may have been little more than a revision in names.

The use of a bat was not an inherent feature of early baseball. Players originally used their bare hands to strike the ball, as was then common in stool-ball and possibly tut-ball as well. Most likely, the bat's use in such popular pastimes as trap-ball, cat, and cricket influenced its adaptation to base-ball. Enterprising children must have readily recognized the greater fun to be had by swinging a big stick. Some regional varieties of stool-ball had begun to incorporate the bat by the 1730s, which may also have encouraged its crossover to base-ball in the following decades.

By the mid-eighteenth century, base-ball was one of innumerable simple pastimes played by children in Great Britain. From Lady Hervey we know that English adults of that era may also have been experimenting with the game, although probably on a very limited basis. It was also at that time that base-ball's transfer to America began to get under way, a tiny splash within a sweeping tide of cultural migration. Along with many aspects of their folklore, successive generations of English settlers brought familiar childhood games with them to the New World. These included base-ball, but also varieties of trap-ball and the game of cat. (Stool-ball was already diminishing in importance by the mid- to late eighteenth century.) The rules and features of the imported games varied by their year of import and their English county of origin. In the American colonies, as had been the case in England, ball games were locally formed. Each community's pastimes reflected the backgrounds of its population, and ball play grew and evolved under the influence of each new wave of immigrants. Flavoring the English mix were contributions by Dutch and German settlers, as well as variations introduced by new arrivals from Ireland and Scotland.[4]

At home in England, base-ball had been a popular activity for both sexes. Once arrived in the American colonies, however, its play was apparently denied to girls due to more rigid standards for ladylike behavior. Unsurprisingly, this deprivation paralleled the stirrings of interest in the game among American adults. Evidence uncovered by the historian Thomas Altherr demonstrates that by the time of the Revolutionary War baseball had moved beyond being the exclusive purview of boys to become a diversion for soldiers and other young men.[5] Thanks to Altherr we also know that the pastime gained a foothold on college campuses during these years. Altherr noted an especially intriguing example in a March 1786 diary entry by a Princeton student named John Rhea Smith: "A fine day, play baste ball in the campus but am beaten for I miss both catching and striking the ball."[6] The noted baseball author John Thorn unearthed a further indication of baseball's stature in the late eighteenth century among the early records of Pittsfield, Massachusetts. Seeking to protect the windows of their newly constructed meeting house, the town authorities passed a by-law in 1791 forbidding within eighty yards of the precious structure "any game of wicket, cricket, base-ball, bat-ball, foot-ball, cats, fives, or any other game played with ball."[7]

At the turn of the nineteenth century, ball play in the young United States was undoubtedly among the most commonplace of pastimes. It was also nearly invisible within the annals of the times. Like many aspects of social and cultural history, especially those involving the diversions of children, baseball was not deemed of any great significance and was not worth writing about. Among the few glimpses available to us are those found in children's chapbooks from the early nineteenth century, in which small woodcut engravings occasionally depicted scenes of boys playing with bat and ball.[8] Descriptions of how to play baseball did not begin appearing in American books until the 1830s. This lag was due, in part, to the immaturity of the country's publishing industry, which placed a low priority on producing titles intended for children. Also, the many localized variants and names for baseball in those days may have discouraged its selection for the few books devoted to children's activities.

Town-ball, round-ball and base ball were the three most common designations for American baseball in the first half of the nineteenth century. As with the old-cat games, the ubiquity of town-ball is documented mainly through the later recollections of old-timers rather than in primary accounts. The earliest references to the game thus far located come from two unlikely sources. The first is an 1841 Louisiana newspaper article praising the athletic virtues of quoits — a pastime similar to horseshoes — in which the author urged the players, "Keep it up gentlemen; if you weary at it and want variety, form a cricket club, devote an hour to town-ball, or resort to the row boats of the river."[9] This reference was found in the *Daily Picayune* of New Orleans, which had borrowed the quoits story from an obscure rural Louisiana newspaper, the *Concordia Intelligencer*, published in the small Mississippi River town of Vidalia. The second sighting of town-ball pops up in an equally improbable venue — gold rush San Francisco. There, in 1852, a writer for the *California Sunday Dispatch* reminisced: "A game of 'town ball' which was had on the Plaza during the week, reminded us of other days and other scenes. Those who played with us on the old school house green, where are they?"[10] The game was already evoking nostalgia, but our knowledge of its earlier history under that name remains exceptionally thin.

A common explanation for the origin of the name "town-ball" is that it came to be used to describe the ball games played when communities gathered for town meetings. While this may be a plausible theory, it is purely speculative and not supported by any actual historical evidence. The term "town-ball" has been casually applied to forms of early baseball played in different regions of the United States. Occasionally writers have equated the name with the Massachusetts variety of baseball, although old-time ballplayers from the New England area who submitted testimony to the Spalding Commission recalled using only the name "round-ball."

By contrast, substantial evidence exists to show that "town-ball" was the principal term for early baseball in the Philadelphia area. The Olympic Ball Club of that city was chartered in 1833, and although later accounts universally agreed that the game they played was known locally as town-ball, their constitution does not specifically mention the term.[11] The following short passage, published in a newspaper article toward the end of the nineteenth century, reportedly described the Olympic club's game:

> The bases, if they may be so called, were five sticks planted as to form a circle, the diameter of which was about thirty feet. The striker was compelled to make a complete circuit upon each hit in order to score. The runner was put out by hitting him with the ball, which was much lighter and softer than the ball of the present time.[12]

From all available indications, the term "town-ball" was simply one of several regional aliases for baseball before 1845. In those years, the game was a localized and generally unorganized activity. Two teams in neighboring communities might have called their respective games town-ball but played under different sets of rules. By the same token, their rules could have been identical, but one might have called it "town-ball" and the other "base ball." Following 1845, when the Knickerbocker Base Ball Club codified rules for the New York game, the term "town-ball" lingered as the label for the Philadelphia version of the sport. It also survived for decades in scattered rural areas as a generic title for older folk varieties of baseball.

"Round-ball," as we have seen, was the name most commonly applied to early baseball played in the New England region. As was the case with town-ball, there is little indication that the actual methods of playing round-ball before 1845 differed materially from forms practiced in other parts of the country, regardless of what they were called. In the 1834 children's *Book of Sports*, published in Boston, the author Robin Carver equated round-ball with "base or goal ball." Even as far afield as New Orleans, a writer for the *Daily Picayune* in 1841 used the term "round ball" interchangeably with "base" in a long column discussing the importance of ball playing for both men and boys.[13]

Impervious to the Knickerbockers' innovations of 1845, New Englanders continued to play their traditional variety of baseball, a game played without foul lines and featuring a square infield and the practice of soaking. By the 1850s New England ball clubs following these older rules began to adopt structures and constitutions along the same lines as clubs in the New York area, and round-ball became known more formally as "the Massachusetts game of base ball." However, the curtain began to close toward the end of the decade, when some New England clubs started experimenting with the New York rules. By the conclusion of the Civil War, the separate New England version of baseball, along with Philadelphia town-ball, were on the road to extinction, and from coast to coast the country adopted the New York game as the national standard.

Most knowledge about the early-nineteenth-century practice of baseball in New England comes from the documented recollections of old-timers recorded many years afterward. Contemporaneous accounts of ball playing in the region before the 1850s are extremely scarce, a sign of the lack of importance accorded the pastime by sporting writers of the era. Bucking this pattern were the efforts of a few pioneering New England writers and editors in the 1830s who chose to include fledgling descriptions of baseball or round-ball within the pages of children's books.¹⁴ These noteworthy examples from Boston, New Haven, and Providence constitute the only attempts by American publishers before 1845 to explain to their readership how baseball was actually played. By contrast, the few fleeting references to the game that appeared in New England newspapers between 1820 and 1850 were typically so brief that no real content could be gleaned from them. The historian Preston Orem cited one unusually robust report from the Bangor, Maine, *Whig* in 1844 that recounted a match game of round-ball between two picked teams. The captain of one side was reputed to be Samuel Cony, a future governor of the state. Unfortunately, the article did not describe how the game was played, mainly concerning itself with the elaborate method the players used to decide a winner after darkness arrived with one side not having completed its at-bat.¹⁵

A few small traces of early baseball from the New York area have survived to the present. In 1823 a Manhattan newspaper called the *National Advocate* published the following extraordinary report:

I was last Saturday much pleased in witnessing a company of active young men playing the manly and athletic game of "base ball" at the Retreat in Broadway (Jones'). I am informed they are an organized association, and that a very interesting game will be played on Saturday next at the above place, to commence at half past 3 o'clock, p.m. Any person fond of witnessing this game may avail himself of seeing it played with consummate skill and wonderful dexterity. It is surprising, and to be regretted that the young men of our city do not engage more in this manual sport; it is innocent amusement, and healthy exercise, attended with but little expense, and has no demoralizing tendency.¹⁶

This clear evidence of young men playing organized baseball in New York City was followed in 1825 by another announcement in an upstate New York newspaper that a team of nine players from the town of Hamden wished to challenge the team of any other town in Delaware County to a game of "bass-ball."[17] These examples strongly suggest that throughout the period of time leading up to the advent of modern baseball the favored name for the game in the New York region was, in fact, "base ball." There is no evidence that the names "town-ball" and "round-ball" ever took hold in the immediate vicinity of New York City. Ultimately, the scarcity of references in New York and elsewhere to any of these terms offers an insight into the nomenclature of the era: most players in most regions probably eschewed the nominal local names for the sport in favor of the generic and ubiquitous phrase "playing ball."

And what about "rounders"? There is no historical evidence in England or the United States of that term's ever being applied to a bat-and-ball game before its appearance in *The Boy's Own Book* in 1828. Other than American reprints of *The Boy's Own Book*, there is no record of the name "rounders" being used in this country during the long era of baseball's advent and maturation. Given that the name "base-ball" predated "rounders" in England by nearly a hundred years, it is time to finally put to rest the tired old axiom that baseball descended from that "ancient" English pastime.

By the 1840s baseball's long ascent from simple English folk game was about to shift into warp speed. Over the next thirty years the game underwent an unprecedented expansion and transformation. This process was especially accelerated in the immediate aftermath of the Civil War, when the popular New York version of the game spread rapidly to all corners of the nation. Baseball was now everywhere, in schoolyards and sandlots, and in large new ballparks built to hold the crowds flocking to see the heroes of the new professional leagues.

With every passing decade the country grew ever more passionate about the National Pastime, and by the time the nineteenth century rolled into the twentieth, it had become far more than a game. Baseball was now a hallmark of America, a cherished and indelible component of the nation's cultural life. Given this eminence, it is no surprise that the issue of the game's origins came to matter so deeply to its most influential boosters. Spalding, Chadwick, Rankin, and Ward, along with others mentioned in these pages, endeavored to outfit the

National Pastime with a pedigree worthy of its stature, albeit one attuned to their respective egos and political agendas. And whether their theories entailed glorifying the ingenuity of the American Boy, or hailing the creative genius of a Civil War hero, or honoring the noble and ancient Old Country game of rounders, they paid little heed to the strictures of historical fact.

I must confess to sharing with these would-be genealogists the belief that baseball merits a creditable pedigree. Like them, I have been inspired by the game's larger-than-life importance to me and to many of my fellow citizens. Yet I also yearn for a time when the enduring folk tales and misguided notions of baseball's beginnings will finally fade into the background, supplanted by a consensus vision of the game's evolution that is faithful to the details of history. In tribute to the pioneering work of Robert Henderson, and indebted to the many amazing discoveries of fellow early baseball historians, I hope with this book to edge us a little closer to that dream. After so many missteps, I believe we are finally turning the corner and heading home in our search for the roots of our beloved National Pastime.

EARLY BASEBALL BIBLIOGRAPHY

ROOTS OF THE GAME IN PRE—CIVIL WAR LITERATURE

At first, this entire book was to be a bibliography. My plan was simply to compile a list of very old books containing information relevant to baseball's history. I would then add some comments about each book, obtain some illustrations, and go to press. I knew that it would not be a very big book, just a booklet really, but that was all that was needed to fill in a small gap in the spectrum of baseball bibliographies.

But as matters unfolded, the modest project gained some momentum and turned into a full-blown book. Information I gleaned from my bibliographic research inspired the assorted observations on baseball's origins that occupy the greater portion of this work. Nevertheless, to me the heart of this effort is, and has always been, the bibliography.

It is a work of love. Love of baseball. Love of history. Love of old books. Writing a bibliography was a natural outgrowth of these passions. Taking an early retirement gave me the time to pursue the project. Discovering that no one had covered the territory before meant that it might actually be useful to others.

Why have I chosen the Civil War as my end point? My focus was "early baseball," and the war provided a natural boundary between early and modern baseball because it was then that soldiers from different regions became exposed to, and fell in love with, the New York variety of the game, turning it into a national phenomenon. It was also a practical matter to close off my bibliography at 1860, because that year has been the customary starting point for many other baseball bibliographies.

I began by drawing upon my own collection of early baseball books and those of friends, and then expanded my list by making an inventory of older titles that were cited as sources in existing baseball histories. I had hoped to produce a detailed checklist for fellow collectors and researchers. What surprised me was finding a significant number of old books with baseball-related content that had not been reported previously.

Many of these discoveries were works published in Europe. Given the game's English origins, this should not have been unexpected. Yet, until now, researchers looking for early baseball books have focused on American titles, undoubtedly because the sport is so closely associated with this country.

I had originally intended to start my chronological list with *A Little Pretty Pocket-Book*, the landmark children's book first published in 1744, which contains the earliest known mention of the word "base-ball." Along the way, however, I lapsed into a bibliofrenzy that drove me to document many titles bearing references to baseball's ancient predecessors — stool-ball, trap-ball, and numerous others. This wound up extending the start date of the bibliography back to the fifteenth century.

I should mention here that for the most part I have ignored books dealing with cricket. While it is a lovely sport, I'm sure, and arguably shares a rung or two with baseball on the evolutionary ladder, it was just too much to handle. The vast amount of cricket literature would have overwhelmed everything else and dramatically shifted the focus of my study.

Bibliographies are an ancient scholarly pursuit, with time-honored formats, syntax, and abbreviations. Don't look for any of those here. My scholarly expertise is limited to my familiarity with early baseball books and does not branch into bibliographic science. I give you the basics: the title, author, publisher, date of publication, and the number of pages. I also provide a description of the book and its relevance to baseball history. I occasionally comment on the rarity of a particular title, although given the age of these books it should be obvious that none of them is common.

Aside from books, the written record of baseball history includes journals, diaries, letters, magazines, and newspapers. While these are all valuable sources, they are not, for the most part, included in this work. The sheer number of newspaper references alone would take volumes to capture. Perhaps the most important contributors in this category were American sporting journals that began reporting on baseball in the 1850s. I have appended a brief overview of these publications following the bibliography.

In the late 1840s and 1850s, the new emerging baseball clubs often published constitutions and by-laws for the use of their membership. I have included a separate listing of all the extant publications of this type that I have thus far identified.

While many different types of book are included in this bibliography, there are several broad categories that merit comment. The first is the children's chapbook of the early nineteenth century, which was among the first form to embrace games and pastimes as subject matter. In those days, in both England and the United States, religious disapproval of frivolous play remained potent. Nonetheless, a few publishers on both sides of the Atlantic were producing tiny, paper-covered booklets intended for small children. These generally consisted of a few simple verses, accompanied by illustrations of everyday objects and activities. Among the many chapbooks produced, a handful included charming woodcuts of children playing with bat and ball.

Anthologies of children's games, sports, and pastimes are also well represented in the bibliography. This category of book also battled religious strictures, and examples did not begin appearing until the early nineteenth century. These works generally listed a wide variety of entertaining activities for children, typically including a small selection of bat-and-ball sports. It should be noted, however, that books in this category are exclusively European in origin. In those days the American publishing industry was still relatively immature, and firms desiring to release books of this type simply reprinted or adapted material that had appeared in England. I have yet to find a completely original work on games and sports published in the United States before the Civil War.

A third category, one that was of American origin, consists of early children's schoolbooks, primarily readers. Beginning in the 1820s, the primers designed for beginning readers occasionally featured woodcut illustrations showing scenes of children playing with bat and ball. More than any other category, these children's texts have historically been overlooked by those tracking baseball content in early American imprints.

Researching this bibliography has been enormously enjoyable. I have rummaged through bookstores and libraries and the far reaches of the Internet to be as comprehensive as possible. But as I ship my manuscript off to the publisher, I know with utmost certainty that there are many omissions. I have no doubt there are collectors and researchers reading this who will go to their bookshelves and say, "Hey, he forgot this one." I am equally certain that there are many early books out there with baseball content still waiting to be discovered. That's why God invented second editions.

1450 *How thow schalt thy paresche preche,* by John Myrc (Mirk). London. This is an early poetic instruction for priests that includes a mandate against fun and games in the churchyard. The author warns: "Bal and bares and suche play, / Out of chyrcheyorde put a-way." Shortly after publication, another writer inserted a note into the text that elaborated on the ban: "Danseyng, cotteyng, bollyng, tenessyng, hand ball, fott ball, stoil ball & all manner other games out cherchyard." Myrc's fifteenth-century Middle English instructions were actually a translation of the fourteenth-century Latin text "Pupilla Oculi" written by the churchman William de Pagula.

1567 *Horace His Arte of Poetrie, Pistles, and Satyrs Englished, and to the Earle of*
Ormounte, by Thomas Drant. London: Thomas Marsh, 283 pp. This early
English translation of Horace is printed in a Middle English gothic type-
face and contains the following swatch of verse:

The stoole ball, top, or camping ball
If suche one should assaye
As hath no mannour skill therein,
Amongste a mightye croude,
Theye all would screeke unto the frye
And laughe at hym aloude.

1575 *The Posies of George Gascoigne Esquire, Corrected, perfected, and augmented*
by the Authour, by George Gascoigne. London: Richard Smith, variously
paged. Gascoigne's poem "The Fruites of Warre" is among the first to
mention the game tut, or tut-ball, an early relative of baseball.

No jarre (good sir) yes yes and many jarres,
For though my penne of curtesie did putte,
A difference twixt broyles and bloudie warres,
Yet have I shot at maister *Bellums* butte,
And throwen his ball although I toucht no tutte:
I have percase as deepely dealt the dole,
As he that hit the marke and get the gole

1591 *Bibliotheca hispanica : containing a grammar, with a dictionarie in Span-*
ish, English, and Latine, gathered out of diuers good authors : very profitable for
the studious of the Spanish toong, by Richard Perciule (Perceval). London:
Richard Watkins, 2 vols. in 1. This early Spanish dictionary includes the
following English equivalents:

paleta — a trapsticke
paletilla — a little trapsticke

1598 *A Survay of London: Contayning the Originall, Antiquity, Increase, Mod-*
erne Estate, and Description of That Citie: written in the yeare 1598, by Iohn
Stow. London: Iohn Wolfe, 483 pp. This classic work presents a sweeping
physical, historical, and cultural picture of London on the threshold of the
seventeenth century. Among the many topics explored by the author are
the sports and pastimes enjoyed by the citizenry, and among these he
notes that on Shrove Tuesday "after dinner all the youthes go into the
fields to play at the bal." Apparently, this was no ordinary contest but one
worthy of keen spectator interest. Stow writes: "The schollers of euery
schoole haue their ball, or baston, in their hands: the auncient and wealthy
men of the Citie come foorth on horsebacke to see the sport of the young

men, and to take part in the pleasure in beholding their agilitie." According to the *Oxford English Dictionary*, the term "baston" was the first of several transitional spellings of what was later to become the word "baton," meaning "cudgel, club, bat or truncheon." Stow's *Survey of London* was reissued in 1599 and 1603, and publishers have produced new editions of the original in every succeeding century.

1598 *A world of wordes or Most copious, and exact dictionarie in Italian and English*, by John Florio. London: Edward Blount, 462 pp. This Italian-English dictionary contains the following English equivalent for the word *lippa*: "a cat or trap as children use to play with."

1610 *Greuel der Verwüstung des menschlichen Geschlechts* (The horrors of the devastation of the human race), by Hippolytus Guarinoni. Ingolstadt, Austrian Empire: Andreas Angermayr, 1,330 pp. From this book's foreboding title you would never guess that deep within its many pages lies an extraordinary description of an early bat-and-ball game. The author was a well-traveled Austrian physician who considered himself an authority on how to live a healthy and pious life. He undertakes to tutor his readers in these virtues, and to this end devotes one large section of the book to the promotion of various games and physical activities.

The jewel among these is a description of a ball game Dr. Guarinoni had witnessed students playing in the city of Prague around the year 1600. This unnamed game utilized a hard ball that was "the size of a quince" and made of leather. Players divided into two sides and one party arranged themselves around a playing field in all directions at distances up to one hundred paces. One player threw the ball to a batter on the opposite team, who tried to hit it with a rounded and tapered four-foot club. If the struck ball was caught in the air by one of the fielders, the sides reversed.

The author does not indicate whether base running was part of the game, although this could be inferred from his comment that the pastime "is good for tender youth which never has enough of running back and forth." Guarinoni states that he has seen the game played only in Bohemia (present Czech Republic), never in Italy. He further observes that the best players were Poles and Silesians, speculating that the game may have originated in those regions of the Austrian Empire.

Although unrelated to this description, it is important to note that Guarinoni played a role in history that was far more serious and sinister than his innocent observations on health and sports. The early seventeenth century in central Europe was a time rife with superstitions and religious fanaticism. In 1621 Guarinoni turned his attention to an old rumor in the Tyrol region that blamed Jews for the local disappearances of children. He wrote about a "dream" that Jews had stolen and murdered a boy named Anderl of Rinn in the year 1462, and then drained the child's blood for use in religious ceremonies. Coming from a respected doctor and author, this story resonated among the populace and precipitated the creation of a widespread anti-Semitic cult in Austria. The Brothers Grimm embellished Guarinoni's story in one of their children's tales, and Pope Benedict XIV endorsed the cult in the eighteenth century — though he stopped short of canonizing the "martyr" Anderl. The cult's strength continued into the twentieth century and provided an ideological inroad for the Nazi Party in Austria. Although the cult of Anderl was officially banned in 1994, devotees to this day pay homage at the boy's grave.

1611 A *Dictionarie of the French and English Tongues*, by Randle Cotgrave. London: Adam Islip, 966 pp. This French-English dictionary defines the word *martinet* as "the game called cat and trap." "Martinet" was a seventeenth-century term for the military device that hurled large stones at a castle under siege, and this apparently was seen as a good analogy for the game trap-ball.

1614 *I Would, and Would Not*, by Nicholas Breton. London: Thomas Bushell, 22 leaves. Stanza 79 of this early poetic work reads as follows:

I would I were an honest Countrey-Wench,
That only could make Curtsey, smoile, and blush,
And sit me downe upon a good-Ale bench,
And answere wanton *Tomkin* with a Tush.
And well, Go-too, and How-now? Pary-away,
And for a *Tanzey*, goe to *Stoole-Ball*-play.

1616 *The whole works of Homer : prince of poetts, in his Iliads, and Odysses*, by George Chapman. London: Nathaniell Butter. This is an early six-volume English translation of the works of Homer, best known today for having provided a subject for a well-known poem by John Keats. In "The Sixth Booke of Homers Odysses," the translator describes a scene in which a group of maids go down to the river, take off all their clothes, wash them, lay them down on the bank to dry, and then eat dinner.

Yet still watcht when the Sunne, their cloaths had dride,
Till which time (having din'd) *Nausicae*
With other virgins, did at stool-ball play;
Their shoulder-reaching head-tyres laying by.
Nausicae (with the wrists of Ivory)
The liking stroke strooke; singing first a song.

Meanwhile, Ulysses is sleeping nearby in the bushes, and Minerva, planning to pair him with Nausicae, hatches a plan to wake him:

Her meane was this, (though thought a stool-ball chance)
The Queene now (for the upstroke) strooke the ball
Quite wide off th' other maids; and made it fall
Amidst the whirlpooles. At which, out shriekt all;
And with the shrieke, did wise *Ulysses* wake.

So we owe thanks to an ancient Greek poet not only for recording the earliest known splash hit but also for leaving us his name as a term to describe baseball's mightiest blast.

1619 *Pasquils Palinodia, and His Progresse to the Taverne; Where, after the Survey of the Sellar, You are Presented with a Pleasant Pynte of Poeticall Sherry.*
London: Thomas Snodham, 35 pp. This ode celebrating self-indulgence
and alcoholic consumption was probably written under its influence. The
author chose to remain anonymous but was likely one of the prominent
poets of the early seventeenth century. The historian Robert W. Henderson
cites this poem to support his hypothesis that the roots of the game of
stool-ball are traceable to ancient pagan festivals:[1]

It was the day of all dayes in the yeare
That unto Bacchus hath its dedication,
When mad-brained Prentices, that no men fear,
O'erthrow the dens of bawdy recreations . . .
It was the day when Pullen go to block,
And every spit is fill'd with belly timber,
When cocks are cudgelled down with many a knock,
And hens are thrashed to make them short and tender,
When country wenches play with stoole and ball,
And run at *Barley-breake* untill they fall:
And country lads fall on them, in such sort
That after forty weekes the rew the sport.

The game of barley-break is often associated with stool-ball in poems of
the seventeenth and eighteenth centuries. Both games were part of traditional spring courtship rituals in the English countryside. Barley-break,
also known as "the last couple in hell," was not a ball game but involved
three couples vying for position on a playing area divided into three sections. The middle section, obviously the one to be avoided, was called
"hell."

1625 *Memorialium Commercatoris* (A merchant's memoirs), by Zbigniew Stefanski. Amsterdam: Adreasa Bickera. The experiences of a handful of

skilled Polish workingmen in early colonial Jamestown, Virginia, provide the subject matter of this memoir written by one of them. An entry for the year 1609 describes how the men entertained themselves one day by playing the Polish game *pilka palantowa* (bat ball) before an audience that included Native Americans.

1629 *The Wedding. As it was lately acted by her Maiesties seruants at the Phenix in Drury Lane*, by James Shirley. London: John Groue, 85 pp. In this early Shirley comedy, one character, Lodam, has just accepted a challenge to fight another character, Rawbone. After Rawbone has departed the scene, Lodam is trying to decide whether to follow through with the duel:

> Lodam: Whether I am bound to meet him or no? I will consult some
> o' the swordmen, and know whether it be a competent challenge.
> Camelion!
> Camelion: Sir!
> Lodam: Has the rat, your master that was, any spirit in him?
> Camelion: Spirit! the last time he was in the field a boy of seven year
> old beat him with a trap-stick.
> Lodam: Say'st thou so? I will meet him then, and hew him to pieces.

This may be the earliest recorded example of a ball bat used as a weapon.

1634 *The Two Noble Kinsmen*, by John Fletcher and William Shakespeare. London: John Waterson, 88 pp. There have always been questions as to whether this play was actually cowritten by Fletcher and Shakespeare, as both were deceased at the time it was first performed and published. One scholar has described the play as "a Jacobean dramatization of a medieval English tale based on an Italian romance version of a Latin epic about one of the oldest and most tragic Greek legends." Sounds like Shakespeare to me. In act 5, scene 2, a young maid (Daughter) and her Wooer are having a conversation with a doctor standing by:

> Daughter: How far is is't now to th' end o' th' world, my masters?
> Doctor: Why a day's journey, wench.
> Daughter (to Wooer): Will you go with me?
> Wooer: What shall we do there, wench?
> Daughter: Why, play at stool-ball; What is there else to do?
> Wooer: I am content, If we shall keep our wedding there.
> Daughter: 'Tis true,
> For there, I will assure you, we shall find
> Some blind priest for the purpose, that will venture
> To marry us, for here they are nice and foolish.

Besides, my father must be hanged tomorrow
And that would be a blot i'th' business.

Aside from the daughter's appearing somewhat indifferent to her father's fate, this passage is notable for its "play at stool-ball" double entendre. The euphemistic usage of stool-ball to signify sexual intercourse was common in the literature of the era, deriving from the game's association with springtime flirtations and courtship. This example is particularly risque in that it is the woman extending the "stool-ball" invitation.

1637 *A Divine Tragedie Lately Acted; or, A collection of sundry memorable examples of Gods judgements upon Sabbath-breakers, and other like Libertines, in their unlawfull sports, happening within the realme of England, in the compass only of two yeares last past, since the booke was published, worthy to be knowne and considered of all men, especially such, who are guilty of the sinne or archpatrons thereof,* by Henry Burton and William Prynne. London, 46 pp. The title is a mouthful, but gets to the point of the book, which is to denounce King Charles's "Declaration of Sports." This was a royal edict that granted the English public the right to practice sports after church on Sundays. Conservative Protestants like Burton and Prynne were horrified at what they saw as a violation of the Sabbath. Among the "memorable examples of Gods judgements" upon Sabbath breakers was this: "Sundry Youths playing at Catt on the Lords day, two of them fell out, and the one hitting the other under the eare with his catt, he therwith fell downe for dead." The "catt" in this case was clearly the cat-stick, and while there are many other examples of unlucky souls being brained by ball bats, this may be the earliest recorded instance of a fatality.

1637 *Hide Park: a comedie,* by James Shirley. London: Andrew and William Cooke, 72 pp. In this play, a brash and beautiful young woman, Mistress Carol, is teasing two of her male servants who are enamored with her. After making fun of one young man, she turns to the other, named Rider, and addresses him:

Mis. Car.: You would have some?

Rid.: Some testimony of your love, if it please you.

Mis. Car.: Indeed, I have heard you are a precious gentleman, And in
your younger days could play at trap well.

1648 *Hesperides: or, The Works both Humane & Divine of Robert Herrick, Esq.,* by Robert Herrick. London: John Williams, 398 pp. The following ditty appears on page 280 of this book of witty verse, and may be the earliest poem completely dedicated to a ball game:

1. At Stool-ball, *Lucia*, let us play,
For Sugar-cakes and Wine;
Or for a Tansie let us pay,
The losse or thine, or mine.

2. If thou, my Deere, a winner be
At trundling of the Ball,
The wager thou shalt have, and me,
And my misfortunes all.

3. But if (my Sweetest) I shall get,
Then I desire but this;
That likewise I may pay the Bet,
And have for all a kisse.

1652 *A Short Relation of a Long Journey Made Round or Ovall*, by John Taylor. London, book 4, 24 pp. An account of a round-trip journey from London to Wales by way of various English counties, as told by "The Water Poet," John Taylor. This poetic travelogue of the author's experiences recounts, with some humor, the punishments doled out in certain English villages to women and children for avoiding church and playing games on the Sabbath. To which he adds: "There is no such zeal in many places and parishes in Wales; for they have neither service, prayer, sermon, minister, or preacher, nor any church door opened at all, so that people do exercise and edify in the churchyard at the lawful and laudable games of trap, cat, stool-ball, racket, &c., on Sundays."

1653 *The Spanish Gipsie*, by Thomas Middleton and William Rowley. London: Richard Marriot, 71 pp. This English play is set in Spain. One character, Pedro, asks another, Sancho, where he intends to get money to buy some maps. Sancho responds: "If my woodes being cut down cannot fill this pocket, cut 'em into trapsticks." This suggests that the term "trapstick" for a trap-ball bat was already in common usage.

1665 *Scarronnides, or, Virgile travestie a mock-poem, in imitation of the fourth book of Virgils Æneis in English, burlesque*, trans. Charles Cotton. London, E. Cotes, 156 pp. In this English translation of book four of Paul Scarron's mid-seventeenth-century French parody of Virgil's Aeneid, the author fashions the following depiction of Mercury:

This said, *Jove* need not bid him twice,
Away he trips it in a trice,

To make him ready to be gone;
And first his pumps he fastned on;
Which being neatly pinckt and cut,
And finely fitted to his foot:
Had wings tyde on with thongs of leather,
Or Taching ends, I know not whether.
Which he could flie withall as well,
As he'd been brought up too't from th' shell:
Then in his hand he take a thick Bat,
With which he us'd to play at Kit-cat;
To beat mens Apples from their trees,
With twenty other rogueries;
Besides (as Rake-hells will abuse dayes)
To throw at Cocks upon *Shrove-Tuesdayes.*

In addition to the early description of Air Jordans, this passage contains a rare reference to the game "kit-cat," a three-base bat-and-ball game that was a forerunner to the American game three-old-cat. The verse also provides yet another example of how early ball bats were put to violent use.

1666 *Grace abounding to the chief of sinners, or, A brief and faithful relation of the exceeding mercy of God in Christ, to his poor servant John Bunyan,* by John Bunyan. London: George Larkin, 94 pp. In this autobiography, Bunyan demonstrates that his own religious awakening was the basis for the adventures of his character Christian in *The Pilgrim's Progress.* He recalls one pivotal incident when he had been engaged in frivolous ball play and was interrupted by someone he needed to pay attention to:

> The same day as I was in the midst of a game of cat, and having struck it one blow from the hole, just as I was about to strike the second time a voice did suddenly dart from Heaven into my soul which said: "Wilt thou leave thy sins and go to Heaven or have thy sins and go to Hell?" [2]

1672 *The Life and Death of Mr. Tho. Wilson, Minister of Maidstone in the County of Kent, M.A.,* by George Swinnock. London, 99 pp. This biography is listed more for what it doesn't contain than what it does. Since the mid-twentieth century, this book has been the basis of an oft-repeated quotation that was purported to include the first recorded appearance of the word "baseball." Actually the quotation, which was cited in Robert W. Henderson's *Ball, Bat, and Bishop* in 1947, is attributed to Reverend Wilson himself, not his biographer, and is reputed to have been written in 1700, not 1672. Henderson quotes Wilson as having written in his diary:

"I have seen Morris-dancing, cudgel-playing, baseball and cricketts, and many other sports on the Lord's Day."[3] Subsequent to Henderson, a number of other writers have cited the quotation in baseball histories.

Henderson's source for the sentence was an article entitled "The Origin of Cricket" that appeared in *Baily's Magazine of Sports and Pastimes* in July 1901. The author of that article, C. F. Woodruff, quotes the identical words that were later cited by Henderson, and also attributes them to Reverend Wilson. Unfortunately, Woodruff neglects to mention where he found the quotation.

As it turns out, the same sentence, or at least most of it, first appeared more than two hundred years earlier in the Wilson biography. Therein Mr. Swinnock wrote: "Maidstone was formerly a very prophane town, insomuch that I have seen Morrice dancing, Cudgel playing, *Stool-ball*, Crickets, and many other sports openly and publickly on the Lords Day" (italics mine). So instead of "baseball," the original version contains the word "stool-ball," not an insignificant difference! How did this change come about? Possibly some enlightened nineteenth-century editor elected to modernize Swinnock's language, substituting the voguish game of baseball for the obsolete game of stool-ball. Perhaps this was done by Woodruff himself or possibly Woodruff took the quotation from an as yet unknown reprinting of the biography. It is also mystifying why credit for the quotation shifted from its actual author Swinnock to his subject Wilson, and why its purported date of origin switched from 1672 to 1700. These changes appear purposeless, and may have resulted from nothing more sinister than editorial carelessness.

1677 *Poor Robin 1677. An almanack after a new fashion*, by Poor Robin (W. Winstanley). London, 48 pp. This early almanac features the following Easter verse:

> Young men and maids,
> Now very brisk,
> At barley-break and
> Stool-ball frisk.

1680 *Honest Hodge and Ralph Holding a Sober Discourse in Answer to a late Scandalous and Pernicious Pamphlet, Called a Dialogue Between the Pope and a Phanatick Concerning Affairs in England*, by "a person of quality." London: John Kidgell, 39 pp. This anonymous political-religious essay, written in the form of a conversation between two men (Honest Hodge and Ralph), seeks to discredit an earlier pamphlet. The author's stance is that the Pope is meddling in English affairs with the purpose of rekindling the civil war.

Ralph: Why then, what will you make of this *Dialoguing Pamphlet?*

Hodge: Why what I should do, that it is a perfect *Mock Cant* and Juggle, a meer *trap-stick* to bang the *Phanaticks* about. You see, the very first leaf of him presents you with his main design, to *trouble* the *Waters* of our *peace* and *quiet,* that so he might *fish* in them the more *securely* and pass *undiscovered.*

Another early example of a ball bat serving as a convenient literary weapon.

1690 *The Pagan Prince: or a Comical History of the Heroik Atchievements of the Palatine of Eboracum.* Amsterdam, 144 pp. The author of this humorous work of prose chose to remain anonymous, identified only as "the Author of the Secret History of King *Charles* II and K. *James* II." One passage discusses security arrangements for the Palatine:

Sir . . . you have three Pagan Deities at Command, St. *Loyola,* St. *Dominick,* and St. *Francis,* there's not a straw to choose. Ply any one of these, and they will as surely send you a Life Guard of four Arch Angels. . . . These Arch Angels will guard ye, one before, another behind, and one of each side, and when they see a Cannon Bullet coming toward ye from any corner of the Wind, will catch it like a Stool-Ball, and throw it to the Devil.

1694 *The comical history of Don Quixote, as it is acted at the Queens theatre in Dorset-Garden, by Their Majesties servants,* by Thomas D'Urfey. London: Samuel Briscoe, pagination erratic. In this musical play, based upon Cervantes's novel, D'Urfey (apparently the Bob Dylan of the Restoration) unleashes this long, silly, bawdy rap song on the occasion of "Mary the Buxom's" wedding (possibly anticipating the tune of "Subterranean Homesick Blues"):

Come all, great, small, short tall, away to Stoolball;
Down in a Vale on a Summer's day, all the Lads and
Lasses met to be Merry, a match for Kisses at
Stoolball play, and for Cakes, and Ale, and Sider, and
Perry. Will and Tom, Hall, Dick and Hugh, Kate,
Doll, Sue, Bess and Moll, with Hodge, and Briget,
and James, and Nancy; but when plump Siss got the
Ball in her Mutton Fist, once Fretted, she'd hit it
Farther than any; Running, Haring, Gaping, Staring

Reaching, Stooping, Hollowing, Whooping; Sun a
setting, all thought fitting, by consent to rest 'em;
Hall got Sue, and Doll got Hugh, all took by
turns their Lasses and Buss'd 'em. Jolly Ralph wass
in with Peg, tho' Freckl'd like a Turkey Egg, and
she as right as is my Leg, still gave him leave to
towze her. Harry then to Katy, swore, her Duggs were
Pretty, tho' they were all sweaty, and large as any
Cows are. Tom Melancholy was with his Lass; for
Sue do what e'er he cou'd, wou'd not note him.
some had told her, b'ing a Soldier in a Party,
with Mac-carty, at the Siege of Limrick, he was
wounded in the Scrotum. But the cunning Philly
was more kind to Willy, who of all their Ally,
was the ablest Ringer; He to carry on the Jest, be-
-gins a bumper to the best, and winks at her of
all the rest, and squeez'd her by the Finger. Then
went the Glasses round, then went the Lasses down, each
Lad did his Sweet-heart own, and on the Grass did
fling her. Come all, great small, short tall,
a-way to Stool Ball.
    Whew!

1706 *The Scotch rogue; or, The life and actions of Donald Macdonald, a High-
land Scot.* London: R. Gifford, 24 pp. This is a tale about the adventurous
life of Mr. Macdonald, beginning with how he was found abandoned on
a road as a baby and raised by a kindly couple. His adulthood is filled
with misadventures and fortune hunting, heroic actions, and great love
affairs—all in all, quite a potboiler. As a young man he makes this
statement:

I was but a sorry proficient in learning: being readier at *cat and doug,*
cappy-hole, riding the *burley hacket,* playing at *kyles and dams, spang-*
bodle, wrestling and *foot-ball* (and such other sports as we use in our
country) than at my book.

Cat and doug (cat and dog) was an early two-base version of the game of cat
that was most commonly played in Scotland. It was the likely forebear of
the American game two-old-cat.

1709 *Poor Robin 1709. An almanack after a new fashion,* by Poor Robin
(W. Winstanley and successors). London. Another selection from this

popular almanac that illustrates the springtime entwining of ball sports
and courtship rituals.

> Thus harmless country lads and lasses
> In mirth the time away so passes;
> Here men at foot-ball they do fall;
> There boys at *cat* and trap-ball.
> Whilst Tom and Doll aside are slank,
> Tumbling and kissing on a bank;
> Will pairs with Kate, Robin with Mary,
> Andrew with Susan, Frank with Sarah.
> In harmless mirth pass time away,
> No wanton thoughts lead them astray,
> But harmless are as birds in May.

1719 *Wit and Mirth: or Pills to Purge Melancholy*, by Thomas D'Urfey. London:
J. Tonson, six vols, 2,075 pp. In volume 3 of this expansive collection of
songs and verse appears an untitled little ditty that begins:

> Thus all our lives long we're Frolick and gay,
> And instead of Court Revels we merrily Play
> At Trap and Kettles and Barley-break run,
> At Goff, and at Stool-ball, and when we have done
> These innocent Sports, we Laugh and lie down,
> And to each pretty Lass we give a green Gown.

"Green gown" is a euphemism for loss of virginity, an allusion to the grass
stains that would inevitably show up on a maiden's dress as a result of a
roll in the meadow.

1733 *The London Magazine*, vol. 2, December 1733. London: J. Wilford. On
page 637 of this monthly publication begins an extended poem entitled
"Stool-Ball or the Easter Diversion," which offers by far the most complete
and detailed portrayal of the game to date.[4] The information revealed in
the poem includes the following:

> The earliest evidence of a stool-ball player actually using a bat.
>
> New details about the method of play. In this version there are no base
> runners. The batters are young ladies who remain at the plate (the
> stool) until they are retired. This could happen if a batted ball is
> caught on the fly or on a bound, or if a defender retrieves the ball
> and successfully hits the stool. The fielders are of both sexes, with
> the young men positioned deeper because they are said to have
> stronger throwing arms.

A wonderful poetic description of the setting for the game, including the playing field and the cheering assembled audience.

A dramatic narration of the contest itself, the building tension and the climactic role of individual players, somewhat anticipatory of "Casey at the Bat."

A paean to the benefits of good clean fun, fresh air, and exercise.

1737 *The Natural History of North-Carolina*, by John Brickell. Dublin: J. Carson, 408 pp. The author reports on everything he could observe about North Carolina, including the games played by Indians. He writes: "They have [a] game which is managed with a *Battoon*, and very much resembles our *Trap-ball*."

1740 *Poor Robin 1740. An almanack after a new fashion*, by Poor Robin (W. Winstanley and successors). London, 48 pp. Yet another citation from this long-running almanac:

> Much time is wasted now away,
> At pigeon-holes, and nine-pin play,
> Whilst hob-nail Dick, and simpring Frances,
> Trip it away in country dances;
> At *stool-ball* and at barley-break,
> Wherewith they at harmless pastime make.

1744 *A Little Pretty Pocket-Book, Intended for the Instruction and Amusement of Little Master Tommy and Pretty Miss Polly*, [by John Newbery]. London: John Newbery, 95 pp. This amazing book not only contains the first known appearance of the word "base-ball" in print but also is considered to be the first children's book intended primarily for entertainment. In 1744 John Newbery, who later became a renowned children's publisher, created a small book describing thirty-two youthful games and activities. He placed them one to a page and accompanied each with a woodcut illustration, a poem describing how to play, and a brief moral lesson or "rule of life." Of course, this was still the age of piety, when frivolous play was frowned upon by many church authorities. Accordingly, half the book is devoted to various devotional activities, as well as guidelines for children's behavior.

Nevertheless, the book was a breakthrough of never before described fun for children. Its "Base-Ball" page features a woodcut showing three players and three bases marked by posts. One player stands ready to pitch the ball (although none of the others is holding a bat). The short poem following reads:

> The ball once struck off,
> Away flies the boy

To the next destined post.

And then home with joy.

Besides baseball, *A Little Pretty Pocket-Book* devotes separate pages to the games of stool-ball, trap-ball, and tip-cat, each with a woodcut engraving and accompanying verse. The woodcuts are the first known illustrations of each of these games, and, taken together with the information provided by the poetry, provide valuable snapshots of these pastimes at an early moment in their histories.

Apparently, no copies of the original 1744 edition, nor of eight subsequent editions, have survived. Single copies of the 10th, 11th, and 12th English editions, from 1760, 1763, and 1767, respectively, exist in library collections, as well as two copies of a 1770 edition. Pirated American editions were produced in 1762 by the New York printer Hugh Gaine and in 1786 by the Philadelphia publisher W. Spotswood. No copies of either edition are known. In 1787 the well-known publisher Isaiah Thomas issued the first major American edition in Worcester, Massachusetts. A small number of copies of this edition in both hardcover and paper wraps can be found in libraries and private collections.

1755 *A dictionary of the English language in which the words are deduced from their originals, and illustrated in their different significations by examples from the best writers : to which are prefixed, a history of the language, and an English grammar*, by Samuel Johnson, London: J. and P. Knapton et al., 2 vols. This renowned early English dictionary contains the following simple definitions

"stoolball"—"A play where balls are driven from stool to stool."

"trap"—"A play at which a ball is driven with a stick."

1776 *Juvenile Sports and Pastimes*, by Michel Angelo, London: T. Carnan, 104 pp. This rare early title on the subject of children's pastimes features a trapball section that includes a woodcut of five gents in three-cornered hats playing the game. The humorous and surprisingly sarcastic text derides *"gentlemen"* for ruining what had once been a challenging boys' game. The author explains that by mechanizing the trap and using a broad flat bat instead of a thin round one, these *"gentlemen"* had disgraced the game by making it too easy to play. The author's wit is also noted in his choice of *nom de plume*, Michel Angelo. The title page identifies the book as a second edition. There is no record of a first.

1787 *The Royal Primer; or, An Easy and Pleasant Guide to the Art of Reading*. Worcester MA: Isaiah Thomas, 72 pp. This tidy early reader by the renowned Worcester publisher Isaiah Thomas is filled with woodcut illustrations, though unfortunately none of them depicts a ball game. On the last page of the book, however, Thomas printed an advertisement for his selection of children's titles. This begins with a paean to the importance of parents encouraging their children to read, and then concludes with the following paragraph:

> Isaiah Thomas, Bookseller in Worcester, Massachusetts, Always keeps for SALE a large Assortment of BOOKS, for CHILDREN of all Ages and Capacities. All little Masters and Misses, by Consent of their Parents, are invited to his Store, where, if they have only a few Pennies to spend, they may be suited with Something more valuable than Cakes, prettier than Tops, handsomer than Kites, more pleasurable than Bat and Ball, more entertaining than either Scating or Sliding, and durable as Marbles.

The question of whether a book is more pleasurable than bat and ball is certainly debatable. Nevertheless, one must salute Thomas's enthusiasm for the joys and importance of reading. Fortunately, there is ample room in life for the pleasures of books and baseball alike.

1795 *An Historical, Geographical, Commercial and Philosophical View of the American United States, and of the European Settlements in America and the West Indies,* by William Winterbotham. London: J. Ridgway, H. D. Symonds, and D. Holt, 4 vols. This epic work offers a comprehensive overview of life in the young United States. Thumbnail baseball histories of the type that appear on the Internet occasionally cite this book as possessing a valuable early indication of the game's presence in America. These quote Winterbotham as having written that the game of "bat and ball" was common in America before the Revolutionary War, and that "by the time of the Revolution, it was commonly called 'base' or 'baste,' and it wasn't necessarily a game for boys anymore." Such a finding, if confirmed, would constitute a very important early reference to the game in North America. The problem is that several researchers, including myself, have never been able to locate the quotation among the book's 1,200 pages. Thus far the only verified comments by Winterbotham regarding ball games appear in his sections on New England and Tennessee. In the former, on page 17 of volume 2, he writes: "The healthy and athletic diversions of cricket, foot ball, quoits, wrestling, jumping, hopping, foot races, and prison bars, are universally practiced in the country, and some of them in the most populous places, and by people of almost all ranks." In the Tennessee section in volume 3, page 235, he refers to the citizenry's fondness for sports, including "playing at ball," but does not elaborate further.

This was a widely circulated book, much reprinted in both England and the United States.

1796 *Spiele zur Uebung und Erholung des Körpers und Geistes für die Jugend, ihre Erzieher und alle Freunde Unschuldiger Jugendfreuden* (Games for the exercise and recreation of body and spirit for the youth and his educator and all friends of innocent joys of youth), by Johann Christoph Friedrich Gutsmuths. Schnepfenthal, Germany: Verlag der buchhandlung der Erziehungsanstalt, 492 pp. This wonderfully detailed book on games and sports contains the first known published rules for a game called "baseball." Written by the German physical education pioneer J. C. F. Gutsmuths, the book includes a chapter entitled: "Ball mit Freystäten (oder das englische Base-ball)," which literally translates to "ball with free station, or English base-ball."

Even though the book was intended for a German audience, there is no indication that the game was actually played in Germany. Still, the fact that Gutsmuths, working from a small town in central Germany, was familiar enough with baseball to include it in his book suggests that the game was already well established in England.

The version of baseball described by Gutsmuths contained some features that have changed considerably over the years. For example, the bat was two feet long and oddly shaped, the number of bases varied with the number of players, and the batting team was entitled to only one out before the side was retired. Nevertheless, at its core, *das englische Base-ball* is very familiar. A pitcher served to a batter, who had three attempts to put the ball in play. Once striking the ball, the batter ran counterclockwise from base to base as far as possible without being put out. His objective was to complete a circuit of the bases and return to home. Outs were tallied by catching the ball, touching the runner with the ball, or throwing to a base (as well as a couple of other methods that have not survived the test of time).

Dimensions and scale of *das englische Base-ball* were smaller than in today's game. The pitcher stood only five or six steps from the batter and lobbed the ball in an arc. The bases were ten to fifteen paces apart and irregularly spaced, and the short bat had a four-inch flat face at the hitting end. Home base was an area rather than a specific spot, and apparently all players from the hitting team gathered there, not just the individual who was batting.

The 492-page book also includes coverage of many other ball games and youth activities, including a lengthy description of *das deutsche Ball-*

spiel or "the German ball game," a cousin of baseball, also known as "ball-stock." The German ball game was popular in the late eighteenth century, and while it continued to be played into the 1900s, it is now virtually extinct. Gutsmuths's documentation of the game is an important contribution to baseball history, because it is the strongest surviving evidence of an ancient family of European ball games that may have influenced the inception of baseball in England. The German ball game is also uncannily similar to a ball game of Stone Age vintage discovered by an Italian researcher in North Africa in the 1930s.[5]

Gutsmuths dwells on the relative aspects of *das englische Base-ball* and the German ball game. He writes that English baseball "is smaller in scale and requires less strength in hitting, running, etc. At the same time, it demands an equal amount, if not more, attentiveness, and is much more bound by numerous small rules." He observes, "The German ball game will never be able to fully repress English base-ball, as pleasant as ours may be."

Gutsmuths goes so far as to devote a separate short chapter to promote his suggestion of an improved hybrid game that would "unite both forms." It would be based upon the rules of English baseball but would adapt the longer, stronger bat of the German ball game so that the ball could be hit with greater power. He recommends, in addition to a home base, a fixed layout of four bases arranged in a square pattern. (In fact, his proposal is similar to later rounders and town-ball configurations.) He believed these improvements would make the game more appealing to German players.

The book includes diagrams of numerous games, including one each of *das englische Base-ball* and the German ball game. The first edition of this book appeared in April 1796, with a second edition following in October of the same year. A third edition, essentially unchanged from the first two, appeared in 1802, followed by numerous subsequent editions throughout the nineteenth century.

1797 *Illustrations of the Manners and Expences of Ancient Times in England; In the Fifteenth, Sixteenth, and Seventeenth Centuries, Deduced from the Accompts of Churchwardens,* by John Nichols. London: printed for John Nichols, 515 pp. Listed in the financial records for the parish of St. Margaret's, Westminster, is the following entry from the year 1658: "Item to *Richard May*, 13 shillings for informing of one that played at trap-ball on the Lord's day." Apparently during the Reformation, some churches actually paid people for snitching out ballplayers on the Sabbath!

1799 *Battleridge*, by Cassandra Cooke. London: G. Cawthorn, 2 vols. On the
second page of this historical novel appears the following passage: "This
time twenty years, when my clerkship ended with Lawyer Colson, never
shall I forget it, I came to bid adieu to my old playmate, Sir Ralph Vesey:
how kindly did he part with poor Jack Jephson, as he called me! 'Ah!' says
he, 'no more cricket, no more base-ball, they are sending me to Geneva.'"
Cooke's early use of the term "base-ball" is noteworthy in its own right, but
there is an added curiosity about it because of her acquaintance with fellow author Jane Austen. This relationship is evidenced in an October 1798
letter written by Austen to her sister (also named Cassandra), in which she
writes that Cooke had complained to her about having some problems
with Cawthorn, the publisher of *Battleridge*. The timing of Austen's letter
is significant because she was then in the midst of writing her own novel
Northanger Abbey (not to be published until 1818), in which she also em-
ploys the term "base-ball." Given that the term was virtually unknown in
contemporary literature, its application in the same year by two authors
who were corresponding raises the question of whether their mutual em-
ployment of "base-ball" was coincidental.

1800 *The Prize for Youthful Obedience*. London: Darton and Harvey, 48 pp.
This popular early children's book consists of simple tales with moral lessons. In one story, a visiting hermit praises some children for their good
behavior while playing, and says: "If you do me the honour of another visit,
I shall endeavour to provide bats, balls, &c . . . " The first American edition
was issued by Jacob Johnson of Philadelphia in 1803, and a number of subsequent editions followed in both countries.

1801 *Glig-gamena Angel-deod. Or, The Sports and Pastimes of the People of England; Including the Rural and Domestic Recreations, May-games, Mum-
meries, Pageants, Processions, and Pompous Spectacles, from the Earliest Period to the Present Time*, by Joseph Strutt. London: T. Bensley for White and
Co., 301 pp. This epic folio work is the first major scholarly effort in English to chronicle games and sports. It includes references to several of
baseball's precursors and cousins, including stool-ball, cricket, trap-ball,
and tip-cat. Of special interest is Strutt's theory that a medieval game
called "club ball" was the ancestor of cricket and other bat-and-ball games.
The only proof Strutt can offer that a specific pastime called "club ball"
ever existed, however, is a fourteenth-century proclamation released during the reign of Edward III that banned ball games played with the hand,
the foot, or a club. Because of this tenuous evidence, some modern historians consider the club-ball theory a disingenuous attempt by Strutt to ad-

dress the origins of bat-and-ball games for which he had no other satisfactory explanation.

Sports and Pastimes of the People of England features a full-page plate depicting illustrations of men and women playing "club ball" dating back to the fourteenth century. One of these Strutt describes as "a female figure in the action of throwing the ball to a man who elevates his bat to strike it; behind the woman at a little distance appear in the original delineation several other figures of both sexes, waiting attentively to catch or stop the ball when returned by the batsman." Strutt does not actually picture the group of fielders, explaining that the original plate was damaged and of poor quality. Strutt copied his image from a manuscript in Oxford's Bodleian Library. It turns out that the copied manuscript, *The Romance of Alexander*, was French in origin, and thus not likely to have been illustrating English club-ball. Far more startling is the fact that, while copying the image, Strutt made a significant alteration. Where he depicted a woman holding a ball in her hand, the original clearly shows that the woman is holding a jug.

Strutt's work became the authoritative reference on ball sports in both England and America in the nineteenth century. His descriptions of games such as trap-ball and tip-cat reappeared in numerous other books of the era. He describes an interesting variation of trap-ball called "Essex trap ball," which utilized a round, slender bat instead of the typical flat-faced bat. Strutt reports that this resulted in balls being hit "astonishing" distances. One of the versions of tip-cat he describes featured multiple bases with a batsman at each base. This appears to link tip-cat with the family of old-cat games that were emerging in America during the same period, with the main difference being that the former used a wooden cat while the latter used a ball.

A second edition of Strutt's work appeared in 1810, and there were numerous subsequent editions.

1801 *Youthful Recreations.* London: W. Darton and J. Harvey, 32 pp.; also, 1802 and 1810, Philadelphia: J. Johnson. A wonderful early chapbook depicting a number of children's games, it features fifteen full-page engravings, including one of trap-ball.

1801 *Youthful Sports.* London: W. Darton and J. Harvey, 36 pp.; also, 1802, Philadelphia: J. Johnson. This chapbook is similar to *Youthful Recreations* above. The American edition of 1802 contains 59 pages. This work does not include trap-ball, but in his description of cricket the author editorializes: "Bat and ball is an inferior kind of cricket, and more suitable for little children, who may safely play at it, if they will be careful not to break windows."

1804 *Youthful Sports.* London: W. Darton and J. Harvey, 47 pp. Despite its identical name and publisher, this is a completely different work from the 1801 title. This chapbook contains a series of wonderful copperplate engravings, including one of trap-ball. No American edition appeared until many years later, and when it did the copperplates had been replaced by simple woodcuts. Mahlon Day of New York produced editions in 1825 and 1830, and S. Crane, also of New York, in 1847.

1805 *The Book of Games, or, a History of Juvenile Sports: Practised at the Kingston Academy.* London: Tabart, 156 pp. This book contains a charming collection of rules and descriptions for twenty-four outdoor children's games, each accompanied by a high-quality copperplate engraving. Trap-ball and cricket are among the games included. What is particularly captivating about the presentation of the games in this book is that most of the rules are explained by means of dialogue among a returning cast of children. For example, the following is an excerpt from the book's eight-page section on trap-ball:

> Thomas: What are we to do? I have forgot what little I have heard of the game.
>
> George: Well then I will tell you; you know, of course, that when I hit the trigger, the ball flies up, and that I must then give it a good stroke with the bat. If I strike at the ball and miss my aim, or if, when I have struck it, either you or Price catch it before it has touched the ground, or if I have hit the trigger more than twice, without striking the ball, I am out and one of you take the bat, and come in, as it is called.

Additional English editions were produced in 1810 and 1812, with the subtitle changed to *A History of Juvenile Sports Practised at a Considerable Academy near London.* The 1810 edition was by the same publisher as the first edition, but the 1812 was from Richard Phillips of London. The first American edition was issued by Johnson and Warner of Philadelphia in 1811 using the "Kingston Academy" subtitle. Several additional American editions were produced in the 1820s by various publishers.

1810 *Youthful Amusements.* Philadelphia: Johnson and Warner, 47 pp. This chapbook, not to be confused with the similar titles above, describes thirty games and includes a charming engraving of trap-ball.

1811 *Remarks on Children's Play.* New York: Samuel Wood and Sons, 48 pp. This extraordinary chapbook devotes each of its pages to a separate game, sport, or activity, each accompanied by a small woodcut. The trap-ball page is especially intriguing. While the text describes typical early-nineteenth-century rules for playing the game, the illustration, although labeled "trap ball," clearly depicts a baseball scene. No trap is evident, and instead the woodcut shows a pitcher delivering the ball to a waiting batter, with a catcher positioned close behind. A fielder also stands at the ready. Subsequent editions were issued in 1812, 1814, 1816, 1817, and 1819, as well as an undated edition from about 1820.

1815 *Taschenbuch für das Jahr 1815 der Liebe und Freundschaft*, by Johann Stephan Schütze. Frankfurt am Main: Friedrich Wilmans, 298 pp. This "almanac of love and friendship" was one of a series that was issued annually. The book celebrates each month of the year with a poem or story, accompanied by an illustration. For April it features a wonderfully whimsical copperplate engraving of children in a field dancing around and playing a bat-and-ball game. On one side of the image, a whole troop of younger kids parade out of a nearby school, bats in hand, ready to join the game. There is only one known library copy in the United States.

ca. 1815 *Les Jeux des jeunes garçons, représentés par un grand nombre d'estampes* (Games of young boys, represented by a great number of prints). Paris: Chez Nepveu, Libraire, 4th ed., 95 pp. According to Robert W. Henderson, this book "holds the distinction of being the first book, so far located, to contain the printed rules of a bat and ball base-running game."[6] The game he refers to — *la balle empoisonée* — was unquestionably a variant of early baseball and was similar in some respects to the description of *das englische Base-ball* that appeared in the 1796 book *Spiele zur Uebung und Erholung*. While it is clear that Henderson was unaware of the earlier German book, there is no doubt that *Les Jeux des jeunes garçons* is a significant work. It contains rules and descriptions of numerous children's games and pastimes, accompanied by twenty-four poems and charming aquatint engravings.

The earliest known copies of this book are undated and labeled *Quatrième édition*. Henderson believed these dated to about 1815. Fifth and sixth editions appeared in the early 1820s with a different set of engravings. There are no known copies of any earlier editions.

La balle empoisonée (poisoned ball) was a game with two methods of play. One variety involved rolling a ball into holes similar to the old game of nine holes. The second variety is more familiar, featuring batting, fielding, and base running. The number of bases was fixed at four, unlike some of the other early versions of baseball, which employed five bases or a variable number. Base runners could be retired by being struck with a thrown ball, which was a universal feature of early baseball-like pastimes. A team was allotted only one out per at-bat, similar to *das englische Baseball*. Another similarity was the quirky rule that allowed a batting team, after being retired, to retain its at-bat by retrieving the ball and then striking one of the fielding team players before they had left the field. The author of *Les Jeux des jeunes garçons* observes that the game works best if played in an enclosed court, complaining that in an open field "it is inconvenient to have to run too far to field the ball, and the team at bat is apt to have too long an innings."

Extant copies of *Les Jeux des jeunes garçons* vary as to their illustrations of *la balle empoisonée*. The fifth edition shows the roll-the-ball-in-a-hole version of the game. The sixth edition has no illustration at all. The fourth edition portrays the baseball-like variation, picturing a batter standing at home plate attempting to swat a pitched ball with his bare hand. This raises the question whether a bat was employed in the game. Henderson defines *la balle empoisonée* as a bat-and-ball pastime. The French text is ambiguous on the point, simply stating that the batter "repels" the ball. While it is possible that the illustrator was in error, it is far more likely that the game simply did not use a bat, as in the early form of baseball illustrated in *A Little Pretty Pocket-Book* in the eighteenth century. On the other hand, a later German book, *Jugendspiele zur Erholung und Erheiterung*, published in 1845, describes another game called *der Giftball* as identical to *la balle empoisonée*. The illustration of *der Giftball* pictures a bat.

1816 *Talisman des Glückes oder der Selbstlehrer für alle Karten- Schach- Billard-, Ball- und Kegel-Spiele* (Lucky charm, or self-instructor for all card, chess, billiard, ball, and bowling games), by Christian Gottfried Flittner von Düben. Berlin: Societäts-Buchhandlung. Gambling and card games are the main attractions in this large and diverse collection of games and activities. It also covers chess, billiards, and bowling and has a small section on ball games. Included in the latter is the same detailed description of *das deutsche Ballspiel* (the German ballgame) that was originally published in *Spiele zur Uebung und Erholung* in 1796.

1817 *The Gaping, Wide-mouthed, Waddling Frog: A new and entertaining game of questions and commands*. London: E. and J. Wallis, 16 leaves. This chapbook features a clever rhyming riddle game. The answer to one of the riddles itemizes a list of people and objects, with the number of each incremented by one in sequence (similar to what "my true love gave to me" in "The Twelve Days of Christmas"). Among this list are "Fourteen Boys at bat-and-ball, some short and some tall." The book also contains fifteen hand-colored illustrations, including one portraying a game of trap-ball that includes a batter, a trap, and half a dozen boys standing ready in the field. A second edition published in London by Dean and Munday appeared circa 1820.

1818 *Northanger Abbey and Persuasion*, by Jane Austen. London: John Murray, 631 pp. In *Northanger Abbey*, Austen's first novel (drafted between 1798 and 1799, though not published until 1818), she writes: "It was not very wonderful that Catherine, who had by nature nothing heroic about her, should prefer cricket, base ball, riding on horseback, and running about the country at the age of fourteen, to books." This is the first reference to baseball cited in the *Oxford English Dictionary*, whose editors chose to ignore the earlier *A Little Pretty Pocket-Book*. *Northanger Abbey* was released initially as the first two volumes of a four-volume set that also included the novel *Persuasion*.

1820 *Children's Amusements*. New York and Baltimore: Samuel Wood and Sons, 30 pp. Of the pre-1830 chapbooks covering games and pastimes, this stands above the rest in quality and content. The author clearly reveled in the joys of childhood pleasure, as signaled by the couplet on the title page that reads: "When school is over for the day, / The sprightly boys run off to play." The book describes many games and activities, most accompanied by masterful engravings by the woodcut pioneer Alexander Anderson. Of central importance is the first appearance of the landmark woodcut "Playing Ball," which depicts a pitcher serving the ball to a batter, with several other children waiting in the field.

The pages measure 4 inches by 5 inches, larger than most chapbooks of the era. It is somewhat unusual that more space and detail are devoted to "playing ball" than to cricket, which at the time was a more established game. The illustration of "playing ball" fills one full page and bears the caption: "With bat and ball some boys we find, / T' amuse themselves are much inclin'd." The following text appears on the facing page:

> Playing ball is much practised by school boys, and is an excellent exercise to unbend the mind and restore to the body that elasticity and spring which the close application to sedentary employment in their studies within doors, has a tendency to clog, dull or blunt. But when practised as is the common method, with a club or bat, great care is necessary, as some times sad accidents have happened, by its slipping from the hand, or hitting some of their fellows. We would therefore, recommend Fives as a safer play, in which the club is not

used and which is equally good for exercise. The writer of this, beside other sad hurts which he has been witness of in the use of
clubs, knew a youth who had his skull broke badly with one, and it
nearly cost him his life.

The 1820 edition and an 1822 edition are both extremely rare.

ca. 1820 *Juvenile Recreations*. London: Hodgson, 12 leaves. Engaging book of
games and pastimes illustrated by hand-colored woodcuts. A charming
engraving of trap-ball is followed by these lines:

Then Master Batt he did decide,

That they might one & all,

Since Rosebud fields were very wide,

Just play Trap bat & ball,

Agreed said all with instant shout,

Then beat the little ball about.

ca. 1820 *Juvenile Sports or Youth's Pastimes*. London: R. Miller, 12 pp. A small
children's chapbook containing beautiful hand-colored woodcut engravings. On one page an illustration of trap-ball is followed by a little verse:

With bat and trap, the Youth's agre'd

To send the ball abroad with speed,

While eager with his open hands,

To catch him out his playmate stands.

1820 *School-boys' Diversions: Describing Many New and Popular Sports; with
Proper Instructions for Engaging in Them*. London: A. K. Newman; also,
Dean and Munday, 54 pp. A cute little book that describes numerous
games and activities. Its description of trap-ball is accompanied by a woodcut that shows a trap and bat in the foreground. Each publisher dates its
edition April 1820 on the title page, but Dean and Munday also identifies
theirs as the second edition.

1821 *Letters of Mary Lepel, Lady Hervey*. London: John Murray, 332 pp. Lady
Hervey was a beautiful and witty royal courtier in eighteenth-century England. At a young age she became maid of honor to the Princess of Wales,
and, after her marriage, remained devoted to the royal family. During her
lifetime she became acquainted with many leading intellectuals of the era
including Alexander Pope, Voltaire, and Horace Walpole. She was an active correspondent, and her collected letters were published in book form
in 1821. One of these, dated November 14, 1748, reveals the following
about the family of the then-current Prince of Wales: "The Prince's family
is an example of innocent and cheerful amusements. All this last summer
they played abroad; and now, in the winter, in a large room, they divert

themselves at base-ball, a play all who are, or have been, schoolboys, are well acquainted with. The ladies, as well as gentlemen, join in this amusement." This 1748 example is only the second known mention of the word "base-ball."

1821 *Little Ditties for Little Children*, by Nancy Sproat. New York: Samuel Wood and Sons, 23 pp. This children's book is filled with numerous woodcuts and poems. On one page is an illustration of three children getting ready to play with bat and ball, with the following verse underneath:

How bright is the morning, how fair is the day,
Come on little Charley, come with me and play
And yonder is Billy, I'll give him a call,
Do you take the bat, and I'll carry the ball.
But we'll make it a rule to be friendly and clever
Even if we are beat, we'll be pleasant as ever,
'Tis foolish and wicked to quarrel in play,
So if any one's angry, we'll send him away.

1823 *Good Examples for Boys.* New York: Mahlon Day, 30 pp. A cute chapbook that conveys moral lessons for children. The book's first tale is the apocryphal George Washington–cherry tree story, which had been dreamed up by Parson Weems in 1806. It is followed by a similar story about a boy who decided to play fungo with a bat and ball *inside* his house, in a room with a looking glass! Of course, he breaks the mirror and then confesses to his father, who promptly forgives him because he told the truth. The tale is illustrated with a nice woodcut showing the boy with bat in hand getting ready to slam the ball into the mirror. The 1823 edition is extremely rare. The publisher reissued a slightly modified version of the book under the name *Good Examples for Children* in 1828.

1823 *New York Primer, or Second Book.* New York: Samuel Wood, 33 pp. This is an early children's reader with paper covers. Gracing the back page is a reprint of the wonderful woodcut "Playing Ball" that first appeared in *Children's Amusements* 1820. Many editions of this work were published, but the baseball woodcut apparently appeared only in the 1823 version.

1823 *Suffolk Words and Phrases*, by Edward Moor. Woodbridge, England: J. Loder for R. Hunter, 525 pp. This work contains the passage: "We have [in Suffolk] . . . a great variety of games, active and sedentary. . . . Omitting games so universal as Cricket, Leap-frog, Marbles, etc., we have . . . Bandy, bandy-wicket, Base-ball, Bandy-ball, Bubble-hole . . . Foot ball, Hocky, Nine holes . . . " and so on through a long list of names.

1824 *Juvenile Pastimes or Sports for the Four Seasons.* London: Dean and Munday, 16 pp. This beautiful, paper-covered children's book features thirty engravings with original hand-coloring. The book depicts a variety of games, each accompanied by a snippet of verse and an illustration. These include cricket and "trap and ball." The cricket verse reads: "Cricket's the noblest game of all, / That can be play'd with bat and ball." For trap-ball, the lines are: "This is a pleasing, healthy sport, / To which most boys with glee resort." Both are illustrated by lovely colorful images featuring boys holding bats in a very baseball-like style. The 1824 London edition is particularly rare. Publishers in the United States decided to divide the already small book into two tinier volumes, Parts I and II, each devoted to two of the four seasons. These were published in 1828 and 1832 by Morgan and Yeager of Philadelphia and Marshall and Hammond in Providence. Bibliographies of children's literature referencing this work suggest that it was an original American imprint, but analysis of the book's content, as well as the discovery of the earlier London edition, confirm its English derivation.

1824 *Our Village*, by Mary Russell Mitford. London: R. Gilbert, 292 pp.; also, 1828, 1st American ed., New York: E. Bliss. In one passage of this novel Mitford observes: "Better than playing with her doll, better even than baseball, or sliding or romping, does she like to creep of an evening to her father's knee." This early literary reference to baseball provides additional confirmation that in England it was a game for both boys and girls.

1825 *Picture of the Manners, Customs, Sports and Pastimes of the Inhabitants of England from the Arrival of the Saxons Down to the Eighteenth Century*, by Jehoshaphat Aspin. London: J. Harris, 296 pp. Just as the title promises, the book focuses primarily on pageants and tournaments, secondarily on field sports. Regarding the history of ball sports, Aspin repeats the theory first advanced by Joseph Strutt in *Sports and Pastimes of the People of England* that an ancient pastime called "club ball" was the ancestor of other bat-and-ball games.[7] Aspin published a virtually identical book in 1835 under the title *Ancient Customs, Sports, Pastimes of the English*, containing the same section on ball games.

ca. 1825 *Sports and Pastimes for Children.* Baltimore: F. Lucas, Jr., 14 pp. A wonderful chapbook which associates a children's pastime with each letter of the alphabet. For some reason, however, the pastimes have no relationship to the letters they are matched with. For example, next to the letter "D" is a cricket illustration (which, if not for the presence of a wicket, more closely resembles a baseball scene). Next to the letter "F" is "Trap and

Ball", which also is illustrated. The cricket and trap-ball scenes are both accompanied by the same brief little verses that appeared the previous year in *Juvenile Pastimes or Sports for the Four Seasons*. The illustrations in the two books are different, however.

1827 *Manuel complet des jeux de société* (Complete manual of social games), by Elisabeth Celnart. Paris: Roret, 403 pp. This work offers an encyclopedic presentation of the games and pastimes of French children of the era. Two pages describe *la balle empoisonée* (poisoned ball), the baseball-like game first referenced in *Les Jeux des jeunes garçons*, ca. 1815. The description of the game in *Manuel complet* is virtually identical to that of the earlier book, and it is evident that Celnart borrowed the passage. A number of subsequent editions appeared between 1830 and 1867, including one in Spanish in 1839. There are no illustrations.

1827 *Philosophy in Sport Made Science in Earnest, Being an Attempt to Illustrate the First Principles of Natural Philosophy by the Aid of the Popular Toys and Sports of Youth*, by J. A. Paris. London: Longman, Rees, Orme, Brown, and Green, 3 vols., 837 pp. The title is a mouthful, but it neatly sums up the purpose of the book. The work includes a wonderfully detailed illustration showing the construction of a trap used in trap-ball. Various publishers released many editions of this book on both sides of the Atlantic, with the first American version appearing in 1847.

1828 *The Boy's Own Book; a Complete Encyclopedia of All the Diversions, Athletic, Scientific, and Recreative, of Boyhood and Youth*, by William Clarke. London: Vizetelly, Branston, 2d ed., 462 pp.; also, 1829, 1st American ed., Boston: Monroe and Francis. This book contains the first printed description in English of a bat-and-ball base-running game played on a diamond. The game was called rounders, but as Robert W. Henderson has commented in *Ball, Bat, and Bishop*, "The fact that the name 'rounders' was selected, instead of the earlier name 'base-ball', indicates that the former name was in more general use about the year 1829 [sic]".[8] Clarke's description of rounders was not included in his first edition, but was added as part of an expanded second edition, which, like the first, was issued in 1828. In the mid-1830s variations of this same rounders description reappeared in three American children's books. In two of those, the game was renamed as "'base' or 'goal ball.'" In the third it was called "base ball."

The Boy's Own Book served as a central piece of evidence in Henderson's historic refutation of the Doubleday Myth in 1939. Henderson proved that Doubleday couldn't have invented baseball in 1839 by demonstrating that rules for a baseball-like game had been published a decade earlier.[9]

Boys in England and the United States made *The Boy's Own Book* one of the most popular titles of its era because it offered rules and descriptions for hundreds of games and activities, including baseball's cousins "trap, bat and ball," "tip-cat," and "northern spell." The pivotal second English edition is extremely rare, with only a handful of copies known to exist. According to Henderson, the book "ran through seven editions by 1832, twenty by 1849, and netted the publishers £600 a year for many years."[10] American editions were nearly as numerous and continued to appear through the 1880s. In at least one later English edition (1849), the shape of the playing field reverted from a four-base diamond to a five-base pentagon configuration, while the American editions continued to describe rounders with four bases.

ca. 1830 *Juvenile Pastimes in Verse*. New York: Mahlon Day. This small chapbook presents several popular games by means of poetry and woodcut engravings. It includes a nice illustration of trap-ball. There was also an 1847 edition issued by S. M. Crane in New York.

ca. 1830 *My Father*. New York: Mahlon Day. A tiny chapbook that displays a woodcut on the back cover of a boy hitting a ball with a bat inside his house. This was the same illustration that appeared in 1823 in *Good Examples for Boys*, by the same publisher. There is no reference to the picture in the book.

ca. 1830 *Sports of Childhood*. Northampton MA: E. Turner, 18 pp. This chapbook features numerous woodcuts of games and sports. One with the caption "trap ball" portrays the same baseball-like scene that first appeared in *Remarks on Children's Play*, 1811. Publisher Sidney Babcock of New Haven produced a similarly titled chapbook in 1840 (*The Sports of Childhood; or Pastimes of Youth*), but its content is different and it lacks the baseball woodcut.

1831 *Festivals, Games, and Amusements*, by Horatio Smith. New York: J. and J. Harper, 355 pp. This work spans a broad spectrum of subjects ranging from folk dancing to the games of ancient Olympia. Initially published in England by Henry Colburn and Richard Bentley in 1831, the book focuses exclusively on "old world" traditions. To augment the first American edition published that same year, however, Samuel Woodworth of New York contributed several appendices describing holiday traditions in the United States and the growing popularity of games in various regions of the new country. He included the following statement: "The games and amusements of New England are similar to those of other sections of the United States. The young men are expert in a variety of games at ball — such as cricket, base, cat, football, trap ball . . . " This is the first known book reference to "base ball" in which the venue of play is clearly situated in the United States. Subsequent editions of this book were published in both England and America throughout the 1830s.

1832 *The Child's Own Book*. Boston: Munroe and Francis, 4 parts, 64 pp. each part, 256 in total. This is an elementary spelling and reading book issued by the same publisher that produced the first American edition of *The Boy's Own Book*. Other than the similar title, however, this work is entirely different from the earlier book. In part four of *The Child's Own Book*, two ball games are pictured and briefly described. Cricket is given the greater attention of the two, with a large engraving and interesting write-up that includes a commentary about a woman passing out fruit to the players. The second example features a small woodcut showing boys playing a bat-and-ball game in front of a school. The attached text reads: "This picture is intended to represent the Franklin school house in Boston. It is now recess time, and some lads are playing at ball on the green lawn before the portico of the brick building."

1832 *Easy Lessons; or, Leading Strings to Knowledge*, by Sarah Trimmer. Boston: Monroe and Francis, 223 pp. This children's story book includes a three-page tale entitled "Playing at Trap Ball." In it, a first-person narrator explains the order of the game to two other children and admonishes them to play fairly by measuring the length of their hits very accurately. It includes a simple illustration of a trap. This work is undoubtedly of English origin, but I have not been able to identify its original year of publication.

1832 *Mary's Book of Sports*. New Haven: S. Babcock, 8 pp. This is the first in a series of chapbooks issued by the New Haven publisher Sidney Babcock that feature the same simple but accurately rendered woodcut of boys playing baseball. The timeless image shows one player pitching a ball underhanded to an awaiting batter, with a fielder and base runner arrayed behind them. The engraving was the handiwork of the artist Alexander Anderson; it found its way into at least ten other chapbook titles over the following ten years. In *Mary's Book of Sports* the woodcut bears the title "Playing at Ball" and is followed by the following brief message, whose supercilious tone must have annoyed the book's juvenile readers:

What! more boys at play! I should not think you could see to play. Oh, it is too late to play at ball my lads. The sun has set. The birds have gone to roost. It is time for you to seek your homes. Get up early in the morning. Then say your prayers, and ask to be led in the way of good boys.

There were also 1833 and 1834 editions of *Mary's Book of Sports*.

1832 *William Johnson; or, The Village Boy*, New Haven: S. Babcock, 24 pp. This chapbook features the *Mary's Book of Sports* baseball woodcut on its title page. The image has nothing whatsoever to do with the story.

1833 *The Easy Reader; or Introduction to the National Preceptor*, by J. Olney. New Haven: Durrie and Peck, 144 pp. An early children's reader that features an illustration of boys playing a bat-and-ball game. Three of the players in the image are shown attempting to catch a fly ball, while a fourth holds a strange looking curved bat. The woodcut appears in the book twice, on the cover and on an inside page.

1833 *The Field Book; or, Sports and Pastimes of the British Islands*, by William Maxwell. London: Effingham Wilson, 616 pp. Typical of most English books devoted to "field" or "rural" sports during the era, this work dwells primarily on fishing, horses, hunting, and other blood sports. Within its short section on cricket, however, the author issues a criticism of theories raised by the historian Joseph Strutt in *Sports and Pastimes of the People of England*, published in 1801. Maxwell scoffs at Strutt's comments that cricket originated from the ancient game of "club ball," and that the game of trap-ball predated both of these. Maxwell states that cricket is far older than Strutt acknowledged, and adds: "The game of club-ball appears to be none other than the present, well-known bat-and-ball, which, with similar laws and customs prescribed in the playing at it, was doubtless anterior to trap-ball. The trap, indeed, carries with it an air of refinement in the 'march of mechanism.'" Maxwell suggests that a primitive rural game similar to tip-cat was actually the ancestor of cricket, a game that used a single stick for a wicket, another stick for a bat and a short three-inch stick for the ball. He is probably alluding to the game of cat and dog, which other historians have credited as one of cricket's progenitors.

1833 *The Picture Exhibition*. New Haven: S. Babcock, 24 pp. This chapbook — not the same book as an identically titled English work from the same time period — is one of those containing the *Mary's Book of Sports* baseball woodcut.

1833 *The Picture Reader; Designed as a First Reading Book, for Young Masters and Misses*. New Haven: S. Babcock, 48 pp. This small children's primer includes a reduced-size version of the Alexander Anderson baseball woodcut that had appeared in *Mary's Book of Sports*. Babcock also released an undated edition of this work, which was followed by an 1844 edition by William T. Truman of Cincinnati and an 1850 edition by Wm. N. Wiatt of Philadelphia.

1833 *A Pleasing Toy for Girl or Boy.* New York: Mahlon Day, 8 pp. This tiny chapbook of children's pastimes features a football woodcut on its cover. Inside is an illustration of boys playing trap-ball followed by this short verse:

> Who'll play at Ball
> I, says Jack Hall,
> I am nimble and tall,
> I'll play at Ball.
>
> Here is Jack Hall,
> With his Bat and Ball.

1833 *Stories for Emma; or Scripture Sketches.* New Haven: S. Babcock, 24 pp. A chapbook that displays a tiny baseball woodcut on its front wrap.

1833 *Watts' Divine and Moral Songs.* New York: Mahlon Day, 16 pp. Tucked into this chapbook of moral poems is an interesting woodcut portraying boys playing a slightly ambiguous bat-and-ball game that is possibly baseball. A pitcher is shown getting ready to serve the ball to a batter. Another boy waiting his turn stands nearby with bat in hand. Two other boys are in the field. A goal in the ground near the batter might be a wicket, but it more closely resembles an early baseball goal such as the type pictured in *A Little Pretty Pocket-Book.* Subsequent editions of this work were published by Mahlon Day in 1834 and 1836. Dr. Watts's moral songs were reproduced by many publishers in both England and the United States over the course of a century following the author's death in 1748. These works were of various lengths and sizes, but, to the best of my knowledge, only the sixteen-page chapbooks from Mahlon Day contain the baseball woodcut.

1833 *The Young Florist; or Conversations on the Culture of Flowers and on Natural History,* by Joseph Breck. Boston: Russell, Odiorne, 68 pp. This book is all about flowers, but it also, for no discernible reason, contains a lovely engraving of boys playing baseball. The image depicts a pitcher throwing overhand to a batter, who holds a slightly crooked bat, with a catcher standing behind. No references to baseball are found in the text.

1834 *The Book of Sports,* by Robin Carver. Boston: Lilly, Wait, Colman, and Holden, 164 pp. This is one of the crown jewels of early baseball books because it contains the first description in English of a game identified as baseball, specifically "'base' or 'goal ball.'" The children's author Robin

Carver set out to create a work of sports and activities for children that was both accessible and affordable. In his preface he states: "For a portion of my materials . . . I have been indebted to the English edition of *The Boy's Own Book*, the price of which work places it beyond the reach of most young people in this country."

For his description of baseball, Carver borrows almost verbatim the rules for rounders first published six years earlier in *The Boy's Own Book*. In introducing the sport, however, he makes the following distinction: "This game is known under a variety of names. It is sometimes called 'round ball.' But I believe that 'base' or 'goal ball' are the names generally adopted in our country." This marks the first time that the name "base ball" was associated with a diamond-shaped infield configuration. Carver's *The Book of Sports* also marks the first appearance of a uniquely American illustration of baseball, a woodcut showing boys playing the game on the Boston Common. This scene was reproduced in several other books over the following decade. *The Book of Sports* is prized by collectors as a great American rarity, with only about a dozen copies known to exist.

1834 *The Complete Farmer and Rural Economist*, by Thomas G. Fessenden. Boston: Lilly, Wait, and Company, and George C. Barrett, 374 pp. Yes, this book is all about farming. But it was issued in the same year and by the same publisher as the above-described *Book of Sports*, and accordingly it features a full-page advertisement for the works of Robin Carver. *The Book of Sports* is the focus of the ad, which reproduces the woodcut of boys playing baseball on the Boston Common. The ad also includes a number of testimonials to the virtues of *The Book of Sports* that had appeared in various periodicals. *The Complete Farmer* went through a number of subsequent editions by various publishers, but the advertisement only appears in its first edition of 1834.

1834 *Deutsches A B C- und Bilder-Buch für Kinder* (German ABC and picture book for children). Cincinnati: Truman, Smith, 34 pp. This German-language chapbook contains the same popular baseball woodcut that first appeared in *Mary's Book of Sports* in 1832.

1835 *The Boy's Book of Sports; a Description of the Exercises and Pastimes of Youth*. New Haven: S. Babcock, 24 pp. Along with Robin Carver's *Book of Sports*, published a year earlier, this simple chapbook is considered one of the two most historically important American baseball books to come forward in the first half of the nineteenth century. While the Carver book describes a game called " 'base,' or 'goal ball,' " *The Boy's Book of Sports* takes the further step of calling it "base ball." In appearance, the chapbook is similar to other children's offerings of the era, small in size with paper covers and illustrated throughout by woodcut engravings. In introducing a section entitled "Games at Ball," the editor writes that there are a great number of games, "but the limits of our book will only allow us to describe the most common." That the first game he lists is "base ball" confirms that the pastime was already quite popular by 1835. The book's actual description of "base ball" is based on the one in *The Book of Sports* from 1834. The editor of *The Boy's Book of Sports* makes some significant modifications, however, in addition to the change in name. He updates and clarifies the rules for playing, including the noteworthy change of reversing the direction of base running from clockwise to counterclockwise. Additionally, this book introduces the first known applications of the terms "innings" and "diamond" to the game of baseball. As an added feature in the book, the editor also chose to reprint the classic illustration of boys playing baseball on the Boston Common that had first appeared in the Carver work.

In the section following "base ball," *The Boy's Book of Sports* describes another game called "drive ball." In this activity, two boys with bats face each other, taking turns fungoing the ball. When one boy hits the ball, the other has to retrieve it as quickly as he can, then fungo it back from the spot he picked it up. The idea was to advance forward by a combination of hitting the ball as far as possible past your opponent and also retrieving the opponent's ball before it could get too far behind you.

This is apparently the only known description of drive ball, a game which would be of little interest except for one small historical connection. In 1862, during the Civil War, L. N. Rosenthal, an artist from Philadelphia, created an engraving of a Union Army encampment named Camp Doubleday. The illustration depicts the headquarters of the Seventy-sixth Regiment of New York State Volunteers, who had named their camp after their highly respected commanding officer, General Abner Doubleday.[11] In the foreground of the illustration two soldiers face each other with bats, one striking a ball. Since no other players are involved, the only game that seems to correlate to the image is, in fact, drive ball. If not for Abner Doubleday's association, we would pay this little heed, but it is a matter of curiosity, if not amusement, to place baseball's legendary noninventor in such close proximity to a game involving bat and ball.

The 1835 edition of *The Boy's Book of Sports* features bright orange- or rose-colored paper covers. Only a handful of copies are known to exist. The subsequent 1838 and 1839 editions are slightly smaller in format, with dark green covers, and are also quite rare.

1835 *Boy's and Girl's Book of Sports.* Providence: Cory and Daniels, 24 pp. This is another important chapbook that reprints the rules of baseball (called "base or goal ball"), including the diamond-shaped diagram, from Carver's *The Book of Sports.* Subsequent editions by Geo. P. Daniels appeared in 1836, 1843, 1845, and 1847. There was also an 1841 edition by J. S. Hammond of Providence.

ca. 1835 *The Child's Song Book.* Cincinnati: Truman and Smith, 16 pp. This is another chapbook that features the *Mary's Book of Sports* woodcut, but unlike most of the others it was not published by Sidney Babcock of New Haven.

1835 *The First Lie, or Falsehood Its Own Punishment. Shewing the Misery Occasioned by Disobedience to Parents.* New Haven: S. Babcock, 24 pp. This is a religious chapbook produced by the American Sunday School Union. It reprints the Boston Common baseball illustration that first appeared in *The Book of Sports* in 1834 with the caption "the play ground of Mr. Watt's school."

ca. 1835 *Happy Home.* New York and Philadelphia: Turner and Fisher, 8 pp. This delightful children's chapbook features original hand-colored illustrations. A pastoral sporting scene unfolds on two facing pages, accompanied by a short selection of verse. On the first of these pages, a boy greets his mother in the foreground while two boys behind them are engaged in a game of cricket. On the following page, several children read a book while, in a field behind them, a boy pitches a ball to a waiting batter and two girls play at battledore and shuttlecock (badminton). The descriptive verse reads as follows:

At length the happy time draws near,
When George is to return,
Back to his cheerful sports and see
His parents and his home.

Next day, well pleased, they pass their time,
With books and pictures gay,
At battledore, or bat and ball,
And in the garden play.

ca. 1835 *Rose of Affection.* New York and Philadelphia: Turner and Fisher, 8 pp. This cute little chapbook features a woodcut engraving of boys playing with bat and ball captioned by an equally charming snippet of verse. The illustration ostensibly pictures a game of trap-ball, based upon the presence of a trap, but it also appears to depict one boy pitching to another, as in baseball. The batter is armed with a short, one-handed bat. The accompanying verse reads as follows:

With a bound, see the ball go,
Now high in the air as hit it just so,
No catch is Jo.; oh, how he lingers,
He'll soon have the name of old butter fingers.

Of interest here is the author's use of the term "butter fingers." The *Oxford English Dictionary* cites usage of the phrase as early as the year 1615 to denote a clumsy person, but its appearance in *Rose of Affection* in 1836 may have been the first time it was applied to a player prone to fumble a ball in a ball game. Not long thereafter, however, Charles Dickens employed the term, using it to characterize a clumsy cricket player in his 1837 novel *The Pickwick Papers*.

1835 *Sports of Youth; a Book of Plays*. New Haven: S. Babcock, 8 pp. A miniature chapbook which describes several children's games. One page entitled "playing ball" features the same baseball woodcut that had appeared in *Mary's Book of Sports*. A description under the image reads: "One of them stands ready to toss the ball — one to knock it, and two to run after it, if they fail to catch it." There was also an 1838 edition.

1835 *Two Short Stories, for Little Girls and Boys*. New Haven: S. Babcock, 16 pp. This chapbook is another that includes the baseball woodcut from *Mary's Book of Sports*.

1836 *Die reinste Quelle jugendlicher Freuden, oder 300 Spiele zur Ausbildung des Geistes, kräftigung des körpers und zur geselligen Erheiterung im Freien wie im Zimmer* (The purest source of juvenile joy, or 300 games for the training of the spirit, strengthening of the body, and companionable amusement outdoors and in), by Johann A. L. Werner. Dresden and Leipzig: Arnoldi, 228 pp. This onmibus collection of three hundred games and sports is notably unoriginal. The editor, Herr Werner, borrows liberally from the contributions of earlier authors, in particular J. C. F. Gutsmuths. Of greatest interest is Werner's reprinting of the earliest rules for baseball, which he calls *Ball mit Freistätten*. Gutsmuths had first published the same rules forty years earlier under the name *Ball mit Freystäten (oder das englische Base-ball)*. The primary difference between the two renditions, other than the modernized spelling of the word *Freistätten*, is that Werner did not use the phrase *englische Base-ball* throughout the text, as had Gutsmuths. At the end of his description, however, Werner acknowledges: "This game originates by way of England, where it bears the name base-ball, and is played there very frequently." Werner's book, printed in the older gothic

German typeface, also includes many of the other ball games that Gutsmuths had described years earlier. Among these is baseball's German cousin *das deutsche Ballspiel* (the German ball game), as well as Gutsmuths's suggested hybrid of the two sports, which he refers to as "the German-English ball game."

1836 *Little Lessons for Little Learners*. New Haven: S. Babcock, 16 pp. This chapbook includes a woodcut with a scene of trap-ball in the background. There were also 1837 and 1839 editions.

1837 *Female Robinson Crusoe, A tale of the American Wilderness*. New York: Jared W. Bell, 286 pp. This book purported to be an account of the travels of a teenage girl, Lucy Ford, who was lost somewhere in the American wilderness. While almost certainly fictitious, the book contains an intriguing description of a ball game played by Indians. The "witness" to the game is a young boy, also lost, who is a captive of the Indians. The activity resembles baseball and may be the first published American portrayal of a bat-and-ball base-running game that was truly original and not a reworking of the description of the game rounders that first appeared in the second London edition of *The Boy's Own Book* in 1828.

1837 *Games and Sports; Being an Appendix to Manly Exercises and Exercises for Ladies*, by Donald Walker. London: 369 pp. This work focuses primarily on gymnastic exercises but also contains a short description of trap-ball. It includes several simple illustrations, though none of ball games.

1837 *The Jewel, or, Token of Friendship*, by Edward Gallaudet. New York: Bancroft and Holley, 246 pp. This small collection of children's stories contains what may be the earliest known reference to the legendary game one-old-cat. The following sentence appears on page 90 in a story entitled "The Barlow Knife": "Just then, two of his playmates coming along with a ball, Dick put his knife into his pocket, and went to join them in a game of '*one-old-cat*.'" The brief mention in this story is noteworthy because, despite the game's reputed popularity during the first decades of the nineteenth century, no other reference to the name can be found before 1850. One-old-cat was a form of scrub baseball that required as few as three players and may have been played in America as early as the colonial era. It descended from a family of "cat" games played in England; in these games, instead of a ball, the object struck (the cat) was a short piece of stick.

My citation of the 1837 edition of *The Jewel* is a presumption, because no copies of that edition have been located. The one-old-cat reference appears in an 1839 edition, published in New York by R. Lockwood, and bibliographic references indicate that this edition was a direct reprint of the

1837 edition. Subsequent New York editions with a length of 248 pages each were published in 1843 and 1844 by R. P. Bixby. The book was retitled in the 1840s and 1850s as *The Juvenile Forget-Me-Not*. It should be noted, however, that the titles *The Jewel, or, Token of Friendship* and *The Juvenile Forget-Me-Not* were both popularly applied to a variety of children's books during the mid-nineteenth century, yet only those containing the story "The Barlow Knife" had the reference to one-old-cat.

1838 *Home as Found*, by James Fenimore Cooper. Philadelphia: Lea and Blanchard. In this, one of Cooper's lesser-known novels, the author describes a dispute between a homeowner and a group of young workers who are playing a game of ball on his lawn. Although Cooper does not provide enough detail to establish firmly that the game is baseball, it is not unreasonable to reach such a conclusion based upon the few particulars he does furnish. These include the facts that the ball is "struck," that the game can be suitably played on either a lawn or in the street, and that there is a tendency to lose balls in the shrubbery. The locale of this incident is also noteworthy. The lot on which the disputed game transpired is situated in the fictional village of Templeton near the shore of Lake Otsego in New York State. Cooper clearly modeled Templeton after Cooperstown, the mythical birthplace of baseball. The author grew up there, and Cooperstown takes its name from his father, who founded the village. It is a curious coincidence that the date of the novel, 1838, predates by only one year the mythic invention of baseball in the same spot by Abner Doubleday.

1838 *The Poetic Gift; or Alphabet in Rhyme*. New Haven: S. Babcock, 16 pp. This chapbook includes the same baseball woodcut that first appeared in *Mary's Book of Sports* in 1832. There were also 1840, 1842, 1844, and undated editions.

1838 *The Youth's Encyclopædia of Health: with Games and Play Ground Amusements*, by W. Montague. London: W. Emans, 490 pp. Identified on its front cover simply as *The Book of Amusement*, this work is a large, excellent, and unusual anthology of children's games. Its primary distinction is that the author provides original text for all the games described, whereas most similar books of the period cloned or rewrote text from earlier titles. *The Youth's Encyclopædia* includes a short but detailed description of trapball that paid particular attention to all the ways in which a batter could be put out.

A more unusual aspect of the book is a short passage describing a game called squares, which was nearly identical to early baseball and rounders. The text depicts four bases laid out as a square, although it is ambiguous as to whether home plate was one of the four bases or a separate location. The bases are described as being a "considerable distance" apart, which suggests that the dimensions may have been larger than other versions of early baseball. To the best of my knowledge, this is the only instance of the name "squares" being used as a pseudonym for baseball or rounders. The author was obviously not impressed with the pastime, concluding his description with the comment: "There is nothing particular[ly] fascinating in this game."

1839 *The Saturday Magazine*. London: no. 430, March 16, 1839. A detailed article entitled "Games with a Ball" appears in this issue of the weekly English publication. Serious treatment of the subject of ball playing was highly unusual for the era, and this may have been the earliest magazine piece devoted entirely to the topic. The opening sentence reads as follows:

> There are but few exercises more delightful and invigorating than games played with a ball in the open air. Every muscle is exerted — the eye is accurately directed towards a particular spot — and the attention of all the players is fully roused. Unlike many other games, it is seldom that wrangling or churlish feelings are engendered by the course of the sport; and there can be no doubt that the physical powers are strengthened by the exercise.

I can agree generally with these words, excepting the occasional wrangling or display of churlish feelings I have witnessed. The anonymous author of this piece describes a number of ball games that were popular in England during the nineteenth century. A good portion of his material is drawn from Joseph Strutt's *Sports and Pastimes of the People of England* from 1801. He borrows Strutt's description of stool-ball, but adds: "This differs but very little from the game of *rounders* which is much played at the present day in the west of England." It is curious that the author equates rounders and stool-ball, since the former utilized a bat while Strutt's sketch of stool-ball stated that the ball was struck by the bare hand.

The article also contains standard descriptions of trap-ball, tip-cat, and a number of other games. Two woodcut engravings accompanying the text illustrate trap-ball and the mythical game of club-ball. Both are hand-copies of earlier copies made by Strutt from original medieval manuscripts.

1840 *The Book of Seasons, A Gift for the Young. Autumn*. Boston: William Crosby, 70 pp. A softbound book of children's verse that includes a frontispiece engraving of boys playing an early variety of baseball. The scene depicts three players: a pitcher, a fielder, and a striker standing ready with a short, one-handed bat.

1840 *The Child's Own Story Book, or Simple Tales.* New Haven: S. Babcock. One of the woodcuts in this chapbook shows a scene of trap-ball in the background. There were also 1842 and undated editions.

1840 *An Encyclopædia of Rural Sports,* by Delabere P. Blaine. London: Longman, Orme, Brown, and Longmans, 1,200 pp. This thick book is an exactingly detailed study of field sports, mostly hunting. It contains a tiny section on ball games, including this sentence on page 131: "There are few of us of either sex but have engaged in base-ball since our majority." This confirms prior indications that early baseball in England was a pastime practiced by both genders.

ca. 1840 *Juvenile Melodies.* New York and Philadelphia: Turner and Fisher, 8 pp. A larger-format chapbook whose content is similar to that of *Rose of Affection* from 1835. This includes the woodcut showing a baseball-like game and the verse containing the reference to "butter fingers."

1840 *The School Reader, First Book,* by Charles W. Sanders. New York: Mark H. Newman, 118 pp.; also, a slightly modified edition, 120 pp., was issued later in 1840 simultaneously by the following: New York: Ivison and Phinney; Chicago: S. C. Griggs; Buffalo: Phinney; Cazenovia NY: Crandall and Moseley; Auburn NY: J. C. Ivison; Detroit: A. M'Farren; Cincinnati: William H. Moore. The cover illustration of this primer shows two boys playing with bat and ball amid a schoolyard scene. Subsequent editions of the book feature the same illustration on inside pages, including an 1846 printing that shows the playground scene captioned and described in the German language.

ca. 1840 *The Spring of Knowledge or the Alphabet Illustrated.* Mark's Edition, Smithfield (London): J. L. Marks, 16 pp. This larger-format ABC chapbook places a quality engraving next to each letter of the alphabet. Pictured below the letter "R" is a smartly attired young man, complete with ruffled collar, hitting a ball with a bat. A trap appears on the ground between his feet. The caption reads: "Master Richard with his ball and bat." This is an extremely rare title.

1840 *The Village Green; or Sports of Youth.* New Haven: S. Babcock, 8 pp. This relatively common miniature chapbook of children's games features the same well-used baseball woodcut that first appeared in *Mary's Book of Sports* in 1832. In *The Village Green* it is accompanied by the following verse:

Now ascends the favorite ball;
High it rises in the air,

Or against the cottage wall,
Up and down it bounces there.

Now a knock, and swift it flies
O'er the plain the troop are flying,
Joy is sparkling in their eyes,
As to catch it all are trying.

There was also an edition in 1843 and others that were undated.

1841 *The Every Boy's Book, a Compendium of All the Sports and Recreations of Youth*, by J. L. Williams. London: Dean and Munday, 448 pp. This excellent book contains rules for hundreds of children's pastimes, including detailed accounts of three early variations of baseball: feeder, rounders, and a German cousin, ball-stock (ball-stick in English). Some aspects of these are noteworthy. For one, rounders is described differently than in *The Boy's Own Book* thirteen years earlier. Instead of a four-base diamond-shaped infield, it now had five bases laid out as a pentagon. In addition, base runners ran counterclockwise, as in modern baseball. *The Every Boy's Book* was a pivotal work in its era, as evidenced by the fact that its original and well-written descriptions show up regularly in other books on games published in the years to follow.

1841 *The Gift of Friendship*. New Haven: S. Babcock, 24 pp. A chapbook that includes a tiny scene of boys playing baseball on the cover.

1841 *Instruction and Amusement for the Young*. New Haven: S. Babcock, 24 pp. Another Babcock chapbook that includes a tiny scene of boys playing baseball on its cover. A poem entitled "Papa's Advice to Herbert; or Good Rules for Little Boys" appears on page 23. The third stanza reads:
When grandmamma calls,
Give up bats and balls,
And quickly your lesson begin;
Endeavor to spell,
And try to read well,
And then a good name you will win.
Further undated editions of this work were issued during the 1840s.

1841 *The School Reader, Third Book*, by Charles W. Sanders. New York: Mark H. Newman, 250 pp. This reader contains a schoolyard illustration captioned "Sports Out of School," which depicts a batter and pitcher.

1841 *The Snow-Drop: A Collection of Rhymes for the Nursery*, by Ann Gilbert and Jane Taylor. New Haven: S. Babcock, 24 pp. A chapbook that exhibits a woodcut showing a scene of trap-ball in the background. It also includes a very small baseball image among a series of children's activities pictured on the cover.

1841 *Specimens of Penmanship.* Bridgeport CT: J. B. Sanford. Printed on the cover of this simple tablet of blank writing paper is the well-known illustration of baseball on the Boston Common that first appeared in Carver's *Book of Sports* in 1834. Reissued in 1842 by E. Hunter, Middletown CT.

1842 *Cobb's New Spelling Book, in Six Parts,* by Lyman Cobb. New York: Caleb Bartlett, 168 pp., and also released shortly thereafter in 1842 by various publishers in Buffalo, Ithaca, and Cazenovia NY. An engraving on the frontispiece of this book pictures a baseball scene outside of a school building. One boy is shown getting ready to fungo a baseball to two awaiting fielders, while two other boys stand around with bats in their hands. A crowd of other boys and girls looks on.

1843 *Children at Play.* Cincinnati: William T. Truman, 16 pp. This chapbook of children's games includes a unique little woodcut depicting children playing baseball. The accompanying text reads:

> Here are some boys playing at ball. They have just come out of school, and are very eager to spend all the recess in play. Well, boys, it is a good exercise; but you must not think too much about your play while in school. Bat and ball is a very good play for the summer season.

ca. 1843 *Sports for All Seasons.* New York: T. W. Strong, 12 pp. This children's chapbook is a bit different from most in the genre. It features better-quality woodcuts and heavier paper stock than was typical and also aims at a somewhat older audience. On one page is a vignette entitled "The Accident." A woodcut depicts several children playing outside of a house, with an air-borne ball zeroing in on a window. A woman peering out of another window watches with alarm. The paragraph below reads: "Trap ball and Cricket are juvenile Field Sports, and not fit to be played near the houses, much to the annoyance of the neighbours, where it generally ends in the ball going through a window; then you find, too late; that you have been 'doing more mischief in a minute, than you can mend in a month'; after having their pocket money stopped for some time to replace the glass they had broken, they pitched their traps and wickets in a more suitable place for the game." The language and appearance of this book suggest that it may have been drawn from an earlier English work.

1844 *The Boy's Treasury of Sports, Pastimes, and Recreations,* by Samuel Williams. London, D. Bogue, 464 pp. This book is almost identical to *The*

Every Boy's Book published in 1841, including the coverage of rounders, feeder, and ball-stock. A second English edition of *The Boy's Treasury of Sports* appeared in 1847. A Philadelphia publisher, Lea and Blanchard, issued the first American edition in 1847, and additional editions by various publishers on both sides of the Atlantic appeared almost every year from 1848 to 1855.

1844 *McGuffey's Newly Revised Eclectic First Reader*, by Wm. H. McGuffey. Cincinnati: Winthrop B. Smith, 108 pp. This renowned early primer uses a simple little woodcut of boys playing baseball to illustrate a reading lesson. The accompanying text reads: "The boys play with balls. John has a bat in his hand. I can hit the ball." This baseball content does not appear in the 1836 first edition of this reader. An 1853 edition repeats the woodcut and text of the 1844 edition.

1844 *The Pictorial Elementary Spelling Book*, by Noah Webster. New York: George F. Coolidge and Brother, 168 pp. A woodcut in this work pictures a scene of children on a village green playing various games including baseball.

1845 *The History of a Day*, by Thomas Teller. New Haven: S. Babcock, 64 pp. A tiny illustration of boys playing baseball appears on the paper cover of this children's book.

1845 *Jugendspiele zur Erholung und Erheiterung* (Boys' games for recreation and amusement). Tilsit, Germany: W. Sommerfeld. 95 pp. This is a small, attractive German-language book of children's games. It includes a game called *der Giftball*, which is described as identical to the early French game of *la balle empoisonée* (see *Les Jeux des jeunes garçons*, ca. 1815). A color illustration of two boys playing *der Giftball* shows it to be a bat-and-ball game.

1845 *The Knickerbocker*, vol. 26, November 1845. New York: Peabody, pp. 426–27. It is fitting, though coincidental, that in the very year the Knickerbocker Base Ball Club was organized, a magazine of the same name yielded a reference to baseball. The publication's witty essays were meant to amuse New York's rising class of educated young merchants and professionals, although what may have passed for humor in those days now seems smug and arrogant. The baseball reference pops up in a rambling article entitled "The New Philosophy," in which the author spends several pages bemoaning how the wearing of a "tournure" distorts the grace and beauty of a woman's stride. A tournure was a type of bustle worn in the rear beneath a skirt, and the author is so aghast at its unflattering impact on a woman's gait that he uses numerous analogies to illustrate his point. Of particular interest is the following:

I scarcely ever walk down Broadway behind a lady, without being inclined to exclaim with Fulton, (when he first beheld the so-called
perpetual-motion machine,) "It is a crank motion." The truth is,
there is some mistake in the situation, or some defect in the application of the machinery. Perhaps the system of tight lacing has
something to do with the matter. . . . The motion very much resembles that of one who, in playing "base," screws his ball, as the
expression is among boys; or of a man rolling what is known among
the players of ten pins as a "screw ball."

Notwithstanding the obnoxiousness of the source, this may be the earliest
allusion to the practice of curving a baseball pitch.

1845 *The Mischievous Boy; a Tale of Tricks and Troubles*, by Thomas Teller. New
Haven: S. Babcock, 64 pp. On the cover of this chapbook are numerous
tiny engravings of children's games, including baseball.

1846 *The Every Boy's Book of Games, Sports, and Diversions, or, The Schoolboy's Manual of Amusement, Instruction, and Health*, London: G. Vickers,
546 pp. This original and unusual collection of games and pastimes is
completely different from a similarly titled book published in 1841. It includes a lengthy description of standard trap-ball and also details the rare
"Essex" version of the game first mentioned in Strutt's *Sports and Pastimes
of the People of England* in 1801.

Of greater interest and rarity is the description of rounders. It differs
from any variety of rounders described elsewhere, although it is very similar to a version of the game tip-cat first reported by Strutt. For starters, the
number of bases (actually, holes in the ground) varies from four to eight
depending upon the number of players. Also, the ball is referred to as a cat.
This might lead one to conclude that it was actually a short piece of stick
as in tip-cat, except that the final sentence of the description states that "a
smooth round stick is preferred by many boys to a bat for striking the ball."
The similarity to tip-cat also extends to the positioning of players with bats
at every base. A feeder in the field pitched to one of them, and when the
cat was hit, the batters started to run around the bases. When a defensive
player retrieved the cat, he could retire a runner who was between bases by
throwing it anywhere between the two bases, or sometimes players made
a rule that the runner had to be stuck by the ball. A "score" was gained any
time one of the base runners reached the next base successfully.

In its four-base form, this version of rounders is remarkably similar to
the American game of four-old-cat. Yes, the very game that Albert Spalding classified in 1905 as the immediate predecessor to town-ball, and

which was part of his proof that baseball could not have descended from "the English picnic game of rounders," was, at least in this one instance, identified as none other than rounders.

This version of *The Every Boy's Book* was reissued by two different London publishers in 1852, J. Kendrick and R. Grieves.

1846 *Sanders' Pictorial Primer, or, An Introduction to "Sanders' First Reader"*, by Charles W. Sanders. New York: Newman and Ivison, with simultaneous editions by other publishers in New York, Philadelphia, and Newburgh NY, 48 pp. This elementary primer reprints the same illustration of two boys playing with bat and ball in a schoolyard that first appeared in Sanders's *School Reader* in 1840. There was also an 1846 German-language edition.

1847 *The Book of Sports*. Philadelphia: Edward W. Miller, 191 pp. One of several different works bearing the same title, this example is a miniature children's book with gilt-edged pages and covered with gilt-decorated red cloth. It measures barely two by three inches. The tiny volume contains dozens of thumbnail sketches of juvenile activities, including one called "bat and ball." The simple description states that the game "is played by two parties, one throwing the ball in the air, the opposite boy tries to strike it with his bat; if he fails it counts one against the party to which he belongs, and in this manner the game is carried through." Subsequent editions of this work were issued in 1850 by Clark, Austin and Smith in New York as part of its "Tom Thumb" series, and in the same year by Peck and Bliss in Philadelphia.

1847 *Charles' Journey to France and Other Tales*, by Mrs. [Anna Leticia] Barbauld. Worcester MA: Edward Livermore, 72 pp. This small, hardcover volume of children's tales was part of the series "Uncle Thomas' Stories for Good Children." One chapter entitled "The Ball Players" features a slightly strange poem celebrating generic ball play, with obscure references to the game "fives." Illustrating the poem are several woodcuts borrowed from earlier children's books. One is a baseball scene that first appeared in *Remarks on Children's Play*, 1811, where it was mislabeled as "trap ball." In *Charles Journey to France* the trap-ball designation is dropped. Two other illustrations accompanying the poem feature cricket and fives, respectively. Immediately following the poem is a larger woodcut, also appropriated from an earlier work. The image, showing two boys, one with a bat, the other with a ball, first appeared in *Little Ditties for Little Children* in 1821. A second edition of this scarce book appeared in 1850.

1847 *A Dictionary of Archaic and Provincial Words*, by James Orchard Halliwell. London: John Russell Smith, 2 vol., 960 pp. The inclusion of the word "base-ball" in this classic early reference may have marked its inaugural appearance in a dictionary. Regrettably, the accompanying definition does not measure up to the occasion. All Halliwell bothers to say is that it is "a country game mentioned in Moor's Suffolk Words, p. 238." But baseball advocates shouldn't feel slighted because Halliwell also gives rounders scant respect, calling it simply "a boy's game at balls." The dictionary offers similarly brief definitions of several other bat-and-ball games, including tut-ball, which is defined as "a sort of stobball."

1847 *Natural History of Wiltshire*, by John Aubrey. London: J. B. Nichols and Son, 132 pp. Although apparently not published before 1847, the manuscript of this reference work was completed in 1685. According to Alice Gomme in *The Traditional Games of England, Scotland, and Ireland*, this seventeenth-century text contains the earliest description of the game of stool-ball:[12]

> It is peculiar to North Wilts, North Gloucestershire, and a little part of Somerset near Bath. They smite a ball stuffed very hard with quills and covered with soale leather, with a staffe, commonly made of withy, about three feet and a half long. Colerne Down is the place so famous and so frequented for stobball playing. The turfe is very fine and the rock (freestone) is within an inch and a halfe of the surface which gives the ball so quick a rebound. A stobball ball is of about four inches diameter and as hard as a stone.

Notwithstanding Ms. Gomme's appraisal, it is not certain whether this was actually stool-ball or another game, stow ball, which Strutt speculated might be similar to golf.

1848 *Boy's Own Book of Sports, Birds, and Animals*. New York: Leavitt and Allen, 548 pp. Probably seeking to economize, the publisher of this work combined three separate children's titles under one cover. They are, in order of placement, *The Boy's Book of Sports and Games*, *The Book of Birds*, and *The Book of Animals*. As one might expect, it is the first of these that warrants mention here. *The Boy's Book of Sports and Games*, attributed to the author "Uncle John," contains more than two hundred descriptions of children's games and activities, including rounders, trap-ball, and stool-ball. The version of rounders the book presents is generally consistent with others from the period, with perhaps a little more detail than most. It specifies the number of bases as four or five and describes a bat of only two feet in length.

The derivation of *The Boy's Book of Sports and Games* is somewhat mysterious. The book's language, references, and choice of games unmistakably establish it to be the work of an English author. Yet I find no evidence of its publication in Great Britain prior to the appearance of this New York edition. The book's American provenance is also a little confusing, given that its 1848 copyright is attributed to a Philadelphia publisher, George S. Appleton, and yet no record of an Appleton edition is found until 1851. In 1850, a 184-page solo edition of *The Boy's Book of Sports and Games* was issued by the publisher Henry Allman of London. The title page of that edition lists "Uncle Charles" as its author and bears the subtitle: *Containing Rules and Directions for the Practice of the Principal Recreative Amusements of Youth*. ("Uncle Charles" may have been the pen name for Charles D. Mallary, the author of other similar children's books.) The 1851 Philadelphia edition by George Appleton reverts to the "Uncle John" pseudonym used in 1848, but in other respects is virtually identical to the 1850 London edition.

1848 *Holiday Sports and Pastimes for Boys*, by H. D. Richardson. London: William S. Orr, 112 pp. This is a nice little collection of descriptions of games and activities for boys that was completely original in content. In the section "Games with Toys" the author offers two unique descriptions of rounders. The first of these is of a somewhat cricket-like game. A wicket of two "stumps" or sticks, with no crosspiece, was set up behind the batter, with three other stumps as corners of an equilateral triangle in front of the batter. A bowler served the ball, as in cricket, and, if the batter hit it, he attempted to touch each of the stumps in succession, as in baseball. The batter was out if he missed the ball, if the struck ball was caught on the fly, or if a fielder touched one of the stumps with the ball before a base runner reached it. It is noteworthy that this cricket-baseball hybrid did not include the practice of "soaking" or "plugging" the base runner with the thrown ball.

The book's second version of rounders is a more traditional variety, with no wicket behind the batter. It featured a home base and three others marked with sticks as in the previous version. The author distinguishes this form of rounders from the other in its use of a "pecker or feeder" rather than a "bowler." He also points out that "in this game it is sought to strike, not the wicket, but the player, and if struck with the ball while absent from one of the rounders, or posts, he is *out*." (Of all the known published descriptions of the game in the nineteenth century, this is the only one to use the term "rounders" to denote bases.) This second version of the game also featured "taking of the rounders," which elsewhere was generally known as "hitting for the rounder." This option was exercised when all members of a side but one were out, and the star player then had three pitches with which to attempt to hit a home run. If he was successful, his team retained its at-bat.

This is a small, hard-bound volume with an ornately decorated paper cover. The 1848 edition of *Holiday Sports* was apparently the only one produced.

ca. 1849 *Juvenile Pastimes; or Girls' and Boys' Book of Sports.* New Haven: S. Babcock, 16 pp. The precise publishing date of this chapbook is not certain because the title page shows 1849 while the cover shows 1850. The book contains a section called "Playing Ball," which includes the passage: "There are a great number of games played with balls, of which base-ball, trap ball, cricket, up-ball, catch ball and drive ball are most common." It contains two woodcuts of "base-ball," one showing a rudimentary scene of a game and the second "a party of ballplayers."

1850 *The Boy's Book of Sports and Games, Containing Rules and Directions for the Practice of the Principal Recreative Amusements of Youth,* by Uncle Charles. London: Henry Allman, 184 pp. Please see the particulars for this work under the 1848 title *Boy's Own Book of Sports, Birds, and Animals* listed above.

ca. 1850 *The Broken Bat; or, Harry's Lesson of Forgiveness.* Philadelphia: American Baptist Publication Society, 8 pp. This small religious chapbook conveys a moral lesson that revolves around a boy's dearest possessions: his bat and ball. The tale begins when a lad named Harry expresses resentment at being the object of another boy's spite. Harry's mother counsels him to have a more pious attitude, and Harry pledges to respond with forgiveness should a similar situation arise. His resolve is quickly tested by an assault on his precious treasures. "I've got a new ball and a new bat, too," he tells his cousin. "The bat's made of hard wood, and varnished — a real tip-top one, and the ball, covered with red morocco. My father gave them to me for a birth-day present last week." Predictably, Harry's equipment is stolen and trashed by the same spiteful boy whom Harry had vowed to forgive. "On the ground lay Harry's hand-some new bat, broken in two, and his bright red ball stained and cut, and perfectly ruined." Harry is ready to slug the kid, but his mother reminds him of his earlier resolution, so Harry, naturally, expresses forgiveness to his nemesis. The guilty boy, of course, is now struck with shame and remorse, and determines "in his own mind that he would never rest until he had got another ball and bat for Harry Donaldson, and that as long as he lived he would never be guilty of such another act."

ca. 1850 *Grandpapa Pease's Pretty Poetical Spelling Book.* Albany: E. H. Pease, 8 pp. This is a large but very thin paper-covered ABC book. The author wrote a few simple verses to teach children the letters of the alphabet and illustrated these with hand-colored woodcuts. In one image a boy is shown holding a bat and ball; the accompanying verse reads:

The letter B you plainly see,
Begins both Bat and Ball;
And next you'll find the letter C
Commences Cat and Call.

An extremely rare title.

ca. 1850 *Frank's Adventures at Home and Abroad.* Troy NY: Merriam and Moore, 43 pp. Among the children's stories in this small hard-bound book is one entitled "Frank and the Cottage," which contains a woodcut showing boys playing baseball. A second story, "Cousin Richard," is illustrated with a woodcut of two boys, one holding a bat, being confronted by a woman whose window they have just broken with a ball.

ca. 1850 *Frank and the Cottage.* Troy NY: Merriam and Moore, 12 pp. A paper-covered chapbook that contains one of the stories and illustrations from the previous work.

ca. 1850 *Jeux et exercices des jeunes garçons* (Games and exercises of young boys). Paris: A. Courcier, 64 pp. This French book of games and sports contains the same description of the baseball-like game *la balle empoisonée* (poisoned ball) that first appeared in *Les Jeux des jeunes garçons,* ca. 1815.

1850 *The Knickerbocker,* vol. 35, January 1850. New York: Peabody, p. 84. The editor of this New York men's magazine included the following sentence in his introduction to a report about gambling in San Francisco:

As we don't know one card from another, and never indulged in a game of chance of any sort in the world, save the "bass-ball," "one" and "two-hole-cat," and "barn-ball" of our boyhood, matching "dominoes" and for needful and effective exercise, an occasional "taste" of bowling at ten-pins, in this period of our early manhood, we are not quite certain that the accompanying extract of a letter from a correspondent recently returned to "the States" from San Francisco, may be of interest.

While this is a rather late appearance for the colloquial spelling "bass-ball," it is one of the earliest references to the old-cat games.

1850 *The Little Boy's Own Book; Consisting of Games and Pastimes, with Directions for the Breeding and Management of Rabbits, , Pigeons, etc. for the Recreation and Amusement of Good Boys,* by Charles D. Mallary (Uncle Charles).

London: Henry Allman, 200 pp. This is a curious collection of games and pastimes intermixed with lessons on animal husbandry. The section on outdoor games includes a passage describing "rounders; or, feeder" which the author adapted and shortened from a description that had first appeared in *The Boy's Own Book* in 1828.

ca. 1850 *Louis Bond, the Merchant's Son.* Troy NY: Merriiam and Moore, 12 pp. This chapbook contains the same baseball illustration that appeared in *Frank and the Cottage*, by the same publisher.

1852 *Little Charley's Games and Sports.* Philadelphia: C. G. Henderson, 32 pp. A small book on children's games and activities that features numerous woodcuts. The illustration of trap-ball shows a tiny bat that looks more like a Ping-Pong paddle and bears the caption "bat ball." The text contains the sentence: "He also plays at cricket, and bass ball, of which the laws or [sic] quite too complicated for me to describe." There were also 1854 and 1858 editions.

1852 *My Little Guide to Goodness and Truth,* by Benjamin C. Fernald. Portland ME: Sanborn and Carter. This is a larger-format religious chapbook designed to be used as a Sunday school reader. It features a detailed woodcut depicting a group of boys playing baseball. The illustration shows a fielder reaching for a ball in the air off the bat of a left-handed batter. Also in view are a pitcher, a second fielder, and a boy waiting on deck leaning on a bat. The lesson below the image reads: "Boys will play cheerfully when influenced by good spirits. What fine sport these boys are having at recess."

1852 *Southern Literary Messenger,* vol. 18, no. 2, February 1852. Richmond VA, p. 96. This literary journal contains a poem entitled "Mournful Musings on an Old School-Stile." The following appears in the fifth stanza:

How they poured the soul of gay and joyous boyhood
Into roaring games of marbles, bat and base-ball!
Thinking that the world was only made to play in, —
Made for jolly boys, tossing, throwing balls!

An early poetic baseball reference, and from the South!

1852 *Stray Leaves from an Arctic Journal; or, Eighteen Months in the Polar Regions, in Search of Sir John Franklin's Expedition, in the Years 1850-51,* by Lieut. Sherard Osborn. London: Longman, Brown, Green and Longmans, 320 pp. On page 77 the author describes games played during long, sunny polar nights, including rounders. "Shouts of laughter! roars of 'Not fair, not fair! run again!' 'Well done, well done!' from individuals leaping and clapping their hands with excitement, arose from many a ring, in which 'rounders' with a cruelly hard ball, was being played."

1853 *Dongens! Wat zal er gespeld worden? Handboekje voor knapen bij hunne Onderlinge Oefeningen en Spelen* (Boys! What shall we play? Handbook for young boys for their exercise and games). Leeuwarden, The Netherlands: G. T. N. Suringar, 163 pp. This wonderful Dutch-language book of sports and games for boys is loaded with hand-colored engravings. A section on ball games includes *Engelsch balspel* (English ball game), essentially a Dutch translation of the rules for rounders or baseball as published in *The Boy's Own Book* in 1828. Included is a diagram of a diamond-shaped playing field. Many other games are described, including *De kat (Het tippelspel)*, which is the English tip-cat. Another game is called *De wip* (the whip), which is a variety of trap-ball. The illustration accompanying *De wip* shows an older, nonmechanical form of trap. Rare title.

1853 *The Illuminated A, B, C.* New York: T. W. Strong, 10 pp. This comic-book-sized children's title features a poem and one or more elaborate woodcuts of games for each letter of the alphabet. For the letter "B" a small trap-ball illustration is followed by this verse:

My name is B, at your beck and call,
B stands for battledore, bat, and ball;
From the trap with your bat, the Tennis ball knock,
With your battledore spin up your light shuttlecock.
I beg you'll excuse me for making so free,
Remember, they call me the great bouncing B.

1853 *The School Reader, First Book*, by Charles W. Sanders. Newburg NY: T. S. Quackenbush, 120 pp.; also published simultaneously in New York by Ivison and Phinney; Chicago by S. C. Griggs; and Philadelphia by Sower, Barnes. This edition of the primer contains an illustration entitled "Boys Playing Bat and Ball" with a full-page lesson describing the game. The baseball image and text are different from those in earlier editions of Sanders.

1854 *Little Charley's Picture Home Book: or Treasury of Amusement and Pleasing Instruction.* Philadelphia: C. G. Henderson, 214 pp. This book combines several smaller works published earlier by the same publisher. One is *Little Charley's Games and Sports*, originally issued in 1852, which includes references to "bat ball" and "bass ball." There were also 1857 and 1858 editions.

1854 *Uncle John's Panorama.* Philadelphia: C. G. Henderson, 26 pp. Another book from the publisher C. G. Henderson to reprint the material from *Little Charley's Games and Sports*. In this one, the pages are attached accordian-style and the illustrations are hand-colored.

1855 *Book of Sports*. New York: Leavitt and Allen, 16 pp. This tiny chapbook is a different work from several earlier books bearing the same title. It describes a small assortment of children's games accompanied by woodcut illustrations. These include a simple write-up for "trap, bat and ball," which features the same illustration of this game that first appeared in *Little Charley's Games and Sports* in 1852.

1855 *Leaves of Grass*, by Walt Whitman. Brooklyn: Rome Brothers, 95 pp. In this, one of the greatest of all American poetical works, Whitman's vision takes him coursing across the national experience, including the following:

> Approaching Manhattan, up by the long-stretching island,
> Under Niagara, the cataract falling like a veil over my countenance,
> Upon a door-step . . . upon the horse-block of hard wood outside,
> Upon the race-course, or enjoying pic-nics or jigs or a good game of
>   base-ball . . .

1855 *Manual of British Rural Sports*, by Stonehenge (J. H. Walsh). London: G. Routledge, 720 pp. This work focuses on hunting, fishing, and other field sports, but also has a nice detailed description and diagram of the game of rounders. This version of the game featured a pentagon-shaped five-base layout, with base runners proceeding in a counterclockwise direction. The rules were generally consistent with other accounts of rounders and pre-1845 baseball. This book's description of rounders was the one quoted by Henry Chadwick in his well-known 1867 article in *The Ball Players' Chronicle* entitled "The Ancient History of Base Ball."

The publishing date of 1855 for this book's first edition is presumptive, as no copy of it has been located. The second edition, dated 1856, is the earliest known. Numerous later editions were issued. The first from an American publisher, retitled *The Encylopedia of Rural Sports*, contains a section on baseball. It was produced by Porter and Coates of Philadelphia and, although undated, is believed to be from 1867.

ca. 1855 *Sports for All Seasons, Illustrating the Most Common and Dangerous Accidents That Occur During Childhood, with Amusing Hints for Their Prevention*. London: J. March, 6 leaves. The subtitle of this wonderful little book conveys its humorous treatment of children's pastimes. Divided into sections for each of the four seasons, the book uses verse, prose, and woodcut engravings to depict different games and the dangers they might represent. The game of trap-ball is placed in the autumn segment, with a picture of a group of boys playing the game in front of a house with several large windows. One of the players has just struck a ball, which is heading directly at one of the windows. The verse underneath reads:

School's up for to day, come out boys and play I'll put my trap here on the grass;

Look out John Thatcher, here comes a catcher, oh dear! it will go through the glass.

1856 *Jeux des adolescents*, by Par G. Beleze. Paris: Librairie de L. Hachette et Cie, 359 pp. This heavily illustrated major work on games and sports for youth includes an extensive section on ball games. Among these are the pastimes *la balle au camp ou balle empoisonnée*, and *la balle au bâton*. The author's description of the former is similar to earlier portrayals of *la balle empoisonnée* (poisoned ball), including the acknowledgment that the game had several known variants. The primary method was reminiscent of early baseball, in that two teams took turns striking and fielding in a large playing area with a four- or five-base infield. Outs were recorded by catching balls on the fly or soaking runners between bases. The major difference from baseball was that the striker was not armed with a bat but relied upon his bare hand to propel the ball.

On the other hand, the game *la balle au bâton* did feature a bat, as the name implies. The author reveals it in other ways, however, to be a scrub activity. Players were not divided into teams, and each individual fended for himself. If a batter reached base, he earned another trip to the plate once he came around to score. Fielders could bat if they successfully retired another player by soaking him on the base paths. No pitchers were involved. Batters struck the ball by one-handed fungo hitting. The author comments on the game's simplicity: "It can be seen that this game is in many of its rules and circumstances similar to field ball [*la balle au camp*, which in this version is the same as *la balle empoisonnée*], but, compared to that game, this one seems to us far inferior . . . less varied in its combinations, and especially less animated because there is no contest between two sides." Of some interest is the author's remark that the bat "is called *tèque* in Normandy, the principal place where the game is played." This would seem to make *la balle au bâton* analogous to the Norman game known as *tèque* or *thèque*, although there were some discrepancies. Other works depict *thèque* as a two-team pastime, requiring a pitcher. Also, the term *thèque* is typically equated with the ball, rather than the bat, as in this example.

1856 *The Progressive First Reader*, by Salem Town and Nelson M. Holbrook. Boston: Sanborn, Carter, Bazin (alternatively identified as O. Ellsworth, or

Bazin and Ellsworth), 112 pp. This children's elementary school book contains an illustration depicting boys playing baseball in a schoolyard.

1857 *Arctic Explorations: the Second Grinnell Expedition in Search of Sir John Franklin, 1853, '54, '55*, by Elisah Kent Kane. Philadelphia: Childs and Peterson, 2 vols., 467 pp. This was the second book to chronicle the search for the long-missing Franklin. In his second volume, while describing a scene in an "Esquimaux" village, the author observes "children, each one armed with the curved rib of some big amphibion, are playing ball and bat among the drifts." An engraving illustrates the children playing a baseball-like game with the long, curved bones.

1857 *The Progressive Pictorial Primer*, Salem Town and Nelson M. Holbrook. Boston: Oliver Ellsworth (alternatively identified as Sanborn, Carter, Bazin, Hobart and Robbins), 64 pp. This is the primer from the same series as *The Progressive First Reader* (1856) It offers a different illustration of boys engaged in baseball.

1858 "The Base Ball Polka." Buffalo: Bodgett and Bradford; 5 pp. This is the earliest known published baseball sheet music, a polka written for piano and composed by J. R. Blodgett of the Niagara Base Ball Club. On the title page, under an emblem of two crossed bats above a baseball, is a dedication "To the Flour City B. B. Club of Rochester, N.Y. by The Niagara B. B. Club of Buffalo."

1858 *Games for All Seasons*, by George Pardon. London: James Blackwood, 208 pp. This comprehensive and detailed anthology of sports and games includes the full spectrum of baseball's English relatives. Of particular interest is the author's description and diagram of the game rounders, which depicts five bases *plus* a home plate. This culminates a thirty-year metamorphosis of the game's infield configuration that began with the four-base diamond-shaped layout illustrated in *The Boy's Own Book* in 1828 and progressed through various five-base arrangements in the 1840s and 1850s. This also exemplifies the steady divergence of rounders and baseball during those decades to the point of becoming two distinct sports.

1858 *The Little One's Ladder, or First Steps in Spelling and Reading*. New York: George F. Cooledge, 61 pp. This children's reader includes a nice woodcut of a schoolyard scene with a baseball game in progress. The caption reads: "Now, Charley, give me a good ball that I may bat it."

1858 *Manual of Cricket and Base Ball*. Boston: Mayhew and Baker, 24 pp. This booklet with paper covers is devoted principally to cricket, allocating only the final four pages to baseball. It presents rules for the Massachusetts game of baseball, along with a rudimentary diagram of the ball field. Its historical significance lies in the fact that this was the first treatment of baseball as a pastime for adults in a book made available to the general public.

1859 *Amherst Express, Extra.* Amherst MA: July 1, 2, 1859. A two-page broadsheet that reported on competitions between Williams and Amherst colleges in both baseball and chess, all under the headline "Muscle and mind!" Only four copies are known to exist.

1859 *The Base Ball Player's Pocket Companion.* Boston: Mayhew and Baker, 36 pp. Following the publication of the *Manual of Cricket and Base Ball* a year earlier, Mayhew and Baker issued this follow-up volume totally focused on the game of baseball. It devotes space to both the Massachusetts and New York versions of the game, although it is clear that the New England–based publisher favors the former. The introduction to the Massachusetts game states: "The game of base ball, as adopted by the 'Massachusetts Association of Base Ball Players,' May 1858, which has ever been the favorite and principal game played throughout New England, differs in many points from the New York game, though it requires equal skill and activity, and deservedly holds the first place in the estimation of all ball players and the public."

The paragraph introducing the New York game contains generic comments about baseball: "It is fast becoming in this country what cricket is to England, a national game, combining, as it does, exciting sport and healthful exercise at a trifling expense." The book contains rules, regulations, and by-laws of both versions of the game, including diagrams of the playing fields. It also features four simple illustrations of uniformed players: a "thrower" on page 9, a "striker" holding a very small bat on page 17, a "catcher" (simply a player catching a ball) on page 24, and a "base tender" on page 31. The latter stands next to the "base" — a waist-high pole. These four images may be unique in their depiction of adults attired for the soon-to-be-extinct New England variety of baseball. The *Pocket Companion* is covered in dark, textured cloth embossed with gold lettering and a "catcher" figure. The book was reissued in 1860 and 1861. It is a landmark work, fiercely prized by collectors, and a great rarity.

1859 Advertising prospectus for *The Base Ball Player's Pocket Companion.* Boston: Mayhew and Baker. This four-page brochure was issued by the publishing house of Mayhew and Baker to advertise their newest publications. One of the four books advertised is *The Base Ball Player's Pocket Companion.* The ad fills a 5½-inch-by-9½-inch page, and features two of the illustrations from the book: one a uniformed player throwing a ball, the

other a player catching a ball. Of the three other advertisements in the brochure, one features *The Cricket Player's Pocket Companion* and includes a
nice woodcut of a cricket game in progress. The other two ads are for a
book of essays and for a handbook for correcting grammatical errors.
There is only one known copy of this booklet.

1859 *The Boy's Own Toy-Maker.* London: Griffith and Farran, 153 pp. This
book offers detailed instructions for making many different types of toys,
including sporting equipment. It devotes two pages to the game of tip-cat
and three to "trap, bat and ball." These feature not only specific guidance
for making the equipment but also information on the development of
the games. One of the varieties of tip-cat described is the multiple-base,
multiple-bat, "old-cat" version first detailed in Strutt's *Sports and Pastimes
of the People of England* in 1801, which was nearly identical to the unusual
form of rounders featured in *Every Boy's Book of Games, Sports, and Diversions*, 1852. The Boston publisher Shepard, Clark and Brown released the
first American edition of *The Boy's Own Toy-Maker* in 1859, and further
editions by various publishing houses in both England and the United
States appeared during the following decade.

1859 *The Cricket Field: or, The History and Science of Cricket*, by James Pycroft.
Boston: Mayhew and Baker, 238 pp. While this is an excellent little volume
about cricket, its inclusion in this bibliography has nothing to do with that
particular old English sport. Originally published in London in 1851, *The
Cricket Field's* American debut was an 1859 edition produced by the Boston firm of Mayhew and Baker, a publisher better known to baseball collectors for its historic title *The Base Ball Player's Pocket Companion.* The
Mayhew and Baker edition of *The Cricket Field* sports a multipage advertisement for *The Base Ball Player's Pocket Companion.* It features a full page
of descriptive information about the historic guide, and the following four
pages picture the *Pocket Companion's* four distinctive images of uniformed
players outfitted for the Massachusetts game of baseball.

The *Cricket Field's* initial chapter is entitled "The Origin of the Game of
Cricket" and is, if not the earliest, one of the finest early studies of cricket
history. The author exhumes a great number of references to cricket and
its antecedents dating back to the year 1300 and scientifically traces several
possible evolutionary paths for England's national sport. This work stands
in stark contrast to the embarrassingly biased and amateurish attempts to
recount the origins of America's National Pastime that issued from writers in this country through the remaining decades of the nineteenth
century.

1859 *Games and Sports for Young Boys.* London: Routledge, Warne and Routledge, 106 pp. This cute little book describes all kinds of activities, accompanied by numerous whimsical woodcuts. It includes all the contemporaneous English relatives of baseball, including rounders, feeder, trap-ball, and northern spell. The descriptions were lifted verbatim from the 1841 title *The Every Boy's Book.*

1860 *Beadle's Dime Base-Ball Player: A Compendium of the Game, Comprising Elementary Instructions of the American Game of Ball,* by Henry Chadwick. New York: Irwin P. Beadle, 40 pp. "In presenting this work to our readers, we claim for it the merit of being the first publication of its kind." So writes Henry Chadwick, the "father of baseball," in his introduction to the 1860 *Beadle's Dime Base-Ball Player.* He clearly had a feeling that history was being made by his contribution to the first annual baseball guide, a form of publication that would become an American institution.

This first issue of *Beadle's Dime* included multiple sets of rules. Besides the newest rules of the National Association of Base Ball Players, Chadwick also printed the original Knickerbocker rules of 1845, the rules for the Massachusetts version of the game, and even the rules of rounders. The book also contains detailed guidance for laying out a baseball field, playing each position, and batting.

Chadwick also presents a brief history of the game, clearly stating it to be of "English origin" and "derived from rounders," but also saying that it had changed so much in America that it hardly resembled its former self "beyond the mere groundwork of the game." Nevertheless, his suggestion that baseball was of foreign origin carried tremendous weight. For twenty-five years his pronouncement remained the accepted definition of the game's origins. Then the controversy erupted. First John Montgomery Ward and later Albert Spalding attacked Chadwick's theory. Ultimately, their jingoistic efforts saddled the nation with the Doubleday Myth.

The first Beadle's guide is very rare due to a small print run and the fragility of its paper covers.

1860 *The Bobbin Boy; or, How Nat Got His Learning,* by William M. Thayer. Boston: J. E. Tilton, 310 pp. This is an important early example of a fictional work containing references to baseball. The book is typical of the material written for adolescent audiences during that era, with its objective the teaching of moral lessons. Beginning on page 51, several pages are devoted to "a game of ball." This culminates with the author's description of a player hitting a home run, and then trotting around the bases in a manner that today would guarantee a knock-down pitch the next time he came to the plate: "'There, take that,' said Nat, as he sent the ball at first bat, over the heads of all, so far that he had time to run round the whole circle of goals, turning a somerset as he came in."

1860 *Owed 2 Base Ball in Three Cant-Oh's!* Philadelphia: McLaughlin Brothers, 16 pp. This humorous baseball narrative poem was published in booklet form. Dated December 25, 1860, with its subject the Mercantile Base Ball Club of Philadelphia, it was probably issued for the club's Christmas banquet. All nine of the club's starters are mentioned in the body of the poem. The booklet has a glossy paper cover printed in gold-leaf ink. Only two copies are known.

1861 *Beadle's Dime Base-Ball Player for 1861,* by Henry Chadwick. New York: Ross and Tousey. The second annual baseball guide, it was actually published late in 1860 in anticipation of the following season. It was the first guide to print baseball statistics (team and player averages for 1860). It also contains rule revisions for 1860. Like the 1860 issue, this title is very rare because of a small print run and the fragility of its paper covers.

1861 *Lessons in Life, a Series of Familiar Essays,* by Timothy Titcomb (J. G. Holland). New York: Charles Scribner, 344 pp. In an essay entitled "The Rights of Women," the author challenges the argument that a woman "has no right to engage in base-ball." He writes that the faulty notion was based upon the perceived physical shortcomings of women, which he attributes to the denial of training and opportunity. In an awkward attempt to make his point, he states, "I have seen negro slave women at work in the field with a muscular development that would be the envy of a Bowery boy."

CONSTITUTIONS AND BY-LAWS

Most of the newly emerging organized baseball clubs in the mid-nineteenth century published booklets for their membership. These contained rules, regulations, and/or the club constitution. Each member was expected to know the team rules and comport himself in a gentlemanly manner. From club to club, the constitutions were similarly structured, with only slight variations. Beginning in 1858 the incipient National Association of Base Ball Players published a yearly set of general rules that were agreed upon at the annual convention. These were made available to the individual teams, and also, possibly, to the general public.

The following is a listing of the published constitutions and by-laws I have identified of which there is at least one surviving copy:

1838 *Constitution of the Olympic Ball Club of Philadelphia*. Philadelphia: John Clark. Later accounts attest that this club played town-ball, although that name is not found in the constitution.)

1848 *By-laws and Rules of the Knickerbocker Base Ball Club*. New York: W. H. B. Smith Book and Fancy Job Printer; revised editions by Wilbur and Hastings, 1858-60, and Biglow and Bleecker, 1861. These landmark rules were established September 23, 1845, but no earlier printing than the 1848 edition is known.

1852 *By-laws and Rules of the of the Eagle Ball Club, 1852*. New York: Douglass and Colt; revised edition 1854, Oliver and Brother. The cover of Eagle's 1852 rule book says that the club was established in 1840. It is not certain whether the club actually played ball from its inception.

1854 *Constitution, by-laws and rules of the Empire Ball Club: organized October 23d, 1854*. New York: The Club.

1855 *Constitution and By-laws of the Pioneer Base Ball Club of Jersey City*. New York: W. and C. T. Barton.

1856 *Constitution and By-laws of the Excelsior Base Ball Club*. Brooklyn: George Scott Roe; revised yearly through 1861.

1856 *Rules and By-laws of Base Ball.* New York: Hosford. These were generic, not specific to a club.

1856 *Rules and By-laws of Base Ball.* Putnam Base Ball Club. Brooklyn: Baker and Godwin.

1858 *By-laws, Rules and Regulations of the Mazeppa Base Ball Club.* Stamford CT: E. Hoyt.

1858 *By-laws and Rules and Regulations of the Newburgh Base Ball Club.* Newburgh NY: Gray and Lawson.

1858 *Constitution and By-laws, with Rules and Regulations of the Louisville Base Ball Club.* Hanna.

1858 *By-laws of the Independent Baseball Club.* New York: Bowne.

1858 *By-laws and Rules of Order of the Takewambait Base Ball Club of Natick.* Natick MA: G. W. Ryder. Rules for the Massachusetts game of baseball.

1858 *Constitution and By-laws of the Olympic Base Ball Club of South Brooklyn.* New York: William D. Roe; revised edition in 1859.

1858 *Revised Constitution, By-laws and Rules of the Hamilton Base Ball Club.* Jersey City: William B. Dunning.

1859 *Constitution and By-laws of the National Association of Base Ball Players.* New York: Wilbur and Hastings; also 1860 and 1861 editions.

1859 *By-laws of the Harlem Base Ball Club.* New York: William Manwaring.

1859 *Constitution and By-laws of the Mercantile Base Ball Club.* Philadelphia: Grattan.

1860 *Constitution, By-laws and Rules and Regulations for Playing, of the Granite Base Ball Club.* Manchester NH: Daily Mirror Office.

1860 *Revised Constitution, By-laws and Rules.* Quinnipiack Base Ball Club, New Haven CT.

1861 *By-laws, Regulations and Rules of the New York Base Ball Club.* New York: J. A. H. Hasbrouck and Company.

SOME COMMENTS ON
SPORTING JOURNALS OF THE 1850S

Among the earliest newspapers to initiate comprehensive coverage of organized baseball in the United States were a handful of weekly publications devoted to literature, theater, and the sporting world. Researchers digging into baseball's emergence in the 1850s have found these journals to be gold mines of information. Although a number of daily newspapers in the New York City area also initiated coverage of local ball clubs during those years, the breadth and depth of their reporting typically fell short of that of the sporting weeklies. While a thorough review of these publications is beyond the scope of this work, what follows is an itemization of the journals that initiated coverage before 1860 and a commentary on their contents and relative importance.

The Spirit of the Times. A Chronicle of the Turf, Field, Sports, Literature and the Stage, founded by William T. Porter. New York, December 1831–June 22, 1861. This is the granddaddy of the group, already an oldster by the time baseball burst upon the New York scene in the 1850s. Like the other sporting journals of the era, the paper gave extensive coverage to field sports, boxing, and horse racing, as well as the gentlemanly game of cricket, which enjoyed rising popularity in the 1840s. (The *Spirit's* editor, William T. Porter, was personally connected to cricket through his appointment as president of the newly founded New York Cricket Club in 1844.) *The Spirit of the Times*, known later as the "Old" Spirit, was slow to embrace baseball. A letter to the editor published in the July 9, 1853, issue reports the outcome of a match between the Knickerbocker and Gotham clubs. The game commenced on July 1 but was suspended because of a rain storm. It was resumed and completed on July 5. The letter to the *Spirit* includes a box score that lists the names of players and the number of runs and outs recorded by each of them.

A second letter, published in the December 23, 1854, issue, extols "the advantages of this noble game." It describes the activities and playing grounds of the three practicing clubs in New York — the Knickerbockers, the Eagles, and the Gothams. The letter is signed "W.H.V.C."; those are the initials of William Cauldwell, a sportswriter for the *New York Mercury*, who was the first journalist to cover baseball on a regular basis. A further small notice appearing in the paper on June 2, 1855, observes that the number of active baseball clubs had increased to four. From then on, until its demise six years later, the "Old" Spirit gradually increased its coverage of the game but never approached its namesakes, listed below, in the quantity or quality of reporting.

Porter's Spirit of the Times. A Chronicle of the Turf, Field, Sports, Literature and the Stage, founded by William T. Porter and George Wilkes. New York, September 6, 1856–August 17, 1861. This similarly named journal was founded when the aging Porter, along with his brash protégé George Wilkes, parted ways with the "Old" Spirit. Perhaps as a way of distinguishing itself from its namesake, the new *Porter's Spirit* began reporting on baseball within its first weeks of publication. This early coverage includes publication of the New York rules of baseball in the December 6, 1856, issue, followed by a rebuttal arguing the merits of the Massachusetts variety of the game in the December 27 issue.

For the remainder of the 1850s, *Porter's Spirit* excelled in its baseball coverage, recording several pioneering firsts. Most noteworthy is the front page of its September 12, 1857, issue, which features the earliest illustration of adults playing a baseball match. The image, which depicts a game between the Eagle and Gotham clubs played on the Elysian Fields in New Jersey, scooped by one week the engraving of the same contest that appeared in *Porter's Spirit's* rival *The New York Clipper*. *Porter's Spirit* encouraged correspondents from other regions of the country to send in baseball reports, and soon box scores from New England, upstate New York, Canada, and even New Orleans began appearing in its pages. In this, the first early heyday of the game, *Porter's* set such a high standard for baseball coverage that even the legendary *Clipper* could not, at first, keep up.

Wilkes' Spirit of the Times. A Chronicle of the Turf, Field, Sports, Literature and the Stage, founded by George Wilkes. New York, September 10, 1859–December 13, 1902; title changed July 4, 1868, to *Spirit of the Times*. Yet another entry in the Spirit of the Times parade, this version originated when George Wilkes had a falling out with the publishers of *Porter's Spirit* following the death of William Porter a year earlier. Incredibly, for a short while, all three of the Spirits were publishing in New York simultaneously. However, *Wilkes' Spirit* quickly ascended to the fore, and its two rivals soon ceased publication. Wilkes continued the rich baseball coverage that he had supervised in *Porter's*, and his publication continued to be an important repository for news of the game.

California Spirit of the Times and Fireman's Journal. San Francisco, July 25, 1857–August 20, 1870; from 1857 to 1859 named *California Spirit of the Times*, after which it merged with the *Fireman's Journal*. This rare and little-known paper was a West Coast variation of its more famous New York namesakes. The depth of its baseball coverage has not yet been fully explored because few libraries hold copies of it and microfilming has been very limited. Many of its early issues cannot be located and may no longer exist. However, indications from the scattered issues that have been examined suggest that this journal remains an untapped reservoir of clues to early West Coast baseball. For example, the February 11, 1860, edition, located in the Bancroft Library at the University of California in Berkeley, contains several intriguing references to organized baseball activity. These would seem to challenge the generally accepted assessment that the earliest contest on the West Coast was one played on February 22, 1860, in San Francisco.[1] The *California Spirit* reported the following three items eleven days earlier on page two:

> A Base Ball Club Match is to be played at Mariposa to-day. The stakes are $25 a side, but there has been considerable outside betting.

> We shall republish next week the entire set of rules governing Base Ball matches and playing. All clubs desiring any number of the papers containing the rules, will do well to notify us in time, as this will be the third publication we have made of the rules.

> The Union Club of Sacramento met at the house of Protection No. 2, and elected the following officers for the ensuing two months: President, Converse Howe; Vice President, N. G. Millman; Secretary, J. S. Smith; Treasurer, M. McManus. The club hold their regular meetings on Saturday night each week.

Taken together, these items strongly suggest that organized baseball in California predated the 1860s. One only wonders what else could be learned when and if other early issues of the *California Spirit* are located and examined.

The New York Clipper, founded by Frank Queen and Harrison Trent. New York, May 14, 1853–July 12, 1923. This journal was similar to the respective Spirits of the Times in many respects, although its coverage of the entertainment world broadened over the decades. Ultimately, in 1924 *The Clipper* merged with its counterpart, the newspaper *Variety*, which remains the premier journal of the entertainment industry to this day. The *New York Clipper*'s baseball coverage is legendary, in part due to its long association with Henry Chadwick, the "father of baseball," who was among the most prominent and influential journalists to write about the National Pastime. Chadwick joined the staff of the *Clipper* in 1858 at the behest of Frank Queen, and he remained in that position almost uninterrupted until 1886, when his responsibilities to other publications necessitated his resignation. Chadwick had earlier separated from the *Clipper* for a short stint in the 1860s, during which time he published the short-lived *Base Ball Players' Chronicle*. During Chadwick's years of service, the *Clipper* rose to the forefront of baseball journalism, eclipsing *Wilkes' Spirit of the Times*, which was the only remaining member of the New York Spirit trilogy. The *Clipper* initiated its baseball coverage on July 16, 1853, with a summary and box score of the match between the Gotham and Knickerbocker clubs, completed on July 5, that had been reported a week earlier on the pages of the Old Spirit. However, despite starting at that early date, the quality of the *Clipper*'s reporting did not outstrip that of *Porter's Spirit of the Times* until Chadwick's influence began to take hold in the late 1850s.

"A PLACE LEAVEL ENOUGH TO PLAY BALL"

Baseball and Baseball-type Games in the Colonial Era,
Revolutionary War, and Early American Republic

Thomas L. Altherr

In the spring of 1779, Henry Dearborn, a New Hampshire officer, was a member of the American expedition in north central Pennsylvania, heading northwards to attack the Iroquois tribal peoples. In his journal for April 3rd, Dearborn jotted down something quite different than the typical notations of military activities: "all the Officers of the Brigade turn'd out & Play'd a game at ball the first we have had this yeare. — " Two weeks later he entered something equally eye-catching. On April 17th, he wrote: "we are oblige'd to walk 4 miles to day to find a place leavel enough to play ball."[1] On the face of it, the two journal entries might not seem all that startling, but to baseball historians they should be sort of front-page news.[2] For Henry Dearborn was one of several, if not more, soldiers who played baseball, or an early variant of it, during the Revolutionary War, a good sixty years before another military man, one Abner Doubleday, allegedly invented the game in the sleepy east central New York village of Cooperstown.

Dearborn's two notations, meager as they were, suggest that the game of ball they played was more than whimsical recreation. Tom Heitz, the long-time historian and librarian at the National Baseball Library at the Hall of Fame, has speculated that baseball-type games at this stage were like pulling a hacky-sack out of a backpack and kicking it around or playing frisbee on the college quad.[3] But what if the game was more serious, more important than that? Indeed Dearborn's writings warrant a second look. First, the earlier one reveals that the men were familiar with the game, having played it before, at least during some previous year. Moreover the remark hints that they were eager to play again, that the weather or other circumstances had delayed their "opening day," if you will. The second entry also reflects on the place of the game in their lives. Any historian of the Revolution knows that average soldiers, and even some of the officers, despite their well-known heroism, grumbled about carrying out daily duties. In this case, however, the prospect of playing ball was so important that they hoofed it four miles, during a time when a good day's march might have been fifteen miles, to locate a spot flat enough to get in the game. Clearly this game meant something more to Henry Dearborn and his assemblage.

Although most current Americans probably still believe in the "immaculate conception" theory of baseball's origins, that one June day in 1839 in Elihu Phinney's farm field in Cooperstown, Abner Doubleday drew up the rules, laid out the diamond, and taught the villagers his new game, Americans had been playing baseball and its variants long before then. In fact, bat and ball games are actually quite ancient and in spite of Albert Spalding's fervid wishes, not even particularly American. In his 1947 book, *Ball, Bat, and Bishop*, Robert Henderson demolished the Cooperstown origins story by pointing to numerous examples of bat and ball–type games in medieval Europe and Great Britain before and during colonization of the Americas.[4] Soon Denver historian Phil Goodstein will place another nail in the coffin with more evidence about the unreliability of the Mills Commission's "star witness," Abner Graves, whose unsavory connections in the West were many.[5] Folklorist Erwin Mehl pushed the antiquity of baseball back even further than Henderson would. In a 1948 article "Baseball in the Stone Age," Mehl located evidence of ancient bat and ball games not only in western Europe, but also in North Africa, Asia Minor, India, Afghanistan, and northern Scandinavia. "The spectators at an American baseball game, cheering a Ty Cobb or a Babe Ruth, may have had counterparts in the Stone Age," he surmised.[6] The terminology for baseball may also be quite more ancient than expected. English vicar Robert Crowley, in his 1550s poem "The Scholar's Lesson," may have referred to baseball in his advice to pupils on the advantages of healthful recreation:

To shote, to bowle, or caste the barre,
To play tenise, or tosse the ball,
Or to rene base, like men of war,
Shal hurt thy study nought at al.[7]

English professor Robert Moynihan has suggested other examples of the antic linguistic derivations of baseball terms dating to ancient, medieval, and Shakespearean times.[8] Along with other fragmentary evidence such as a hieroglyphic scene of a bat and ball game in ancient Egypt, a 1344 French illustration of nuns and monks lined up for a ball game, a 1400s Flemish painting showing women playing a bat and ball game, eighteenth-century English diary writers' references to the game, and mention of "baseball" in Jane Austen's novel, *Northanger Abbey*, Henderson and Mehl's writings make it clear that baseball existed long before and outside an American context.[9] So, then, why not the probability of the existence of the game and its variants within the American context?

Problems of definition arise. As O. Paul Mockton pointed out in *Pastimes in Time Past*, "The very fact that so many early pastimes were all played with balls, causes great confusion, in attempting to investigate the history of these old games. Old historians were very loose in their descriptions of the way the different games were played in mediæval times."[10] Some of the "ball games" may have been actually soccer or a combination of foot-and-hand ball sports, but in the absence of firm proof, it is just as reasonable to assume that "ball play" among Euroamericans involved a stick and a ball. Indeed, in my research for an encyclopedia of pre-1820 North American primary source sports documents, I found that the sources made distinct references to football, cricket, bandy (a type of field hockey), and fives (a forerunner of modern handball) when they meant those sports. In a couple of instances they referred to "base," "baste ball," or "baseball," leaving the possibility that the term "ball" or "to play ball" referred fairly regularly to baseball-type games.[11]

Certainly Europeans, perhaps mostly the children, but probably even adult men and women, took a swing at a variety of pre-baseball folk games: stool ball, trap ball, catapult ball, which became one-o'cat (and two-o'cat, three-o'cat, etc.), kit-cat, munchets, tip cat, round ball, sting ball, soak ball, burn ball, barn ball, rounders, town ball, and base, or baste, ball, and possibly others called whirl and chermany.[12] Balls were easy to make out of rags and leather and wood and feathers, and bats were paddles or tree branches.[13] Farm fields or the cozier confines of streets and alleys sufficed for the playing field. Bases were trees, chairs (hence "stool ball"), stones, and stakes. Rules were immensely flexible. For example, sources described trap ball as a "simple batting game," in which a batter hit a ball resting on a stake, much like in modern T-ball, and fielders attempted to catch the ball in order to come to bat themselves, much as in the modern game of work-up.[14] Yet other sources, namely children's books in the 1810s, depicted trap ball as a much more elaborate game in which batters tried to outhit their opponents over a series of consecutive hits, guess the lengths of their opponent's hits, or hit or pitch the ball into a special trap. The games then were mostly spontaneous. There were no long, grueling playing seasons nor extended tournaments. But the quality of spontaneity and irregularity did not signify whimsicality. The games held importance for the players and the community. These folk games fit into the interstices of work patterns, ceremonial days, and longer leisure stretches.[15]

The first recorded instance of a baseball-type game in Anglo-America took place in 1621, in of all places, Plymouth, Massachusetts, on, of all days, Christmas Day. Plymouth may have a spurious claim to being the starting place of "American" history, but it may have a solid claim on the start of baseball in the English colonies. The Separatists, as with many other English Reformation dissenters, did not celebrate Christmas, but rather saw it as just another day. Thus the governor, William Bradford, took a work crew out that morning. The non-Separatist English in the group begged off and Bradford relented, only to find them hard at play, playing stool ball among other sports. Bradford scolded them and recalled the episode in his journal:

> On the day called Chrismasday, the Governor caled them out to worke, (as was used,) but the most of this new-company excused them selves and said it wente against their consciences to work on that day. So the Governor tould them that if they made it a mater of conscience, he would spare them till they were better informed. So he led away the rest and left them; but when they came home at noone from their worke, he found them in the streete at play, openly; some pitching the barr, & some at stoole-ball, and shuch like sports. So he went to them, and took away their implements, and tould them that if they made the keeping a mater of devotion, let them kepe their houses, but ther should be no gameing or revelling in the streets. Since which time nothing has been atempted that way, at least openly.[16]

Bradford and his successors may have had some success in curtailing ball games, but probably never totally suppressed them. The Dutch also played, according to Esther Singleton, in her book, *Dutch New York*, "all varieties of ball games" in New Netherlands.[17] After the turn of the century, Boston magistrate Samuel Sewall reported games of "wicket" and made one tantalizing reference to trap ball in 1713: "The Rain-water grievously runs into my son Joseph's Chamber from the N. Window above. As went out to the Barber's I observ'd the water to run trickling down a great pace from the Coving. I went on the Roof, and found the Spout next Salter's stop'd, but could not free it with my Stick. Boston went up, and found his pole too big, which I warn'd him of before; came down a Spit, and clear'd the Leaden-throat, by thrusting out a Trap-Ball that stuck there."[18] Caesar Rodeney, an East Dover, Delaware, resident, mentioned playing trap ball, indeed quite well, twice in his journal for August 1728. On August 24th, he scribbled, "Hart and I & James Gordon went to a Trabbal [trap ball] Match In John Willsons old feild I out Plaid them all" and a week later, he noted, "To Tim Harons: Where James Gordon & I Plaid at Trabbal against John Horon and Th Horon for an anker of Syder We woun We drunk our Syder."[19] Clearly the British were familiar with these games, as evidenced in Irish doctor John Brickell's comment about a bat and ball game that indigenous people in North Carolina were playing about 1737: "They [indigenous peoples] have another Game which is managed with a *Battoon*, and very much resembles our *Trap-Ball*; . . ."[20] It is tempting to wonder if this was a pre-contact game or the tribal people adapted it from early European Carolinians. Farther north, in Scarborough, Maine, and in later decades, indigenous people played against Euroamericans, according to town historian William Southgate: "The game of 'base' was a peculiar favorite with our young townsmen, and the friendly Indians, and the hard beach of 'Garrison Cove' afforded a fine ground for it."[21]

About midcentury, however, the frequency of references to baseball and baseball-type games increased. Three groups in particular, children's book writers, soldiers, and students, seem to have made the most major contributions to spreading the game. In his study of sport in colonial and Revolutionary era New England, Bruce Daniels contended that ball sports gained less acceptance than other sports such as horseracing, but that due to "soldiers in the militia, mischievous adolescents, and the students at Harvard and Yale," the games "were on the verge of legitimacy." Daniels did not refer specifically to baseball and its variants, but mentioned wicket, bowling, shinny, fives, and football.[22] Baseball-type games were definitely in the mix. Future Philadelphia physician Benjamin Rush played so much that it caused him to lament all the time spent: "I have been ashemed likewise, in recollecting how much time I wasted when a boy in playing cat and fives . . ."[23]

Indeed it was a children's book that gave Americans their first *American* visual expression of the games of stool ball, baseball, and trap ball. A 1767 revised edition of a 1744 book, *A Pretty Pocket-Book, Intended for the Amusement of Little Master Tommy and Pretty Miss Polly*, featured engravings of scenes of boys playing each of the three games and appended the following moral verses below them:

STOOLBALL

THE *Ball* once struck with Art and Care,
And drove impetuous through the Air,
Swift round his Course the *Gamester* flies,
Or his Stool's taken by *Surprise*.

RULE OF LIFE
Bestow your Alms whene'er you fee
An Object in Necessity.

BASE-BALL
THE *Ball* once struck off,
Away flies the *Boy*
To the next destin'd Post,
And then Home with Joy.

MORAL
Thus *Britons* for Lucre
Fly over the Main;
But, with Pleasure transported,
Return back again.

TRAP-BALL
TOUCH lightly the *Trap*,
And strike low the *Ball*;
Let none catch you out,
And you'll beat them all.

MORAL
Learn hence, my dear Boy,
To avoid ev'ry Snare,
Contriv'd to involve you
In Sorrow and Care.[24]

It is impossible to gauge just what effect a children's book had on the growth of baseball-type games, but by 1771 the province of New Hampshire felt compelled to prohibit boys and adolescents playing ball in the streets on Christmas Day for fear of damage to windows. The law, as opposed to William Bradford's 1621 remonstrances in Plymouth, did not outlaw the game, but rather asked the players to remove to a safer location. Ball playing had apparently become an accepted Christmastide recreation. The New Hampshire law read as follows:

An Act to prevent and punish Disorders usually committed on the twenty-fifth Day of December, commonly called Christmas-Day, the Evening preceding and following said Day, and to prevent other Irregularities committed at other Times. *WHEREAS as it often happens that many disorders are occasioned within the town of Portsmouth, . . . by boys and fellows playing with balls in the public streets:* . . . And any boys playing with balls in any streets, whereby there is danger of breaking the windows of any building, public or private, may be ordered to remove to any place where there shall be no such danger.[25]

Yet it would be inaccurate to assume that only children, lazy adults, and indigenous people played baseball-type games. Revolutionary War troops were apparently enthusiasts for ball, even walking for miles to find a place level enough to play, as did Henry Dearborn and his compatriots. The Revolutionary War contained, as do most, long stretches of boredom and busywork, camp duty and drill for the troops. They sought out recreation to alleviate this tedium. As long as the game did not involve gambling, which George Washington prohibited and prosecuted, or trample on public safety, soldiers could resort to such exercises. Presumably, as their diaries and memoirs show, baseball was in that category. The level of formality to the games was probably low.

Certainly there were no organized teams nor leagues, but the embryonic pattern for such may have lain behind what soldiers saw played and played themselves at Valley Forge, in the Wyoming valley of Pennsylvania, and elsewhere.

The notations were often simple, as in the case of Sharon, Connecticut, soldier Simeon Lyman, who recorded his ball playing in New London on September 6, 1775, quite tersely: "Wednesday the 6. We played ball all day."[26] Even a quick entry, however, is revealing in its information that they played *all day*. Similarly, Joseph Joslin, Jr., a South Killingly, Connecticut, teamster, observed ball playing, on April 21, 1778, while carrying out his duties for the army: "I took care of my oxen & then I went to Capt grinnels after oats and for a load of goods and then S W Some cloudy and I See them play ball . . . "[27] In like manner, Samuel Shute, a New Jersey lieutenant, jotted down his reference to playing ball in central Pennsylvania sometime between July 9 and 22, 1779: " . . . until the 22nd, the time was spent in playing Shinny and Ball."[28] Incidentally Shute distinguished among various sports, referring elsewhere in his journal to "Bandy Wicket." He did not confuse baseball with types of field hockey and cricket that the soldiers also played.

Other soldiers made several references to playing. For example, Lieutenant Ebenezer Elmer, a New Jersey officer, chronicled ball playing in New York state, in September 1776 and in New Jersey, in May 1777. On September 18, 1776, he wrote: " . . . The Regiment exercised 'fore and afternoon, and in the afternoon the Colonel, Parsons, and a number of us played whirl . . . "

Two days later the troops played again and Elmer suffered a jaw injury: "At 9 o'clock, A. M., the Regiment was paraded, and grounded their arms to clear the parade; after which we had a game or two more at whirl; at which Dr. Dunham gave me a severe blow on my mouth which cut my lip, and came near to dislocating my under jaw . . . " "In the afternoon again had exercise, . . . Played ball again." A week later Elmer returned to the theme in his September 28th entry: "We had after exercise a considerable ball play — Colonel, Parsons and all. Parade again at 2 o'clock, but soon dismissed." Two days later, the ball play resulted in a rhubarb: "The day was so bad and so much labor going on, that we had no exercise, but some ball play — at which some dispute arose among the officers, but was quelled without rising high." The next spring, Elmer was playing ball again. His diary citation for May 14, 1777, noted: "Played ball, &c., till some time in the afternoon, when I walked up to Mr. DeCamp's, where I tarried all night."[29]

Benjamin Gilbert played ball with about the same frequency. Gilbert, a Brookfield, Massachusetts, sergeant who ironically settled later near Cooperstown, recounted ball playing in the lower Hudson River valley in the Aprils of 1778 and 1779. On April 28, 1778, he entered in his journal: "In the fore noon the Serjt went Down the hill and plaid Ball." Two days later, duty hindered his desire to play: "In the Morning I went Down the Hill to play Ball and was Called up immediately to Gather watch coats." The next April, however, found him hard at play. On April 5, 1779, he wrote: "Our Regt Mustered at 3 oClock after noon. After Muster went to the store and plaid Ball with serjt. Wheeler." And the next day: "In the after noon the serjt. of our Regt. Went to the Comsy. store to play Ball." A week later, on the 14th, Gilbert wrote about ball again: "Fair and Clear. In the afternoon we went to the Comissary Store and Plaid Ball." Three years later, on April 7, 1782, Gilbert noted once again: "plaid at Ball severely." Whatever "severely" meant is anyone's guess; it may have been a misspelling for "severally."[30]

Indeed baseball is associated with the heights of patriotism in the war. In 1778, at Valley Forge, after that terrible winter of deprivation, George Ewing, a New Jersey ensign, recorded that the troops played baseball. In what might have been the first written use of the term "base" in North America, Ewing wrote that April: "Attested to my Muster Rolls and delivered them to the Muster Master excersisd in the afternoon in the intervals playd at base . . . "[31] Even the commander of the whole Continental Army apparently had a penchant for throwing the old horsehide around. Commenting on George Washington's character while observing him at camp at Fishkill in September, 1779, the newly-arrived secretary to the French legation, François, Comte de

Barbé-Marbois, wrote, "To-day he sometimes throws and catches a ball for whole hours with his aides-de-camp."[32]

The patriots, however, did not have a monopoly on baseball; even loyalists played. Enos Stevens, a Charlestown, New Hampshire, loyalist lieutenant serving near New Utrecht on Long Island, mentioned baseball several times in his journal. On May 2, 1778, he penned: "at hom all day play ball sum." On May 31st: "Lords dy. I omit puting down every dy when their is nothing meteriel happens good weather for ball Play." Apparently Stevens saw ball play, even when the Sabbath prevented it, as more important than "nothing meteriel." On June 2nd: "fine plesent weather play ball." On June 5th: "play ball." And on June 8th: "play ball in afternoon." The next May 3rd, he recorded "in the after noon [illegible words] play ball." And in 1781, he returned to the game. On March 22nd, the entry read: "in the after noon played Wickett." And a week later, Stevens wrote "playd ball."[33]

Some of the soldiers and officers observed ball playing while they were prisoners-of-war. Lieutenant Jabez Fitch, a Connecticut officer, witnessed ball playing during his imprisonment in the New York City area in March and April, 1777. On March 14th, he wrote: "In the Morning Lt: Blackleach made us a short Visit; this forenoon I went with Capt: Bissell down to Capt: Wells's Quarters where I procured some paper &c; on our way we lit of a number of our Offrs: who were Zealously Engaged at playing Ball, with whom we staid some time; We came home to our Quarters at about one." The next day the scene was much the same: "This Forenoon Col. Hart & Majr: Wells came to our Quarters, & we went with them down Street as far as Johanes Lotts, where there was a large number of our Offrs: collected, & spent some Time at playing Ball." About a month later, on April 12th, Fitch again saw the officers at play: "Toward Night I took a walk with Lt: Brewster down as far as Capt: Johnsons Quarters, where there was a number of our Offrs: Assembled for playing Ball; I came home alittle after Sunset."[34] Some Americans watched or played the game while imprisoned in England. Charles Herbert, a Newburyport, Massachusetts, sailor, thus referred to ball playing as a prisoner-of-war in Plymouth, England, on April 2, 1777: "Warm, and something pleasant, and the yard begins to be dry again, so that we can return to our former sports; these are ball and quoits, which exercise we make use of to circulate our blood and keep us from things that are worse."[35] Jonathan Haskins, a Connecticut surgeon who was also in an English prison, witnessed one of the odder occurrences of a baseball-type game. On May 23, 1778, a game of ball took an odd and potentially deadly twist. Haskins wrote in his journal for that day: "23rd. This forenoon as some of the prisoners was playing ball, it by chance happened to lodge in the eave spout. One climbed up to take the ball out, and a sentry without the wall seeing him, fired at him, but did no harm."[36] Note that it was the prisoners, that is, the Americans, who were playing the ball game, not their colonial overlords.

Perhaps the most intriguing evidence about soldiers playing during the Revolution came from the memoirs of Samuel Dewees, a Pennsylvania captain, who in 1781 and 1782 was a teenager guarding the British prisoners-of-war at Lancaster, Pennsylvania. Dewees recalled that the Convention Army officers had a passion for ball playing:

> These officers were full of cash, and frolicked and gamed much. One amusement in which they indulged much, was playing at ball. A Ball-Alley was fitted up at the Court-House, where some of them were to be seen at almost all hours of the day. When I could beg or buy a couple of old stockings, or two or three old stocking-feet, I would set to work and make a ball. After winding the yarn into a ball, I went to a skin-dressers and got a piece of white leather, with which I covered it. When finished, I carried it to the British officers, who would *"jump at it"* at a quarter of a dollar. Whilst they remained at Lancaster, I made many balls in this way, and sold them to the British officers, and always received a quarter a-piece.

Dewees's passage is remarkable for a number of reasons. It suggested that ball playing was quite common and an activity that players could invest with a passionate intensity. Second, skill in making balls was also apparently commonplace, as a fifteen-year-old boy easily knew how to fashion them. And it is astonishing to find out that players were playing with white leather balls as early as 1781 or 1782! Dewees also recorded a brouhaha among the officers during a ball game: "Whilst the game of ball was coming off one day at the Court House, an American officer and a British officer, who were among the spectators, became embroiled in a dispute."[37]

It is unclear whether or not the Revolutionary War accelerated the familiarity of baseball in North America, as the Civil War clearly did eighty some years later. It would be useful to ascertain if prisoners-of-war taught their captors how to play the games and learned from each other during those incarcerations. Similarly, did officers play the games more often than enlisted men, or vice versa? Were the officers' games more formalized than those of the troops? The sources indicate that both sets of soldiers played, but don't make any detailed distinctions. What is discernible is that during the war, baseball-type games provided needed recreation for troops within a matrix of other sports. As Montague, Massachusetts, farmer Joel Shepard recalled baseball at a bivouac near Albany, New York, late in the war, about 1782: "We passed muster and layed in Albany about six weeks and we fared tolerable well, and not much to doo, but each class had his amusement. The officers would bee a playing at Ball on the comon, their would be an other class piching quaits, an other set a wrestling, . . . "[38]

Like the soldiers, students at the academies and colleges took a shine to the ball games. Students probably played the games, taking advantages of study breaks and lapses in college discipline to pour out onto the common for a match or two. The practice apparently could get quite rowdy. Some colleges attempted to ban the ball games because of potential property damage to windows and buildings. As early as 1764, Yale College tried to restrict hand and foot ball games. The statute, in Latin at first, and in later laws in English, read: "9. If any Scholar shall play at Hand-Ball, or Foot-Ball, or Bowls in the College-Yard, or throw any Thing against [the] Colege by which the Glass may be endangerd, . . . he shall be punished six Pence, and make good the Damages." Later renditions changed the monetary amount to eight cents and this restriction carried into the next century with little change.[39] Dartmouth College followed suit with its own ordinance in 1780: "If any student shall play at ball or use any other diversion the College or Hall windows within 6 rods of either he shall be fined two shilling for the first offence 4 for the 2d and so no [on] at the discretion of the President or Tutors —"[40] In 1784, the University of Pennsylvania acknowledged that the yard was "intended for the exercise and recreation of the youth," but forbid them to "play ball against any of the walls of the University, whilst the windows are open."[41] Williams College followed suit in 1805: " . . . the students in the College and scholars in the Grammar School, shall not be permitted to play at ball, or use any other sport or diversion, in or near the College Edifice, by which the same may be exposed to injury." Violations would result in fines and possibly dismissal.[42] Bowdoin College added its own prohibition in 1817: "No Student shall, in or near any College building, play at ball, or use any sport or diversion, by which such building may be exposed to injury, on penalty of being fined not exceeding twenty cents, or of being suspended, if the offence be often repeated."[43]

Students continued to play, however, as Sidney Willard, son of Harvard president Joseph Willard, and himself later a Harvard professor, remembered in two passages in his 1855 memoirs. Referring to the campus Buttery of the 1760s, Willard wrote, "Besides eatables, everything necessary for a student was there sold, and articles used in the play-grounds, as bats, balls, &c." Then recalling the campus play fields of the last decade of the century, he noted,

"Here it was that we wrestled and ran, played at quoits, at cricket, and various games of bat and ball, whose names perhaps are obsolete, and leaped and jumped in rivalry.[44] Diarist John Rhea Smith recorded at least one baseball game at Princeton College in March, 1786: "A fine day, play baste ball in the campus but am beaten for I miss both catching and striking the ball."[45] Daniel Webster referred to "playing at ball" during his Dartmouth College years at the turn of the century.[46] Baltimore poet Garrett Barry placed ball play in verse lament about college days, "On Leaving College":

> I'll fondly trace, with fancy's aid,
> The spot where all our sports were made,
> When in our gay . . . our infant years,
> While strangers yet to pain and tears,
> When toil had "lent its turn to play,"
> The little train forever gay,
> With joy obey'd the pleasing call,
> And nimbly urged the flying ball.[47]

On April 11, 1824, Bowdoin College student and future poet Henry Wadsworth Longfellow wrote to his father, who was in Washington, about a surge in ball playing on the campus:

> This has been a very sickly term in college. However, within the last week, the government, seeing that something must be done to induce the students to exercise, recommended a game of ball every now and then; which communicated such an impulse to our limbs and joints, that there is nothing now heard of, in our leisure hours, but ball, ball, ball. I cannot prophesy with any degree of accuracy concerning the continuance of this rage for play, but the effect is good, since there has been a thorough-going reformation from inactivity and torpitude.[48]

Williams Latham played at Brown in the mid-1820s. On March 22, 1827, he declared, "We had a great play at ball to day noon." But a couple of weeks later, on April 9th, he was complaining about the quality of the play and pitching: "We this morning . . . have been playing ball, But I never have received so much pleasure from it as I have in Bridgewater. They do not have more than 6 or 7 on a side, so that a great deal of time is spent runing after the ball, Neither do they throw so fair ball, They are affraid the fellow in the middle will hit it with his bat-stick."[49] Oliver Wendell Holmes, Sr., played at Harvard in 1829.[50] Yale was not to be outdone, as a March 1837 letter from student Josiah Dwight Whitney, later an eminent geologist in the American West, showed:

"It is about the time now for playing ball, and the whole green is covered with students engaged in that fine game: for my part, I could never make a ball player. I can't see where the ball is coming soon enough to put the ball-club in its way." Anson Phelps Stokes, who also reprinted the letter in a book on Yale students, dismissed the game as "merely 'one-old-cat' or 'two-old-cat,'" because he believed in the Doubleday origins story. But the game in which Whitney had such trouble placing the bat on the ball, a problem recognizable to us moderns, could have as easily been baseball.[51] Older scholars may have had some interest in the game as well. Connecticut lexicographer and writer Noah Webster may have been referring to a baseball-type game when wrote his journal entry for March 24-25, 1788: "Take a long walk. Play at Nines at Mr Brandons. Very much indisposed."[52]

Indeed, the sabbath restrictions against ball playing were breaking down. In 1836, a Georgetown University student wrote to a friend, ". . . the Catholics think it no harm to play Ball, Draughts or play the Fiddle and dance of a Sunday . . . "[53] Such was the case apparently even in Rhode Island, according to James B. Angell: "[Sunday] was the day for visiting relatives and friends and largely for fishing and hunting and ball-playing."[54] At least one minister played the game. In his diary, Rev. Thomas Robbins detailed his ball play and that of local boys, while a divinity student at Williams College and during his teaching days. "I exercise considerable, playing ball," he wrote on April 22, 1796. In February and March, 1797, he noted that the Sheffield, Connecticut, boys were playing ball, apparently "smartly" on one occasion. The April 24th entry recorded: "Play ball some. The spring as yet rather backward." Three years later, at Danbury, Connecticut, on an unseasonably warm January day, Robbins remarked, "My boys play ball freely." And right around Christmas that same year, in another warm spell, the boys were at it again. For December 27th, Robbins wrote: "Boys play at ball till night without the least inconvenience."[55]

There was some dissent about the moral uses of the game. On August 19, 1785, Thomas Jefferson urged his nephew Peter Carr to avoid ball games and take up hunting as recreation. "Games played with the ball and others of that nature, are too violent for the body and stamp no character on the mind," the future president counseled.[56] Despite Jefferson's opinion, however, children's books continued to recommend or at least document baseball-type games for youths. Edgar and Jane, the protagonists of a British children's book, published in Baltimore in 1806, *The Children in the Wood*, wandered into a British town where some children "were playing at trap and ball."[57] In an 1806 book of poems for children, Ann Gilbert described some sort of ball play as common on the village commons:

THE VILLAGE GREEN
Then ascends the worsted ball;
High it rises in the air;
Or against the cottage wall,
Up and down it bounces there.[58]

In a sequel volume published the next year, Gilbert included one warning boys about breaking windows during ball play:

BALL
MY good little fellow, don't throw your ball there,
You'll break neighbour's windows I know;
On the end of the house there is room and to spare;
Go round, you can have a delightful game there,
Without fearing for where you may throw.

Harry thought he might safely continue his play,
With a little more care than before;
So, forgetful of all that his father could say,
As soon as he saw he was out of the way,
He resolved to have fifty throws more.

Already as far as to forty he rose,
And no mischief happen'd at all;
One more, and one more, he successfully throws,
But when, as he thought, just arriv'd at the close,
In popp'd his unfortunate ball.

Poor Harry stood frighten'd, and turning about,
Was gazing at what he had done;
As the ball had popp'd in, so neighbour popp'd out,
And with a good horsewhip he beat him about,
Till Harry repented his fun.

When little folks think they know better than great,
And what is forbidden them do;
We must always expect to see, sooner or late,
That such wise little fools have a similar fate,
And that one of the fifty goes through.[59]

In an 1807 edition of *The Prize for Youthful Obedience*, a hermit who had been watching some children playing ball games approved of their play and promised "to provide bats, balls, &c." at his next visit."[60] An 1802 volume, *Youthful Sports* actually touted cricket as a sport superior to what it called "bat and ball":

CRICKET

THIS play requires more strength than some boys possess, to manage the ball in a proper manner; it must therefore be left to the more robust lads, who are fitter for such athletic exercises. It must be allowed to be good diversion, and is of such note, that even men very frequently divert themselves with it. Bat and ball is an inferior kind of cricket, and more suitable for little children, who may safely play at it, if they will be careful not to break windows.[61]

Two succeeding children's recreation manuals in 1810 painted a rosier picture of trap ball. *Youthful Amusements* recommended it highly:

TRAP BALL

Without any exception, this is one of the most pleasing sports that youth can exercise themselves in. It strengthens the arms, exercises the legs, and adds pleasure to the mind. If every time the ball be bowled to the trap, the striker be permitted to guess the number of bat's lengths from the trap, it greatly contributes to teach lads the rule of *addition*. And should he be so covetous as to overguess the distance, he will, as he deserves to do, forfeit his right to the bat, and give it to another playmate.[62]

Youthful Recreations went even further, offering that it should be the right of every child to have an hour of recreation each day with sports, among bat and ball-type games: "To play with *battledore* and *shuttlecock* or with a *trap* and *ball*, is good exercise; and if we had it in our power to grant, not only to the children of the affluent, but even such of the poor as are impelled by necessity to pick cotton, card wool, to sit and spin or reel all day, should have at least one hour, morning and evening, for some youthful recreation; and if they could obtain neither battledore nor shuttlecock, trap, bat, nor ball, they should at least play at *Hop-Scotch.*"[63] The next year, *The Book of Games*, a look at sports at a British academy, gave a ringing endorsement to trap ball and supplied the most detailed description of it in the period.[64] *Remarks on Children's Play*, in 1819, repeated the same comments of the 1810 *Youthful Amusements* book.[65] By the time *The Boy's Own Book* and Robin Carver's *The Book of Sports* appeared in 1829 and 1834 respectively, with their descriptions of baseball, the game was probably quite familiar to the youth of the Early Republic.[66]

At the turn of the century, baseball-type games continued to provoke clashes in cities, towns, and villages. Some of their governments responded with prohibitions on such games, much as did the province of New Hampshire for Christmas Day in 1771. At its town meeting in March, 1795, Portsmouth, New Hampshire, attempted to abolish cricket and any games played with a ball. The ordinance read as follows:

> VOTED III, That if any person or persons shall after the thirty-first day of May next, within the compact part of the town of Portfmouth, . . . play at cricket or any game wherein a ball is used, . . . he, she, or they, so offending, on conviction thereof shall forfeit and pay to the overseers of the porr of said town for the time being, for each and every offence, a sum not exceeding three dollars and thirty cents, nor less than fifty cents, and costs of prosecution . . . [67]

By the 1830s, however, players consumed egg-nog "between intervals of base-ball playing" on nearby Shapleigh's Island and taunted the temperance forces.[68] Down the coast, Newburyport, Massachusetts, passed a similar restriction in 1797, adding soccer to its list of offending games: "12th. Voted and ordered, that if any person shall play at foot-ball, cricket or any other play or game with a ball or balls in any of the streets, lanes, or, alleys of this town, such person shall forfeit and pay a sum not exceeding one dollar nor less than twenty-five cents."[69] In 1805 the town of Portland, Maine, promulgated a more detailed prohibition entitled "A By Law to check the practice of playing at Bat and Ball in the Streets": " . . . [N]o person shall play at the game of bat and ball, or shall strike any ball with a bat or other machine in the streets, lanes, or squares of the town, on penalty of *Fifty Cents* for each offense."[70] By 1828, however, a Portland newspaper referred to boys playing at "bat-and-ball."[71] Twelve years earlier and fifty miles inland, Worcester, Massachusetts, considered outlawing playing ball because of numerous complaints:

> At a legal meeting May 6, 1816
> To see if the said Inhabitants will adopt any mode, or make such regulations as will in future prevent the playing Ball and Hoops in the public Streets in said Town, a practice so frequent and dangerous, that has occasioned many great and repeated complaints.[72]

Note that the town council characterized ball playing as *frequent*. Troy, New York, restricted baseball-type games in 1816: "[N]o person or persons shall play ball, beat, knock or drive any ball or hoop, in, through or along any street or alley in the first, second, third or fourth wards of said city; and every person who shall violate either of the prohibitions . . . shall, for each and every such offence, forfeit and pay the penalty of ten dollars."[73] Down the Hudson, New York City outlawed ball play in the Park, Battery, and Bowling-Green in 1817.[74] The crowning irony to all of this came a month later in, of all places, Cooperstown, when that village promulgated an ordinance forbidding the playing of ball in the center of town fully twenty-three years before Abner Doubleday supposedly drew up his diamond and rules! The June 1816 ordinance read as follows: "*Be it ordained*, That no person shall play at Ball in Second or West street, in this village, under a penalty of one dollar, for each and every offence."[75] Tom Heitz has suggested that the one dollar fine was equivalent to the cost of replacing a window in those days, so perhaps the law was setting up an insurance program of sorts to cover breakage and had little hope of completely discouraging players from playing.[76]

Still boys and men continued to play ball. Keene, New Hampshire, farmer Abner Sanger noted in his journal entry for April 27, 1782: "Caleb Washburn, young Benjamin Hall, Tom Wells, the younger and El play ball before my barn."[77] Ball games were familiar enough in northern New England that Vermonter Levi Allen could write to his brother Ira from Quebec on July 7, 1787: "Three times is Out at wicket, next year if Something is not done I will retire to the Green Mountains . . . "[78] The games went on at the private academies. At the turn of the century ball-playing at Exeter Academy was commonplace, according to a historian of that school: "The only games seem to have been old-fashioned 'bat and ball,' which, in the spring, was played on the grounds around the Academy building, and football. The former differed widely from the modern game of base ball, which was introduced later. The old game had fewer rules, and was played with a soft leather ball."[79] Note, however, the author's characterization of the game as old-fashioned, implying a longevity of familiarity. In 1836 Albert Ware Paine recalled playing in Bangor, Maine, in the 1810s and 1820s: "But a day seems to have elapsed since meeting with our neighboring boys, we took delight in flying our kite and prancing our horses on the green or engaged ourselves in the more active sports of 'playing ball' or 'goal.'"[80] New York City octogenarian Charles Haswell reminisced that if "a base-ball was required, the boy of 1816 founded it with a bit of cork, or, if he were singularly fortunate, with some shreds of india-rubber; then it was wound with yarn from a ravelled stocking, and some feminine member of his family covered it with patches from a soiled glove."[81] By the late 1830s, Buffalo, New York, boys were even using fish noses for the ball cores, according to Samuel L. Welch: " . . . the fish I bought as a small boy at that time, at one cent per pound, mainly to gets its noses for cores for our balls, to make them bound, to play the present National Game," he wrote in 1891.[82]

Sometimes memoirists mentioned baseball only to say that they avoided the game or regretted what they considered a waste of time and industry. Thus Wilmington, Delaware, ship captain John Hamilton wrote about his boyhood in the 1790s that reading about foreign countries "took precedence [over] Kites, Marbles, Balls, Shinny Sticks, and all other Boyish Sports."[83] Similarly, Cannon's Ferry, Delaware, doctor William Morgan remarked about his adolescence in the 1790s, "My sixteenth, seventeenth and eighteenth yeares were spent in youthfull folley. Fidling, frolicking, ball playing and hunting as far as I could be spared by my father from his employ. These are called inocent amusements and ware not caried very far by me."[84] Sometimes, however, ball games led to further adventures. Jonathan Mason, Jr, a Boston merchant, remembered a special game of ball on the Boston Commons in the 1790s or early 1800s:

> Another early remembrance of the common besets me. One morning, the day after what was called the Negro election, Benj Green, Martin Brimmer, George E Head, Franklin Dexter and myself were playing ball on the common before breakfast: and the ball fell into a hole where one of the booth's stakes had been driven the day before, which was filled up with paper, rubbage etc. putting the hand down something jingled and we found several dollars in silver which had probably been put there for safety and the owner becoming intoxicated late in the day had gone off and forgotten them. I can't recollect that we advertised them. We were small boys then all of us, and I was the youngest.[85]

And even though he claimed he had never heard the word "baseball" in the 1820s, Middletown, Connecticut, resident John Howard Redfield remembered that baseball-type games were pervasive:

> The remainder of Election week was given more or less to relaxation and amusement. This period usually coincided with the vacation, or gap between the winter and summer terms of school. Ball was the chief amusement, and if weather permitted (and my impression is that it generally *did* permit) the open green about the meeting-house and the school-house was constantly occupied by the players, little boys, big boys, and even *men* (for such we considered the biggest boys who condescended to join the game), . . . These grown-up players usually de-

voted themselves to a game called "wicket," in which the ball was impelled along the ground by a wide, peculiarly-shaped bat, over, under, or through a wicket, made by a slender stick resting on two supports. I never heard of baseball in those days.[86]

Clearly, as these prohibitions, depictions in children's books, and remembrances indicate, baseball and its predecessors were entrenched in the young republic's athletic repertoire by 1820.

Other evidence hints that the games had spread to the South and to Canada. John Drayton, a South Carolina politician and historian, referred to ball playing in his state about 1802: "[A]musements are few; consisting of dancing, horse racing, ball playing, and rifle shooting."[87] Another South Carolinian, Charles Fraser, recalled, in 1854, how vibrant were the sports of his childhood in Charleston in the early part of the century: "The manly sports of ball, shinee, jumping, running, wrestling, and swimming, are now laid aside as unworthy of modern refinement. But they were as common among the elder boys of my time, as marbles, tops and kites were among the little ones."[88] Ely Playter, a York, Ontario, tavernkeeper, may have meant baseball or a baseball-type game when he wrote in his diary for April 13, 1803: "I went to Town . . . walk'd out and joined a number of men jumping & playing Ball, perceived a Mr. Joseph Randall to be the most active . . . "[89] Incipient commercialism may also have been invading the games. The New York *Evening Post* for September 20, 1811, contained an advertisement for "Trap Ball, Quoits, Cricket, &c." at Dyde's Military Ground.[90]

The most bizarre bit of evidence of baseball's spread may have occurred in conjunction with a tragic incident just after the close of the War of 1812. The British were still housing numerous American prisoners at Dartmoor Prison in England, awaiting repatriation arrangements. Needless to say, tempers ran high, and the British officers occasionally tormented the Americans. As had other prisoners-of-war before them, some of the Americans whiled away their incarceration by playing baseball. For example, American prisoners-of-war back in North America at Cornwall, Ontario, mixed ball with their boxing. Wrote one prisoner, "The men remained in the gaol yard and fought several times and in fact played [ball — the editor mistakenly translated the word as "hell"] all day."[91] Similarly one prisoner, Benjamin Waterhouse, recalled the Americans at Dartmoor were in "high spirits and good humour" about going home and reflected it in their play: "I distinctly remember that the prisoners appeared to enjoy their amusements, such as playing ball and the like, beyond what I had before observed."[92] The previous June, the British commander had opened the yards on the south side of the enclosure, which, according to prisoner Charles Andrews, "would admit of many amusements which that of No. 4 would not, such as playing ball, &c."[93]

On April 6, 1815, some of the prisoners were at such play. As inmate Nathaniel Pierce recalled, " . . . first part of this day the Prisoners divirting themselves Gambling playing Ball &c."[94] During the afternoon, however, things went awry. A batter hit the ball over one of the interior walls and the British sentries would not allow the players to retrieve it. As prisoner Andrews later wrote, " . . . some boys who were playing ball in No. 7 yard, knocked their ball over into the barrack-yard, and on the sentry in that yard refusing to throw it back to them, they picked a hole in the wall to get in after it."[95] Another inmate, Joseph Valpey, Jr., described the scenario in more detail:

On the 6th day of April 1815 as a small party of prisoners were amusing themselves at a game at ball, some of the number striking it with too much violence it went over the wall fronting the prison the Centinals on the opposite side of the same were requested to heave the ball back, but refused, on which the party threatened to brake through and regain the ball and immediately put their threats in execution, a hole was made in the wall sufficiently large enough for a man to pass through . . . [96]

The "Judicial Report of the Massacre at Dartmoor Prison" concluded indeed that ball playing figured in the incident: "It unfortunately happened, that in the afternoon of the 6th of April, some boys who were playing ball in No. 7 yard, knocked their ball over into the barrack yard: on the sentry in that yard refusing to throw it back to them, they picked a hole in the wall to get in after it."[97] The British officers misconstrued this breach of the interior wall as some sort of riot and ordered troops to fire at the ball players. By the end of the melee there were seven dead and thirty-one wounded prisoners. A poem by John Hunter Waddell, which ran in New York and Boston newspapers in June, 1815, referred to the ball playing as commonplace and summed up the tragedy:

Forsooth, there was great fear to dread, he [the British captain]'d search'd
    and found in wall
A hole was made for boy to creep, and get again a ball,
Which oft was thrown by boys at play, their usual daily sport,
In pastime who at prison wall, did ev'ry day resort;

And frequent would their balls bounce o'er out of the prison yard,
To get again their balls for sport, their pastime and their play,
And so their joy, was oft times spoilt, and ended for the day.
The boys thus baulk'd, and being griev'd to lose their balls and play,
Contriv'd to make a hole to gain, and get their balls again.[98]

By the 1820s, the games were taking on the more organized form of clubs. In his autobiography, New York politician Thurlow Weed claimed to have been a member of a town ball club in Rochester in 1825:

> Though an industrious and busy place, its citizens found leisure for rational and healthy recreation. A base-ball club, numbering nearly fifty members, met every afternoon during the ball-playing season. Though the members of the club embraced persons between eighteen and forty, it attracted the young and the old. The ball-ground, containing some eight or ten acres, known as Mumford's meadow, by the side of the river above the falls, is now a compact part of the city.

Weed went on to list ten of the better players on that club and point out that a couple of them rose to prominence as lawyers in New York City.[99] Although some historians think that the mounting popularity of baseball in the intervening decades may have colored Weed's memoir, Samuel Hopkins Adams, in the story, "Baseball in Mumford's Pasture Lot," in his book, *Grandfather Stories*, corroborated Weed with a scene in which Grandpa Adams informed his grandson and friends that he had played baseball back in Rochester in 1827. "When I first came here, the Rochester Baseball Club met four afternoons a week. We had fifty members. That was in 1827," the old man recounted. The club played in "Mumford's pasture lot, off Lake Avenue." Furthermore, he told them, "The cream of Rochester's Third Ward ruffleshirts participated in the pastime," which was clearly baseball, not town ball, as the old man described the positioning of the fielders and mentioned that it took three outs to retire the batting side.[100]

Yet it would be a mistake to see baseball and baseball-type games as very modern by the 1820s, at least not in the sense that sport historians such as Allen Guttmann have stipulated. Presumably there was an equity in the rules, that each player played under the same conditions, but there may have been exceptions to that. There was certainly no bureaucratization overseeing baseball-type games. There may or may not have been specialization; players most likely played nonspecific positions on the playing field and probably the pitcher, or "feeder," was not a very important position yet. How much players were experimenting to perfect the rules or methods of playing the game is also unclear. Quantification, at least in the form of statistics that carried over time, was nonexistent, and if there were any "records," they didn't make it into any "recordbook."[101] Local players may have kept up an oral memory of great players and great plays, but it is just as likely that the emphasis was on play, spontaneity, and communal recreation. Baseball and similar games were still folk games, with all their rubbery aspects and irregular patterns. That does not mean, however, that they were any less important to the populace than are modern sports today. Baseball and baseball-type games existed with some degree of frequency, because they filled a cultural hunger for physical play and communal recreation, a yearning of time immemorial. The above sources, and probably others still undiscovered in the record, attest to the American phase of this long process. Henry Dearborn and his fellow soldiers deserve thanks not only for helping to convince the British to lose the war, but for marching four miles that day in April 1779 "to find a place leavel enough to play ball," and all the ball-playing students merit our remembrances as well.

Finally, though, the origins of the game may have to remain shrouded in mystery. Perhaps, as Harold Seymour wrote, "To ascertain who invented baseball would be equivalent to trying to locate the discoverer of fire."[102] Perhaps it was an entirely "natural" occurrence. As James D'Wolf Lovett stated, "It seems to be the natural instinct of a boy as soon as he finds the use of his arms, to want to 'bat' something."[103] Possibly the instinct is quite deep-seated and the Freudians and other psychoanalysts can weigh in with theories such as Adrian Stokes's provocative interpretation that cricket developed as a form of sexual sublimation.[104] Or maybe Kenneth Patchen's explanation in his poem, "The Origin of Baseball," comes as close as any:

Someone had been walking in and out
Of the world without coming
To much decision about anything.
The sun seemed too hot most of the time.
There weren't enough birds around
And the hills had a silly look
When he got on top of one.

The girls in heaven, however, thought
Nothing of asking to see his watch
Like you would want someone to tell
A joke — "Time," they'd say, "what's

That mean — time?", laughing with the edges
Of their white mouths, like a flutter of paper
In a madhouse. And he'd stumble over
General Sherman or Elizabeth B.
Browning, muttering, "Can't you keep
Your big wings out of the aisle?" But down
Again, there'd be millions of people without
Enough to eat and men with guns just
Standing there shooting each other.

So he wanted to throw something
And he picked up a baseball.[105]

THE LETTERS OF ABNER GRAVES

❖

The following are the two letters submitted by Abner Graves in 1905 describing the purported invention of baseball by Abner Doubleday. The first of these was addressed to the editor of the Akron, Ohio, Beacon-Journal *newspaper in response to an article by Albert Spalding that appeared in that paper. The second letter was sent directly to Spalding. I have adhered to Graves's original spelling and punctuation.*

LETTER I

Abner Graves

Mining Engineer

32 Bank Block

P.O. Box 672

Denver, Colo.

April 3rd, 1905

Editor Beacon Journal

Akron, Ohio,

Dear Sir: —

I notice in Saturdays "Beacon Journal" a question as to "origin of "base ball" from pen of A G Spalding, and requesting data on the subject be sent to Mr J E Sullivan, 15 Warren Street, New York.

The American game of "Base Ball" was invented by Abner Doubleday of Cooperstown, New York, either the spring prior, or following the "Log Cabin & Hard Cider" campaign of General Harrison for President, said Abner Doubleday being then a boy pupil of "Green's Select School" in Cooperstown, and the same, who as General Doubleday won honor at the Battle of Gettysburg in the Civil war. The pupils of "Otsego Academy" and "Green's Select School" were then playing the old game of "Town Ball" in the following manner.

A "Tosser" stood beside the home "goal" and tossed the ball straight upward about six feet for the batsman to strike at on its fall, he using a four inch flat board bat, and all others who wanted to play being scattered all over the near and far field to catch the ball, the lucky catcher then taking his innings at the bat while the losing batsman retired to the field. Should the batsman miss the ball on its fall and the tosser catch it on its first bounce he would take the bat and the losing batsman toss the ball.

When the batsman struck the ball into the field he would run for an out goal about fifty feet and return, and if the ball was not caught on the fly, and he could return to home goal without getting "plunked" with the ball thrown by anyone, he retained his innings same as in "old cat". There being generally from twenty to fifty boys in the field, collisions often occured in attempt of several to catch the ball. Abner Doubleday then figured out and made a plan of improvement on town ball to limit number of players, and have equal sides, calling it "Base Ball" because it had four bases, three being where the runner could rest free of being put out by keeping his foot on the flat stone base, while next one on his side took the bat, the first runner being entitled to run whenever he chose, and if he could make home base without being hit by the ball he tallied. There was a six foot ring within which the pitcher had to stand and toss the ball to batsman by swinging his hand below his hip. There was eleven players on a side, four outfielders, three basemen, pitcher, catcher, and two infielders, the two infielders being placed respectively a little back from the pitcher and between first and second base, and second and third base and a short distance inside the base lines. The ball used had a rubber center overwound with yarn to size some larger than the present regulation ball, then covered with leather or buckskin, and having plenty of bouncing qualities, wonderful high flys often resulted. Anyone getting the ball was entitled to throw it at a runner and put him out if could hit him.

This "Base Ball" was crude compared with present day ball, but it was undoubtedly the first starter of "Base Ball" and quickly superceded "town ball" with the older boys, although we younger boys stuck to town ball and the "old cats". I well remember several of the best players of sixty years ago, such as Abner Doubleday, Elihu Phinney, John C Graves, Nels. C Brewer, Joseph Chaffee, John Starkweather, John Doubleday, Tom Bingham and others who used to play on the "Otsego Academy Campus" although a favorite place was on the "Phinney farm" on west shore of Otsego lake.

"Baseball" is undoubtedly a pure American game, and its birthplace Cooperstown, New York, and Abner Doubleday entitled to first honor of its invention.

Abner Graves
32 Bank Block, Denver, Colorado.

Abner Graves

Mining Engineer

32 Bank Block

P.O. Box 672

Denver, Colo.

November 17th 1905

A G Spaulding Esq.

126 Nassau Street, New York City

Dear Sir:

Your letter of 10th regarding origin of Base Ball received and contents noted. You mention sending me copy of "Spaldings Base Ball Guide for 1905", which I have not received, although I would like it to note the discussion mentioned. I am at loss how to get verification of my statements regarding the invention of base ball made in my letter of April 3rd 1905 to the "Akron, Ohio, Beacon-Journal", the carbon copy of my original draft of which I herewith enclose, this giving full particulars, and which after using, please return for my files.

You ask if I can positively name the year of Doubledays invention, and replying will say that I cannot, although am sure it was either 1839, 1840 or 1841, and in the spring of the year when we smaller boys were "playing marbles for keeps" which all stopped when ball commenced, as I remember well Abner Doubleday explaining "base ball" to a lot of us that were playing marbles in the street in front of Coopers tailor shop and drawing a diagram in the dirt with a stick by marking out a square with a punch mark in each corner for bases, a ring in center for pitcher, a punch mark just back of home base for catcher, two punch marks for infielders and four punch marks for outfielders, and we smaller boys didnt like it because it shut us out from playing, while Town Ball let in everyone who could run and catch flies, or try to catch them. Then Doubleday drew up same diagram on paper practically like diagram I will draw on back of another sheet and enclose herewith. The incident has always been associated in my mind with the "Log Cabin and Hard Cider" campaign of General Harrison, my Father being a "Militia" Captain and rabid partisan of "Old Tippecanoe".

I know it was as early as spring of 1841 because it was played at least three years before April 1844 when I started for Leyden Mass. to live that summer with my Uncle Joseph Green, the last prominent thing that I remember before starting being a big game of Base Ball on the "Phinney Farm" half a mile up the west side of Otsego Lake, between the Otsego Academy boys (Double-day then being in the Academy), and Professor Green and his Select School boys. Great furore and fun marked opening of the game on account of the then unprecedented thing of "first man up, three strikes and out". Elihu Phinney was Pitcher and Abner Doubleday Catcher for Academy, while Greens had innings and Prof. Green was first at bat, and Doubleday contrary to usual practice stood close at Green's back and caught all three balls, (Green having struck furiously at all with a four inch flat bat and missing all, then being hit in the back by the ball as he started to run.

While everyone laughed and roared at Green's three misses he claimed that Doubleday caught every ball from in front of the bat so there was no ball to hit, and that made the furore greater. I was an onlooker close up to catcher, and this incident so impressed me with the glories of Base Ball that on arriving at Leyden, Mass. I tried to get up a game but couldnt find anywhere near 22 boys so we had to play "Old Cat". Abner Doubleday unquestionably invented Base Ball at Cooperstown, N.Y., as an improvement on Town Ball so as to have opposing sides and limit players, and he named it Base Ball and had eleven players on each side. If any Cooperstown boys of that time are alive they will surely remember that game between the "Otsego's" and "Green's" which I surely identify as early in April 1844 before my start to Massachusetts, and I am certain it had been played at least three years earlier under same name and the larger boys had become proficient at it. Although I never saw any mention of ball playing in a newspaper when I was young, it might be that some mention of the game was made in the "Otsego Republican" about that time, said paper then (and now) being leading paper in Cooperstown.

Abner Doubleday was I think about 16 or 17 years old when he invented the game: he lived in Cooperstown but I do not know if born there. His cousin "John Doubleday" (a little younger) was born there and his father was a merchant with store in the main four corners in Cooperstown. The Phinneys were running a large Book Bindery there, and I believe one in New York at same time. Of course it is almost impossible to get documentary proof of the invention, as there is not one chance in ten thousand that a boys drawing plan of improved ball game would have been preserved for 65 years as at that time no such interest in games existed as it does now when all items are printed and Societies and Clubs preserve everything.

All boys old enough to play Base Ball in those days would be very old now if not dead, and this reminds me of a letter. I have a letter dated April 6th 1905, from Mary, wife of "John C Graves" mentioned in my printed letter saying, "Dear Cousin, I received a paper this eve from Akron, Ohio, with an article you wrote about Base Ball! Every one of the boys you named are dead except John, and perhaps you do not know that John has been sick over a year with the gout, and now his mind is very weak so sometimes he does not know me". She was mistaken in saying all for I am aware that Nels C Brewer whom I mentioned now lives in Cleveland, Ohio, and I think his address is 230 Superior Street, or near that, and although he is aged he may possibly remember about the Base Ball: John C Graves is about 85 and still lives in Cooperstown.

Also I have a brother (Joseph C Graves) still in business in Cedar Rapids, Iowa. I have added a few years experience since Base Ball was invented, but am still young enough to make a lively hand in a game, as I did last July, and I attribute my youth to the fact that I left Cooperstown and New York early in winter of 1848-9 for the Goldfields of California and have lived in the west ever since where the ageing climate of New York hasn't touched me. My Typewriter thinks this is a pretty long letter on one subject and I guess that is about correct, but your letter asked for as full data as possible and I have given you all the items I can in a rambling sort of way, but I think you have head enough to pick out the gist of it and be better satisfied than if I had been less explicit or prolix. Just in my present mood I would rather have Uncle Sam declare war on England and clean her up rather than have one of her citizens beat us out of Base Ball.

Yours truly
Abner Graves, E.M.

DR. ADAM E. FORD'S LETTER TO *SPORTING LIFE*

❖

Published May 5, 1886

*A Game of the Long-ago Which Closely
Resembled Our Present National Game. Denver, Col.,
April 26. Editor Sporting Life.*

The 4th of June, 1838, was a holiday in Canada, for the Rebellion of 1837 had been closed by the victory of the Government over the rebels, and the birthday of His Majesty George the Fourth was set apart for general rejoicing. The chief event at the village of Beechville, in the County of Oxford, was a base ball match between the Beechville Club and the Zorras, a club hailing from the townships of Zorra and North Oxford.

The game was played in a nice, smooth pasture field just back of Enoch Burdick's shops. I well remember a company of Scotch volunteers from Zorra halting as they passed the grounds to take a look at the game. Of the Beechville team I remember seeing Geo. Burdick, Reuben Martin, Adam Karn, Wm. Hutchinson, I. Van Alstine, and, I think, Peter Karn and some others. I remember also that there were in the Zorras "Old Ned" Dolson, Nathaniel NcNames, Abel and John Williams, Harry and Daniel Karn, and, I think, Wm. Ford and William Dodge. Were it not for taking up too much of your valuable space I could give you the names of many others who were there and incidents to confirm the accuracy of the day and the game. The ball was made of double and twisted woolen yarn, a little smaller than the regulation ball of to day and covered with good honest calf skin, sewed with waxed ends by Edward McNamee, a shoemaker.

The infield was a square, the base lines of which were twenty-one yards long, on which were placed five bags. The distance from the thrower to the catcher was eighteen yards; the catcher standing three yards behind the home bye. From the home bye, or "knocker's" stone, to the first bye was six yards. The club (we had bats in cricket but we never used bats in playing base ball) was generally made of the best cedar, blocked out with an ax and finished on a shaving horse with a drawing knife. A wagon spoke, or any nice straight stick would do.

We had fair and unfair balls. A fair ball was one thrown to the knocker at any height between the bend of his knee and the top of his head, near enough to him to be fairly within reach. All others were unfair. The strategic points for the thrower to aim at was to get it near his elbow or between his club and his ear. When a man struck at a ball it was a strike, and if a man struck at a ball three times and missed it he was out if the ball was caught every time either on the fly or on the first bound. If he struck at the ball and it was not so caught by the catcher that strike did not count. If a struck ball went anywhere within lines drawn straight back between home and the fourth bye, and between home and the first bye extended into the field the striker had to run. If it went outside of that he could not, and every man on the byes must stay where he was until the ball was in the thrower's hands. Instead of calling foul the call was "no hit."

There was no rule to compel a man to strike at the ball except the rule of honor, but a man would be despised and guyed unmercifully if he would not hit at a fair ball. If the knocker hit the ball anywhere he was out if the ball was caught either before it struck the ground or on the first bound. Every struck ball that went within the lines mentioned above was a fair hit; everyone outside of them no hit, and what you now call a foul tip was called a tick. A tick and a catch will always fetch was the rule given strikers out on foul tips. The same rule applies to forced runs that we have now. The bases were the lines between the byes and a base runner was out if hit by the ball when he was off of his bye. Three men out and the side out. And both sides out constituted a complete inning. The number of innings to be played was always a matter of agreement, but it was generally from 5 to 9 innings, 7 being most frequently played and when no number was agreed upon seven was supposed to be the number. The old plan which Silas Williams and Ned Dolson (these were grayheaded men then) said was the only right way to play ball, for it was the way they used to play when they were boys, was to play away until one side made 18, or 21, and the one getting that number first won the game. A tally, of course, was a run. The tallies were always kept by cutting notches on the edge of a stick when the base runners came in. There was no set number of men to be played on each side, but the sides must be equal. The number of men on each side was a matter of agreement when the match was made. I have frequently seen games played with 7 men on each side and I never saw more than 12. They all fielded.

The object in having the first bye so near the home was to get runners on the base lines, so as to have the fun of putting them out or enjoying the mistakes of the fielders when some fleet-footed fellow would dodge the ball and come in home. When I got older I played myself, for the game never died out. I well remember when some fellows down at or near New York got up the game of base ball that had a "pitcher" and "fou's" etc., and was played with a ball hard as a stick. India rubber had come into use, and they put so much into the balls to make them lively that when the fellow tossed it to you like a girl playing "one-o'd-cat" you could knock it so far that the fielders would be chasing it yet, like dogs hunting sheep, after you had gone clear around and scored your tally. Neil McTaggert, Henry Cruttenden, Gordon Cook, Henry Taylor, James Piper, Almon Burch, Wm. Harrington and others told me of it when I came home from the University. We, with a "lot of good fellows more," went out and played it one day. The next day we felt as if we had been on an overland trip to the moon. I could give you pages of incidents, but space forbids. One word as to prowess in those early days. I heard Silas Williams tell Jonathan Thornton that old Ned Dolson could catch the ball right away from the front of the club if you didn't keep him back so far that he couldn't reach it. I have played from that day to this, and I don't intend to quit as long as there is another boy on the ground.

Yours, Dr. Ford

BATTINGBALL GAMES

Per Maigaard

❖

This study by Per Maigaard of Denmark was the first modern attempt to compare, classify, and trace the origins of games played with bat and ball. The author's command of written English was somewhat awkward. The following article, first published in 1941, is presented in its original, unedited form.

Only a few students of games have in a greater degree taken up the study of *Battingball* games and some are of opinion that these games are of comparatively recent date. Nobody knew that such a game was played in Africa.

Now Professor Corrado Gini, chief of an Italian expedition for demographic investigation in Libya, has brought to light a Berber *Battingball*-game, which proves that the games in question date a long way back.[1] In the following paper I shall give a short account of these games specially as played in N. Europe, their home.

The implements used in the games in question are the bat and the ball (fig. 1). A bat may be simply a round stick, 30 to 115 cms. long, 2 to 6 cms. thick, but often flattened below the handle, and then as a rule broader there. Generally a curved bat is not used. It is held with one hand or with both.

The ball, now as a rule made of leather or rubber, has a size of 6 to 8 cms. Formerly a ball of woollen yarn was generally used or instead of that a billet or a "cat" (a double conical piece of wood) or a piece of horn.

Plain batting consists in striking the ball with the bat, the ball being held in the left hand, then tossed into the air and struck with the bat when it is falling, but before it reaches the ground, or, still more simply, the ball is struck at the moment the left hand leaves hold of it, as used also in *Tipcat*.[2] In other cases a special player, the "pitcher" tosses the ball, the batsman only strikes at it. In others again the pitcher stands at a distance and throws the ball for batting or to get it into a hole in the ground or to hit a goal which the batter has to defend.

Batting has become an important element in a multitude of games, in all

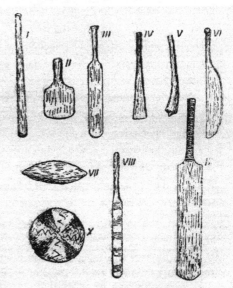

Fig. 1.

I. Common bat for *Longball* and *Baseball* (60 - 115 cms.).
II. Danish longball-bat, about 35 by 15 cms.
III. Common plattened longball-bat.
IV. Old english bat - 13th century.
V. Old (french?) bat.
VI. Rounders - bat (and old cricket-bat).
VII. A «Cat», 7 to 10 cms. long.
VIII. Rounders - bat from Br. Columbia (Thompson Indians).
IX. Modern cricket-bat.
X. Danish ball, sewed with woollen garn in different colours.

the *Tipcat*-games, in the *Hole*-games, and in the real *Battingball*-games, in very plain games and in the most composite and developed games.

The real composite *Battingball*-games will here be spoken of:

1) *Longball*, including *Om el mahag*
2) *Rounders*, incl. *Baseball*
3) *Cricket*.

I. LONGBALL.

In the common form *Longball* is a team game with 4 to 20 players, divided into two teams. As a rule this division takes place as follows:

First two captains are appointed, then as a rule the captains in turn pick out one player at a time for their teams. In some places, as the island of Anholt in the Kattegat, all the players divide themselves, or are divided into pairs, usually two players of equal age or ability making a pair, then each team gets one of them.

The playing ground is 20 to 70 metres long by 6 to 30 metres in breadth, a road or street was formerly often used, side-lines thus being unnecessary. Goal- or base-lines were not generally used, only the "homes" or "goals" were marked out by stones or the like, — at one end of the ground the batting or in-goal (or home), at the other the running or out-goal (fig. 2 — I and II).

The ball and the bat are described above.

The two teams decide by lot who has the right of first innings. The home- or batting-team take up its position in the batting home. The fielding team spread all over the field, only one player, the pitcher, with the ball in his hand stands at the batting home facing the batsman, who stands near the home line with his left side towards the field. The pitcher standing just at a safe distance from the batsman now must deliver the ball so that it falls in front of the batsman, convenient for him to bat. If not so the batter may refuse to strike. But if he strikes, the ball is "fair." The batter holds the bat with both his hands or with his right hand only, this according to the local customs (A one-hand-bat is 30 to 70 cms. long, a two-hands-bat 80 to 115 cms.). When missing the stroke he usually is allowed a second and a third stroke. But after the last stroke allowed he drops the bat to the ground. If succeeding in a good stroke, either the first or the second or third, he immediately starts running for the running-home. If not making a good stroke, in most cases he is allowed to wait for a good stroke made by one of his team-mates. When running to the out-goal he may return at once to the batting-home, or he may remain there waiting for another good stroke, and then run back and again take up his position behind the row of his team-mates, and now he is allowed to bat again in his turn.

The batting-team can lose its positions in two manners: by being "caught out" or by "hit out." If a striker's ball is caught by a fielder, this fielder drops the ball to the ground — in a manner agreed on — and the fielders run to the homes, each to the one nearest. The batters run out into the field, pick up the ball as quickly as possible and throw it at an adversary who has not yet reached a home. The team hit last is always allowed retaliation until the opponents are all in the homes and they are now the batting-team.

When a batted ball is not caught, but falls to the ground, one of the fielders picks it up quickly. If one or more batters are now running, he has to throw the ball to hit a runner. If he thinks it is too difficult to do so, as a rule he is not allowed to run with the ball in his hand for a better place, but he may throw the ball to a team-mate in a better position. If somebody hits a runner, the batting-team is hit out, but has the right of retaliation as above described.

In the case that all the batters are in the running-home, a chance is usually given them to get back to the batting-home. In many places this is done by "lyring," i.e. the pitcher tosses the ball into the air, at least a few metres,

Diagram of playing-grounds of some « Battingball » games.

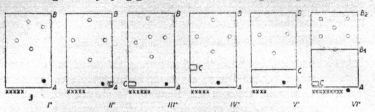

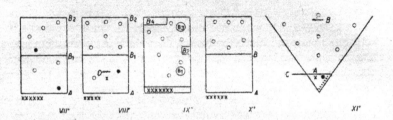

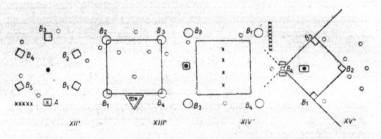

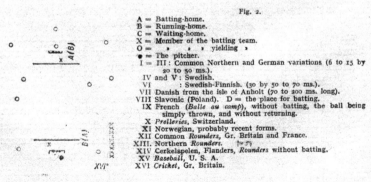

Fig. 2.

A = Batting-home.
B = Running-home.
C = Waiting-home.
X = Member of the batting team.
O = , , , yielding ,
● = The pitcher.
I = III : Common Northern and German variations (6 to 15 by 20 to 50 ms.).
IV and V : Swedish.
VI : Swedish-Finnish. (30 by 50 to 70 ms.).
VII Danish from the isle of Anholt (70 to 200 ms. long).
VIII Slavonic (Poland). D = the place for batting.
IX French (*Balle au camp*), without batting, the ball being simply thrown, and without returning.
X *Prolleries*, Switzerland.
XI Norwegian, probably recent forms.
XII Common *Rounders*, Gr. Britain and France.
XIII. Northern *Rounders*.
XIV Cerkelspelen, Flanders, *Rounders* without batting.
XV *Baseball*, U. S. A.
XVI *Cricket*, Gr. Britain.

and catches it again. It must be repeated several times, and in the meantime the batting-team or some of its members have to run back to the batting-home. At the moment, however, when they leave the running-home, the pitcher finishes his "lyring" and throws the ball to hit one of the runners or passes it to a fielder. If he or a mate succeeds in hitting a runner, the runners team is out (if retaliation is not made). If not, the batters are still batters.

In former days the object of the batters was to go on batting as long as possible. Runs were not scored as is now in use at schools.

This is an account of the common traditional team-game. But there are (or were) many variations with small differences. It is not possible here to describe them all.

Some peculiar variations it is however necessary to deal with.

In a great many variations especially in the North there are besides the two ordinary homes a third near the batting-home in which the batters having batted, but not run, may stay waiting for running (fig. 2 — II and III). In some places in Sweden this home is situated about 8 paces forward as a mark or as a line across the playground (fig. 2 — IV and V). In a great many Slavonic variations this home is found still more forward about the middle of the ground (fig. 2 — VIII). The same is the case in some Northern variations but here not as a place of refuge but as a running-borderline, as also known among the Slavs (fig. 2 — VI and VII). In France the middle home is common. Here we also find variations with more than three homes. But here we are at the borderland of the rounders-games (fig. 2 — IX).

An account of *Om el mahag* is certainly unnecessary here in view of Professor Gini's excellent account. The peculiar traits in that variation of *Longball* are only two:

1) When a runner is hit, the fielding party runs to the running-home, the captain only to the batting-home.
2) When all the batters are in the running-home, the captain takes a three-step lead and tries to steal home (I suppose the pitcher with the ball standing at the running-goal).

As far as I know, the first is unknown elsewhere. To the second we have relations in the North.

Besides the team-games spoken of hitherto there were played individual variations for two, three etc., to 12 to 14 players. In these games the common rule was that when a batter was caught or hit out, he and he alone became a fielder, while a fielder became batsman after he was caught or hit. These games are found especially in Denmark and N. E. Germany.

Rounders is very much like *Longball*. No doubt it is *Longball* mixed with some details from W. European games. But let me describe the ordinary form of *Rounders*.

Gomme has:

A round area is marked out by boundary sticks, and a chosen point of the boundary, the base, is fixed (fig. 2 — XII). This is marked out independently of the boundary, but inside it, sides are chosen. One side are the "ins" and strike the ball, the other side are the "outs" and deliver the ball, and endeavour to get their opponents, the "ins," out as soon as possible. The ball (an india rubber one) is delivered by the "feeder," by pitching it to the player who stands inside the base armed with a short stick. The player endeavours to strike the ball as far away as possible from the fielders or scouts. As soon as the ball is struck away he runs from the base to the first boundary stick, then to the second, and so on. His opponents in the meantime secure the ball and endeavour to hit him with it as he is running from stage to stage. If he succeeds in running completely round the boundary before the ball is returned it counts as one rounder. If he is hit, he is out of the game. He can stay at any stage of the boundary as soon as the ball is in hand, getting home again when the next player of his own side has in turn hit the ball away. When a ball is returned the "feeder" can bounce it within the base, and the player cannot then run to any new stage of the boundary until after the ball has again been hit away by another player. If a player misses a ball when endeavouring to strike at it, he has two more chances, but at the third failure he runs to the first boundary stick and takes his chance of being hit with the ball. *If a ball is caught, the whole side is out at once*, otherwise the side keeps in until either all the players have been hit out with the ball or until the base is "crowned." This can be done by bouncing the ball in the base whenever there is no player there to receive the delivery from the feeder. When a complete rounder is obtained, the player has the privilege either of counting the rounder to the credit of his side or of ransoming one of the players who has been hit out, who then takes his part in the game as before. When all but one of the players are out, this last player in hitting the ball must hit it aways so as to be able to make a rounder, and return to the base before his opponents get back the ball to crown the base.

Gomme's account although quite clear is not sufficient. He doesn't tell how many boundary sticks there are in use, where the "feeder" is standing while pitching, or how the bat and the base are formed.

In Pick and Aflalos Encyclopaedia of Sport (about 1900) the article about *Rounders* says that the bases are arranged 15 to 20 yards apart and that the feeder stands in the middle of the ground, the fielders outside the bases, and one behind the batter. The pitcher is allowed to feign a toss. The batter has one or three strikes. If he misses, he is out. There is counted one point for each base. The batsman only, not his team, is out when the ball is caught. In case of a long strike the ball going outside the border, into trees or so, there must not be counted more than four points. The number of players are 10 to 30. Nor do we here hear anything about the number of bases.

Gutsmuths tells us (1796) that as a rule there are as many bases as there are players in one party. He doesn't mention his source, but generally he is well informed and is surely right. His account is the oldest we possess. The bat he says is for one hand, flattened below the handle, length 45 cms., breadth 10 cms. thickness about 2.5 cms. The bases were sticks 10 to 15 paces apart, arranged casually (but probably forming a round). The pitcher stands 5 to 6 paces from the batsman and pitches in a flat curve. The batsman can get out of play in three manners:

1) His ball is caught by the fielders (*and then his team too, is out*).
2) He is hit by the ball when outside the bases.
3) He forgets to touch a base. Then this can be "burnt," i.e. the ball is thrown on it.

Moreover it should be noted that no more than one player is allowed to stand safe on one base. In the contrary case the fielders may hit the players or "burn" the base. When the teams are changing, retaliation-hit is allowed.

Gutsmuths mentions the game as *Baseball*. Gomme has in addition to *Rounders* also the names *Baseball, Cuckball, Pizeball* and *Tutball. Baseball* he [*sic*] mentions as a Suffolk game.

In France several variations of *Rounders* are played and several transitional forms of *Rounders-Longball*. The best known *Rounders*-game is *La grand thèque*. In Flanders too is found a *Rounders*-game in plain form, played without bat, the *Cerkelspelen* (fig. 2 — XIV).

The famous American form of *Rounders* has got the name *Baseball* (fig. 2 — XV). It is a game with four homes or bases, modernized and reorganized in the last century. It has hard and rather flat pitching from a distance of about 15 metres. The bat is about 106 cms. long, round and about 7 cms.

in diam. The bases are situated in a square with sides of about 30 metres. There are 9 players each side. The batsman can be played out in three manners, as well as for infringement of the rules:

1) The fielders catch the batted ball in the air.
2) A fielder picks up the ball and reaches the base before the batsman.
3) The running batsman is touched with the ball in a fielders hand outside the bases.

Townball is no doubt a younger brother of *Baseball*.

Two variations of *Rounders* or *Baseball* are recorded from two Indian tribes, the Navaho in Arizona and the Thompson Indians in Br. Columbia, both with four bases.

The Navaho game was played with an inverted Hockey-stick like a walking-stick with curved handle. The players were allowed four strikes in each round. But the batter stood in the middle of the ground and there were two pitchers, the batter standing between them. The ball might be struck in any direction. The batter had to run in one direction, the opposite of the manner in *Baseball*. One circuit meant a point, the runner might run in curves, dodge, jump, indeed he might knock the ball out of his opponent's hand. If the runner, however, was hit or touched with the ball, *his whole team was out*.

The Thompson Indians used a flattened straight bat for one hand only, four bases marked out with stones about 20 yards apart. The pitcher stood in the middle of the ground. Each player had one stroke only at one round. The description is however insufficient, but it is recorded that the base runner was out when struck with the ball.

A Hawaiian *Rounders*-game is recorded by Culin as a game similar to *Baseball* but without bat.

CRICKET.

As *Baseball*, *Cricket* has become a modernized game within the last century and a half, it is scarcely necessary to explain the game all through.

The most peculiar traits in Cricket are the two batting homes and the two batsmen, at the same time running in opposite direction (fig. 2 –XVI). Moreover a "wicket" in each batting-home which the batsman has to defend against the ball. The bat is long, broad and heavy, and throwing from about 20 metres is hard and flat. The ball is rather hard, and the runners are not to be struck or touched with it. But the batter can be caught out, or the ball can be thrown at the wicket by a fielder while the runner is out from home, besides be can be put out for infringment of the rules.

Longball, Rounders and *Cricket* are the most complicated games of ball ever seen. They evidently make one common group, typologic and also genetic. The similarities are too many to the justify belief in an independent origin for any of them.

The similarities are:

The batsman is the central player of the game.

He has to strike the ball in the air and then to run to one or more spots agreed on.

If the batted ball is caught, the batsman or his party is "out."

If he himself is hit or touched with the ball outside his safe places, he or his party is out, or in a few cases: if his safe places, when he himself is, outside them, are touched with the ball, he is out.

The differences between the variations are:

I.   – The pitching is short and high, a toss only, in *Longball*. In *Rounders* it is longer but still curved, while in *Baseball* and *Cricket* it is flat and hard and 15 to 20 metres long.

II. – Numbers and situation of the homes are different. In *Longball* there are two homes, in some cases three. In *Cricket* two. In *Rounders* four or more.

III. – The runner's route is in *Longball* (and *Cricket*) right forward and back. in *Rounders* it goes in a circle or a polygon.

IV. – In some *Rounders*-games (*Baseball*) and *Cricket* the runners may not be hit with the ball, instead their homes may be touched. In some cases the runners are to be touched with the ball in the fielders hand.

V.   – In *Cricket* the batter may strike the ball in any direction. In most *Rounders*-games and in *Longball* the ball must be struck in a forward direction within the side borderlines of the playing ground.

VI. – In *Longball* retaliation throws are allowed, in *Rounders* this is not the rule, except in a few cases.

VII. – In *Longball* the task is to keep the bat and bat as often as possible by means of the runs. In *Rounders* on the contrary the task is by means of the batting to run as often as possible, each run counting a point.

The rules of *Battingball* games tell us something about their development. The games centre round the batting. Next comes the catching of the ball. Then the run and the throwing for hitting the runners. The retaliation, the "lyring" and the like rules, and the want of hitting in some games, tell us that this last detail was once new and not taken as so important a detail as the catching which invariably gets the batter out, and consequently must be taken for older. In reality we find games consisting of batting only, as *Trap-ball* in England in which the players compete for the longest stroke. We find moreover games consisting of batting and catching only, in Europe, Persia and India. At that stage the games probably met with *Hitting* games. These are specially known in Germany, Poland and the North in numerous forms. A very simple form consists of the runners moving within the limits of the playing ground, and the throwers standing around this place and throwing at the runners. In a single variation in Denmark the throwers mix with the runners, the last defending themselves each with a short broad bat (*Rotten and Fresh —* Jutland). Here we have the retaliation detail in *Longball* as an independent game. Furthermore a catchplay with runs between two places of refuge is very well known in Denmark and probably elsewhere. So the principles of all the details of *Longball* were present.

In Great Britain and Flanders a group of games are known, the essential stamp of which is much like that of *Rounders* and *Cricket*: Cudgels, *Kit-Cat, Stool-ball, Munchets*, etc. and *O'Cat* in U.S.A. A similar game in Flanders is *Keitslaen*. As an instance I shall explain *Cat and Dog*.

There are three players, two of these have small clubs and each a hole in the ground 8 to 9 metres apart. The third player has a "cat" i.e. a double-conical billet, about 10 cms. long, 2 to 3 cms. in diam. He stands at the one hole and throws the cat at the other which the owner has to defend with his club. If the cat goes into the hole, the defender has lost it to the pitcher and becomes the pitcher himself.

But if the defender strikes the cat away, he and the second batsman change holes as many times as possible while the pitcher goes for the cat, each run counting for a point.

In other similar games there are more players, all but one with [*sic*] and the runs going in a circle.

But is not *Cat and Dog, Cricket* in miniature?

And what does the game need but more players in order to become *Rounders?* The number of clubs reduced to one, the "Cat" changed with a ball, the batting stronger, the fielders added. In reality it is quite likely that a meeting between those probably Celtic games and *Longball* gave rise to *Rounders* and *Cricket*. *Cricket* has got only the stronger batting, *Rounders* also the hitting of the runners, the burning of the bases being known in the Hole-games. The touching too is known in such a game as *Munshet*, or it has come into use on account of the drawbacks of being hit with a hard ball.

HISTORY.

The *Battingball* games are European games. Plain batting as used in *Tipcat* had reached N. America in Precolumbian times as *Hockey, Football* and some *Shuttlegames* had. Connection or not with Precolumbian American culture is one of the few good data for determining the age of the games. But fully developed *Battingball* games are not to be found outside Europe — save the *Om el mahag* which is described by Professor Gini (fig. 3). The few instances of such games among Red Indians and in Hawaii must be taken as imported from Europe. In Persia, India and perhaps China and Japan plain batting with ball is, or was, surely known, but no developed game, except the Russian importation of *Longball* to Siberia and E. Turkestan. After all, the games in question are European, probably Northern and Central-European. But as those parts of the continent in former times were rather isolated, *Battingball* may very well have existed there without reaching the great highways of culture along the Southern coasts of Eurasia, or the Nomadic route from Persia-Turan toward E. Asia and the Bering sea. So *Battingball* games may be of rather ancient date.

Hitherto I have supposed them not to be more than some 1500 years old. Professor Jusserand, France, was of opinion that they were not known before the 13th to 14th centuries in France. The occurence of the *Om el mahag* tells us however they must be older. Professor Gini is right: it is not probable that *Om el mahag* is a recent importation. Thus it must be either a survival from a greater area of *Battingball* or an earlier importation. The first theory is not probable, because if the game had been known around the Mediteranean sea in the time of the ancient civilizations it would be strange that it had not spread to the negroes and the Arabs, to E. Asia and America as did other games, and none of the ancient Greek or Roman authors tell anything about the game. It is true that they say nothing about Hockey, and *Hockey*, we learn from archeologists, was known. But we also know that *Hockey* spread all over the world, *Battingball* games did not — as far as we know. Until we possess

Map of the world showing the spreading of « Batting » games, primitive and developed. Boundary lines very uncertain.

Map of the world showing the spreading of « Batting » games, primitive and developed. Boundary lines very uncertain.

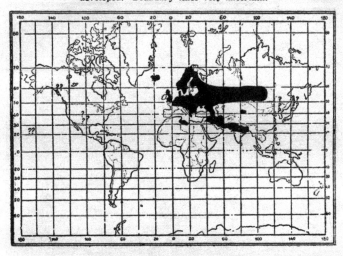

Fig. 3.

N. B. As regards the query marks for China and Japan :
Bushan states, without any explanation, that *Battingball* is known in Japan.
Helen Gunsaulas speaks of «swinging bats for ballplay», also without further
information. A single author, Martin, writing about China, speaks of *Cricket*
at the time of the Tartar or Mongolian siege of Peiping, when *Cricket* may
have been played there. Culin, our greatest authority, however says nothing,
nor does Giles. Thus *Batting* probably is or has been known in East-Asia
but, as long as we know nothing certain about it, we must consider it as a
primitive from of *Battingball*-games.

evidence to the contrary we must stick to Europe the present home of the
games as their ancient home. As a comparison between *Longball* and
Rounders (fig. 4) make it probable that *Longball* is the older, we must take
the Teutonic or Slavonic peoples or their ancestors as the inventors of the
game. But as the German Slavs seem to play German variations of *Longball*,
and as the East Baltic peoples do not seem to know the game, it would seem
that the Slavs are not the inventors but more probably the blond North European Race.

If this is so then the blond peoples would have imported the game to North
Africa. When did that take place? We don't know, but all probability goes to
show that the migration of tribes southwards from Northern Europe took
place in cold or rainy periods, after the last glacial period, in the Atlantic pe-

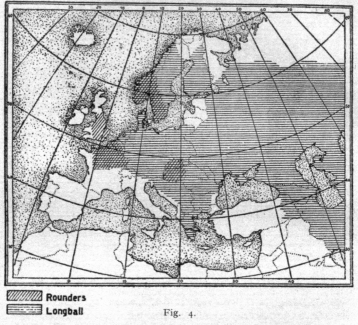

▨▨▨ **Rounders**
▤▤▤ **Longball**

Fig. 4.

Map of Europe showing the spread of developed or as a rule developed *Battingball*-games as far as we know it. The information for the Slavonic peoples and the Balkans is taken from Professor E. Piasecky, Poland. The boundary lines are uncertain.

riod (6th to 3rd millennniums B.O.E,) in the subatlantic period in the last centuries B.O.E., and during the great migrations of nations. Nothing goes to show that migrations towards Africa have taken place in periods of dry climate.

The blond strain among the Berbers, the Guanchos, the capsien culture, the megalitic culture, etc. make it probable that from the oldest times connection between the two continents has taken place, and surely migrations too, the directions of which were particularly determined by changing climatic conditions. The last migration from Europe to Africa by people from N. Europe, and the only one about which we know anything definite, is that of the Vandals in the 5th century. From the point of view above spoken of, it is not probable that *Longball* is a very ancient game in Africa. The most probable conclusion would then be that the Vandals brought the game to Africa, and that some Berber tribes learnt it.

The Vandals primeval home no doubt was the North. They settled on the stretches of the Vistula near the Goths, and afterward they went westward through Germany and France to S.E. Spain and at last to Africa, some of them probably settling down on the way.

One might ask why the Goths did not bring *Longball* to N. Spain and S. France, the Lombards to Italy.

Perhaps they did. We don't know whether the game was known in those countries and later became extinct. Games do not easily become extinct among their own peoples and in their own country with its own customs and traditions. But when a nation migrates and mixes with other nations in a higher stage of culture, it is another matter.

At any rate, as *Om el mahag* was included in ritual festivals it can hardly have come to Africa later than the time of the Vandals. The Berbers' way of dividing the players into teams is identical with the manner known in the North. The term "rotten" applied to the players who have batted but not run, is also known, at any rate, in Denmark and surely not elsewhere. In the North too the game was used in festivals connected with the cults of fertility in the spring. In Denmark we have instances of the game being played in the rural churchyard at Easter, probably a tradition from preChristian times.

So it is probable that this Berber-*Longball* came to Africa with the Vandals at the latest. The form of the game and the terms used, lead us to consider it probable that the game came from Northern Europe.

Jusserand's theory that the game came into existence at the French universities in the 13th to 14th centuries can not be correct. Neither can Dr. Schnells theory of the game being a special German game, only known in the neighborhood of Germany. In Germany there are no variations with the middle home as in France, among the Slavs and in the North. There exists only one where all the peculiar details are found and it is in the North, i.e. Denmark and Sweden. In view of the general inclination of authors who have written about these games to attribute their origin to their own country, I am not very glad to draw this conclusion. I am also sorry to be co-responsible for the Vandals. But facts are facts. With the knowledge we so far possess we must conclude that *Longball* came into existence in the North and that is has gone southwards with Goths, Vandals, Burgundians, etc., brought from the Goths to the Slavs from the Vandals or Burgundians to the Alemans, Franks, etc. With the Angles and Saxons it went to England, mixed with Celtic games, and became *Rounders* and *Cricket*. *Rounders* again crossed the Atlantic and became *Baseball* in America.

The oldest complete account of a *Battingball*-game is that of Gutsmuths in 1796. From older times we only hear about *Batting* without further explanation, the oldest from the 11th century in Germany. Not until the 19th century did the folklorists take up the matter. And still now we want further investigations in many places before we can know all the variations, the terminology, etc.

Longball and *Rounders* are now in Europe as a rule children's games. Formerly they were the most considerable games of ball among the Teutonic and Slavonic peoples, although they were never fashionable games played by kings and "the upper ten" as were *Tennis, Golf, Maill*, etc. But when *Football, Hockey*, etc. were modernized in England and became very well organized games, easy to learn and with dramatic events, *Battingball*-games were frequently superceded in their own countries, and either went out of use altogether, or led a languishing existence.

But in modernized athletic form as *Cricket* and *Baseball* and as *Bo-ball* in Finnland they are still very much alive.

NINE SURVIVING DESCRIPTIONS OF
BASEBALL-LIKE GAMES WRITTEN AND
PUBLISHED BEFORE 1845

❖

1. *"Ball mit Freystäten (oder das englische Base-ball)"* (Ball with free station, or English base-ball), from the book *Spiele zur Uebung und Erholung des Körpers und Geistes für die Jugend, ihre Erzieher und alle Freunde Unschuldiger Jugendfreuden* (Games for the exercise and recreation of body and spirit for the youth and his educator and all friends of innocent joys of youth), by Johann Christoph Friedrich Gutsmuths (Schnepfenthal: Verlag der buchhandlung der Erziehungsanstalt, 1796).
Translated by Mary Akitiff.

In the description of this game I can be brief, for it is mostly equivalent to the German ball game. Thus I am aiming my description at those players who already understand the German game.

Almost everything about this form of base-ball (which is very often played in England) is smaller in scale and requires less use of strength in hitting and running, etc. At the same time it demands an equal amount, if not more, attentiveness, and is much more bound by numerous small rules. The German ball game will never be able to fully repress the English one, as pleasant as ours may be.

One plays the game with two teams, of which one is serving the ball, the other batting (as with ours). Likewise the process is as in the German ball game: hitting, running, etc. That which is different can be summarized as follows: the bat is lighter, a little under two feet in length, four inches wide at its widest point, and about one inch thick (item Y in the drawing). For this reason, one can make only short, light hits. The pitcher stands five to six steps from the batter and lobs the ball to him in an arc.

The line of the curve from A to B in the drawing constitutes the home plate. From here the ball is hit, as in the German ball game. Instead of a limited fielding area, one finds on the field as many bases, marked with handkerchief-covered stakes, as there are members of each team. However, in this game, the home plate is counted as a base as well. They are marked in the drawing with the numbers 1, 2, 3, 4, and 5, and are arranged ten to fifteen feet apart in a variable pattern.

The batter has three attempts to hit the ball while at the home plate. Even if he touches the ball so lightly that one can hear only a slight crackling, or if he pushes the ball through even light contact out of the home plate area, or if he has struck three times without hitting the ball, then he must begin to run. His path is from A to B through all of the bases in order until he comes back to the home plate. If many people are on a single team, then there are more bases, and the length of the track is thus longer. The serving team stands in a variable fashion behind, next to and between these bases as indicated by the letters a, b, c, d, e, because the ball is hit to those places.

The at-bat can be lost by the batting team in three ways: by having the ball caught, by "burning," or by having a runner touched by the ball. I will clarify these three situations, for that will constitute the rules and laws of the game.

1. Catching: When the ball, which has been hit, is caught by any member of the serving team, it makes no matter who (as with the German game), then the other team has lost that at-bat. In this way the out is the most securely and incontrovertibly achieved. But he who has caught the ball must yell to his teammates: "in! in!" or "into the home plate!" And as they run there, and have almost arrived, then he must throw the ball over his head backward, so that the team making out does not grab it from him (see the explanation below under 3e) and run back into the home plate themselves. The ball is thrown backward so that it cannot be thrown too far.

2. Burning: This happens in two ways.

   a. When a running batter has forgotten to touch a base with his hand, then the best-positioned member of the serving team who has noticed this runs to the base (after having received the ball from his teammates without any outward show, or perhaps very subtle waving) and yells to his teammates, "in! in!" and throws the ball with the exclamation, "burned!" to the base. The throw must be executed such that the ball goes forward very gently, after which the thrower must then run quickly into the home plate. The reason for this can be seen in part 3e below.

   b. When there are no batters in the home plate area, then the pitcher takes the ball, yells to his fellow members of the serving team, "in!" and then throws the ball with the exclamation, "burned!" at an angle toward the ground of the home plate, so that it continues to move and does not stay lying still on the ground. (Reason for this under 3e.) He himself is not allowed to stand within the arc of A and B when he throws, but must spring back within it right after he has thrown the ball.

3. Touching and Throwing at a Runner: No hitter may have the ball touch him outside of the home plate, for if he does, then his party has lost the at-bat. This rule is very effective and can be seen in the following cases.

   a. If the batter has hit the ball, then he runs from 1 to 2 to 3, etc., until the ball is thrown into the home plate, at which precise moment he may not go farther, but rather must stand still at the base he has reached until a new hit is made, or until the ball in some other way comes out of the home plate. If he lets himself be hit by any member of the serving team, then the at-bat is lost for his team. It has already been stated above that the hitter has the right to three swings while in the home plate, but if he does not hit the ball at all, then he must run, and since the pitcher has the ball right in his hand, he usually throws it directly at the hitter. If he hits the runner before he has gotten to the base, then the at-bat is lost. Exactly the same applies when the hitter touches the ball so lightly that it barely goes forward.

   b. When several hitters have already hit and run, then several bases are occupied. Let us assume that this is the case with numbers 3 and 4. Thus it sometimes happens that when a new hit occurs, the person in 3 runs farther, whereas the person in 4 stands still (either due to inattentiveness or because the serving team is too near to him with the ball), the result of which is that two people are standing in base 4. This once again calls for the order of the game: there can be only one person at one base at any time. If, in this case, the person at base 4 does not quickly run to base 5, or if the recently arrived runner does not return to base 3, then the best-positioned member of the serving team in possession of ball can run toward them and either hit one of the individuals or burn one of them in the manner described above, in which case the at-bat is lost.

c. Once the ball has been hit, the batter can run from one base to another until the ball has been thrown back to the home plate by the serving team. However, then he must stay at the base where he is. If he has already gone farther — more than halfway to the next base — then he can run ahead all the way to the next base. If he ignores this, and runs farther even after the ball has arrived in the home plate without quickly running back, then any member of the serving team can move quickly to either touch him with the ball or burn the base. In both cases, the at-bat is lost. The very same occurs when he is hit with the ball while running back toward the base.

d. When the hitter does not have the permission of the pitcher to leave the home plate, then the pitcher can likewise touch him with the ball, and the at-bat is lost.

e. If team A, already in the hitting position, loses the at-bat in any one of the ways mentioned in 1, 2, and 3 above, then, from that moment on, the team that was formerly serving is seen as the batting team. Thus, all of the members of team B who are still standing on the field must run into the home plate area the moment they get the out, for if someone from team A gets hold of the ball and touches any member of team B who is still outside of the home plate with it, then B has once again lost the at-bats, and A is once again the batting team. Similarly B has, once again, the right to touch any member of A with the ball, and if they do, then they once again become the batting team. In this way a fun, short-lived fight ensues, and the team that wins at the end is the one that has the last throw. This is the reason why when one catches the ball one must throw it backward, and why when one burns or touches a runner for an out, the ball must be thrown such that no one from the opposing team can grab it and thus throw it again.

From the above it is clear what each team has to do. This game has all of the complexities of the German game, but it requires less use of strength and more attentiveness, because it is bound by more rules.

2. *"La balle empoisonée"* (poisoned ball), from the book
*Les Jeux des jeunes garçons, représentés par un grand nombre
d'estampes,* 4th ed. (Paris: Chez Nepveu, Libraire, ca. 1815)
Translated by Xavier Glon.

Eight or ten children divide themselves into two teams. In a courtyard, or in a large square area, four corners are marked, one as the home base and the others as bases which the runners must touch in succession. Straws are drawn; the team that wins occupies the home base. The players of the other team place themselves among the other bases at suitable distances. One of their team serves the ball to one of the players at the home base. This one repels the ball, and runs to the first base, to the second, and to others if he has time. Another player repels the ball in turn and reaches the first base while his teammate reaches the second, and so on. However, two members from the batting team may not stand together on the same base at the same time.

Players from the team on the field must pick up the ball as promptly as possible in order to touch or hit one of the runners before he reaches base. In that case, the player who has been hit by "the poisoned ball" suspends his running, and his team has lost the home base. His team then becomes the serving team unless, on the spot, he or one of his teammates is sufficiently skilled to pick the ball up and hit one of their adversaries before he reaches the home base. In this case the batting team may continue to bat. If a player who repels the ball does it so carelessly that one of the players from the other team catches it before it touches the ground, then his side is out and has to leave the home base.

This game is a great exercise in a large courtyard, whose four corners mark the bases. When played in a large field, stacks of clothes mark the bases, but then you have the inconvenience of having to run too far to fetch the ball, and the team at home base tends to remain batting too long.

3. "Rounders," from *The Boy's Own Book,* by William Clarke,
2d ed., (London: Vizetelly, Branston, 1828).

In the west of England this is one of the most favourite sports with the bat and ball. In the metropolis, boys play a game very similar to it, called Feeder. In Rounders, the players divide into two equal parties, and chance decides which shall have first innings.

c

b   *d*

e

a

Four stones or posts are placed from twelve to twenty yards asunder, as *a*, *b*, *c*, *d*, in the margin; another is put at *e*; one of the party which is out, who is called the pecker or feeder, places himself at *e*. He tosses the ball gently toward *a*, on the right of which one of the in party places himself, and strikes the ball, if possible, with the bat. If he miss three times, or if the ball, when struck, fall behind *a*, or is caught by any of the out players, who are all scattered about the field except one who stands behind *a*, he is out, and another takes his place. If none of these events take place, on striking the ball he drops the bat, and runs toward *b*, or, if he can, to *c*, *d*, or even to *a* again. If, however, the feeder, or any of the out players who may happen to have the ball, strike him with it in his progress from *a* to *b*, *b* to *c*, *c* to *d*, or *d* to *a*, he is out. Supposing he can only get to *b*, one of his partners takes the bat, and strikes at the ball in turn; while the ball is passing from the feeder to *a*, if it be missed, or after it is struck, the first player gets to the next or a further goal, if possible, without being struck. If he can only get to *c*, or *d*, the second runs to *b* only, or *c*, as the case may be, and a third player begins; as they get home, that is to *a*, they play at the ball in rotation, until they all get out; then, of course, the out players take their places.

c

b   d

e

a

4. "Base, or Goal Ball," from *The Book of Sports*, by Robin Carver,
(Boston: Lilly, Wait, Colman, and Holden, 1834). Repeated nearly
verbatim in *The Boy's and Girl's Book of Sports* (Providence:
Geo. P. Daniels, 1835). This description was based upon the one
of rounders in the 1828 *Boy's Own Book*, differentiated only
by a few word substitutions.

This game is known under a variety of names. It is sometimes called "round
ball," but I believe that "base," or "goal ball" are the names generally adopted
in our country. The players divide into two equal parties, and chance decides
which shall have first innings. Four stones or stakes are placed from twelve to
twenty yards asunder, as *a, b, c, d*, in the margin; another is put at *e*.

One of the party, who is out, places himself at *e*. He tosses the ball gently
toward *a*, on the right of which one of the *in-party* places himself, and strikes
the ball, if possible, with his bat. If he miss three times, or if the ball, when
struck, be caught by any of the players of the opposite side, who are scattered
about the field, he is out, and another takes his place. If none of these accidents take place, on striking the ball he drops the bat, and runs toward *b*, or
if he can, to *c, d*, or even to *a* again. If, however, the boy who stands at *e*, or any
of the out-players who may happen to have the ball, strike him with it in his
progress from *a* to *b, b* to *c, c* to *d*, or *d* to *a*, he is out. Supposing he can only
get to *b*, one of his partners takes the bat, and strikes at the ball in turn. If the
first player can only get to *c*, or *d*, the second runs to *b*, only, or *c*, as the case
may be, and a third player begins; as they get home, that is, to *a*, they play at
the ball by turns, until they all get out. Then, of course, the out-players take
their places.

*

2   4

3

5. "Base ball," from *The Boy's Book of Sports* (New Haven:
S. Babcock, 1835). This was also based upon the 1828 description
of rounders in the *Boy's Own Book*, but modified to a greater degree
than the previous example.

"Base ball" is played by a number, who are divided into two parties by the
leader in each choosing one from among the players alternately. The leaders
then toss up for the innings. Four stones for gaols [*sic*] are then placed so as
to form the four points of a diamond, as seen in the margin:

The party who are out then take their places; (*see picture.*) one stands near
the centre of the diamond, to toss the ball for one of the in-party who stands
with his bat at *. Another stands behind the striker to catch the ball, if he fail
to hit it. A third stands still farther behind, to return the ball when necessary.
The remainder of the out-party are dispersed about the field to catch the ball
when knocked, or to return it if not caught. If the striker miss the ball three
times, or if he knock it and any of the opposite party catch it, he is out, and
another of his party takes his place; if none of these accidents happen, then,
on striking the ball, he drops his bat and runs to 2, or, if the ball be still at
some distance, to 3, or 4, or even back to *, according to circumstances; but
he must be cautious how he ventures too far at a time, for if any of the opposite party hit him with the ball while he is passing from one goal to another,
he is out. When the first has struck the ball, another takes the bat and strikes

and runs in like manner; then a third, and so on through the party, and as they arrive at * one after another, each, who are not out, take their turns again, until all are out. Then, of course, the other party takes their places.

6. Unnamed Indian ball game, from *Female Robinson Crusoe,*
A tale of the American Wilderness
(New York: Jared W. Bell, 1837).

Some of the male adults were playing ball, which article was, as he afterwards ascertained it to be on examination, portion of a sturgeon's head, which is elastic, covered with a piece of dressed deerskin. Another ball which he noticed, was constituted of narrow strips of deerskin, wound around itself, like a ball of our twine, and then covered with a sufficiently broad piece of the same material.

In playing this game, they exhibited great dexterity, eagerness, and swiftness of speed. The party engaged, occupied an extensive surface of open ground, over whose whole space, a vigorous blow with the hickory club of the striker, would send the ball, and also to an amazing height. On its coming down, it was almost invariably caught by another player at a distance, and as instantly hurled from his hand to touch, if possible, the striker of the ball, who would then drop his club, and run, with a swiftness scarcely surpassed by the winds, to a small pile of stones, which it was part of the game for him to reach. If the runner succeeded in attaining to the desired spot, before the ball touched him, he was safe. Otherwise, he had to resign his club to the fortunate thrower of the ball against him, and take his place to catch. The runner, by watching the coming ball, was almost always enabled to avoid its contact with him, by dodging or leaping, which was effected with all the nimbleness of one of the feline race. If that was effected, another person, in his own division of the playing party, (there being two rival divisions,) assumed the dropped club, to become a striker in his turn.

Their principal object seemed to be, to send the ball as far as possible, in order to enable the striker of it, to run around the great space of ground, which was comprised within the area formed by piles of stones, placed at intervals along the line of the imaginary circle.

7. "Squares," from *The Youth's Encyclopædia of Health:*
with Games and Play Ground Amusements,
by W. Montague (London: W. Emans, 1838).

At some considerable distance from each other, 4 stones are placed so as to form a large square — and a boy is stationed at each. There are also — out-players, by one of whom the ball is thrown, and if the boy struck misses it, or if it is caught by an enemy — he is out. — If it is not caught he must contrive to run to a stone — or home again if possible. He should drive the ball so far, that it may be rendered scarcely possible to hit him with it as he runs from stone to stone. While he is at a stone one of his partners takes up the bat and plays, — but if, while running, he is hit by an enemy, he is out. All must be out on one side or the other before the game is concluded. There is nothing particular fascinating in this game. —

8. "Feeder," from *The Every Boy's Book,*
by J. L. Williams (London: Henry Allman, 1841).

In this game, four or five stones or marks must be placed on the ground, as in the annexed figure A, B, C, D, E, about twelve or fifteen yards asunder; these marks are called bases, and one of them, as A, is styled "home."

The players next toss up for the office of "feeder," who takes his place about two yards in front of "home," as at F, and the rest of the players stand at and round the home. The feeder then calls out "Play!" and pitches the ball to the first player, who endeavours to strike it with a bat, as far as he possibly can; should he succeed in hitting the ball, he immediately drops the bat, and runs to the first base on his right hand, as E, while the feeder is going after the ball; but if he can run all the bases and then home, before the ball is in hand, so much the better. If, however, the feeder obtains the ball soon enough to throw it at, and strike him with it as he is running from base to base, the player is out; he is also out if the feeder catches the ball; in either case the player becomes feeder, and the latter runs home to join his playmates. Should any of the other players be out at the bases, when one is caught or struck out, they also must run home. If the first player could only reach the base E, after striking the ball, he should, when the second player strikes it, run to the base D, as it is not allowable for two persons to be at one base at one and the same minute; he proceeds in the same manner to the third and fourth bases, until

C ·   D °

B ∧   E °

F ·

A °

he arrives home again, thus enabling the others to get to their bases and home in their respective turns. The player with the bat is not obliged to take every ball the feeder chooses to give him; if he does not like a throw, he catches the ball and throws it back again. He is not allowed to make more than three "offers" at the ball; if he does so he is out, and must be feeder.

9. "Rounders," from *The Every Boy's Book*, by J. L. Williams (London: Henry Allman, 1841)

This game very much resembles Feeder, differing only in the following particulars; the players divide into two equal parties, and toss up for innings, the winners taking their position at the home. The opposing party stations a "feeder" and also a player behind the home, to catch missed balls and "tips," (when a ball is slightly touched by the corner or end of the bat, it flies off either to the side or behind the home, and is then termed a "tip;") this player's office is to endeavour when one of the in-party runs, after making a tip, to strike him out before he reaches the first base; the rest of the out-party station themselves out in the field, at various distances from the bases, to field, or throw up the ball, and catch out or strike out the players while they are running between the bases. Each player is allowed three "offers" — that is to say, he may strike at the ball three times, but if he fails to hit it the third time he is out. In most places it is usual when all the players but one have been caught or struck out, for him to take the "rounder" — *i.e.*, strike the ball so far that he can run round to all the bases and then home before the opposite party can get the ball, and "ground" it, or throw it down on the "home." In taking the rounder the player is allowed three hits, but when the ball is thrown to him the third time, he *must* run, even if he does not strike it five yards. If he succeeds in getting the "rounder," his party resume their innings, if not, their opponents take their turn.

In other places, it is the custom when two or three are out, if one player can obtain the rounder three times, for the player who was struck out first to come in again, and if any more players get the same number of rounders, for the others who were out to resume their places, so that it often happens that the in-party thus regain all their lost partners. If two players happen to be at one base at the same time, the out-player who has picked up the ball should stand about the length of a horse and cart, or as near that measure as he can guess, behind the base; one of the boys at the base, after making several feints in order to deceive the one with the ball, runs off to the next base, and as he does so the other throws the ball at him; if the ball strikes him, he is of course out; if not, he continues in the game. The rules of rounders respecting catching and striking out are precisely the same as in Feeder. A smooth round stick is preferred by many boys to a bat for striking the ball with.

NOTES

❖

1. UNCERTAINTY AS TO THE PATERNITY

1. *Porter's Spirit of the Times*, November 15, 1856, 176.

2. *Porter's Spirit of the Times*, January 31, 1857, 357.

3. *Porter's Spirit of the Times*, October 24, 1857, 117.

4. The letter was the first in a series that the anonymous writer contributed to *Porter's*; most evaluated the various baseball clubs in the New York area. "X" claimed to have been an observer of baseball during "the last four years of the Ball-playing mania," and this suggests he may have been William Cauldwell, the journalist who inaugurated regular coverage of the game. Cauldwell began to cover baseball for the *New York Mercury* in 1853.

5. "Saints and Their Bodies," *Atlantic Monthly*, March 1858, 593.

6. "The Gymnasium," *Atlantic Monthly*, May 1859, 541.

7. Henry Chadwick, *Beadle's Dime Base-Ball Player* (New York: Irwin P. Beadle, 1860), 5.

8. Charles A. Peverelly, *The Book of American Pastimes* (New York: self-published, 1866), 338.

9. "The Philosophy of the 'National Game,'" *The Nation*, August 26, 1869, 167–68. This article was published anonymously, but in *Base-ball: How to Become a Player*, John M. Ward credited the authorship to Sedgwick.

10. Two-old-cat, like its siblings one-, three-, and four-old-cat, was an early variety of informal "scrub" baseball played in the United States.

11. Rankin's article appeared in various newspapers during the summer of 1886. In some it bore the title "Our National Game," and elsewhere it was called the "Early History of Baseball." A reprint of the latter is located in Box 8, "New York Clipper articles by Rankin, 1904–1912" among the baseball scrapbooks originally included in the Charles W. Mears Collection on Baseball at the Cleveland Public Library and is also found within the "Scrapbook of William Rankin's Weekly Base Ball Letters, 1904–1912," Part 9 of the *Baseball Scrapbooks* microfilm collection, University of Notre Dame Memorial Library, South Bend IN.

12. Ibid.

13. Ibid.

14. William M. Rankin, letter dated March 25, 1908 (published April 2, 1908), "Rankin's Weekly Base Ball Letters."

15. William M. Rankin to Albert G. Spalding, January 15, 1905, John Doyle Papers, National Baseball Hall of Fame Library, Cooperstown NY.

16. John Montgomery Ward, *Base-ball: How to Become a Player* (Philadelphia: Athletic Publishing, 1888), 9–23. Ironically, Ward's contrarian contention that baseball preceded rounders is identical to the theme advanced in Chapter 2 of this book, albeit arrived at from a very different rationale.

17. Ibid., 18.

18. Ibid., 19–21.

19. Ibid., 21–23.

20. John Montgomery Ward, "Our National Game," *The Cosmopolitan*, October 1888, 443.

21. H[enry] C[hadwick], "Baseball and Rounders," *Brooklyn Eagle*, July 1, 1888, 7.

22. "What Is Said of Sports, The Late Richard A. Proctor on Base Ball," *Brooklyn Eagle*, December 30, 1888, 7.

23. The tour was an ambitious venture, with the traveling players performing exhibitions of American baseball to audiences around the globe. Their itinerary took them to Hawaii, New Zealand, Australia, Ceylon, Egypt, Italy, France, and England before returning to New York. The party consisted of Spalding's Chicago team, headed by Cap Anson, and, as their opponents, an all-star team captained by John Montgomery Ward of New York. The players were accompanied by their wives, various representatives of baseball, and a coterie of sporting journalists, including Henry Chadwick. The group traveled first class, with Spalding shouldering much of the cost. The tour was intended to spread the popularity of America's National Pastime around the globe, ostensibly for nationalist and cultural purposes. But Spalding may have envisioned his sporting goods company, the world's largest producer of baseball equipment, as the venture's ultimate beneficiary.

24. "Testimonial Banquet to Mr. A. G. Spalding and His Party of Base Ball Players, Monday, April 8, 1889," A. G. Mills file, National Baseball Hall of Fame Library, Cooperstown NY.

25. Harold Seymour, *Baseball*, vol. 1, *The Early Years* (New York, Oxford University Press, 1960), 9.

26. W. I. Harris, "Origin of the Game," in *Athletic Sports in America, England, and Australia* (Philadelphia: Hubbard Brothers, 1889), 24–25.

27. "From This Came Our Baseball," article from unnamed newspaper,

dated December 7, 1889, Henry Chadwick Scrapbooks, Spalding Collection, New York Public Library.

28. The only two North American Indian ball games bearing a resemblance to baseball were both likely the products of European influence. The first was called aqejólyedi (run around ball), also known as Navaho baseball. This activity featured a square infield and shared many characteristics of early American town-ball, including the practice of retiring base runners by hitting them with a thrown ball. Stewart Culin, who conducted an exhaustive study of Indian games at the turn of the twentieth century, stated: "In spite of tribal traditions, it appears that the Navaho learned the game from the whites when they were imprisoned at the Basque Redondo after 1863." A second similar game, observed being played among the Thompson Indians of British Columbia, is believed to have been adapted from a form of early baseball or rounders imported into the territory by early English settlers. Stewart Culin, "Games of the North American Indians," *Twenty-fourth Annual Report of the Bureau of American Ethnology, 1902–1903* (Washington DC: Government Publishing Office, 1907), 789–791.

29. *Spalding's Official Base-Ball Guide, 1878* (Chicago: A. G. Spalding and Bros., 1878), 5.

30. A. G. Spalding, "In the Field Papers: Base Ball," *The Cosmopolitan*, October 1889, 50.

31. Ibid.

32. Ernest Bell, *Handbook of Athletic Sports*, vol. 4 (London: George Bell and Sons, 1892).

33. *Spalding's Official Base Ball Guide, 1890* (Chicago: A. G. Spalding and Bros., 1890), 7.

34. Albert G. Spalding, "What Is the Origin of Base Ball?" *Spalding's Official Base Ball Guide, 1905* (Chicago: A. G. Spalding and Bros., 1905), 5.

35. Albert G. Spalding, "The Origin and Early History of Base Ball," *Spalding's Official Base Ball Guide, 1905* (Chicago: A. G. Spalding and Bros., 1905), 15–27.

36. Rankin, "Early History of Baseball."

37. "Played Baseball in Bible Times," undated 1905 newspaper column, John Doyle Papers.

38. Myron W. Townsend, "Sportographs," *Boston Traveler*, January 16, 1905.

39. The commission members included three former presidents of the National League, Abraham G. Mills, N. E. Young, and Morgan G. Bulkeley, who was also a sitting United State senator from Connecticut. Other mem-

bers included a second U.S. senator, Arthur P. Gorman of Maryland, along with the legendary baseball figures A. J. Reach and George Wright. James E. Sullivan, president of the Amateur Athletic Union and also a Spalding employee, was named the commission's secretary.

40. Albert G. Spalding to John Lowell, November 5, 1904, John Doyle Papers.

41. Abner Graves to Editor, *Beacon Journal* (Akron OH), April 3, 1905, John Doyle Papers.

42. Albert G. Spalding to Abner Graves, November 10, 1905, John Doyle Papers.

43. Abner Graves to Albert G. Spalding, November 17, 1905, John Doyle Papers.

44. "Origin of Baseball; Special Commission Decides It Is Strictly American," *New York Daily Tribune*, March 20, 1908, 4.

45. Upon learning the news, an aging and ailing Chadwick wrote to commission member Abraham Mills: "I read you [sic] decision in the case of Chadwick Vs. Spalding, contained in Spalding' guide — just out today — with great interest, and I want to say to you that it is a masterly piece of special pleading, which lets my dear old friend Albert escape a bad defeat. I notice that the italicised paragraph, which closes your dictum in the case, dates your strongest witness's evidence at 1839, whereas it is well known that the old Philadelphia town ball club played under the rounders rule in 1831, eight years earlier. How about that? I was so sure of my case that I failed to present detailed evidence. The fact is, the whole matter was a joke between Albert and myself, for the fun of the thing. As for the judges Reach and Wright, they mean well but they don't know!" March 20, 1908, John Doyle Papers.

46. Will Irwin, "Baseball: 1. Before the Professionals Came," *Collier's*, May 8, 1909, 12–13.

47. Exchange of letters between Albert G. Spalding and William M. Rankin, January 1905, John Doyle Papers.

48. Alfred H. Spink, *The National Game*, 2d ed. (St. Louis: The National Game, 1911), 54.

49. Chadwick died April 20, 1908, one month to the day after the commission released its findings. Spalding passed away on September 9, 1915.

50. Robert W. Henderson, "Baseball and Rounders," *Bulletin of the New York Public Library*, April 1939, 303–13.

51. John Kieran, "A Challenge to History," Sports of the Times column, *New York Times*, April 15, 1939, 13.

52. Contained in Robert W. Henderson, *Baseball: Notes and Materials on Its Origin* (New York: New York Public Library, 1941), unpaginated.

53. The Knickerbocker Base Ball Club was chartered in 1845 by a group of young professional workers and tradesmen who had already been playing ball together informally for several years in New York. The club has long been regarded as the first organized baseball team, although that designation has been cast into doubt by recent discoveries of other organized teams in New York dating as early as 1823. Nevertheless, the Knickerbocker team produced and ultimately published a set of rules for a variety of baseball that became known as the "New York game." This version of baseball was distinguished from other forms of the game by several innovations, including the elimination of the practice of "soaking" (throwing the ball at a base runner), replacing it with the familiar method of tagging or forcing runners at a base.

54. Harold Peterson, "Baseball's Johnny Appleseed," *Sports Illustrated,* April 14, 1969, 56–78.

55. Peterson uncovered a 1796 German book entitled *Spiele zur Uebung und Erholung* by J. C. F. Gutsmuths that described an early cousin of baseball called "the German ball game." Ironically, the same book mentioned a game called "English base-ball," which Peterson inexplicably ignored. Harold Peterson, *The Man Who Invented Baseball* (New York: Scribner's, 1973), 37–40. Peterson also uncovered rare articles by the European researchers Corrado Gini and Per Maigaard, which are discussed in Chapter 7.

56. See, in particular, John Thorn, "The True Father of Baseball," *Elysian Fields Quarterly* 11, no. 1 (Winter 1992): 85–91, who credits Doc Adams as the primary author.

57. See SABR UK, Web site for Society for American Baseball Research (UK Chapter), http://www.sabruk.org/.

58. George A. Thompson, Jr., "New York Baseball, 1823," *National Pastime,* Society for American Baseball Research, no. 21 (2001): 6–8.

59. Thomas L. Altherr, "'A Place Leavel Enough to Play Ball': Baseball and Baseball-type Games in the Colonial Era, Revolutionary War, and Early American Republic," *Nine: A Journal of Baseball History and Social Policy Perspectives,* 8, no. 2 (2000): 15–49. The full text can be found in appendix 3.

2. ROUNDERS, SCHMOUNDERS

1. In a number of his writings, Chadwick credited an encounter with baseball in 1856 as the catalyst for his interest in the game, but he occasionally claimed earlier experiences. For example, in 1892 he wrote: "When I first

played base ball at Hoboken, N.J. in 1847, the game was little else than a mere schoolboy pastime." *Spalding's Official Base Ball Guide, 1892* (Chicago: A. G. Spalding and Bros., 1892), 10.

2. Chadwick, *Beadle's Dime Base-Ball Player,* 1860, 5.

3. Henry Chadwick, "The Ancient History of Base Ball, *"The Ball Players' Chronicle,* July 18, 1867, 4.

4. William Clarke, *The Boy's Own Book,* 2d ed. (London: Vizetelly, Branston, 1828), 20.

5. Henderson, "Baseball and Rounders," 313.

6. Ibid., 312, 313.

7. The second known appearance in print of the term "rounders" confirms its regional usage. In an article called "Games with a Ball" appearing in the March 16, 1839, issue of the *Saturday Magazine,* rounders is identified as a pastime "which is much played at the present day in the west of England."

8. Henderson, "Baseball and Rounders," 313.

9. Henderson believed that the rules for rounders first appeared in the third English edition of *The Boy's Own Book,* published in 1829. My research shows that they actually appeared in the second edition of 1828.

10. R. Maillard Stead, "Origin of Baseball Mixed with Contests in England," *Christian Science Monitor,* June 12, 1939, 13.

11. Robert W. Henderson, "How Baseball Began," *Bulletin of the New York Public Library,* April 1937, 291.

12. Robert W. Henderson, *Ball, Bat, and Bishop* (New York: Rockport, 1947), 156, 145.

13. *Daily News* (London), August 17, 1874, 6.

14. Delabere P. Blaine, *An Encyclopædia of Rural Sports* (London: Longman, Orme, Brown, and Longmans, 1840), 131.

15. Seymour, *Baseball,* 1: 4–5.

16. Patrick Carroll, a member of the Society for American Baseball Research (SABR) chapter in the United Kingdom, first raised questions about the dubious credit given to rounders in an article "The Chicken or the Egg?" *SABR UK Examiner* no. 5 (January 1995).

17. Frederick Ivor-Campbell, email message to members of the Society for American Baseball Research Nineteenth-Century Committee, December 3, 2001. Emphasis mine.

18. *Oxford Companion to Sports and Games,* ed. John Arlott (London: Oxford University Press, 1975), 851.

19. Web site of the National Rounders Association, Rounders: History of the Game, http://www.nra-rounders.co.uk/history.html.

20. P. Maigaard, "Battingball Games," *Genus* 5, nos. 1–2 (December 1941): 57–72.

21. Johann Christoph Friedrich Gutsmuths, *Spiele zur Uebung und Erholung des Körpers und Geistes, für die Jugend, ihre Erzieher und alle Freunde Unschuldiger Jugendfreuden* (Schnepfenthal, Germany: Verlag der buchhandlung der Erziehungsanstalt, 1796), 78. See chapter 5.

22. See, for example: David Quentin Voigt, *Baseball: An Illustrated History* (University Park: Pennsylvania State University Press, 1987), 11: "Major league baseball had its origins in British stick-ball games, notably one called rounders"; Warren Goldstein, *Playing for Keeps: A History of Early Baseball* (Ithaca, NY: Cornell University Press, 1989), 10: "The genuine forerunner of American baseball . . . was the English game of rounders"; and John Thorn, *Total Baseball*, 7th ed. (Kingston, NY: Total Sports Publishing, 2001), 1: "Baseball was in its infancy in the 1850s — having just evolved from the boyhood game of rounders." (Thorn has since conducted further research on this topic and has recanted his former assessment. He now maintains that if anything, rounders derived from baseball.)

3. ABNER AND ALBERT, THE MISSING LINK

This chapter is dedicated to the memory of Akira Shimada.

1. Henderson, *Ball, Bat, and Bishop*, chapter 24, "The Myth Exploded," 182, 183.

2. Ibid., 179; Abraham Mills, "Final Decision of the Special Baseball Commission," December 30, 1907, in *Spalding's Official Baseball Guide, 1908*, ed. Henry Chadwick (New York: American Sports, 1908), 47.

3. A. G. Spalding, "Mr. A. G. Spalding Contends That Base Ball Is of American Origin," July 28, 1907, in *Spalding's Official Baseball Guide, 1908*, 41–42.

4. Spalding, "Origin and Early History," 15–17.

5. Albert Spalding to James Sullivan, August 13, 1905, John Doyle Papers.

6. Spalding's report to the Commission states, "It certainly appeals to an American's pride to have had the great national game of Base Ball created and named by a Major General in the United States Army, and to have that same game played as a camp diversion by the soldiers of the Civil War, who, at the conclusion of the war, disseminated Base Ball throughout the length and breadth of the United States, and thus gave to the game its national character." Spalding, "Spalding Contends," 42.

7. The second paragraph of Graves's original letter to the *Beacon Journal* states, "Said Abner Doubleday being then a boy pupil of 'Green's Select School' in Cooperstown, and the same, who as General Doubleday won honor

at the Battle of Gettysburg in the Civil war." Graves to Editor, April 3, 1905. Nevertheless, in a reply to Graves on November 10, 1905, Spalding asked Graves, "Who was Abner Doubleday?".

8. Among Abner Doubleday's writings are *Reminiscences of Forts Sumter and Moultrie in 1860–61* (New York: Harper and Brothers, 1876); *Chancellorsville and Gettysburg* (New York: Scribner's, 1882); and *Gettysburg Made Plain* (New York: Century, 1888). Nor were Doubleday's achievements limited to his military career. He is also credited by some with being a member of the group that obtained a charter for the first San Francisco cable street railway in 1870. David Morgan Ramsey, *The "Old Sumpter Hero": A Biography of Major-General Abner Doubleday*, Ph.D diss., Florida State University, 1980, reproduction (Ann Arbor MI: University Microfilms International, 2002), 195–97.

9. Peter Levine cites newspaper articles that suggest that Spalding was not a believer in Theosophy. A. G. *Spalding and the Rise of Baseball* (New York: Oxford University Press, 1985), 127, n. 15.

10. "General Abner Doubleday," *Harper's Weekly*, February 4, 1893, 115. Actually, Doubleday served as president ad-interim of the Theosophical Society, not as president. Nor is there any evidence that Doubleday described himself as a "Buddhist." The use of the term by the obituary writer was probably due to the difficulty in succinctly summarizing the beliefs of the Theosophists.

11. Ramsey, *The "Old Sumpter Hero,"* 4, quoting from Abner Doubleday, letter, November 20, 1887, Abner Doubleday Papers, Baseball Hall of Fame and Museum Library, Cooperstown NY.

12. John S. McCalmont, "Abner Doubleday," in *Twenty-Fourth Annual Reunion of the Association of the Graduates of the United States Military Academy at West Point, New York, June 9, 1893* (Saginaw MI: Seeman and Peters, 1893), 89, located at Archives, United States Military Academy, West Point NY).

13. Doubleday's subscription to *The Dial* was discovered in a handwritten letter of his that was offered on eBay.com on June 5, 1999, by Rancourts, a St. Petersburg, Florida, autograph dealer. The text reads in part:

Fort Johnson, N.C.
Sept 25, 1843

Sir,
Enclosed I send you $3. for one years subscription to 'The Dial' commencing with the number I have already received for this year.

A. Doubleday, Lieut. 3d U.S. Army

P.S.
Please direct to Smithville Brunswick Co
North Carolina A.D. to James Munroe
Publisher Dial.

14. Ramsey, The "Old Sumpter Hero," 25, 51; McCalmont, "Abner Double-day," 93.

15. Abner Doubleday, My Life in the Old Army: The Reminiscences of Abner Doubleday, ed. Joseph E. Chance (Fort Worth: Texas Christian University Press, 1998), 180.

16. Ramsey, The "Old Sumpter Hero," 105; "General Abner Doubleday."

17. Gerry Van der Heuvel, Crowns of Thorns and Glory (New York: E. P. Dutton, 1988), 127–29; Ruth Painter Randal, Mary Lincoln (Boston: Little Brown, 1953), 292–94; Ishbel Ross, The President's Wife: Mary Todd Lincoln (New York: G. P. Putman's Sons, 1973), 181–85.

18. McCalmont, "Abner Doubleday," 99.

19. Charles J. Ryan, H. P. Blavatsky and the Theosophical Movement, 2d rev. ed. (Pasadena CA: Theosophical University Press, 1975), 18–30.

20. Sylvia Cranston, The Extraordinary Life and Influence of Helena Blavatsky (New York: G. P. Putnam's Sons, 1993), 123–26.

21. Henry Steele Olcott, Old Diary Leaves, 1st ser. (Adyar, India: Theosophical Publishing House, 1895; 3d printing, 1974), 113–22. "Theosophy" comes from the Greek "Theos" (God) and "sophos" (wise) and was defined by Blavatsky as "the archaic 'Wisdom-Religion', the esoteric doctrine once known in every ancient country having claims to civilization." H. P. Blavatsky, "What Is Theosophy? What Are the Theosophists?" Sunrise 40, no. 4 (April–May Special Issue 1991): 102–3, condensed from The Theosophist 1, no. 1 (October 1879): 2–7. Theosophy has been described as "a body of knowledge — accumulated since time immemorial — that answers the great questions of life — Who am I, Where am I going, What am I doing here, What is the nature of the soul, What is the origin of the universe and What can be said about the nature of divinity. The term theosophy (in its Greek and other forms) had been used about 100 or so times over two millennia before its use by Madame Blavatsky." Blavatsky Net Foundation, "Meaning of the word 'Theosophy,'" Blavatsky Net Foundation Web Page, http://www.blavatsky.net/theosophy/word-theosophy.htm.

22. It is very possible that Doubleday had already become acquainted with Colonel Olcott during the latter years of the Civil War, as both were involved

with military commissions that investigated fraud by government contractors. Ramsey, The "Old Sumpter Hero," 188; Stephen Prothero, The White Buddhist (Bloomington: Indiana University Press, 1996), 33–34.

23. Abner Doubleday, "General Doubleday in Defense of Madame Blavatsky," Religio-Philosophical Journal (Chicago), April 28, 1888, 6.

24. Ramsey, The "Old Sumpter Hero," 202. Doubleday joined the society at the same time as one other prominent American, Thomas Alva Edison. Although associates in Edison's employ later denied that Edison was a member, correspondence between Edison, Blavatsky, and Olcott in 1878 confirm that Edison was indeed a member. Thomas Alva Edison to Henry Steele Olcott, April 4, 1878, [TAED D8912], Thomas Alva Edison Papers Website, http://edison.rutgers.edu/taep.htm; Helena Petrovna Blavatsky to Thomas Alva Edison, April 30, 1878, [TAED D7802], ibid.

25. "Faces of Friends," The Path 7 (March 1893): 373; Doubleday, "General Doubleday in Defense of Madame Blavatsky," 6.

26. Michael Gomes, "Abner Doubleday and Theosophy in America, 1879–1884," Sunrise 40, no. 4 (April–May 1991): 152, quoting from Doubleday Notebook 8, pp. 4–5.

27. Photocopies of the Doubleday Notebooks are in the Archives of the Theosophical Society, Altadena CA.

28. Gomes, "Abner Doubleday and Theosophy in America," 153–56.

29. The books were Dogme et Rituel de la Haute Magie (Dogma and ritual of high magic), 10th ed. (Paris: Germer Baillière, 1861), and Fables et Symboles (Fables and symbols) (Paris: Germer Baillière, 1862), both by Éliphas Lévi Zahed (the pseudonym of Alphonse Louis Constant, 1810–75). Doubleday later donated his copies of the Lévi books and sixty-eight other rare books and manuscripts on the occult to the Theosophical Society, and this formed the cornerstone of their library. "Faces of Friends," 373.

30. "Faces of Friends," 374.

31. Doubleday, "General Doubleday in Defense of Madame Blavatsky," 6.

32. "Lying in State," New York Sun, January 31, 1893; "Honors to His Memory," New York Tribune, January 31, 1893.

33. According to a Doubleday family genealogy, General Doubleday's funeral at Arlington took place on a "miserably cold, windy and wet day," which would prove fateful to his family. Among the large group of relatives that attended the funeral, Abner's younger brother, Ulysses, and Ulysses's son-in-law, Charles Weed Cutting, caught pneumonia and subsequently died from their illnesses. Margaret Curfman and Stephen Rockstroh, Doubleday Families of America, 2d ed. (Port Charlotte FL: S. W. D. Rockstroh, 1993), 156.

34. "Faces of Friends," 373.

35. McCalmont, "Abner Doubleday," 100. The obituary of General Doubleday in the *Twenty-Fourth Annual Reunion* makes no mention of Doubleday's involvement in the Theosophical Society or his interest in Theosophy and the occult sciences.

36. Levine, *A. G. Spalding and the Rise of Baseball*, 125.

37. "Mrs. Elizabeth Churchill Spalding Passes Away," *Theosophical Path* 32, no. 1 (January 1927): 96–97.

38. H. P. Blavatsky, *Collected Writings*, ed. Boris de Zirkoff, 2d ed. (Wheaton IL: Theosophical Publishing, 1977), 1: 484–90. Judge and the British-born social reformer Annie Besant had competed for the leadership of the world-wide Theosophical organization; in the split that ensued, most of the American lodges followed Judge, and most of the European and Asian lodges sided with Besant.

39. "Mrs. Elizabeth Churchill Spalding Passes Away." Among the society duties entrusted to Elizabeth was her role as general superintendent of the society's Children's Department, which oversaw the "Lotus Groups," the organization's Sunday schools.

40. The event, which was attended by San Diego's mayor, other dignitaries, and more than a thousand of San Diego's seventeen thousand citizens, drew a great deal of attention from the San Diego press. Emmett A. Greenwalt, *California Utopia: Point Loma, 1897–1942*, 2d rev. ed. (San Diego: Point Loma Publications, 1978), 31–33.

41. Levine, *A. G. Spalding and the Rise of Baseball*, 125; Levine points out that Mary had helped her older brother through difficult times on more than one occasion. She served as the first bookkeeper for A. G. Spalding and Brother (the original name of the sporting goods company), and her marriage to William Thayer Brown, son of a well-to-do Rockford banker, brought Albert access to much-needed capital when the Spaldings bought their first baseball bat factory. It was at this point that Brown was brought into the ownership circle and the company became A. G. Spalding and Brothers. Ibid., 73.

42. *In the Matter of the Application of Albert G. Spalding and Elizabeth C. Spalding, his wife, for leave to adopt Spalding Brown, a minor*, Monmouth County, New Jersey, Orphans' Court, docket no. 2659, Decree, July 5, 1901. Court documents filed in the adoption proceeding indicate that the Spaldings did not reveal the true nature of their relationship to young Spalding Brown. Their sworn adoption petition alleged that Spalding Brown's parents "are now dead," that he had no legal guardian, and that the child was now living with Mr. and Mrs. Spalding in Seabright, New Jersey, the location of Spalding's

summer home. It is also telling that the court just happened to appoint William Thayer Brown, Spalding's brother-in-law and business partner, to be "Next Friend" of Spalding Brown, so as to look after the best interests of the child in the proceeding. Needless to say, Brown readily gave his consent to the adoption of the child by the Spaldings. *In the Matter of the Application of Albert G. Spalding and Elizabeth C. Spalding, his wife, for leave to adopt Spalding Brown, a minor,* Monmouth County, New Jersey, Orphans' Court, Docket #2659, Next Friend's Consent, July 5, 1901. No mention was made in any of the court papers that William Brown, together with Spalding's sister Mary, had raised Spalding Brown in their own home before the death of Spalding's first wife.

43. Levine, *A. G. Spalding and the Rise of Baseball,* 125; "Last Will and Testament of Albert Goodwill Spalding," attached to Certificate of Proof of Will and the Facts Found, July 13, 1917, *In the Matter of the Estate of Albert Goodwill Spalding, Deceased,* San Diego County Superior Court, Case P6464, located in San Diego County Central Records.

44. "Adopted Son Dies in Battle," *New York Herald,* July 8, 1916, 14.

45. *San Diego Union,* June 24, 1900, 5.

46. Levine, *A. G. Spalding and the Rise of Baseball,* 88, 125–26.

47. Greenwalt, *California Utopia,* 47–48; Robert V. Hine, *California's Utopian Colonies* (San Marino CA: Huntington Library, 1953), 44.

48. The SPCC was often criticized as being overzealous in removing children from the care of parents and guardians. Greenwalt, *California Utopia,* 58.

49. Ibid., 56–65; Levine, *A. G. Spalding and the Rise of Baseball,* 127–30.

50. Graves to Editor, April 3, 1905.

51. James E. Sullivan to Abner Graves, April 5, 1905, James Doyle Papers.

52. "Major-General Abner Doubleday," *New Century Path* 8, no. 40 (August 13, 1905): 14. Italics in original.

53. Ibid.

54. The *New Century Path* article's description of Spalding as a member of the society can be viewed as authoritative on the issue, as Spalding had ample opportunity to dispute it. He could have simply walked the short distance from his home to the *Path's* offices and demanded a correction. Other evidence of Spalding's membership can be found in a will contest filed by Keith Spalding, Spalding's son by his first wife, Josie, following Albert's death in 1915. In legal documents Keith claimed his father executed his will under the undue influence of Elizabeth Spalding and Katherine Tingley. In support of this claim, he alleged that shortly after his father's marriage to Elizabeth,

A. G. had been "prevailed upon" to formally join the Theosophical Society. *In the Matter of the Estate of Albert Goodwill Spalding, Deceased,* San Diego County Superior Court, Case P6464, Opposition to Probate of Will, located in San Diego County Central Records. Eventually the will contest was settled out of court. Levine, *A. G. Spalding and the Rise of Baseball,* 144, n. 3; Greenwalt, *California Utopia,* 187.

55. Spalding to Sullivan, August 13, 1905.

56. Albert Spalding to Albert Pratt, August 13, 1905, John Doyle Papers.

57. Spalding, "Spalding Contends," 42.

58. This letter was published in the 1908 *Spalding Guide* and was titled the "Final Decision" of the Special Baseball Commission. Mills, "Final Decision," 47.

4. WAS ABNER GRAVES TELLING THE TRUTH?

1. The Special Base Ball Commission, as it was officially known, comprised well-known and respected members of the baseball establishment who, for the most part, played a negligible role in the actual investigation. Albert Spalding, who controlled virtually every aspect of the process, handpicked all of them, and for this reason the body can most accurately be described as the Spalding commission. Commission member Abraham Mills, former president of the National League, has often been represented as the panel's president. In fact, he played no such role, and "Mills commission" is a misnomer. Mills was reluctant to join the commission — telling Spalding in a March 27, 1905, letter, "I am not inclined to take up the baseball question again in any of its aspects" — but ultimately he acquiesced. His recognition as chairman came about because he was the only member of the body to respond to the commission secretary's summation of the evidence. A letter submitted by Mills containing analysis of the secretary's findings and concluding that Abner Doubleday invented baseball was subsequently signed by other commission members and became known as the "final report."

2. Albert Spalding, "The Origin of the Game of Base Ball," Akron OH *Beacon Journal,* April 3, 1905.

3. Graves to Editor, April 3, 1905.

4. "Abner Doubleday Invented Base Ball," Akron OH *Beacon Journal,* April 4, 1905.

5. Graves to Spalding and the Special Commission, November 17, 1905.

6. Phil Goodstein, "The Fate of Abner Graves" (Denver: unpublished, 1996).

7. Ibid.

8. "Denver Man Played First Baseball Game in History of Sport," *Denver Post*, May 9, 1912.

9. Graves to Spalding and the Special Commission, November 17, 1905.

10. "Denver Man Played First Baseball Game."

11. Ibid.

12. "Would Return Here for Ball Game in 1919," (Cooperstown NY) *Freeman's Journal*, December 18, 1916, 1.

13. "Abner Graves Vents Wrath on Dying Mate Who Offers to Forgive," *Denver Post*, June 17, 1924, 1.

14. Report on Abner Graves's trial, *Denver Post*, June 25, 1924.

15. "Death of Insane Wife-slayer Revealed after Three Months," *Denver Post*, February 2, 1927, 17.

16. The full text of Graves's letters can be found in appendix 4.

17. Peter Morris, *Baseball Fever: Early Baseball in Michigan* (Ann Arbor: University of Michigan Press, 2003), 363–64.

18. [John Newbery,] *A Little Pretty Pocket-Book, Intended for the Instruction and Amusement of Little Master Tommy and Pretty Miss Polly*, 11th ed. (London, 1763; orig. pub 1744), References to an earlier use of the name "base-ball," from the year 1700, are erroneous. This is explained in the annotated bibliography under the listing for *The Life and Death of Mr. Tho. Wilson, Minister of Maidstone in the County of Kent, M.A.*

19. Pittsfield town meeting records, entry for September 5, 1791, Berkshire Athenaeum, Pittsfield MA; Thompson, "New York Baseball, 1823."

20. Robin Carver, *The Book of Sports* (Boston: Lilly, Wait, Colman, and Holden, 1834); *The Boy's Book of Sports* (New Haven: S. Babcock, 1835); *The Boy's and Girl's Book of Sports* (Providence: Cory and Daniels, 1835).

21. The practice of "plugging" or "soaking" a runner in early-nineteenth-century American baseball emanated from a long line of English and European folk games, including stool-ball, cat, and longball.

22. Mills, "Final Decision."

23. *By-laws and Rules of the Knickerbocker Base Ball Club*, September 23, 1845 (New York: W. H. B. Smith, 1848).

24. Curiously, the flat-faced bat and high-lob pitching recounted by Graves were almost identical to features of an early variety of baseball described in a German book in 1796. See Chapter 5.

25. *Sporting Life*, May 5, 1886. The complete text of Dr. Ford's letter can be found in appendix 5. (Ford used the out-of-date Spelling "Beechville.")

26. Nancy Bouchier and Robert Barney, "A Critical Examination of a

Source on Early Ontario Baseball: The Reminiscence of Adam E. Ford," *Journal of Sport History* (Spring 1988): 75–89.

27. William Humber, *Diamonds of the North* (Toronto: Oxford University Press, 1995), 16, 18.

28. Bouchier and Barney, "Critical Examination," 79–80.

29. Chip Martin, "The Adam Ford–Abner Graves Connection in Their Stories on the Origins of Baseball" (London, Ontario: unpublished, 2003).

5. RULES OF BASEBALL

1. Johann Christoph Friedrich Gutsmuths, *Spiele zur Uebung und Erholung des Körpers und Geistes für die Jugend, ihre Erzieher und alle Freunde Unschuldiger Jugendfreuden* (Schnepfenthal, Germany: Verlag der buchhandlung der Erziehungsanstalt, 1796), 78. Translation provided by Mary Akitiff for Gutsmuths's section on *das englische Base-ball*.

2. Ibid. Translation provided by David Ball for Gutsmuths's section on *das deutsche Ballspiel*.

3. The Gutsmuths book is discussed by the author Harold Peterson in *The Man Who Invented Baseball*. Peterson dwells on Gutsmuths's description of "the German ball game," but never mentions the German author's inclusion of "English base-ball." Interestingly, two European researchers working in the 1940s published articles that mentioned Gutsmuths's coverage of English base-ball, but American baseball historians overlooked their findings. See Chapter 7.

4. Gutsmuths, *Spiele zur Uebung und Erholung*, 80.

5. Ibid., 82.

6. Ibid., 83–84.

7. *La balle empoisonée* is first described in *Les Jeux des jeunes garçons, représentés par un grand nombre d'estampes* (Paris, ca. 1815), 104–5.

8. Gutsmuths, *Spiele zur Uebung und Erholung*, 78.

9. This rule from *das deutsche Ballspiel* is remarkably similar to the later practice of "hitting for the rounder," which emerged as a feature of the English game rounders in the 1840s. It may be reasonably surmised that rounders adapted the feature from the older German pastime, which was played on a limited basis in nineteenth-century England under the name "ballstock." S. Williams, *Boy's Treasury of Sports* (London: D. Bogue, 1844), 19.

10. Gutsmuths, *Spiele zur Uebung und Erholung*, 78.

11. [Newbery,] *A Little Pretty Pocket-Book*.

6. HOW SLICK WERE THE KNICKS?

1. Thompson, "New York Baseball, 1823."

2. See, for example, Geoffrey C. Ward and Ken Burns, *Who Invented the Game?* (New York: Knopf, 1994), 8.

3. See, for example, Seymour, *Baseball*, 1: 19–20.

4. These were as follows: "rounders" from Clarke, *The Boy's Own Book*, (first American edition 1829), 20; "base or goal ball" from Carver, *The Book of Sports* (1834), 37–38; "base or goal ball" from *The Boy's and Girl's Book of Sports* (1835), 18; and "base ball" from *The Boy's Book of Sports* (1835), 11.

5. See, for example, David Nemec, *The Rules of Baseball* (New York: Lyons and Burford, 1994), 2.

6. Noah Webster, *An American Dictionary of the English Language* (New York: S. Converse, 1828), 2:[224]. Webster's identically titled 1844 edition carries the same definitions.

7. See Gutsmuths, *Spiele zur Uebung und Erholung*, 78.

8. Clarke, *The Boy's Own Book*; Carver, *The Book of Sports*; *The Boy's and Girl's Book of Sports*.

9. Joseph Strutt, *Sports and Pastimes of the People of England* (London: T. Bensley for White and Co., 1801), 101.

10. *Porter's Spirit of the Times*, December 27, 1856, 276.

11. Gutsmuths, *Spiele zur Uebung und Erholung*, 78.

12. *Revised Constitution, By-laws, and Rules of the Eagle Ball Club* (New York: Oliver and Brother, 1854), 9. The pitching distance was not specified in the Eagle Club's original rule book of 1852.

13. Strutt, *Sports and Pastimes of the People of England*, 99–100.

14. Clarke, *The Boy's Own Book*.

15. Carver, *The Book of Sports*.

16. J. L. Williams, *The Every Boy's Book* (London: Dean and Munday, 1841), 23.

17. *Porter's Spirit of the Times*, December 27, 1856, 276

18. Alice Bertha Gomme, *The Traditional Games of England, Scotland, and Ireland* (London: D. Nutt, 1894–98), 1: 310. Gomme was the foremost authority on this topic.

19. Williams, *The Every Boy's Book*, 26.

20. Gutsmuths, *Spiele zur Uebung und Erholung*, 79.

21. Clarke, *The Boy's Own Book*; Carver, *The Book of Sports*; *The Boy's and Girl's Book of Sports*; *The Boy's Book of Sports*.

22. "Stool-Ball, or the Easter Diversion," *London Magazine*, December 1733, 637–38.

23. Stonehenge [J. H. Walsh], *The Manual of British Rural Sports* (London: G. Routledge, 1856), 500–501.

24. Gutsmuths, *Spiele zur Uebung und Erholung; Les Jeux des jeunes garçons*.

25. Ibid.

26. "Base or goal ball" from Carver, *The Book of Sports*; "base or goal ball" from *The Boy's and Girl's Book of Sports*; "base ball" from *The Boy's Book of Sports*; "squares" from W. Montague, *The Youth's Encyclopædia of Health with Games and Play Ground Amusements* (London: W. Emans, 1838), 11.

27. Gomme, *Traditional Games of England, Scotland, and Ireland*, 1: 310.

28. *New York Morning News*, October 22, 1845.

29. William Cauldwell to William Rankin, February 11, 1905, John Doyle Papers.

30. Clarke, *The Boy's Own Book*.

31. *Constitution of Olympic Ball Club of Philadelphia* (Philadelphia: John Clark, 1838), 8.

32. Tom Shieber, personal communication with author, February 2000.

7. IN THE BEGINNING

1. Claims that baseball may have originated in Ancient Egypt vary from the sensational ("Ancient Egyptians Invented Baseball!" *Weekly World News*, July 6, 1999) to the scholarly. The Egyptologist Peter Piccione, quoted in *Time* magazine as well as in other publications, proposed that a four thousand–year–old Egyptian bat-and-ball game called *seker-hemat* may have been an an-cestor to baseball. Piccione's theory was based upon ancient writings and im-ages showing that players used a bat to hit a ball. However, Piccione's claims of further similarities to baseball were apparently speculative in nature. Franz Lidz, "Balk Like an Egyptian," *Time*, May 5, 2003, 21. Other materials on this subject can be found in the Origins of Baseball file at the National Baseball Library, Cooperstown NY, including the description of an image of a player with bat and ball inscribed upon the ancient Egyptian Temple of Philae.

2. Peterson, *The Man Who Invented Baseball*, 37–50.

3. Corrado Gini, "Rural Ritual Games in Libya," *Rural Sociology* 4, no. 3 (1939): 283–99; Corrado Gini, "Considerazioni ed ipotesi sull'origine del' 'Om el Mahag,' in generale, di giuochi di 'Battingball,'" *Genus* 5, nos. 1–2 (1941): 73–86.

4. Efforts to locate and obtain the film from Gini's organization, *Comitato Italiano per lo Studio dei Problemi Della Popolazione*, have proven unsuccessful.

5. Gini, "Rural Ritual Games," 290, 291.

6. Ibid., 291.

7. Maigaard, "Battingball Games."

8. Gini, "Rural Ritual Games," 284.

9. Maigaard, "Battingball Games," 65.

10. Ibid., 70, 72.

11. Ibid., 68, 72. Emphasis mine.

12. Gini, "Considerazioni ed ipotesi," 77.

13. Erwin Mehl, "Baseball in the Stone Age," *Western Folklore* 7, no. 2 (1948): 145–61.

14. Unrelated to his observations on sports, Guarinoni promulgated an infamous historical lie whose effect lingers to this day. See my descriptive remarks in the Early Baseball Bibliography on his 1610 book *Greuel der Verwüstung des menschlichen Geschlechts*.

15. Erwin Mehl, "Notes to 'Baseball in the Stone Age,'" *Western Folklore* 8, no. 2 (1949): 154. Although Mehl made limited mention of the Prague game in "Baseball in the Stone Age," he published additional notes a year later that included the original German text of Guarinoni's description, as well as an English translation. His original source for the passage was Hippolytus Guarinoni, *Greuel der Verwüstung des menschlichen Geschlechts* (Ingolstadt, Austrian Empire: Andreas Angermayr, 1610).

16. Walter Andrei and László Zolnay, *Fun and Games in Old Europe* (English translation of *Társasjáték és szórakozás a régi Európában*) (Budapest: Corvina, 1986), 110–11.

17. Trans. and excerpted in Arthur L. Waldo, *The True Heroes of Jamestown* (Miami: American Institute of Polish Culture, 1977), 128. The original volume is Zbigniew Stefanski, *Memorialium Commercatoris* (Amsterdam: Adreasa Bickera, 1625).

18. Mehl, "Baseball in the Stone Age," 154.

19. Ibid.

20. Ibid., 151, 152.

8. STOOLS, CLUBS, STOBS, AND JUGS

1. Strutt, *Sports and Pastimes of the People of England*, 97.

2. Quoted ibid., xliii.

3. William Maxwell, *The Field Book; or, Sports and Pastimes of the British Islands* (London: Effingham Wilson, 1833), 129.

4. Henderson, *Ball, Bat, and Bishop*, 60.

5. MS. Bodl. 264, fol. 22r (detail), Bodleian Library, Oxford University.

6. P. H. Ditchfield, *Old English Sports, Pastimes, and Customs* (London: Methuen, 1891), 65.

7. From the original Latin record of the court as translated by the scholar Brian Twyne about the year 1620, published in an Oxford journal in 1891, and reissued by the Rev. H. E. Salter, *Records of Medieval Oxford* (Oxford, 1912), 11.

8. MS. Royal 10 E IV, f. 94v, British Library.

9. Alexander Luders and John Raithby, *The Statutes of the Realm* (London: George Eyre and Andrew Strahan, 1810–1822), v. 2, 462–463.

10. *Oxford English Dictionary*, ed. James Augustus Henry Murray (Oxford: Clarendon, 1933), 5: 59.

11. Joseph A. Baldassarre, "Baseball's Ancestry," *National Pastime*, Society for American Baseball Research, no. 21 (2001): 42–43.

12. *New York Morning News*, October 24, 1845; *New York Herald*, October, 24 1845.

13. *By-laws and Rules of the Knickerbocker Base Ball Club.*

14. Gomme, *Traditional Games of England, Scotland, and Ireland* , 1: 34.

15. Henderson, *Ball, Bat, and Bishop*, 75.

16. John Myrc (Mirk), *How thow schalt thy paresche preche* (London, ca. 1450).

17. Henderson, *Ball, Bat, and Bishop*, 71.

18. William Shakespeare, and John Fletcher, *The Two Noble Kinsmen* (London: John Waterson, 1634), 78.

19. *The whole works of Homer*, trans. George Chapman, (London: Nathaniell Butter, 1616), 152–53.

20. Samuel Johnson, *A dictionary of the English language* (London: J. and P. Knapton, 1755), no pagination.

21. [Newbery,] *A Little Pretty Pocket-Book.*

22. Strutt, *Sports and Pastimes*, 89–90.

23. "Stool-ball, or the Easter Diversion."

24. In his work *A tour thro' the whole island of Great Britain* (London, 1724), the author Daniel Defoe uses the same spelling.

25. John Taylor, *A Short Relation of a Long Journey Made Round or Ovall* (London, 1652), 23.

26. Henry Charles Howard, *The Encyclopædia of Sport* (London: Lawrence and Bullen, 1897), 412.

27. Joseph Wright, ed., *The English Dialect Dictionary* (London: H. Frowde; G. P. Putnam's Sons, 1898–1905), 5: 774; Gomme, *Traditional Games of England, Scotland, and Ireland*, 2: 217; *Oxford English Dictionary*, 10: 1054; Strutt, *Sports and Pastimes*, 95–96.

28. John Aubrey, *Natural History of Wiltshire* (London: J. B. Nichols and Son, 1847), 117. Original manuscript completed in 1685.

29. Edward Chamberlayne, *Angli notitia: or, The present state of England, together with divers reflections upon the antient state thereof,* 3d ed. (London: printed for J. Martyn, 1669), 86 (The full quotation reads: "The Citizens and Peasants have *Hand-ball, Foot-Ball, Skittles,* or *Nine-Pins, Shovel-board, Stowball, Goffe, Trol-Madam, Cudgels, Bear-baiting, Bow and Arrow, Throwing at Cocks, Shuttlecock, Bowling, Quaits, Leaping, Wrestling, Pitching the Barr,* and *Ringing of Bells,* a Recreation used in no other Countrey of the World.")

30. Aubrey, *Natural History of Wiltshire.*

31. John Smyth, *The Berkeley manuscripts. The lives of the Berkeleys, lords of the honour, castle and manor of Berkeley, in the county of Gloucester, from 1066 to 1618* (Gloucester UK: 1883), 2: 290–91, 3: 10. Original unpublished manuscript completed no later than 1640.

32. David Terry, "The Seventeenth Century Game of Cricket, a Reconstruction of the Game," *Sports Historian* 20, no. 1 (May 2000): 33–43.

33. "Rolls of the Court Baron of the Royal Manor of Kirklington," *Bodleian Quarterly Record,* November 15, 1927, 186 (trans. David Ball).

34. *"Nul enfaunt ne autres ne jue, —* a barres," *Rot. Parl.* MS. *Harl.* 7057, as cited in Strutt, *Sports and Pastimes,* 72.

35. Strutt, *Sports and Pastimes,* 72.

36. Ibid.

37. Chadwick, "Ancient History of Base Ball."

9. TRAPS AND CATS

1. Strutt, *Sports and Pastimes of the People of England,* 99–100.

2. Ibid., 100.

3. Signs of trap-ball play in America are occasionally evidenced in the early colonial period. The diarist Samuel Sewell reported one in his entry for June 6, 1713: "The Rain-water grievously runs into my son Joseph's Chamber from the N. Window above. . . . I went on the Roof, and found the Spout next Salter's stop'd, but could not free it with my Stick. Boston went up . . . and clear'd the Leaden-throat, by thrusting out a Trap-Ball that stuck there. Thus a small matter greatly incomodes us; and when God pleases, tis easily remov'd. The Rain that fell the two Nights and Lords-day following was in such Abundance, we had been almost Drown'd, if the Spout had not been cleared." Surely this is the earliest near-drowning blamed on a batted ball. *Diary of Samuel Sewell,* 3 vols. (Boston: Massachusetts Historical Society, 1878–82), 2: 718.

4. Strutt, *Sports and Pastimes*, 100–101; Gomme, *Traditional Games of England, Scotland, and Ireland*, 1: 421–23.

5. Gomme, *Traditional Games of England, Scotland, and Ireland*, 1: 421–23.

6. Strutt, *Sports and Pastimes*, 101–2.

7. Ibid.

8. Spalding, "Origin and Early History," 17.

9. Strutt, *Sports and Pastimes*, 101–2.

10. Peterson, *The Man Who Invented Baseball*, 28–35.

11. *The Every Boy's Book of Games, Sports, and Diversions, or, The School-boy's Manual of Amusement, Instruction, and Health* (London: G. Vickers, 1846), 63–64. Emphasis mine.

12. Gomme, *Traditional Games of England, Scotland, and Ireland*, 1: 63–64, 84, 331.

13. James Pycroft, *The Cricket Field: or, the History and Science of Cricket* (London: Longman, Brown, Green, and Longmans, 1851), 19.

14. John Jamieson, *An Etymological Dictionary of the Scottish Language* (Edinburgh: University Press, 1808).

15. Sidney Oldall Addy, *A Glossary of Words Used in the Neighborhood of Sheffield, Including a Selection of Local Names, and Some Notices of Folk-lore, Games and Customs* (London: English Dialect Society, 1888).

16. Pittsfield town meeting records, entry for September 5, 1791, courtesy of Berkshire Athenaeum, Pittsfield MA; Edward Gallaudet, "The Barlow Knife," *Jewel, or, Token of Friendship* (New York: Bancroft and Holley, 1837), 90.

17. Spalding, " Origin and Early History," 15; Ward, *Base-ball*, 22.

18. Spalding, "Origin and Early History," 15, 17.

19. "Childhood: A Study," *Atlantic Monthly*, October 1866, 392.

20. For example, see "Trap Ball: The Ultimate Root of Baseball," published privately by Kazuo Sayama.

21. *Oxford English Dictionary*, 2: 167.

22. In *A Dictionarie of the French and English Tongues*, by Randle Cotgrave, 1611, the author defines the French word *martinet* as "the game called cat and trap." The *Oxford English Dictionary* (6: 192) cites an obscure usage for the same word as "a military engine for throwing large stones." At first glance, this might be interpreted as proving a link between the words "cat" and "catapult." It is worth noting, however, that the Cotgrave definition also included the term "trap." And clearly, it is this word that equates to a device for throwing objects. For example, the OED (11: 283) defines "trap" as "the pivotal wooden instrument with which the ball is thrown up in a game of trap-ball."

1. Clarke, *The Boy's Own Book*, 20.

2. *Oxford English Dictionary*, 11: 512.

3. *The Priory of Hexham*, vol. 2 (Durham, England: Publications of the Surtees Society, vol. 46, Andrews and Co., 1864), 157 (trans. David Ball). Pennyston (or pennystone) was a variation of the game quoits utilizing a disk-shaped flat throwing piece rather than a hoop.

4. George Gascoigne, *The Posies* (London: Richard Smith, 1575), 159.

5. Wright, *English Dialect Dictionary*, 6: 277.

6. Addy, *Glossary of Words Used in the Neighborhood of Sheffield*.

7. Frederick Ross, Richard Stead, and Thomas Holderness, *A Glossary of Words Used in Holderness in the East-Riding of Yorkshire* (London: English Dialect Society, 1877).

8. T. C. Peter, "MS Collection of Cornish Words" (undated), as cited in Wright, *The English Dialect Dictionary*, 6: 277.

9. James Orchard Halliwell-Phillipps, *A Dictionary of Archaic and Provincial Words, Obsolete Phrases, Proverbs, and Ancient Customs, from the Fourteenth Century* (London: John Russell Smith, 1847), 896.

10. *Horæ Subsecivæ*, MS. (Devonshire, England: 1777), as cited in *Oxford English Dictionary*, 11: 512.

11. Montague, *The Youth's Encyclopædia of Health*, 11.

12. Clarke, *The Boy's Own Book*, 20.

13. Williams, *The Every Boy's Book*, 22.

14. [Newbery,] *A Little Pretty Pocket-Book*.

15. *Letters of Mary Lepel, Lady Hervey* (London: John Murray, 1821), 139–40.

16. Jane Austen, *Northanger Abbey: and Persuasion* (London: John Murray, 1818), 1: 7.

17. Cassandra Cooke, *Battleridge* (London: G. Cawthorn, 1799), 1: 2.

18. Ward, *Base-ball*, 19, 20.

19. Fourteen years before Ward's book, an English observer pointed out the baseball reference in Hervey's letter during the first tour of American baseball players to Great Britain. On August 13, 1874, the *Times* of London, published her letter to the editor: "Sir, — Some American athletes are trying to introduce us to their game of base-ball, as if it were a novelty; whereas the fact is that it is an ancient English game, long ago discarded in favour of cricket. In a letter of the celebrated Mary Lepel, Lady Hervey, written in 1748, the family of Frederick, Prince of Wales, are described as "diverting them-

selves with base-ball, a play all who are or have been schoolboys are well acquainted with. Your obedient servant, GRANDMOTHER."

20. Georgiana C. Clark, *Jolly Games for Happy Homes, to amuse our girls and boys; the dear little babies and the grown-up ladies* (New York: E. P. Dutton, 1881), 110. (Although Ward cited an 1875 London edition of this rare work, only a single copy of an 1881 New York edition can be located in American libraries.)

21. Ibid.

22. Ward, *Base-ball*, 20, 21.

23. "Baseball's most direct ancestors were two British games: cricket, a stately pastime divided into innings and supervised by umpires, and rounders, a children's stick-and-ball game brought to New England by the earliest colonists." Geoffrey C. Ward and Ken Burns, *Baseball: An Illustrated History* (New York: Knopf, 1994), 3.

24. Terry, "The Seventeenth Century Game of Cricket," 33, 36.

25. Ibid., 36.

26. George Dudley Seymour, "The Old-time Game of Wicket and Some Old-time Wicket Players," *Papers and Addresses of the Society of Colonial Wars in the State of Connecticut*, vol. 2 of the Proceedings of the Society (1909): 274.

27. *Porter's Spirit of the Times*, February 14, 1857, p. 388.

28. See, for example, Georges Petiot, *Le Robert des sports: Dictionnaire de la langue des sports* (Paris: Les Robert, 1982), 455.

29. Spalding, "In the Field Papers. "

30. (Quebec City) *Le Soleil*, January 21, 1899, 2.

31. Charles Du Cange, *Glossarium ad scriptoris mediæ et infimæ latinatis* (Niort, France: Léopold Favre, 1887; orig. pub. 1678), 8: 204.

32. Par G. Beleze, *Jeux des adolescents* (Paris: Librairie de L. Hachette, 1856), 68. Translation provided by David Ball.

33. Du Cange, *Glossarium*.

34. Edélestand Du Méril, *Dictionnaire du patois normand* (Caen: B. Mancel, 1849), 204. Translation provided by David Ball.

35. *Trésor de la Langue Française*, ed. B. Quemada (Paris: Gallimard, 1994), 15: 195; *Le Grand Robert de la Langue Française*, 2nd edition, ed. Paul Robert (Paris: Le Robert, 1991), 9: 283.

36. Henry Claremont, *Le Livre des sports athletiques et des jeux de plein air* (Paris: P. Roger, ca. 1909), 320. Translation provided by David Ball.

37. *Les Jeux des jeunes garçons*, 104–5.

38. Clarke, *The Boy's Own Book*, 20.

39. Henderson, *Ball, Bat, and Bishop*, 142. Of course, Henderson was un-

aware of the rules for English base-ball published some twenty years earlier than *Les Jeux des jeunes garçons* in *Spiele zur Uebung und Erholung* by Gutsmuths.

40. A full translation of these rules can be found in appendix 7.

II. BASEBALL BEFORE WE KNEW IT

1. Harold Peterson also explored aspects of baseball's early history in his 1973 book *The Man Who Invented Baseball*, but he neglected to structure his findings or document his sources.

2. The origins of this myth are explored in the bibliography under the listing for the 1672 book *The Life and Death of Mr. Tho. Wilson, Minister of Maidstone in the County of Kent, M.A.* (Shortly before going to press I learned that a fellow researcher had also discovered the flaw in the Reverend Wilson quotation. Martin Hoerchner, a renowned explorer of baseball's English roots and a member of the United Kingdom chapter of the Society for American Baseball Research, reported his findings in the Fall 2003 issue of the *SABR UK Examiner*, no. 13.)

3. *Letters of Mary Lepel, Lady Hervey* , 139.

4. An early report of bat-and-ball play in colonial North America derived from the village of Schoharie, New York, a settlement with a largely Dutch and German population. In 1753 a clergyman from New England observed that some boys in the town were engaged in ball playing despite the fact that prayer services were under way. "I have been at their meetings, when the boys through the service, and even at the celebration of the Lord's-supper, have been playing bat and ball the whole term around the house of God. Coming out of meeting, we observed the lower orders at all sorts of recreation. To us, who had been used to the strictness of a New-England sabbath, it appeared very profane. But custom will make anything familiar." "A Letter from Rev. Gideon Hawley, of Marshpee, containing a Narrative of his Journey to Onohoghgwage in 1753," *Collections of the Massachusetts Historical Society for 1794* I, no. 4.

5. Altherr, " 'A Place Leavel Enough to Play Ball,' " 22–26.

6. John Rhea Smith, "Journal at Nassau Hall," Princeton Library MSS, AM 12800, as quoted ibid., 27.

7. Pittsfield town meeting records, entry for September 5, 1791, courtesy of Berkshire Athenaeum, Pittsfield MA.

8. A full listing of these can be found in the Early Baseball Bibliography.

9. (New Orleans) *Daily Picayune*, August 15, 1841, 2.

10. (San Francisco) *California Sunday Dispatch*, January 18, 1852, 2.

11. *Constitution of Olympic Ball Club of Philadelphia.*

12. "Olympic Ball Club," *Sporting Life*, December 31, 1885.

13. Carver, *Book of Sports*, 37; (New Orleans) *Daily Picayune*, May 25, 1841, 2.

14. A discussion of these titles can be found in Chapter 5, and their respective descriptions of baseball are located in appendix 7.

15. Preston D. Orem, *Baseball (1845–1881), from the Newspaper Accounts* (Altadena CA, 1961), 3.

16. Quoted in Thompson, "New York Baseball, 1823," 6.

17. Delhi (NY) Gazette, July 13, 1825.

EARLY BASEBALL BIBLIOGRAPHY

1. Henderson, *Ball, Bat, and Bishop*, 74.

2. In *The Man Who Invented Baseball*, Harold Peterson erroneously cites *The Pilgrim's Progress* as the source of this passage.

3. Henderson, *Ball, Bat, and Bishop*, 132.

4. The full text of this poem and further commentary can be found in Chapter 8.

5. Gini, "Rural Ritual Games in Libya."

6. Henderson, *Ball, Bat, and Bishop*, 142.

7. Strutt, *Sports and Pastimes of the People of England*, 97.

8. Henderson, *Ball, Bat, and Bishop*, 145.

9. Henderson, "Baseball and Rounders."

10. Henderson, *Ball, Bat, and Bishop*, 144.

11. A. P. Smith, *History of the Seventy-Sixth Regiment of New York State Volunteers* (Cortland NY: Truair, Smith, and Miles, 1867), 48.

12. Gomme, *Traditional Games of England, Scotland, and Ireland*, 2: 217.

APPENDIX 2

1. Dick Dobbins and John Twichell, *Nuggets on the Diamond: Professional Baseball in the Bay Area from the Gold Rush to the Present* (San Francisco: Woodford, 1994), 16–17.

APPENDIX 3

1. Lloyd A. Brown and Howard H. Peckham, eds., *Revolutionary War Journals of Henry Dearborn, 1775–1783* (Freeport NY: Books for Libraries Press, 1969 [orig. pub. 1939]), 149–50.

2. Baseball historians have generally neglected or glossed over the pre-1845 period of baseball history, giving great emphasis to the developments of the New York Knickerbockers. Dean A. Sullivan, in *Early Innings*, did provide a few examples of pre-1845 baseball activities, but even that barely suggests the older lineage and frequency of baseball and baseball-type games. See Sullivan, comp. and ed., *Early Innings: A Documentary History of Baseball, 1825–1908* (Lincoln: University of Nebraska Press, 1995). For a fuller sampling of documentary evidence, see Thomas L. Altherr, ed., *Sports in North America: A Documentary History*, vol. 1, parts 1 and 2, *Early American Sports to 1820* (Gulf Breeze FL: Academic International Press, 1997). The research for that encyclopedia provided the impetus for this article, with the sincere hopes that other baseball historians and scholars will locate additional pre-1839 evidence of baseball and baseball-type games.

3. Tom Heitz, conversations with the author, June and August 1996.

4. Henderson, *Ball, Bat, and Bishop*.

5. Goodstein, a Denver historian who is not particularly a baseball scholar, has uncovered evidence of Graves's involvement in financial misdealings and shooting a spouse, as well as committals for mental illness, in years prior to his testimony for the Mills Commission. The Mills Commission also ignored testimony that baseball existed before 1839, especially a letter from a man who had played the game in Portsmouth, New Hampshire as a school child in 1830. See also "Origins of Baseball" in *The Cultural Encyclopedia of Baseball*, ed. Jonathan Fraser Light (Jefferson NC: McFarland, 1997), 530; Harold Seymour, "How Baseball Began," *New York Historical Society Quarterly* 40, no. 1 (October 1956), 369–85; and Uriel Simri's little-known dissertation, "The Religious and Magical Function of Ball Games in Various Cultures," Ph.D. diss., West Virginia University, 1966.

6. Mehl, "Baseball in the Stone Age," 161; Erwin Mehl, "Notes on 'Baseball in the Stone Age,'" *Western Folklore* 8, no. 2 (April 1949), 152–56.

7. Robert Crowley, "The Scholars Lesson," in *The Select Works of Robert Crowley* ed. J. M. Cowper (London: N. Trubner, 1872), 73.

8. Robert Moynihan, "Shakespeare at Bat, Euclid on the Field," in *Cooperstown Symposium on Baseball and the American Culture (1989)* ed. Alvin L. Hall (Westport CT: Meckler, 1991), 319–23.

9. See Mark Alvarez, *The Old Ball Game* (Alexandria VA: Redefiniton, 1992), 10–12. See also "Origins of Baseball," in Light, *Cultural Encyclopedia*, 528–31.

10. O. Paul Monckton, *Pastimes in Times Past* (Philadelphia: J. B. Lippincott, 1913), 52.

11. Altherr, *Sports in North America*.

12. Ron McCulloch, *How Baseball Began* (Los Angeles: Warwick, 1995), 4, 6; and Maigaard, "Battingball Games," 67. An 1866 book on outdoor games also refers to a game called "ball-stock," which is German in origin and resembles town ball. There is no way of ascertaining, however, from the book, if the game existed before 1839. *The Play Ground; or, Out-Door Games for Boys* (New York: Dick and Fitzgerald, 1866), 112–13.

13. McCulloch, *How Baseball Began*, 3. Ann McGovern, in a book targeted for adolescents, *If You Lived in Colonial Times* (New York: Scholastic, 1992 [orig. pub. 1964]), stated on page 52, without documentation, "Most of all, boys liked to play ball. They played with a leather ball filled with feathers."

14. Mehl, "Baseball in the Stone Age," 147.

15. For an excellent discussion of the place and role of folk games and sports in pre-colonial and colonial English culture, see Nancy Struna, *People of Prowess: Sport, Leisure, and Labor in Early Anglo-America* (Urbana: University of Illinois Press, 1996), passim, but especially chapter 1.

16. William Bradford, *Of Plymouth Plantation*, ed. Harvey Wish (New York: Capricorn, 1962), 82–83.

17. Esther Singleton, *Dutch New York* (New York: Dodd, Mead, 1909), 290.

18. M. Halsey Thomas, ed., *The Diary of Samuel Sewall, 1674–1729*, vol. 2, *1709–1729* (New York: Farrar, Straus and Giroux, 1973), 718.

19. Harold B. Hancock, ed., "'Fare Weather and Good Helth': The Journal of Caesar Rodeney, 1727–1729," *Delaware History* 10, no. 1 (April 1962), 64.

20. John Brickell, *The Natural History of North-Carolina* (Dublin: James Carson, 1737), 336.

21. William S. Southgate, "The History of Scarborough, from 1633 to 1783," *Collections of the Maine Historical Society*, vol. 3 (Portland: Maine Historical Society, 1853), 148–49.

22. Bruce C. Daniels, *Puritans at Play: Leisure and Recreation in Colonial New England* (New York: St. Martin's, 1995), 174.

23. Benjamin Rush to Benjamin Rush Floyd, April 21, 1812, in "Further Letters of Benjamin Rush," ed. Lyman H. Butterfield *Pennsylvania Magazine of History and Biography* 78, no. 1 (January 1954), 43.

24. Newbery, *A Little Pretty Pocket-Book*, 88, 90, 91.

25. "An Act to prevent and punish Disorders usually committed on the twenty-fifth Day of December, . . . " December 23, 1771, *New Hampshire (Colony) Temporary Laws, 1773* (Portsmouth, New Hampshire, [1773–1774]), 53.

26. [Simeon Lyman], "Journal of Simeon Lyman of Sharon Aug. 10 to Dec. 28, 1775," in "Orderly Book and Journals Kept by Connecticut Men

While Taking Part in the American Revolution, 1775–1778," *Collections of the Connecticut Historical Society* (Hartford: Connecticut Historical Society, 1899), 7: 117.

27. [Joseph Joslin, Jr.], "Journal of Joseph Joslin Jr. of South Killingly A Teamster in the Continental Service March 1777–August 1778," ibid., 7: 353–54.

28. [Samuel Shute], "Journal of Lt. Samuel Shute," in *Journals of the Military Expedition of Major General John Sullivan against the Six Nations of Indians in 1779*, ed. Frederick Cook (Freeport NY: Books for Libraries, rpt. 1885 ed.), 268.

29. [Ebenezer Elmer], "Journal of Lieutenant Ebenezer Elmer, of the Third Regiment of New Jersey Troops in the Continental Service," *Proceedings of the New Jersey Historical Society* 1, no. 1 (1848): 26, 27, 30, 31, and vol. 3, no. 2 (1848): 98.

30. Rebecca D. Symmes, ed., *A Citizen-Soldier in the American Revolution: The Diary of Benjamin Gilbert in Massachusetts and New York* (Cooperstown NY: New York State Historical Association, 1980), 30, 49; "Benjamin Gilbert Diaries, 1782–1786," G372, New York State Historical Association Library, Cooperstown NY.

31. [George Ewing], *The Military Journal of George Ewing (1754–1824) a Soldier of Valley Forge* (Yonkers NY: Thomas Ewing, 1928), 35.

32. Eugene Parker Chase, ed., *Our Revolutionary Forefathers: The Letters of François, Marquis de Barbé-Marbois during His Residence in the United States as Secretary of the French Legation, 1779–1785* (New York: Duffield, 1929), 114.

33. Charles Knowlton Bolton, ed., "A Fragment of the Diary of Lieutenant Enos Stevens, Tory, 1777–1778," *New England Quarterly* 11, no. 2 (June 1938): 384–85, but the original, more accurate journal, from which the above notations come, is at the Vermont Historical Society, Montpelier VT.

34. William H. W. Sabine, ed., *The New-York Diary of Lieutenant Jabez Fitch of the 17th (Connecticut) Regiment from August 22, 1776, to December 15, 1777* (New York: privately printed, 1954), 126, 127, 162.

35. [Charles Herbert], *A Relic of the Revolution, Containing a Full and Particular Account of the Sufferings and Privations of All the American Prisoners Captured on the High Seas, and Carried into Plymouth, England, During the Revolution of 1776* (Boston: Charles H. Peirce, 1847), 109.

36. Marion S. Coan, ed., "A Revolutionary Prison Diary: The Journal of Dr. Jonathan Haskins," *New England Quarterly* 17, no. 2 (June 1944): 308.

37. John Smith Hanna, ed., *A History of the Life and Services of Captain*

Samuel Dewees, A Native of Pennsylvania, and Soldier of the Revolutionary and Last Wars (Baltimore: Robert Neilson, 1844), 265, 266.

38. John A. Spear, ed., "Joel Shepard Goes to the War," New England Quarterly 1, no. 3 (July 1928): 344.

39. Collegii Yalensis, Quod est Novo-Portus Connecticutensium, Statuta, a Præside et Sociis Sancita (New Haven: Benjamin Mecom, 1764), 9; and The Laws of Yale-College, in New-Haven, in Connecticut, Enacted by the Prefident and Fellows (New Haven: Thomas and Samuel Green, 1774), 11.

40. Dartmouth College Laws and Regulations, 1780, Dartmouth College Library, Special Collections MS 782415.

41. RULES for the Good Government and Discipline of the SCHOOL in the UNIVERSITY of PENNSYLVANIA (Philadelphia: Francis Bailey, 1784).

42. The Laws of Williams College (Stockbridge MA: H. Willard, 1805), 40.

43. "Of Misdemeanors and Criminal Offences," in Laws of Bowdoin College (Hallowell ME: E. Goodale, 1817), 12.

44. Sidney Willard, Memories of Youth and Manhood, 2 vols. (Cambridge MA: John Bartlett, 1855), 1: 31, 316.

45. John Rhea Smith, March 22, 1786, in "Journal at Nassau Hall," Princeton Library MSS, AM 12800. Smith's use of "baste" instead of "base" is quite intriguing, suggesting a linguistic connection to striking the ball rather than running to a base. Smith was quite literate and an excellent speller. An examination of the rest of his diary reveals no misspelled words. For more on Smith, see Ruth L. Woodward, "Diary at Nassau Hall: The Diary of John Rhea Smith, 1786," Princeton University Library Chronicle 46, no. 3 (1985): 269–91, and vol. 47, no. 1 (1985): 48–70.

46. Daniel Webster, Private Correspondence, ed. Fletcher Webster, 2 vols. (Boston: Little Brown, 1857), 1: 66. See also Vernon Bartlett, The Past of Pastimes (London: Chatto and Windus, 1969), 45.

47. Garrett Barry, "On Leaving College," in Poems, On Several Occasions (Baltimore: Cole and I. Bonsal and John Vance and Company, 1807).

48. Henry Wadsworth Longfellow to Stephen Longfellow, April 11, 1824, in Life of Henry Wadsworth Longfellow with Extracts from His Journals and Correspondence, ed. Samuel Longfellow, 2 vols. (Boston: Ticknor, 1886), 1: 51.

49. Williams Latham, "The Diary of Williams Latham, 1823–1827" (unpublished), quoted in Walter C. Bronson, The History of Brown University, 1764–1914 (Providence: Brown University, 1914), 245. James D'Wolf Lovett remembered that Boston boys in that era didn't find the shortage of players so problematic. If his crowd couldn't summon up enough players for town ball

or baseball, the boys reverted to playing the simpler games of one-old-cat, two-old-cat, three-old-cat, or whatever configuration fit. Lovett, *Old Boston Boys* (Boston: Riverside, 1906) 127–28.

50. John A. Krout, *Annals of American Sport* (New Haven: Yale University Press, 1929), 115.

51. Josiah Dwight Whitney to his sister, Elizabeth Whitney, March 1837, reprinted in Edwin Tenney Brewster, *Life and Letters of Josiah Dwight Whitney* (Boston: Houghton Mifflin, 1909), 20; Anson Phelps Stokes, *Memorials of Eminent Yale Men*, 2 vols. (New Haven: Yale University Press, 1914), 2: 38.

52. [Noah Webster], "Diary," reprinted in *Notes on the Life of Noah Webster*, ed. Emily Ellsworth Fowler Ford, 2 vols. (New York: privately printed, 1912), 1: 227.

53. Georgetown student letter, August 27, 1836, Georgetown University Library, quoted in Betty Spears and Richard Swanson, *History of Sport and Physical Activity in the United States*, 2nd ed. (Dubuque IA: William C. Brown, 1983), 85.

54. James B. Angell, *The Reminiscences of James Burrill Angell* (London: Longmans, Green, 1912), 14.

55. Increase N. Tarbox, ed., *Diary of Thomas Robbins, D.D. 1796–1854*, 2 vols. (Boston: Beacon, 1886), 1: 8, 29, 32, 106, 128.

56. Thomas Jefferson to Peter Carr, August 19, 1785, in *The Papers of Thomas Jefferson*, ed. Julian P. Boyd, 23 vols. (Princeton: Princeton University Press, 1953–), 8: 407.

57. Clara English, *The Children in the Wood, An Instructive Tale* (Baltimore: Warner and Hanna, 1806), 29.

58. [Ann Gilbert], *Original Poems, for Infant Minds*, 2 vols. (Philadelphia: Kimber, Conrad, 1806), 2: 120. Gilbert's verse re-appeared in several later editions and other children's books, and in an 1840 pamphlet, *The Village Green, or Sports of Youth* (New Haven: S. Babcock), 5, with the word "worsted" changed to "favorite" and with an accompanying woodcut showing four boys playing baseball.

59. [Ann Gilbert], *Original Poems, for Infant Minds*, 2 vols. (Philadelphia: Kimber, Conrad, 1807), 1: 88–89.

60. *The Prize for Youthful Obedience* (Philadelphia: Jacob Johnson, 1807), part 2, [16].

61. *Youthful Sports* (Philadelphia: Jacob Johnson, 1802), 47–48.

62. *Youthful Amusements* (Philadelphia: Johnson and Warner, 1810), 37, 40.

63. *Youthful Recreations* (Philadelphia: Jacob Johnson, 1810), no pagination.

64. *The Book of Games; or, a History of the Juvenile Sports Practised at Kingston Academy* (Philadelphia: Johnson and Warner, 1811), 15–20. The full text reads as follows:

TRAP-BALL.

WELL, young men, said the doctor, addressing himself to his two youngest sons, what think you of a game at trap-ball before you go to bed? there is plenty of time, and it is a fine evening for the purpose. Will you not, my dear Thomas, said he, turning to his new guest, accompany them; a little play will do you good after your long ride.

Thomas readily consented, and accompanied the boys into an field, adjoining the house.

"This is our play-place in fine weather," said George Benson, "and a nice one it is. Well what is the game to-night? Trap-ball I believe my father proposed. Do you play at trap-ball, White?" "No," replied White, "I know but little about it."

George Benson. I suppose you know the rules of the game, however, and can join in our party. Who has got the trap?

James Benson. Here it is; but I think I had rather have a game at fives. If you and Price will play at trap-ball, and give White a lesson, Jackson and Seymore, and I, will go the high wall, and have a good game at fives.

George Benson. Very well. Away with you then, and I will hold you both, Price and White. Who has a half-penny, to toss up for the first innings? O, here is one; heads or tails? Tails did you say? Well then I have it, for it is heads. Now, are you ready?

Thomas White. What are we to do? I have forgot what little I have heard of the game; I never played at it but once.

George. Well then I will tell you; you know, of course, that when I hit the trigger, the ball flies up, and that I must then give it a good stroke with the bat. If I strike at the ball and miss my aim, or if, when I have struck it, either you or Price catch it before it has touched the ground, or if I hit the trigger more than twice, without striking the ball, I am out, and one of you take the bat, and come in, as it is called.

White. And we are to try to hit the trap, with the ball, are we not? and you will be out, as soon as we have done so? And do not you reckon one, every time we bowl without being able to hit the trap?

George. Yes, that is the way, *we* usually play: but I believe sometimes the person who is in, guesses how many bat lengths off the ball was stopped, and reckons as many as he guesses, if that is less than the real number; but if he guesses more than there really are, he is cast.

White. I do not clearly understand you.

George. Perhaps I do not clearly explain myself. Indeed I have never played the game in that manner: but Seymore says that they always did at the school he used to go to. Suppose now that I am *in*, and you bowl, and the ball stops there, just where I point, I guess that it is five times the length of the bat from the trap; if you think there are not so many, and order me to measure, should there be only four times, I am out; but if there should happen to be six or eight times, I may reckon them all though I had only guessed five. Now do you understand what I mean; though, it does not signify, as we play the other way?

White. I believe I do. What have you stuck those two sticks in the ground for?

George. To mark the bounds. You know the batsman is out if he does not strike the ball between them, or if it stops short of them; and he reckons one every time the other party miss the trap in throwing the ball. We have three innings a-piece, and he wins who gets most. But as you do not know so much of the game, and as Price is such a little fellow, I will play against you both. Now for it then; but I must take my coat off, for it is so hot. Now I am ready. There catch the ball, boys. Ay, you have missed it.

Price. I thought White would have caught it. Now I will bowl. Oh, it has not hit the trap.

White. Let me bowl this time. There you are out, I think, master George.

George. Upon my word, you bowl well. I am only one. It is your turn to go in now.

White took the bat, but as he was unused to the management of one, he held it very awkwardly, and struck repeatedly at the ball without being able to hit it. George, very good humouredly, shewed him the best method of holding the bat, and let him practise striking the ball several times before they continued their game. When they again began to play, White gave a noble stroke, and sent the ball to such a distance, that George could not, with all his strength, bowl it quite home; and Tom, with great pleasure, counted one. But the next time he hit it so feebly, that George had no difficulty in bowling him out. It was then Price's turn to come in, he also counted only one; for the next time, he drove it outside the boundary sticks.

"Ah, I shall beat you both, I dare say," cried George, good humouredly taking the trap. "There, I think you will not bowl me out this time, White. You have indeed," continued he, as he threw down the bat. "Why, how wonderfully you do bowl. You must have been used to that, I am sure."

White. Yes, my father is fond of playing at bowls. We have got a bowling green, and I have often practised.

The peculiar skill which White possessed in bowling, made him a tolerable match for George Benson, and Tom felt no small degree of pleasure, when victory declared in favour of the two novices. "You have won, I declare," cried George, as he was bowled out by Thomas, after he had been twice in. "I did not expect to be beat by you, as you said you knew nothing of the game. Shall we go now and see what the fives players are about?"

65. *Remarks on Children's Play* (New York: Samuel Wood and Sons, 1819), 32.

66. *The Boy's Own Book* (Boston: Munroe and Francis, 1829), 18–19; Robin Carver, *The Book of Sports* (Boston: Lily, Wait, Colman, and Holden). For a convenient reprinting of Carver's section on "Base, or Goal Ball," see Sullivan, *Early Innings*, 3

67. *By-Laws of the Town of Portsmouth, Passed at their Annual Meeting Held March 25, 1795* (Portsmouth NH: John Melcher, 1795), 5–6.

68. Charles W. Brewster, *Rambles about Portsmouth*, second series (Portsmouth NH: Lewis W. Brewster, 1869), 269.

69. *Bye-Laws of Newburyport; Passed by the Town at Regular Meetings, and Approved by the Court of General Justice of the Peace for the County of Essex, Agreeably to a Law of this Commonwealth* (Newburyport MA: 1797), 1.

70. *The By Laws of the Town of Portland, in the County of Cumberland*, 2nd ed. (Portland ME: John McKown, 1805), 15. Italics in the original source. The 1817 town by-laws still contained this prohibition. "By Law to check the practice of playing at Bat and Ball in the Streets, &c.," in *The By-Laws of the Town of Portland, in the County of Cumberland* (Portland ME: A. and J. Shirley, 1817), 12.

71. Will Anderson, *Was Baseball Really Invented in Maine?* (Portland ME: privately printed, 1992), 1.

72. Worcester MA Town Records, 6 May 1816, rpt. in Franklin P. Rice, ed., *Worcester Town Records, 1801–1816*, vol. 10 (Worcester MA: The Worcester Society of Antiquity, 1891), 337.

73. *Laws and Ordinances of the Mayor, Aldermen, and Commonalty, of the City of Troy. Passed the Ninth Day of December, 1816* (Troy NY: Parker and Bliss, 1816), 42.

74. "A Law relative to the Park, Battery, and Bowling-Green," in *Laws and Ordinances Ordained and Established by the Mayor, Aldermen, and Commonalty of the City of New York* (New York: T. and J. Swords, 1817), 118.

75. Cooperstown NY village ordinance, June 13, 1816, reprinted in the Cooperstown NY *Otsego Herald*, June 13, 1816, 3.

76. Tom Heitz, conversations with the author, June and August 1996.

77. Lois K. Stabler, ed., *Very Poor and of a Lo Make: The Journal of Abner Sanger* (Portsmouth NH: Peter E. Randall, 1986), 416.

78. Levi Allen to Ira Allen, July 7, 1787, in *Ethan Allen and His Kin, Correspondence, 1772–1819*, ed. John J. Duffy, 2 vols. (Hanover NH: University Press of New England, 1998), 1: 244.

79. Frank H. Cunningham, *Familiar Sketches of the Phillips Exeter Academy and Surroundings* (Boston: James R. Osgood, 1883), 281.

80. Albert Ware Paine, "Auto-Biography," rpt. in Lydia Augusta Paine Carter, *The Discovery of a Grandmother* (Newtonville MA: Henry H. Carter, 1920), 240.

81. Charles Haswell, *Reminiscences of an Octogenarian, 1816 to 1860* (New York: Harper and Brothers, 1896), 77.

82. Samuel. L. Welch, *Home History. Recollections of Buffalo during the Decade from 1830 to 1840, or Fifty Years Since* (Buffalo NY: Peter Paul and Brother, 1891), 353.

83. John Hamilton, "Some Reminiscences of Wilm't'n and My Youthful Days —&c., &c." *Delaware History* 1, no. 2 (July 1946): 91.

84. Harold B. Hancock, ed., "William Morgan's Autobiography and Diary: Life in Sussex County, 1780–1857," *Delaware History* 19, no. 1 (Spring–Summer 1980): 43–44.

85. Jonathan Mason, Jr., "Recollections of a Septuagenarian," 3 vols., Downs Special Collections, Winterthur Library, document 30, 1: 20–21.

86. Edmund Delaney, ed., *Life in the Connecticut River Valley, 1800–1840, from the Recollections of John Howard Redfield* (Essex CT: Connecticut River Museum, 1988), 35. Italics in the original source.

87. John Drayton, *A View of South-Carolina, As Respects Her Natural and Civil Concerns* (Charleston SC: W. P. Young, 1802), 225.

88. Charles Fraser, *Reminiscences of Charleston, Lately Published in the Charleston Courier, and Now Revised and Enlarged by the Author* (Charleston SC: John Russell, 1854), 88.

89. [Ely Playter], "Extracts from Ely Playter's Diary," April 13, 1803, rpt. in *The Town of York, 1793–1815: A Collection of Documents of Early Toronto* ed. Edith G. Firth (Toronto: Champlain Society, 1962), 248.

90. New York *Evening Post*, September 20, 1811, 2.

91. G. M. Fairchild, Jr., ed., *Journal of an American Prisoner at Fort Malden and Quebec in the War of 1812* (Quebec: privately printed, 1890), no pagination.

92. [Benjamin Waterhouse], *A Journal of a Young Man of Massachusetts, Late a Surgeon on Board an American Privateer, Who Was Captured at Sea by the British, in May, Eighteen Hundred and Thirteen, and Was Confined First, at Melville Island, Halifax, then at Chatham, in England, and Last, at Dartmoor Prison* (Boston: Rowe and Hooper, 1816), 186.

93. [Charles Andrews], *The Prisoners' Memoirs, or Dartmoor Prison* (New York: privately printed 1815), 92.

94. "Journal of Nathaniel Pierce of Newburyport, Kept at Dartmoor Prison, 1814–1815," *Historical Collections of Essex Institute* 73, no. 1 (January 1937): 40.

95. [Andrews], *The Prisoners' Memoirs*, 110. In another memoir, prisoner Josiah Cobb referred to the ball being thrown over the wall by accident, something that happened somewhat frequently. [Cobb], *A Green Hand's First Cruise, Roughed Out from the Log-Book of Memory, of Twenty-Five Years Standing: Together with a Residence of Five Months in Dartmoor*, 2 vols. (Boston: Otis, Broaders, 1841), 2: 213–14. For the testimony of other prisoners, see John Hunter Waddell, *Dartmoor Massacre* (Pittsfield MA: Phinehas Allen, 1815), 6–21.

96. [Joseph Valpey, Jr.], *Journal of Joseph Valpey, Jr., of Salem, November, 1813–April, 1815* (Detroit: Michigan Society of Colonial Wars, 1922), 60.

97. "The Judicial Report of the Massacre at Dartmoor Prison," rpt. in John Melish, *Description of Dartmoor Prison, with an Account of the Massacre of the Prisoners* (Philadelphia: J. Bioren, 1816), 7.

98. [John Hunter Waddell], *The Dartmoor Massacre* (Boston: privately printed, 1815), 5.

99. Harriet A. Weed, ed., *Life of Thurlow Weed*, 2 vols. (Boston: Houghton Mifflin, 1883), 1: 203. That same year, residents of Hamden, New York, placed a challenge in the Delhi, New York, *Gazette* of July 12th to any men of Delaware County to form a team and play a baseball match. See Sullivan, *Early Innings*, 1–2.

100. Samuel Hopkins Adams, *Grandfather Stories* (New York: Random House, 1955 [orig. pub. 1947]), 146–49.

101. Allen Guttmann, *From Ritual to Record: The Nature of Modern Sports*

(New York: Columbia University Press, 1978), chapter 2; Guttmann, *A Whole New Ball Game: An Interpretation of American Sports* (Chapel Hill: University of North Carolina Press, 1988), 6.

102. Seymour, "How Baseball Began," 376.

103. Lovett, *Old Boston Boys*, 125.

104. Adrian Stokes, "Psycho-analytic Reflections on the Development of Ball Games, Particularly Cricket," *International Journal of Psycho-analysis* 37 (1956): 185–92.

105. Kenneth Patchen, "The Origin of Baseball," in *Selected Poems* (New York: New Directions, 1957), 15–16.

APPENDIX 6

1. Gini, "Rural Ritual Games in Libya."

2. *Tipcat* is the English name for a group of games, similar to primitive *Battingball*-games. Instead of a ball a billet or a "cat" is used, in a few cases a ball of wood. The batsman has to play the billet out from the home-base, i.e. a hole in the ground or a pair of flat stones. There are usually several divisions in the game, one of these only is common batting. The batsman has to defend his home against the billet, thrown back by a fielder, and gets points in proportion to the distance from the home in which the billet falls to the ground. If the fielders catch the billet in the air, the batsman is out. If they in a return-throw hit the home (in the first part of the game) or (in the second part) get the billet to stop within a bat's length from the home, he is out too. *Tipcat* has many variations and is known almost in the same countries where the *Battingball*-games are known, and moreover in Precolumbian America. Games with a "cat" were known, for instance, in Europe, India and America.

PRINCIPAL SOURCES CONSULTED

❖

Altherr, Thomas L. "A Place Leavel Enough to Play Ball." NINE: A Journal of Baseball History and Social Policy Perspectives 8, no. 2 (2000): 15-49.

Dickson, Paul. The New Dickson Baseball Dictionary. New York: Harcourt, Brace, 1999.

John Doyle Papers. National Baseball Hall of Fame Library, Cooperstown NY.

Gomme, Alice Bertha. The Traditional Games of England, Scotland, and Ireland. 2 vols. New York: Dover, 1964. Orig. pub. as part 1 of the Dictionary of British Folk-Lore, vol. 1, 1894; vol. 2, 1898. London: David Nutt.

Grobani, Anton. Guide to Baseball Literature. Detroit: Gale Research, 1975.

Henderson, Robert W. Ball, Bat, and Bishop. New York: Rockport, 1947.

———. Baseball: Notes and Materials on Its Origin. New York: New York Public Library, 1941.

———. Early American Sport. 3rd ed. Teaneck NJ: Fairleigh Dickinson University Press, 1977.

Murray, James Augustus Henry. Oxford English Dictionary. Oxford: Clarendon, 1933.

Palmer, Harry Clay. Athletic Sports in America, England, and Australia. Philadelphia: Hubbard Brothers, 1889.

Peterson, Harold. The Man Who Invented Baseball. New York: Scribner's, 1973.

Peverelly, Charles A. The Book of American Pastimes. New York: published by the author, 1866.

Richter, Francis C. Richter's History and Records of Baseball. Philadelphia: Francis C. Richter, 1914.

Seymour, Harold. Baseball. Vol. 1, The Early Years. New York: Oxford University Press, 1960.

Sloate, Barry. "Rare and Historical Baseball Books." Vintage and Classic Baseball Collector, no. 3 (1995).

Spalding's Official Base Ball Guide. Chicago: A. G. Spalding and Bros., various years.

Spink, Alfred, H. The National Game. St. Louis: National Game Publishing Company, 1910.

Strutt, Joseph. *Sports and Pastimes of the People of England*. London: T. Bensley for White and Co., 1801.

Sullivan, Dean A. *Early Innings*. Lincoln: University of Nebraska Press, 1995.

Ward, John Montgomery. *Baseball: How to Become a Player*. Philadelphia: Athletic Publishing, 1888.

INDEX

❖

An index of titles in the Early Baseball Bibliography follows this index.

Page numbers in italics indicate illustrations.

INDEX OF TITLES IN THE EARLY BASEBALL BIBLIOGRAPHY